Contents

House of Commons

Education and Skills Committee

the

4–05

s, oral and

HC 120
Incorporating HC 1170-i/iii, Session 2003-04
Published on 10 February 2005
by authority of the House of Commons
London: The Stationery Office Limited
£23.00

The Education and Skills Committee

The Education and Skills Committee is appointed by the House of Commons to examine the expenditure, administration and policy of the Department for Education and Skills and its associated public bodies.

Current membership

Mr Barry Sheerman MP *(Labour, Huddersfield)* (Chairman)
Mr David Chaytor MP *(Labour, Bury North)*
Valerie Davey MP *(Labour, Bristol West)*
Jeff Ennis MP *(Labour, Barnsley East & Mexborough)*
Mr Nick Gibb MP *(Conservative, Bognor Regis & Littlehampton)*
Mr John Greenway MP *(Conservative, Ryedale)*
Paul Holmes MP *(Liberal Democrat, Chesterfield)*
Helen Jones MP *(Labour, Warrington North)*
Mr Kerry Pollard MP *(Labour, St Albans)*
Jonathan Shaw MP *(Labour, Chatham and Aylesford)*
Mr Andrew Turner MP *(Conservative, Isle of Wight)*

Powers

The Committee is one of the departmental select committees, the powers of which are set out in House of Commons Standing Orders, principally in SO No 152. These are available on the Internet via www.parliament.uk

Publications

The Reports and evidence of the Committee are published by The Stationery Office by Order of the House. All publications of the Committee (including press notices) are on the Internet at:
www.parliament.uk/parliamentary_committees/education_and_skills_committee.cfm

Committee staff

The current staff of the Committee are David Lloyd (Clerk), Dr Sue Griffiths (Second Clerk), Libby Aston (Committee Specialist), Nerys Roberts (Committee Specialist), Lisa Wrobel (Committee Assistant), Susan Monaghan (Committee Assistant), Catherine Jackson (Secretary) and John Kittle (Senior Office Clerk).

Contacts

All correspondence should be addressed to the Clerk of the Education and Skills Committee, House of Commons, 7 Millbank, London SW1P 3JA. The telephone number for general enquiries is 020 7219 6181; the Committee's email address is edskillscom@parliament.uk

Footnotes

In the footnotes of this Report, references to oral evidence are indicated by 'Q' followed by the question number. References to written evidence are indicated in the form 'Ev' followed by the page number.

1 Summary

During this inquiry, the Committee has become convinced of the value of education outside the classroom in its broadest sense. Outdoor learning supports academic achievement, for example through fieldwork projects, as well as the development of 'soft' skills and social skills, particularly in hard to reach children. It can take place on school trips, on visits in the local community or in the school grounds. Yet outdoor education is in decline. Provision by schools is extremely patchy. Although some schools offer an active and well-planned programme of outdoor education, which contributes significantly to teaching and learning, many are deterred by the false perception that a high degree of risk attaches to outdoor education as well as by cumbersome bureaucracy and issues of funding, time and resources. Neither the DfES or local authorities have done enough to publicise the benefits of education outside the classroom or to provide strategic leadership or direction in this area.

Risk is often cited as the main factor deterring schools from organising school trips. We have found no evidence to support the perception that school trips are inherently risky. Visits organised in accordance with health and safety guidance should not lead to avoidable accidents or unfounded legal claims against teachers. The DfES needs to work with teacher unions and schools to ensure that teachers do not feel vulnerable to vexatious litigation and that they are aware of the law as it now stands. We also strongly recommend that the NASUWT reviews its advice to members not to participate in school trips.

In contrast, the bureaucracy now associated with school trips is a major problem. Some schools and local authorities are demanding excessively lengthy risk assessments and we have found evidence of needless duplication in the system. The Government claims to be actively reducing public sector bureaucracy in general and specifically the burden on schools. We are therefore extremely surprised that it can allow the current situation to persist.

In order to realise its full potential, outdoor education must be carried out properly, with sessions being prepared by well-trained teachers and in accordance with good curriculum guidance as well as health and safety regulations. Teacher training is therefore a vital aspect of outdoor education. We are concerned that out-of-classroom activities should be led by well-qualified people who know how to get the most out of these experiences. We recommend that the DfES engage professional bodies to ensure that teachers have access to appropriate programmes of continuing professional development, which should include curriculum design. We also urge the department to review the place of outdoor education within Initial Teacher Training (ITT) programmes.

Educational Visits Co-ordinators (EVCs) have recently been introduced into schools. An EVC is a teacher who provides advice on the organisation of school trips and ensures that best practice guidance is followed. We welcome this step, which provides a champion for outdoor education within schools, and look forward to EVCs being present in all schools.

Specialised centres for outdoor education are provided by a number of bodies including private companies, voluntary or charitable organisations and LEAs. In recent years, LEA provision has generally declined and this trend looks set to continue as the Government increasingly devolves funding directly to schools. The DfES and the Department for Culture, Media and Sport need to develop a strategy for the long term viability of activity centres, addressing staff retention and links with schools and developing expertise.

School grounds are a vital resource, but our evidence suggests they are sometimes poorly designed. The DfES should ensure that its capital projects, for example, the Building Schools for the Future and Academy programmes, devote as much attention to the "outdoor classroom" as to the innovative design of buildings and indoor space.

Main recommendations

The Department should issue a 'Manifesto for Outdoor Learning', giving all students a right to outdoor learning. This Manifesto should attract a similar level of funding to the Music Manifesto (£30 million) in order to deliver real change. In particular, schools in deprived circumstances should be enabled to enhance their facilities, to offer professional development programmes to their teachers and to fund off site visits.

We further recommend that the DfES set up a structure to champion education outside the classroom at all levels. Within the Department, a dedicated team of officials should have responsibility for outdoor learning across curriculum areas. A high profile 'champion' for outdoor learning should be appointed to lead this team. In each LEA, an Outdoor Education Adviser should be in place, promoting and co-ordinating outdoor learning locally and liaising with the Department. Each school should have a well-trained Educational Visits Co-ordinator, whose role should be strengthened and expanded to act as the local champion for outdoor learning. A nationwide network of support, guidance and innovation would move outdoor education forwards from its current, patchy position to a more uniform provision of high quality opportunities throughout the country.

2 Introduction

1. The Committee announced its inquiry into Education Outside the Classroom on 22 September 2004. We took evidence on a wide range of outdoor learning experiences, from lessons held within the school grounds to residential expeditions abroad, and the place of outdoor learning in the curriculum from the Foundation Stage to Higher Education.

2. During our inquiry, we examined the barriers that deter schools from teaching outside the classroom. These range from the perception of risk associated with school trips, through the resources and curriculum time available for out-of-classroom learning and for teacher training, to the availability and cost of facilities and activity centres. We analyse these difficulties in this report. We also consider how schools could best be encouraged to improve and expand their outdoor education and what action the Department for Education and Skills (DfES) could take in this area. Options include the publication of a 'Manifesto for Outdoor Learning' (suggested by departmental officials, amongst others) or the creation of a curricular entitlement to a certain number of hours outside the classroom. We also consider the funding implications of these alternatives.

3. In the course of our inquiry, we took oral evidence from the Outward Bound Trust; the Real World Learning Campaign; the RSPB; the Field Studies Council; the Secondary Heads Association; the National Association of Head Teachers; the NASUWT; the NUT; Ofsted; Ms Helen Williams and Mr Stephen Crowne, DfES officials and Mr Stephen Twigg MP, then Parliamentary Under-Secretary of State for Schools, DfES. We received written evidence from a wide range of organisations and individuals, a selection of which is printed with this report. We received a very large number of submissions in connection with this inquiry, which is a measure of the diversity of the sector and the strength of feeling on this subject. We have used the information and opinions expressed in these memoranda to inform the conclusions and recommendations of this report.

3 Context

4. We publish this report at a time when outdoor education is the subject of significant media attention, particularly with regard to school trips. Over the past decade, accidents on school trips have been prominently reported in the press. In 1993, four pupils died in a canoeing accident at Lyme Bay. It was subsequently found that the students were not properly supervised and the activity centre had not provided adequately trained staff. The managing director was prosecuted and convicted of manslaughter. In 2000, two pupils died whilst river walking with a school party in Stainforth Beck, Yorkshire. A case against Leeds City Council was brought by the Health and Safety Executive. The Council was found guilty of failing to ensure the safety of the pupils and fined. In 2002, a teacher was jailed for manslaughter following an accident near Glenridding, Cumbria, when a 10-year-old boy was swept away and drowned in a flooded river. The teacher involved was a member of the NASUWT, who, for the past four years, have advised their members against accompanying school trips due to the danger of litigation if something goes wrong. Many of those who contacted us described these accidents as tragic but isolated incidents. They reported that the adverse publicity generated in these cases has seriously deterred schools from organising off-site visits and has led to a decline in education outside the classroom.

5. School trips have been the focus for much media attention, but our inquiry was not confined to off-site visits. We wished to consider education outside the classroom in its fullest sense. Outdoor learning takes place in many different settings within walking distance of the school, such as neighbourhood parks and green spaces, local buildings and community resources as well as within the school grounds themselves. A lack of access to these spaces is as important in the provision of outdoor learning as the decline of school trips.

6. We also recognise the cross-curricular nature of out-of-classroom learning. Outdoor education contributes to learning in a range of areas, including:

- science and geography fieldwork;

- physical education;

- learning through outdoor play, particularly in the early years;

- history and citizenship, through visits to museums and heritage sites;

- art and design, through visits to galleries and experiences of the built environment;[1]

- environmental and countryside education, and education for sustainable development;

- practical or vocational skills that cannot be practised in a classroom environment;

- group activities that build self-confidence and social skills; these may include adventurous activities that teach students how to deal with an element of risk;

- the use of the environment as a tool to enrich the curriculum across subject areas.

---

1   See particularly evidence from CABE, Ev 157.

The value of outdoor learning

7. The conclusions of this report stem from our belief in the value of outdoor learning. Evidence taken by the Committee strongly indicated that education outside the classroom is of significant benefit to pupils. Academic fieldwork clearly enhances the teaching of science and geography, but other subjects such as history, art and design and citizenship can also be brought to life by high quality educational visits. Group activities, which may include adventurous expeditions, can develop social skills and give self-confidence. Furthermore, outdoor education has a key role to play in the social inclusion agenda, offering children who may not otherwise have the opportunity the simple chance to experience the countryside, or other parts of our heritage that many others take for granted.

8. In some cases, the value of outdoor education and the skills students develop outside the classroom is very directly linked to the employment market. For example, The Institute of Ecology and Environmental Management (IEEM) has identified biological recording, survey and monitoring as a growing area that depends greatly on specialist skills being taught in schools, colleges and universities.[2] This link is also in evidence in the bioscience and ecological sectors and the growing environmental protection sector as well as in the numerous other areas of the labour market which require training involving direct contact with the natural world or vocational preparation which cannot be delivered in classrooms.

9. **The broad extent of this inquiry has convinced the Committee that outdoor learning can benefit pupils of all ages and can be successful in a variety of settings. We are convinced that out-of-classroom education enriches the curriculum and can improve educational attainment. Whilst recognising this cross-curricular scope, we conclude that in order to realise its full potential, outdoor education must be carried out properly, with sessions being prepared by well trained teachers and leaders and in accordance with good curriculum guidance as well as health and safety regulations.**

10. Our view of the value of education outside the classroom is supported by research evidence. Ofsted's recent report, *Outdoor education: aspects of good practice,* finds that "outdoor education gives depth to the curriculum and makes an important contribution to students' physical, personal and social education".[3] The recent *Review of Research on Outdoor Learning,*[4] published by the National Foundation for Educational Research (NFER) and King's College London, found that:

> "Those with a statutory and non-statutory responsibility for policy relating to outdoor education should be in no doubt that there is a considerable body of empirical research evidence to support and inform their work [...] Policy makers at all levels need to be aware of the benefits that are associated with different types of outdoor learning. The findings of this review make clear that learners of all ages can

---

2   Ev 192

3   *Outdoor education: aspects of good practice*, Ofsted, September 2004, page 2.

4   *A Review of Research on Outdoor Learning*, Mark Rickinson, Justin Dillon, Kelly Teamey, Marian Morris, Mee Young Choi, Dawn Sanders and Pauline Benefield, (April 2004). The review synthesised the findings of 150 pieces of research on fieldwork/visits, outdoor adventure, and school grounds/community projects, published internationally in English between 1993 and 2003. It was funded by the Field Studies Council, DfES, English Outdoor Council, Groundwork, RSPB, and Wildfowl and Wetlands Trust.

benefit from effective outdoor education. However, despite such positive research evidence and the long tradition of outdoor learning in this country, there is growing evidence that opportunities for outdoor learning are in decline and under threat." [5]

Dr. Peter Higgins of the Outdoor and Environmental Education Section, University of Edinburgh, agreed with these conclusions:

"The weight of evidence from MSc and PhD theses, projects supported by small research grants and Government commissioned studies does generally show benefits in out-of-classroom experiences. Perhaps more importantly this evidence points to a latent and undeveloped potential in relation to both curricular studies and lifelong learning."[6]

11. Many countries, both in Europe and elsewhere, achieve a significantly higher level of outdoor learning in their schools than the UK. Dr Higgins' evidence, quoted above, goes on to cite Australia, Norway and Canada as examples of good practice and notes that:

"in many cases the countries we are familiar with developed their national approach to outdoor learning after detailed consideration of the approach taken in the UK in the 1960s and 1970s. In particular the carefully constructed and wide–scale provision in the Lothian Region of Scotland was widely regarded as the ideal model. Several decades of erosion have left such provision in a poor state, not dissimilar to the rest of the UK, whilst several of those countries which adapted the model to suit their own situation now have extensive curricular provision."

Recent Committee visits to Denmark, Finland and Norway have convinced us that there is much to learn from the provision of outdoor education in these countries. We were particularly impressed by the Danish 'Forest Schools' initiative, which uses the environment as a tool to enrich the curriculum, whist enabling students to experience a carefully monitored element of risk and to become more familiar with the natural world.

12. There are, however, a number of gaps in the research that could usefully be filled by further studies. Most of the data collated by NFER was published abroad and the report notes that "there is a particular need for more UK-based research into a number of aspects of outdoor learning".[7] It also observes that there is relatively little research on the comparative educational benefits of different approaches to education outside the classroom and warns that this is particularly important as "poor fieldwork is likely to lead to poor learning. Students quickly forget irrelevant information that has been inadequately presented."[8]

13. The Department for Education and Skills told us that it is currently undertaking research into outdoor education.[9] We look forward to seeing the results of this study and hope that the data will go some way towards filling the gaps in current research. **Like all**

---

5   ibid, p 5.

6   Ev 112, para 1.5.

7   *A Review of Research on Outdoor Learning*, p 5.

8   ibid, p 2.

9   Ev 59

educational processes, the benefits of education outside the classroom should be rigorously researched, documented and communicated. Positive and reliable evidence of the benefits of outdoor activities would help schools determine the priority to afford to such work.

The decline of education outside the classroom

14. The recent Ofsted report on Outdoor Education, which concludes that education outside the classroom can be of significant benefit to students, notes that many students do not have access to this form of learning: "Outdoor education gives depth to the curriculum and makes an important contribution to students' physical, personal and social education. However, not all students in schools benefit from such opportunities".

15. There has been a general decline in opportunities for education outside the classroom. This decline seems to be affecting all types of outdoor experience. The Committee has received evidence from professional bodies, including the Royal Society and the Field Studies Council, on the diminishing opportunities for fieldwork. It has also heard from organisations such as Learning Through Landscapes, Play Wales and the Children's Play Council that children's day-to-day access to the outdoors is being increasingly restricted.[10] In the past ten years, twenty local authority outdoor education centres have closed. Nonetheless, the DfES asserted that: "most LEAs tell us outdoor activity in their schools is stable or increasing".[11]

16. Perhaps more worryingly still, the Committee has received some evidence to show that education outside the classroom is declining not only in quantity, but also in quality. In oral evidence, Dr Steve Tilling of the Field Studies Council described "a much closer, much more prescribed content than certainly was the situation ten years ago [...] driven by skills and techniques and things which are easily measurable, or measurable in a predictable and, some would say, sanitised way".[12] Dr Anthony Thomas of the Real World Learning Campaign added that in some schools "it is not particularly well planned [...] it is seen as maybe a prize at the end of the year".[13]

17. Despite these generally discouraging trends, the Committee has also heard of much good practice. High quality outdoor education centres run both by LEAs and private or charitable operators have told us that they are regularly oversubscribed and have to turn schools away.[14] Museums and galleries cannot accommodate all those who wish to visit.[15] Many schools are committed to outdoor learning as an integral part of their students' education and put in place what Dr Rita Gardner of the Royal Geographical Society described as:

---

10   Ev 131, 162, 165.

11   Ev 61, Annex A.

12   Q 4

13   Q 4

14   Ev 106, 168, 187.

15   Ev 125, 187.

"a programme of development that is an educational development over a period of years, […] embedded in the culture of the school and the curriculum, a passionate teacher and a really committed head who sees and understands the values, and can convince their governors too, of the values of out-of-classroom learning".[16]

18. This evidence paints a picture of extremely patchy provision. Individual good practice in many schools and local authority areas is set against a more negative national situation. **It is clear to the Committee that outdoor education is a sector suffering from considerable unexploited potential.** In the remainder of this report, we will explore the barriers that prevent schools from developing opportunities for their pupils to benefit from education outside the classroom and make recommendations for action to spread existing good practice amongst all schools.

4 Barriers

Risk and bureaucracy

19. **Many of the organisations and individuals who submitted evidence to our inquiry cited the fear of accidents and the possibility of litigation as one of the main reasons for the apparent decline in school trips. It is the view of this Committee that this fear is entirely out of proportion to the real risks.** High-profile reporting of isolated incidents and some tabloid journalism misrepresents the incidence of serious accidents on school trips, which is actually very low indeed. There have been 57 fatal accidents on school visits since 1985 (this figure includes adults accompanying visits and road traffic accidents en route to or from off-site visits).[17] In England in 2003, there were between seven and ten million 'pupil visits' involving educational or recreational activity, but only one fatality.[18] Whilst every fatality is clearly tragic for those involved, these statistics compare extremely favourably with other routine activities such as driving or being driven in a car, or simply the likelihood of an accident at home or in school.

20. Over the past decade, the DfES has issued new guidance on health and safety on school trips in reaction to accidents that have occurred. A 1998 good practice guide, *Health and Safety of Pupils on Educational Visits* (HASPEV) has been supplemented with new material in 2002 aimed at specific audiences: *Standards for LEAs in Overseeing Educational Visits*, *Standards for Adventure* and *A Handbook for Group Leaders* as well as *Group Safety at Water Margins* (published in 2003 with the Central Council for Physical Recreation).[19] In addition, adults working with under-18s are now subject to Criminal Records Bureau checks.

21. Written submissions and correspondence associated with this inquiry have in general welcomed this new guidance, but some concerns have been expressed that there is still not enough clarity in guidance regarding visits involving children with special educational needs (SEN). Concerns relate specifically to uncertainty over the correct staffing ratios and the right of children with SEN to attend. The NUT publishes additional guidance for the organisation of school trips involving SEN pupils and some have suggested that the DfES should issue a similar document.[20]

22. **We welcome the DfES health and safety guidance which clearly sets out what is expected of all those involved in organising school trips. There remain some concerns relating to guidance on trips involving children with special educational needs, where there could be more specific recommendations on levels of staffing and the right of children to attend. This area is likely to be affected by the enactment of the Disability Discrimination Bill and we recommend that the DfES review its guidance in this context.**

---

17 Ev 137

18 'Pupil visits' is a measure of the number of visits multiplied by the number of pupils participating. Ev 144.

19 Ev 44, para 111.

20 Ev 66, para 33, Ev 70 and unpublished correspondence.

23. Despite new DfES guidance on health and safety, the fear of accidents is still a significant barrier for some. The Committee took evidence from representatives of teacher unions, including Chris Keates, General Secretary of the NASUWT, a union which now advises its members against participating in school trips. She told us that the risk of litigation, should an accident occur, was now too great:

> "For things that we would all in a sensible world simply dismiss as being a genuine accident that has occurred schools are now getting solicitors' letters as a minimum and then finding they are subject to some sort of investigation, and so on, leading up to potential litigation as the end point on that".[21]

24. When pressed on this point, Ms Keates admitted that cases of teachers being taken to court were actually quite rare, but emphasised that the threat of legal or disciplinary action could still be extremely stressful.[22] In oral evidence, she advised us that the number of false allegations made against her members in connection with school visits has remained roughly stable since 1991, when her union began monitoring it.[23] It is important to distinguish between false allegations (claims of an incident which are untrue) and unfounded claims (where an incident has taken place, but there has not been negligence and there is no basis for litigation). It would also help greatly if teachers were given clear guidance about current law in this area. In subsequent communications, the NASUWT were unable to provide us with a statistical breakdown of cases according to these categories, or even between cases on visits and those in schools.[24]

25. The guidance issued by the NASUWT has not been adopted by any other teaching union and many of those who gave evidence to our inquiry spoke out against it. David Bell, Her Majesty's Chief Inspector of Schools and head of Ofsted, told the Committee that the union's position was unhelpful and contributed to the unjustified culture of fear surrounding school trips:

> "I have the utmost respect for the new general secretary of the NASUWT but I disagree with her on this and I disagree with the advice that she has given her members. Our evidence suggested that the teachers—and it was the teachers and the outdoor instructors who were doing this—said that it [school trips] is still do-able [...] I just worry a bit about that advice being given because are we not just fuelling precisely that risk averseness that [we have] been talking about?"[25]

26. The logical consequences of the NASUWT advice to its members not to participate in school trips would be the cessation of any out-of-school activity. Yet Ms Keates acknowledged that her members do continue to participate in school trips despite her advice, as they believe in the educational value of such experiences.[26] **We do not believe that the NASUWT wishes to see the end of all school trips. We therefore recommend**

---

21   Q 206

22   Q 153

23   Q 139

24   Ev 89

25   Q 225

26   Q 147

that the union seriously reviews its advice to members not to participate in school trips, which is not a helpful attitude.

27. We acknowledge that teachers can feel vulnerable to unjustified allegations or the threat of disproportionate legal action. Dr Fiona Hammans, Head of Banbury School, Oxfordshire and representative of the Secondary Heads Association, told us that her school successfully organises a wide-ranging programme of educational visits and outdoor activities, whilst recognising that an element of risk is involved:

"If I am honest, the fear is still there sometimes. Certainly when you are getting to the end of a month's expedition in Madagascar, for instance, and you get a phone call at 3.30 in the morning and they are saying, 'Actually things are okay; we had forgotten the time difference', there is always a moment of panic then, but it is about as a school we do believe we should be doing it. It is about something special and distinct that we can offer our students. There is a risk there, but our parents have opted into the fact that we will do everything we can and more to minimise that risk, but there is no learning without some risk."[27]

Dr. Hammans went on to describe the positive support her school provides to teachers:

"I think it needs the head teacher's backing, because that is the person who is likely to end up in court. So if we are talking about that fear, if the head is going to say quite clearly, 'These are valuable educational activities which we will run at minimum risk for the very best interests educationally of our students', then you are going to take your staff with you. You inevitably will have the backing of your governors anyway for that. If the LEA supports it, plus there are national initiatives and agendas to support it as well, then it is a winning situation, but I think it has to start with the school, much as the evidence from the DfES officials earlier on saying that it is for the school to determine its priorities locally, but, if it can link in with other national priorities, including Ofsted, then that is a stronger argument."[28]

28. It is clear to us that the fear of accidents and subsequent litigation (whether justified or not) is discouraging some schools from organising school trips. This situation can only be resolved through co-operation and collaboration between teaching unions, schools, LEAs and the DfES. When we asked Stephen Twigg MP, then Parliamentary Under-Secretary of State at the DfES and Minister with responsibility for this area, what he was doing to promote this kind of co-operation and to persuade the NASUWT to change its cautious stance, he told us, "We want to persuade them and we think we can persuade them. We are in discussions with them right now on this issue".[29] We look forward to seeing the department's attempts at persuasion bear fruit.

29. Teachers should be able to expect support from their employers in the case of genuine accidents or unfounded claims. To help achieve this, a consistent approach to vexatious litigation must be developed. Frivolous and unfounded claims should be discouraged. **We recommend that the DfES makes it clear to schools and LEAs that it is unacceptable to**

27   Q 196

28   Q 193

29   Q 231

settle frivolous and unfounded claims out of court simply to get rid of the problem. By working with teacher unions, including the NASUWT, the DfES should be able to address their concerns and persuade the unions to move forward from what is in our view, a needlessly obstructive attitude.

30. The fear of accidents in itself is not the only barrier to the expansion of outdoor education. The Committee has also received evidence to show that the risk assessment bureaucracy associated with out-of-classroom education has increased considerably in recent years. Mr Andy Simpson of the RSPB told us that one teacher organising a visit to a reserve was required to fill in 16 different risk assessment forms (for parents, governors, school authorities, LEA, etc.) in order for the visit to go ahead:

> "RSPB is a professional organisation. We take risk assessment very seriously. We automatically send out risk assessments on our sites and for our activities when schools book with us. Sadly the teacher that I am referring to came back to me and said, 'We would like to have used your risk assessment, but it is not in the format that my local authority wants, so I have to dismantle the whole thing and rebuild it'. Can you blame her for not going?"[30]

31. Representatives of the Outward Bound Trust supported this view. Mr William Ripley told the Committee of the large amount of duplication in the system:

> "We have a licensing system and yet a school will apply to come and do a course with us and so there is a process that they go through whereby they will send us their Local Authority forms, 'Will you fill these forms in'. The first question is: 'Do you have an adventures activities licence?' to which the answer is yes. Instead of saying: 'Go to the bottom of the form, because we have had an external agency do all that work', it then says, 'answer all the questions that you have already answered for the licensing authority'. That is the kind of reaction and process that we are in amongst. […] it is relatively easy for [teachers] when they ask an organisation like us to do that service, but when you are looking at trying to do that in the school as well it just compounds the issue. It just compounds the difficulty."[31]

32. Many witnesses made reference to the Adventure Activities Licensing Authority (AALA), which has inspected adventure activity centres for compliance with health and safety regulations since 1996 (its remit does not cover foreign operators, voluntary organisations or schools themselves). Set up in the wake of the Lyme Bay tragedy, AALA is a cross-departmental and cross-border public authority, sponsored by the DfES and operating under the written guidance of the Health and Safety Commission. No child has died at a licensed centre since the AALA was formed. **Given that AALA-licensed centres have undertaken significant risk assessment processes in order to gain their licence, it seems absurd to us that this should have to be repeated at the demand of local authorities.**

---

30   Q 31 and Ev 31.

31   Q 28

33. The burden of bureaucracy is greatest where local authorities require schools to complete lengthy risk assessment forms and where there is duplication between a number of bodies requiring risk assessments. Dr Fiona Hammans described this situation:

> "There needs to be something which is definitive. So if you are looking at the bureaucracy that everybody has to fill in there is the DfES guidelines which need to be met, there is then the local authority set of guidelines which, as has been indicated earlier on, will change and will change somewhat, then you have got again schools' interpretations, plus whichever group you may be going with, whichever partner you will be working with, so you have got a huge amount of bureaucracy".[32]

34. A number of our witnesses called for the DfES to provide generic risk assessments appropriate to each activity in order to reduce the amount of bureaucracy associated with risk assessments. In supplementary written evidence, the DfES said that this is already provided: "DfES guidance contains model assessment forms for risk assessment, which take up just two sides of A4. It is up to LEAs and schools whether they use our forms. Activity providers can, if they wish, encourage schools to use standard forms."[33]

35. Clearly, it is important for school trips to be the subject of a full risk assessment and to be carried out in accordance with Health and Safety Executive guidelines, but in some areas the number of forms that have to be filled in for the simplest activities is unreasonable. **The Government claims to be actively reducing public sector bureaucracy in general and specifically the burden on schools. We are therefore extremely surprised that it can allow the current situation to persist. We recommend that the DfES takes action to streamline the risk assessment system surrounding school trips, promoting its standard forms more vigorously and deprecating bad practice. We further recommend that AALA licensed centres be subject to a much streamlined risk assessment process, and that the DfES consider expanding the AALA licensing scheme to include other sectors, such as foreign and voluntary operators.**

36. Some schools and activity centres have also described difficulties in securing insurance for visits, either because of unaffordable premiums or, in some cases, because no company has been willing to offer cover.[34] On occasion, this seems to have been caused by local authorities 'over-insuring' or requiring a level of insurance cover that is not appropriate to the level of risk involved.[35] Nevertheless, the insurance industry has submitted evidence to the effect that the cost of liability insurance generally has gone up in recent years, due to legal changes like 'no-win no-fee' arrangements and legal judgements increasing the scope of liability. The insurance industry also notes that cover is generally provided to LEAs for all activities under one premium: "in pricing the cover offered to Local Authorities and schools, insurers do not differentiate between in-school activities and those outside the classroom."[36] Overall, claims for accidents on school trips represent a very small proportion of local authority insurance claims (claims from the education sector as a whole

---

32   Q 179

33   Ev 59

34   Ev 164, para 17: Qq 63–69.

35   Q 68

36   Ev 147

total only 3%).[37] The price of premiums therefore seems to bear very little relationship to the level of risk involved in outdoor education.[38]

37. When we asked DfES officials about this issue, Mr Stephen Crowne, Director of the School Resources Group at the DfES, agreed that it was a symptom of more general problems securing affordable insurance cover for public bodies:

> "I think there is an issue there. It is frankly part of a wider issue to do with school insurance where we have a current position which is of concern, that it is difficult and expensive to get insurance cover for a wide range of school activities and so we are working across government and also commissioning some studies on possible options for the future. [...] We have a study in progress now which we hope by the end of this year will illuminate some of the options that might be available. [...] There are market development options using private sector employers, but there are also options around developing local authorities' capacity to insure for themselves."[39]

The Minister confirmed that his Department was holding talks with insurers on this issue. Although he admitted that these were "at quite an early stage" he expressed his confidence in the process: "I think we have good evidence to present to them in terms of the levels of risk on the basis of the statistics that the Committee will be aware of in terms of the very, very small numbers of accidents that do happen."[40]

38. Our evidence on the extent to which insurance is a problem for schools is largely anecdotal. We therefore look forward to learning the results of the current DfES consultation on this subject. Given the small scale of the risks involved, we can see no reason why a market-led solution to school insurance should not exist. **We recommend that the DfES thoroughly investigate the extent to which difficulties securing insurance cover are a barrier to education outside the classroom and develops options to resolve any problems.**

Teacher Training

39. Our evidence has underlined the importance of teacher training to the provision of high quality education outside the classroom. Andy Simpson of the RSPB told the Committee that this was the top priority for the sector:

> "Nearly every workshop that we have convened and brought together practitioners irrespective of where they have come from [...at] the top was teacher training and support for teachers, both continuing professional development of the teachers but also initial teacher training because I think we all recognise that whatever bureaucracy emerges or whatever curriculum changes emerges, what funding emerges, we have had to take the teaching profession with us."[41]

---

37   Ev 191

38   Commercial or voluntary activity centres that require their own insurance may also experience difficulties and would not be covered by blanket LEA premiums.

39   Qq 109, 110.

40   Q 233

41   Q 54

40. When we spoke to teacher unions about this issue, they agreed. Kathryn James of the NAHT said:

> "I would strongly support the notion of teachers receiving training and all staff receiving training in terms of actually running, planning and moving forward with any outdoor education activity. I think that is absolutely essential. We mention in our evidence the OCR training course, which is actually very valuable, and I think the more people that undertake this the better, or something similar."[42]

41. Despite this general support, many teachers are not specifically trained in teaching outside the classroom. Written evidence submitted by the English Outdoor Council stressed the inadequacy of Initial Teacher Training (ITT):

> "While in-service training has been very effective in recent years, we are not convinced that initial teacher training does a good enough job in terms of giving trainee teachers the confidence they need to take their pupils out of the classroom. Standards for Qualified Teacher Status require trainees to be able to plan out-of-school experiences but, in the context that so much needs to crammed into so little time, we are not convinced that this is in practice being delivered consistently and effectively".[43]

42. When we asked the Minister about this issue, he agreed to reconsider the status of outdoor learning within ITT, saying "the concern you have expressed is one that the organisations have raised recently with the Secretary of State, and I understand the meetings are due with Ralph Tabberer at the TTA [Teacher Training Agency] to look at this".[44] **We welcome this review.**

43. Initial Teacher Training programmes must incorporate a diverse range of subjects and operate under significant time constraints. Nevertheless, the Committee is concerned to hear that the amount of time devoted to education outside the classroom has become so limited. Training may be confined to purely theoretical explanations with practical experience only offered on a voluntary basis.[45] Trainee teachers cannot be expected to prioritise outdoor learning or take up opportunities for continuing professional development in this area later in their career unless its value is explored in ITT. **We recommend that the DfES work with the Teacher Training Agency to ensure that Initial Teacher Training courses demonstrate the potential benefits of education outside the classroom and point teachers towards ways to develop their skills in this area as their career progresses.**

44. The Committee has heard of many excellent in-service training courses on education outside the classroom (including the qualification offered by OCR) that are available to teachers as part of their Continuing Professional Development (CPD). The range and diversity of these courses, from mountaineering to risk assessment, have led the DfES to state that "there is no evidence of lack of opportunities" for teachers to develop their

---

42   Q 173

43   Ev 143

44   Q 245

45   Q 17

skills.[46] Despite this assertion, DfES officials admitted that the department holds no data on the volume of CPD in outdoor learning and keeps no records showing how many teachers hold qualifications obtained as a result of courses carried out at school or LEA level.[47] **Any attempt to raise the quantity and quality of outdoor education depends crucially on the skills and motivation of the teachers involved. We therefore recommend that the DfES give an explicit commitment to support Continuing Professional Development in this area. Any Departmental Manifesto for Outdoor Learning that may emerge should include an entitlement to training for teachers. Networks such as Teachers TV can also be of significant benefit in spreading good practice and should be engaged in this project.**

45. The Committee has also taken evidence on the teaching of fieldwork in science subjects. Witnesses have maintained that younger science teachers are not always well prepared to lead fieldwork activities, as many have themselves suffered from the decline of outdoor education as students.[48] Dr Rita Gardner, Director of the Royal Geographical Society said that this deficit is not necessarily remedied in ITT:

> "Many of those that we have consulted suggest that there are issues in the professional training of teachers with limited capacity in very tight PGCE programmes to include training in fieldwork inquiry and skills, and even if a geographer has come through a graduate programme where they are taught fieldwork and taken in the field, that is very different from then taking a group of kids out in the field and teaching them inquiry learning and skills."[49]

46. Dr. Steve Tilling of the Field Studies Council said that fieldwork skills used to be passed on in schools as part of an informal 'mentoring' process, but voiced concerns that the skills could be lost entirely as older teachers leave the profession:

> "there has been an increasing dependence on, if you like, in school training, mentoring within schools, and even within the schools an age and cohort, if you like, perhaps of teachers who had these skills are dropping out the other end [...] So if a new teacher comes into a school and is looking for that sort of support within the school, then the chances are it is no longer there so unless it is delivered through the college then it will not be delivered, and the stance that we have at our fingertips suggests it is also disappearing from college provision."[50]

47. Both Dr Tilling and Dr Gardner suggested that training in fieldwork skills could be provided to new teachers by engaging subject or professional bodies (such as the Association for Science Education, the British Ecological Society or the Royal Geographical Society/Institute of British Geographers). They reported that courses have been run by organisations such as these, with high levels of take-up and good evaluations, but that access has been limited due to a lack of funding.[51] **We recommend that the DfES engage**

---

46   Ev 62

47   Q 79, Q 83.

48   Q 17

49   Q 4

50   Q 17

51   Q 17

teachers' professional bodies and subject associations in the provision of fieldwork training for science and geography teachers, ensuring that appropriate programmes of professional development are on offer to all those teachers who might benefit.

Schools

48. Outdoor learning works best where it is well integrated into school structures, in relation to both curriculum and logistics (for example, the organisation of timetables and supply cover where necessary). In this context, we welcome the establishment of Educational Visit Co-ordinators (EVCs) in schools. The EVC role was introduced by the DfES in 2002. Its principle functions are to liaise with the LEA's Outdoor Education Adviser and to ensure that school staff taking pupils on any kind of educational visit are competent to do so and trained as necessary in pupil safety outdoors. All LEAs in England participate in the programme and some now have an EVC in every school in their area.[52]

49. **Our evidence suggests that EVCs are working well in schools,[53] but we would re-iterate our comments on training. In order to be effective, educational visits co-ordinators must have access to high quality programmes of Continuing Professional Development. We also consider that the EVC role should be developed further into that of a champion for outdoor learning within a school. This should include not only the promotion of off-site visits but also the benefits of using the school grounds as a resource.**

50. Education outside the classroom does not have to mean education outside the school—school grounds are a vital resource. This is particularly true of primary schools, where opportunities for outdoor play can have a significant positive effect on a child's personal and educational development. The Committee was therefore concerned to hear that many school grounds do not provide suitable environments for this development to occur. Learning Through Landscapes, the national school grounds charity, told us that grounds are often inadequate, even in new schools:

> "The new capital spend under Building Schools for The Future and the Academies programme does not guarantee that LEAs and their schools can or will address this chronic school grounds problem [...] some of the new schools, and particularly some of the new Academies, are coming on stream with school grounds that are still substantially below the standard that would be expected of a modern educational establishment.[...]There appears to be a significant presumption in favour of high tech indoor learning provision which leaves little scope for investment in the outdoors. [...] PPP consortia often appear to have a poor understanding of the teaching and learning potential of school grounds and there is a tendency for them to design expensive aesthetic landscapes of little educational value."[54]

51. We were particularly anxious to hear that the new capital building projects initiated by the DfES (including Building Schools for the Future and City Academies) do not

---

52   Ev 42, paras 94–97.

53   Qq 187–189.

54   Ev 133

necessarily exploit the school's outdoor space to its full potential. When we put this concern to the Minister, he responded:

> "We clearly want to get new schools, be they academies or other new schools, to have the very, very best facilities and I have certainly visited schools where that is the case so clearly the picture is a mixed one […] I would have to study the evidence that they have given to the Committee in more detail to then see whether there is a basis for what they are saying and whether something can be done about it in terms of the guidance we give for the development of new schools. Certainly for academies which are directly our responsibility as a Department I think it is critically important that they do include those opportunities, particularly as these are schools focused in areas of great need and generally areas of educational under-performance and under-achievement."[55]

52. The Commission for Architecture and the Built Environment (CABE) has given the Committee persuasive evidence to suggest that students' experience of the built environment has significant and unexploited potential for learning:

> "The built environment is a resource that is perennially available to all, and one with which everyone has a relationship. It has an immense physical and intellectual range that can provide rich, shared learning experiences. Since the built environment is outside of the windows of classrooms and surrounding streets its learning applications are simple to access and need to be promoted more widely."[56]

Visits to buildings and public spaces can benefit students, but the most immediate built environment available to schools is their own grounds.

53. **It appears that some new schools are being built without due regard to the educational potential of school grounds. This is a result of the lack of leadership and strategic planning from the DfES with regard to outdoor learning. We urge the Department to take action to ensure that new capital projects incorporate good design of outdoor spaces into their plans.**

54. The Government is currently encouraging schools to become 'extended schools', providing 'wraparound' services such as breakfast clubs and after school activities and hosting other youth services on their site. There is a potential to increase outdoor education as part of this programme. Schools could enhance students' experience of the outdoors by offering additional activities and linking up with community groups outside their core hours. The DfES should ensure that schools are aware of these possibilities so that this opportunity is not missed.

55. Finally, children spend more time at home than in school and any strategy intended to increase children's access to a variety of environmental settings needs to engage parents and carers. In this context the Government's extended schools initiative has a vital role to play. By reaching out to parent and community groups, schools can link up with wider

---

55   Q 251

56   Ev 158, para 2.2. The Chairman also had a meeting in a representative capacity with Sophie Andreae, Chair of the CABE Education Foundation.

community activities and make the most of children's learning opportunities both in and out of the classroom.

Cost

56. **Much of our evidence cited cost as a significant barrier to the organisation of educational visits, yet we do not believe that cost alone is responsible for the decline of education outside the classroom, or that simply throwing money at the problem would provide a solution.** This conclusion is supported by evidence from the DfES London Challenge programme. As part of this initiative, the Field Studies Council offered full funding to schools to support an off-site educational visit.[57] One third of schools did not take up this offer despite it being effectively free of charge. It seems therefore that an increase in funding alone would not be enough to persuade schools to change their behaviour, but it is clear to us that certain difficulties do exist in this area, which we discuss below.

57. The cost of arranging good quality supply cover for teachers who are absent on a school trip is one area that has been highlighted in evidence. Some have suggested that the recent National Agreement on Workforce Reform may have led to an increase in costs.[58] The Agreement limits the amount of time teachers can be asked to cover for absent colleagues and may therefore mean that supply cover needs to be secured more often. When we asked the Minister about this issue, he gave his view that the Workforce Agreement was having a "mixed" effect, but declined to quantify the scale of the problem:

> "I think the reality is that it is probably a mixed picture on workforce reform. There is the protection that is given in terms of the maximum contact time, so that could have a negative effect, but, on the other hand, part of the reason that workforce reform can happen is that there are all these other adults working in schools or with schools that were not there ten years ago, and that clearly does give opportunities both in terms of people to cover when trips are happening but also for those people to help with the organisation of the trips. I think workplace reform, in all honesty, will have a mixed impact, in some places positive, in some places it could have the negative effect you have described."[59]

We urge the DfES to monitor any unintended consequences of the Workforce Agreement to determine whether it has led to an increase in the cost of arranging supply cover during school trips.

58. A more significant cost is that of arranging transport to and from off-site visits. This cost has also increased in recent years due to the requirement for minibus drivers to hold a PCV licence if they gained their licence after 1997. This means that young teachers coming into the profession are unable to drive school minibuses and drivers must be hired at extra expense.[60] **Parliament is currently legislating on school transport, an area we considered during our previous inquiry into the draft School Transport Bill. As we recommended**

---

57   Q 8

58   Q 46, although Steve Sinnott, General Secretary of the NUT, said he was unaware of any problem in this area.

59   Q 253

60   Ev 130, para 6.5.

in that report, we would expect the DfES to strongly encourage local authorities trialling alternative arrangements for school transport under the new legislative framework to include transport for school trips in their pilot schemes.[61] **This should lead to a reduction in costs.**

59. Educational visits that cannot be funded by a school's budget are generally subsidised by 'voluntary' parental contributions. Parents or carers cannot be required to contribute and their children must not be excluded from a trip if they cannot or do not wish to contribute.[62] Nevertheless, schools often make it clear at the outset that a visit might become unviable if a number of parents who were unable to contribute financially insisted that their children take part. This can result in poorer families struggling to find the money for school trips, or their children missing out. On a larger scale, schools in affluent areas are likely to be able to call upon a much larger reserve of parental contributions, allowing them to organise more adventurous residential visits away from schools, whereas those in deprived areas are confined to their locality.[63] Although there is much to be gained from outdoor learning activities conducted within the school grounds or in the local area, those children who might arguably be said to have the most to gain from experiencing an environment away from their home area are actually less likely to be given the opportunity to do so through their school.

60. It is this potential disparity that has led campaigners to call for ring-fenced funding to be provided for outdoor learning. We tend to agree with this proposal. As we noted earlier in this report, the DfES has mooted the possibility of a 'Manifesto for Outdoor Learning'. Departmental officials suggested that this would be similar in format to the Music Manifesto.[64] We therefore noted with interest the recent announcement by David Miliband, the then Minister of State for School Standards, of a £30 million three-year funding package associated with the Music Manifesto. **Given the strong evidence for the benefits of education outside the classroom, we recommend that a Manifesto for Outdoor Learning should be issued by the DfES, giving all students a right to outdoor learning. This Manifesto should attract a similar level of funding to the Music Manifesto in order to deliver real change. In particular, schools in deprived circumstances should be enabled to enhance their facilities, to offer professional development programmes to their teachers and to fund off site visits.**

Centres and operators

61. Historically, LEAs have been major providers of facilities for school trips through their networks of activity centres. In recent years, many of these centres have closed and the balance of provision has shifted towards private and voluntary operators.[65] This is not a universal trend: the Committee has heard of some local authorities that have expanded

---

61   Education and Skills Select Committee, Third Report of Session 2002–03, *The Draft School Transport Bill*, HC 509.

62   A charge cannot be made for a trip taking place wholly or mainly during normal school hours, or one which is connected with the National Curriculum or religious education, or meets the requirements of the syllabus for a public examination. Extra-curricular residential trips can be offered at a charge.

63   Qq 46, 47.

64   Q 99. The Music Manifesto promises every primary school child the opportunity to learn an instrument.

65   Ofsted, *Outdoor Education: Aspects of good Practice*, paragraph 41.

their provision. This has often been achieved through a process of financial and organisational restructuring, as in the example of Hampshire county council:

> "During the 1980s and 1990s Hampshire bucked the trend of LEAs that sold off or privatised their outdoor centres in the face of budget pressures and protected its centres from changes to educational funding arrangements by moving its centres into a department outside of education. Thus protected from pressures created by the increasing devolution of funding directly to schools, the county was able to grow and develop its outdoor learning opportunities. Additionally, a dedicated staff of experienced professional instructors and teachers have developed at each centre, able to fully support teachers working in the outdoors. A centrally based Outdoor Activities Officer is also employed to ensure consistency of service, operation and risk management across the centres."[66]

62. In the course of this inquiry, private operators have contacted us, advocating an expansion in private provision. They have stated that private operators remove the burden of risk and of bureaucracy from schools. For example, in their evidence, World Challenge Expeditions Ltd challenge the traditional relationship between schools and LEAs, stating that school trips are "widely inaccessible due to restrictive practice and public sector bureaucracy rather than issues of funding":

> "DfES guidance on school trips can allow a teacher or Head to believe that they are personally liable for any incident, and fails to recognize that much provision, and much of the liability, can be outsourced—as with school transport [...] Further difficulties arise over the allocation of funding, where the tendering process for numerous central government initiatives obscures any reasonable chance of a level playing field. Funds are distributed by Connexions partnerships heavily weighted towards local relationships, with no obligation to assess the quality of provision, innovation or particularly the ability of the provider to recruit children. As a result vast sums of money go unspent, except on a limited range of local opportunity – and at much higher cost to the taxpayer because the public sector adds in administration fees, whereas the private sector bid with a fixed inclusive price. The result, apart from being chaotic, also heavily penalizes innovation or private-sector involvement."[67]

63. In oral evidence, Andy Simpson of the RSPB described the way in which voluntary providers had been affected by the decline of central LEA provision:

> "Whilst we want to do more we are very cognisant of the fact that the money has to be raised from somewhere. If one was being critical of Government over the years, one would say that since local management of schools and the demise of many of the local authority field study centres which offered subsidised visits to children—which is how I started—Government has had pretty much of a free ride. It is the NGO sector and other providers that have stepped in to fill that vacuum. We want to do more. We would appreciate some help."[68]

---

66   Ev 105, para 1.

67   Ev 105, para 4.

68   Q 43

64. The provision of activity centres and other facilities is closely linked to the way in which outdoor education, and education more generally, is funded. Some LEAs have cut central services, including school activity centres, in order to comply with Government pressure to delegate more and more funding directly to schools. The recent *Five Year Strategy for Children and Learners* published by the DfES suggests that this pressure will continue and even increase as control over budgets shifts to schools rather than LEAs. In this document, the Government proposes that local authorities will take on a more 'strategic' planning and collaboration role rather than providing services centrally.[69] **In its *Five Year Strategy*, the Government proposes that all secondary schools should become independent specialist schools and that LEAs should lose control over school budgets. We recommend that the DfES give serious consideration to how it will structure funding for central outdoor activity services under this new system, or help schools access private and voluntary provision, so that students still have access to high quality outdoor education.**

65. The DfES has funded some initiatives intended to assist schools in organising trips, which we discuss later in this report. These include the Growing Schools project, which is designed to support teachers using the 'outdoor classroom' as a curriculum resource, GetREAL, which offers residential visits to teenagers over the summer holidays modelled on the US camp experience, and project funding for museums, galleries and activity centres to facilitate school visits. Here too, funding issues have been highlighted as a barrier to expansion. Witnesses have complained that these initiatives are generally only supported by short term project-based funding. Activity centres participating in these initiatives found it difficult to plan for the future and:

> "were only able to employ additional staff on a temporary or casual basis, which meant that skills and expertise were lost when the projects ended. They were not able to develop such strong relationships with schools as a longer-term programme of investment would offer".[70]

It is essential that the DfES and Department for Culture, Media and Sport develop a strategy for the long-term viability of activity centres, helping them to retain staff, build strong links with schools and develop expertise.

---

69   Department for Education and Skills, *Five Year Strategy for Children and Learners*, CM 6272, July 2004.

70   Ev 127, para 2.6. Q 46.

5 The Role of the DfES

66. Our inquiry has revealed that there is currently a very patchy provision of outdoor education in schools. Some schools do well in organising a carefully planned programme of educational experiences outside the classroom, whereas others are put off by perceptions of risk, time-consuming bureaucracy and cost. The good practice of some schools in this area suggests that it would be possible for others to follow suit and that the DfES could expect to be successful in an attempt to share good practice across schools. When we expressed this view to the Minister, he agreed:

> "We want schools to make the very, very best use of the various opportunities that are available and what we know is a lot of schools do but a lot of schools do not. What that says is there is the potential within the framework we have got at the moment to get there. Our role needs to be to see what can be done to encourage all schools to take up the opportunities that are available to them."[71]

67. **We conclude that the DfES has a vital role to play in demonstrating the value of out-of-classroom learning to schools and spreading best practice across all schools. The future of outdoor learning depends on clear direction and leadership from the DfES that has so far been woefully missing.**

68. A key role for Government is the provision of advice concerning the conduct of visits and of health and safety guidance. As we noted earlier in this report, the DfES has recently updated its guidance on a number of occasions. This clear health and safety advice is to be welcomed, but **the Department as well as LEAs should take care to ensure that schools and activity centres are not becoming overloaded with risk assessment bureaucracy from different, overlapping organisations, as this can be a significant deterrent.**

69. We are also concerned that the recent overwhelming focus on risk and health and safety issues may have meant that opportunities for curricular development have been missed. For example, in a written submission to the Committee, Dr Pete Higgins states:

> "The response of the outdoor education sector on issues of safety has been, since the Lyme Bay incident in 1993, to focus almost exclusively on safety-related issues in their professional practice. Whilst such a response is entirely understandable, it has meant that curricular change has gone largely unnoticed and the resulting opportunities unexploited. This has led to a situation where although many experiences outside the classroom can be deemed to be 'safe' they have little or no locus in a curriculum."

The DfES needs to take the lead by demonstrating the low levels of risk attached to school visits. This could perhaps be achieved via a statistical comparison with other everyday activities. Given the relatively low levels of risk attached to outdoor activities, the Department should now give a clear steer to schools that educational innovation outside the classroom is to be welcomed and even to be expected.

71   Q 227

70. The DfES has set up some initiatives aimed at encouraging outdoor learning. Chief among these are GetREAL and the Growing Schools programme. These have been supplemented by projects from other departments, for example Defra's Countryside Access schemes, as well as some innovative work by the Welsh Assembly.[72] In oral evidence, the Minister particularly stressed the importance and success of the Growing Schools project, terming it "a really, really powerful instrument of improvement"[73] and claiming: "We have got 10,000 schools signed up to Growing Schools. Almost half the schools are already part of this. What that means in practice in most schools is going to vary. They are not all at the excellent end of the spectrum but it is pretty impressive to have that number of schools already part of a network. "[74]

71. Although the Minister boasted that 10,000 schools have signed up to Growing Schools, we have some concerns about the limitations of this project. Growing Schools was specifically set up to teach children about food, farming and the environment, to explain how food travels from the farmyard to the dinner table and explore healthy eating and environmental impacts in this context. The Real World Learning Campaign describes the Growing Schools project as a programme "shackled if not dominated by a food and farming agenda", which cannot therefore be expected to resolve the wider problems facing outdoor education, described in this report.[75] In addition, an independent evaluation of the programme by the Council for Environmental Education and Bath University's Centre for Research in Education and the Environment notes the good resources supplied via the Growing Schools website, but questions whether the scheme recognises, or significantly addresses, barriers to effective learning outside the classroom.[76] **The Committee believes that current Government initiatives do not go far enough in overcoming the barriers to outdoor learning. What is needed is a coherent strategy for education outside the classroom that brings together good practice from around the country, rather than a small number of limited, if worthy projects.**

72. Throughout this inquiry, we have been impressed by the number and variety of voluntary, commercial and professional organisations involved in the provision of outdoor education. These include charitable foundations in the heritage and environmental sectors, local and national companies that bring schools into their businesses, commercial providers of educational and adventurous activities and teachers' professional bodies. In developing a strategy for out-of-classroom education, the DfES needs to more effectively engage these partners, exploiting and developing the resources that already exist.

73. In order to reverse the decline of outdoor education, some of our witnesses have called for a national entitlement to a certain amount of hours of outdoor learning within the school curriculum. The National Curriculum already lays down some limited statutory entitlements to outdoor learning, particularly in the Foundation Stage for nursery children, in PE and recently in Geography, where there is now a requirement for an element of fieldwork. Our evidence on the extent to which this requirement is being met or exceeded

---

72   Ev 192, Ev 163.

73   Q 226

74   Q 248

75   Ev 101

76   *Growing Schools—The Innovation Fund Projects (2002–2003): an External Evaluation;* Council for Environmental Education, University of Bath Centre for Research in Education and the Environment, 2003. Ev 176.

varies. The Field Studies Council told us that "the statutory requirement to carry out fieldwork has had a major positive impact on levels of geography fieldwork",[77] yet other witnesses complained that provision is patchy with some schools struggling to reach the bare minimum.[78] We are particularly concerned that these subject-specific requirements do not sit easily with the cross-curricular nature of much outdoor learning and its ability to raise achievement across subject areas.

74. In oral evidence, DfES officials opposed the idea of a cross-curricular statutory entitlement to outdoor learning, saying that an entitlement "does not offer any assurance about the quality or the relevance of the experience. It is an input measure".[79] This response surprised us, as the department has used the concept of an entitlement successfully in the past (for example, with the 'Literacy Hour'). Nevertheless, we would agree that the simple imposition of an entitlement is unlikely to improve matters by itself. It would need to be accompanied by other measures enabling the entitlement to be delivered.

75. As an alternative to an entitlement, DfES officials suggested that education outside the classroom could be expanded and improved by means of a 'Manifesto for Outdoor Learning'. Campaign groups have called for such a commitment, most recently through the Real World Learning Campaign, an alliance of organisations involved in outdoor education. Any manifesto should be part of a national strategy. **The Committee supports the idea of a Manifesto for Outdoor Learning, but it must be more than 'warm words'.**

76. **Whatever mechanism is used, the Department's role must be expanded from its current reactive work to a more proactive function, championing the benefits of outdoor education. We regret that too often in education, the General Teaching Council and professional organisations do not have the will or the capacity to promote best practice effectively and so the Government is left with the responsibility of driving change.**

77. **We recommend that the DfES set up a structure to promote education outside the classroom at all levels. Within the Department, a dedicated team of officials should have responsibility for outdoor learning across curriculum areas and should tap into other Departmental initiatives, such as the extended schools programme and the provision of before/after school activities. A high profile 'champion' for outdoor learning should be appointed to lead this team. In each LEA, an Outdoor Education Adviser should be in place, promoting and co-ordinating outdoor learning locally and liaising with the Department. Each school should have a well trained Educational Visits Co-ordinator, whose role should be strengthened and expanded to act as the local champion for outdoor learning. A nationwide network of support, guidance and innovation would move outdoor education forwards from its current, patchy position to a more uniform provision of high quality opportunities throughout the country.**

---

77   Ev 11, para 3.

78   Q 4

79   Q 97

6 Conclusion

78. In recent years much of the discourse surrounding outdoor education has been focused on issues of risk and safety. Whilst this is clearly a very important issue, we believe that the debate has now become unbalanced and that not enough has been done to publicise the benefits of education outside the classroom. This is a great pity as there is a growing body of research evidence (supported amongst others by Ofsted) to show the potential of outdoor learning to raise standards in all schools, including amongst hard-to-reach children.

79. The decline of outdoor education impoverishes students' learning and represents a missed opportunity for curricular enrichment. Whilst the DfES has set up some small initiatives and voluntary organisations have contributed significantly, the sector is burdened by excessive bureaucracy, a low profile and a distorted perception of risk that is not supported by the facts. Despite this, many schools do continue to offer a varied and positive programme of events. This is an encouraging sign and leads us to conclude that a proper national strategy for outdoor learning would have a positive effect on many schools.

80. The DfES should act to spread good practice by setting up a network of champions at local, regional and national level, by supporting training for teachers and by conducting research into the benefits of different types of out-of-classroom learning. It should also do more to link outdoor education into its other initiatives such as the 'extended schools' programme and its wider youth services policies.

81. The DfES should publish a Manifesto for Outdoor Learning, giving all children a right to education outside the classroom. This Manifesto must be more than 'warm words'. It must be the expression of a coherent national strategy and should be accompanied by a package of measures and funding enabling change to be delivered across the areas of teacher training, access to facilities and curricular innovation.

82. In order to reverse the decline of education outside the classroom, the Department needs to commit appropriate resources to the sector. Further, the Department should review its current funding of activity centres, museums and galleries and other facilities offering educational services to schools. The current short-term funding structure is hampering development in these areas and the DfES should consider how these facilities can be supported over a longer period of time.

7 Conclusions and recommendations

The value of outdoor learning

1.   The broad extent of this inquiry has convinced the Committee that outdoor learning can benefit pupils of all ages and can be successful in a variety of settings. We are convinced that out-of-classroom education enriches the curriculum and can improve educational attainment. Whilst recognising this cross-curricular scope, we conclude that in order to realise its full potential, outdoor education must be carried out properly, with sessions being prepared by well trained teachers and leaders and in accordance with good curriculum guidance as well as health and safety regulations. (Paragraph 9)

2.   Like all educational processes, the benefits of education outside the classroom should be rigorously researched, documented and communicated. Positive and reliable evidence of the benefits of outdoor activities would help schools determine the priority to afford to such work. (Paragraph 13)

The decline of education outside the classroom

3.   It is clear to the Committee that outdoor education is a sector suffering from considerable unexploited potential. (Paragraph 18)

Risk and bureaucracy

4.   Many of the organisations and individuals who submitted evidence to our inquiry cited the fear of accidents and the possibility of litigation as one of the main reasons for the apparent decline in school trips. It is the view of this Committee that this fear is entirely out of proportion to the real risks. (Paragraph 19)

5.   We welcome the DfES health and safety guidance which clearly sets out what is expected of all those involved in organising school trips. There remain some concerns relating to guidance on trips involving children with special educational needs, where there could be more specific recommendations on levels of staffing and the right of children to attend. This area is likely to be affected by the enactment of the Disability Discrimination Bill and we recommend that the DfES review its guidance in this context. (Paragraph 22)

6.   We do not believe that the NASUWT wishes to see the end of all school trips. We therefore recommend that the union seriously reviews its advice to members not to participate in school trips, which is not a helpful attitude. (Paragraph 26)

7.   We recommend that the DfES makes it clear to schools and LEAs that it is unacceptable to settle frivolous and unfounded claims out of court simply to get rid of the problem. By working with teacher unions, including the NASUWT, the DfES should be able to address their concerns and persuade the unions to move forward from what is in our view, a needlessly obstructive attitude. (Paragraph 29)

8. We recommend that the DfES takes action to streamline the risk assessment system surrounding school trips, promoting its standard forms more vigorously and deprecating bad practice. We further recommend that AALA licensed centres be subject to a much streamlined risk assessment process, and that the DfES consider expanding the AALA licensing scheme to include other sectors, such as foreign and voluntary operators. (Paragraph 35)

9. We recommend that the DfES thoroughly investigate the extent to which difficulties securing insurance cover are a barrier to education outside the classroom and develops options to resolve any problems. (Paragraph 38)

Teacher training

10. We recommend that the DfES work with the Teacher Training Agency to ensure that Initial Teacher Training courses demonstrate the potential benefits of education outside the classroom and point teachers towards ways to develop their skills in this area as their career progresses. (Paragraph 43)

11. Any attempt to raise the quantity and quality of outdoor education depends crucially on the skills and motivation of the teachers involved. We therefore recommend that the DfES give an explicit commitment to support Continuing Professional Development in this area. Any Departmental Manifesto for Outdoor Learning that may emerge should include an entitlement to training for teachers. Networks such as Teachers TV can also be of significant benefit in spreading good practice and should be engaged in this project. (Paragraph 44)

12. We recommend that the DfES engage teachers' professional bodies and subject associations in the provision of fieldwork training for science and geography teachers, ensuring that appropriate programmes of professional development are on offer to all those teachers who might benefit. (Paragraph 47)

Schools

13. Our evidence suggests that EVCs are working well in schools, but we would re-iterate our comments on training. In order to be effective, educational visits co-ordinators must have access to high quality programmes of Continuing Professional Development. We also consider that the EVC role should be developed further into that of a champion for outdoor learning within a school. This should include not only the promotion of off-site visits but also the benefits of using the school grounds as a resource. (Paragraph 49)

14. It appears that some new schools are being built without due regard to the educational potential of school grounds. This is a result of the lack of leadership and strategic planning from the DfES with regard to outdoor learning. We urge the Department to take action to ensure that new capital projects incorporate good design of outdoor spaces into their plans. (Paragraph 53)

Cost

15. Much of our evidence cited cost as a significant barrier to the organisation of educational visits, yet we do not believe that cost alone is responsible for the decline of education outside the classroom, or that simply throwing money at the problem would provide a solution. (Paragraph 56)

16. We urge the DfES to monitor any unintended consequences of the Workforce Agreement to determine whether it has led to an increase in the cost of arranging supply cover during school trips. (Paragraph 57)

17. Parliament is currently legislating on school transport, an area we considered during our previous inquiry into the draft School Transport Bill. As we recommended in that report, we would expect the DfES to strongly encourage local authorities trialling alternative arrangements for school transport under the new legislative framework to include transport for school trips in their pilot schemes. This should lead to a reduction in costs. (Paragraph 58)

18. Given the strong evidence for the benefits of education outside the classroom, we recommend that a Manifesto for Outdoor Learning should be issued by the DfES, giving all students a right to outdoor learning. This Manifesto should attract a similar level of funding to the Music Manifesto in order to deliver real change. In particular, schools in deprived circumstances should be enabled to enhance their facilities, to offer professional development programmes to their teachers and to fund off site visits. (Paragraph 60)

Centres and operators

19. In its Five Year Strategy, the Government proposes that all secondary schools should become independent specialist schools and that LEAs should lose control over school budgets. We recommend that the DfES give serious consideration to how it will structure funding for central outdoor activity services under this new system, or help schools access private and voluntary provision, so that students still have access to high quality outdoor education. (Paragraph 64)

20. It is essential that the DfES and DCMS develop a strategy for the long-term viability of activity centres, helping them to retain staff, build strong links with schools and develop expertise. (Paragraph 65)

The role of the DfES

21. We conclude that the DfES has a vital role to play in demonstrating the value of out-of-classroom learning to schools and spreading best practice across all schools. The future of outdoor learning depends on clear direction and leadership from the DfES that has so far been woefully missing. (Paragraph 67)

22. The Department as well as LEAs should take care to ensure that schools and activity centres are not becoming overloaded with risk assessment bureaucracy from different, overlapping organisations, as this can be a significant deterrent. (Paragraph 68)

23.   The DfES needs to take the lead by demonstrating the low levels of risk attached to school visits. This could perhaps be achieved via a statistical comparison with other everyday activities. Given the relatively low levels of risk attached to outdoor activities, the Department should now give a clear steer to schools that educational innovation outside the classroom is to be welcomed and even to be expected. (Paragraph 69)

24.   The Committee believes that current Government initiatives do not go far enough in overcoming the barriers to outdoor learning. What is needed is a coherent strategy for education outside the classroom that brings together good practice from around the country, rather than a small number of limited, if worthy projects. (Paragraph 71)

25.   The Committee supports the idea of a Manifesto for Outdoor Learning, but it must be more than 'warm words'. (Paragraph 75)

26.   Whatever mechanism is used, the Department's role must be expanded from its current reactive work to a more proactive function, championing the benefits of outdoor education. We regret that too often in education, the General Teaching Council and professional organisations do not have the will or the capacity to promote best practice effectively and so the Government is left with the responsibility of driving change. (Paragraph 76)

27.   We recommend that the DfES set up a structure to promote education outside the classroom at all levels. Within the Department, a dedicated team of officials should have responsibility for outdoor learning across curriculum areas and should tap into other Departmental initiatives, such as the extended schools programme and the provision of before/after school activities. A high profile 'champion' for outdoor learning should be appointed to lead this team. In each LEA, an Outdoor Education Adviser should be in place, promoting and co-ordinating outdoor learning locally and liaising with the Department. Each school should have a well trained Educational Visits Co-ordinator, whose role should be strengthened and expanded to act as the local champion for outdoor learning. A nationwide network of support, guidance and innovation would move outdoor education forwards from its current, patchy position to a more uniform provision of high quality opportunities throughout the country. (Paragraph 77)

Formal minutes

Monday 31 January 2005

Members present:
Mr Barry Sheerman, in the Chair

Jeff Ennis	Helen Jones
Mr Nick Gibb	Jonathan Shaw
Mr John Greenway	Mr Andrew Turner

The Committee deliberated.

Draft Report (Education Outside the Classroom), proposed by the Chairman, brought up and read.

Ordered, That the Chairman's draft Report be read a second time, paragraph by paragraph.

Paragraphs 1 to 82 read and agreed to.

Summary agreed to.

Resolved, That the Report be the Second Report of the Committee to the House.

Ordered, That the Chairman do make the Report to the House.

Ordered, That the provisions of Standing Order No. 134 (Select committees (reports)) be applied to the Report.

Several papers were ordered to be appended to the Minutes of Evidence.

Ordered, That the Appendices to the Minutes of Evidence taken before the Committee be reported to the House.

Several Memoranda were ordered to be reported to the House.

The Committee further deliberated.

[Adjourned until Wednesday 2 February at 9.15 am

Witnesses

List of written evidence

List of unprinted written evidence

Additional papers have been received from the following and have been reported to the House but to save printing costs they have not been printed and copies have been placed in the House of Commons Library where they may be inspected by members. Other copies are in the Record Office, House of Lords and are available to the public for inspection. Requests for inspection should be addressed to the Record Office, House of Lords, London SW1. (Tel 020 7219 3074). Hours of inspection are from 9:30am to 5:00pm on Mondays to Fridays.

Blackpool Local Education Authority (EOC 1)

Outposts Ltd (EOC 3)

Anne White (EOC 4)

Birmingham City Council (EOC 5)

Young Explorers' Trust (EOC 7)

Leeds City Council (EOC 11)

Fairbridge (EOC 13)

Shirley Ali Khan and Mike Fawcett (EOC 14)

Smallpiece Trust (EOC 15)

Wilderness Expertise Ltd (EOC 16)

CLEAPSS School Science Service (EOC 18)

Sayers Croft Field Centre (EOC 20 and EOC 33)

Severn Trent Water (EOC 21)

Magilligan Field Centre (EOC 23)

Julia Welchman (EOC 24 and EOC 110)

National Association for Environmental Education (EOC 25)

The Soil Association (EOC 26)

OCR (EOC 27)

Ty'r Morwydd Environmental Study Centre (EOC 28)

RSPCA (EOC 29)

Norfolk County Council (EOC 32)

The Independent Schools Council (EOC 34)

CCPR (EOC 35)

Oxfordshire County Council Learning & Culture Directorate (EOC 37)

Royal Academy of Engineering (EOC 38)

Buckinghamshire County Council (EOC 39)

Flatts Nursery School (EOC 40)

The Woodland Trust (EOC 41)

ISAAA (EOC 42)

Chris Johnson (EOC 43)

Gloucestershire County Council (EOC 45)

Bedfordshire County Council (EOC 46)

Medway Outdoor Education (EOC 47)

Weymouth and Portland Borough Council (EOC 50)

Alan Childs (EOC 51)

Institute for Outdoor Learning (EOC 52)

Royal Botanic Gardens, Kew (EOC 53)

National Council for School Sport (EOC 54)

University of the First Age (EOC 55)

CRAC (EOC 57)

Norwich Union (EOC 58)

Biosciences Federation (EOC 60)

Forest Schools in England (EOC 61)

Institute of Leisure and Amenity Management (EOC 64)

Sport England and Arts Council England (EOC 68)

Bradfords Countryside Service (EOC 69)

Northamptonshire County Council (EOC 72)

Play Matters (EOC 75)

Groundwork (EOC 76)

Education Services of the National Park Authorities of England and Wales (EOC 78)

Chalmers Smith (EOC 79)

Suffolk County Council (EOC 80)

Mersey Basin Trust (EOC 81)

Barnardo's (EOC 82)

Wildlife Trust (EOC 84)

Association for Science Education (EOC 85)

Whitehorse Leadership Training (EOC 86)

Cambridgeshire Environmental Education Service (EOC 87)

RWE npower (EOC 90)

National Youth Agency (EOC 91)

Nottinghamshire Local Education Authority (EOC 92)

National Museum Directors' Conference (EOC 94)

Institute of Biology (EOC 95)

Engineering Education Scheme, Wales (EOC 100)

Shropshire Wildlife Trust (EOC 102)

Outdoor Industries Association (EOC 103)

School Journey Association (EOC 108)

Mr NG and Mrs JR Thorne (EOC 115)

Oral evidence

Taken before the Education and Skills Committee

on Monday 18 October 2004

Members present:

Mr Barry Sheerman, in the Chair

Mr David Chaytor	Helen Jones
Valerie Davey	Jonathan Shaw
Paul Holmes	Mr Andrew Turner

Memorandum submitted by The Outward Bound Trust

BACKGROUND

1. The Outward Bound Trust is an educational charity which has the aim of "inspiring young people to achieve their potential through challenging outdoor experiences".

2. The first Outward Bound® courses were delivered in 1941 at Aberdovey in North Wales and were focused on equipping young merchant seamen with the personal strength and ability to survive life under fire in the North Atlantic. The educational process that underlay the courses was inspired by a German educator, Kurt Hahn, who said, "we are all better than we know, if only we can be brought to realise this we may never be prepared to settle for anything less."

3. In the twenty-first century The Trust still applies the same principles to today's young people. We offer a range of adventurous outdoor personal development programmes to young people from a wide range of backgrounds. These programmes aim to equip them to meet the challenges of every day life. We achieve this by exposing the young people to a series of challenging activities, (which often they don't believe they can succeed at). We encourage young people to reflect on their success, encourage personal capabilities and interpersonal reactions and then consider how such learning relates to everyday life, be it being an effective team member at work, taking up the opportunities that exist at school or college or creatively using their time out of school.

4. On an Outward Bound® course you will see young participants taking part in a range of adventurous activities such as canoeing, climbing, expeditions and sailing, but what is harder to see is the vital process of developing real transferable interpersonal skills. This process of reflective reviewing and learning transfer is central to our courses and makes Outward Bound® a direct contributor to young peoples' lives, rather than just a holiday.

5. An Outward Bound® course is not a solution in itself, but when combined with support in the work place, school or community, in part of a learning package it enables young people to contribute positively. The learning we offer is practical and experiential and whilst it can be supported in the classroom, it can't be replicated in the classroom. There is much evidence, both anecdotal and formal, that indicates the effectiveness of the work we do, but most telling is the testimony from both parents and teachers who see positive change to behaviour in their young people after an Outward Bound® course.

6. Last year we worked with over 30,000 people from across the country delivering courses in our centres in Scotland, England and Wales. Most of the participants took part in courses during school time.

COSTS AND FUNDING

7. The Trust does not receive any core funding and only limited project funding from government (central or local). Access to courses is through the payment of fees. To increase accessibility The Trust raises funds predominantly from the corporate sector to support the financially disadvantaged. Outward Bound® raises approximately 20% of their Young People course fees from charitable contributions. In addition, a further £500,000 is raised each year to meet central, enhancement and capital expenditure.

8. Course costs are approximately £50 per day making a seven day residential course £350 per person. Currently, the majority of fees come from:

— course participants and parents;

— schools and Local Authorities;

— employers (apprentices and trainees);

— revenue grants from government, lottery and charities;

— donations from the corporate sector.

9. Costs are kept as low as possible. Labour is the highest element of cost and this is kept artificially low through low wage rates. A typical professional, qualified outdoor educator earns £13,000 pa.

10. The message in the market place from most schools and colleges is the courses are ideal, but they can't be afforded. Yet a key point for action from the recent Ofsted report *Outdoor Education Aspects of Good Practice*[1] was to "ensure the benefits of outdoor education could be experienced by all students". Cost is a major barrier to this objective.

11. It should be noted that the Ofsted report only looked at LEA-run centres. These centres are in the minority in terms of numbers of participants, in addition they usually operate in a privileged financial environment with at least support for capital resources and often have heavily subsidised direct costs.

12. Outward Bound® whilst a charity operates in a commercial environment generating funds from course revenues and depending heavily for charitable gifts for capital replacement and enhancement and infrastructure for growth. For example, in the recent New Opportunities Fund (NOF) grant round for enhancing capital infrastructure of outdoor education facilities, that was routed through LEA, the Outward Bound Trust was unable to access any funds despite contacting all England LEAs.

13. It should be noted that in recent years there has been a number of DfES or Lottery funded projects such as the U Project and GetReal. Whilst these are welcome, they are typically short-term and consequently involve charities in high levels of risk, often do not hit targets, and are inefficient.

FEAR OF ACCIDENTS AND LITIGATION

14. There is an increasing fear of accidents and litigation amongst schools and this limits access to outdoor education. The level of anxiety associated with this activity is not proportional to the risk. However, teachers, heads and governors perceive an increasing risk and often feel the best protection is to withdraw from this activity. The Campaign for Adventure sponsored by English Outdoor Council (EOC), Institute for Outdoor Learning (IOL) and many outdoor providers is focused on changing this perception.

15. Outward Bound®'s experience is that whilst the focus is on the risk of incident associated outdoor activity, most issues arise from non activity related incidents and behavioural problems. This situation is likely to reflect the position in school.

16. By following DfES guidelines and using responsible providers, this risk can be managed if schools wish to. However, the perception still exists. Following the Lyme Bay tragedy the whole legislative framework for outdoor activity has changed and become much tighter. As a result outdoor providers are required to hold an Adventure Activities Licensing Authority (AALA) Licence to operate. In short, this is a highly regulated industry with a very keen focus on safety and risk management.

17. Issues do however still exist in the non-regulated sector, particularly schools themselves, which do not operate under AALA licensing. For those schools that wish to deliver Outdoor Education themselves, increasingly they need to operate to the standards of professional organisations, such as Outward Bound® to protect themselves against the risk of accidents and litigation.

QUALIFICATIONS AND MOTIVATION OF TEACHERS AND THE EFFECT ON TEACHER WORKLOAD

18. The main issue from Outward Bound®'s perspective is the ability for schools to manage teacher cover for groups on residentials. This is increasingly becoming an issue with the implementation of the "National Agreement on work force reform" in schools. We are already seeing some schools withdraw from residential programmes citing the agreement and the inability to provide teacher cover as the reason. Given the level of support available at Outward Bound® and some other providers, consideration by DfES could be given to lower teacher ratios for some residentials.

THE PLACE OF OUTDOOR LEARNING IN THE CURRICULUM

19. Outward Bound® personal development courses do not have a direct place in the curriculum; however, much of the learning that takes place has a direct read across, for example into citizenship and personal and social development and the PE curriculum. However, the benefits are much wider with outdoor personal development programmes having a significant impact on positive behaviours. The key role of Outward Bound® is to equip young people to maximise opportunities at school and consequently achieve more from the formal curriculum. The learning outcomes of specific Outward Bound® courses are shown in "Outward Bound® Personal Development Courses for Schools and Colleges" pages 8, 10, 12 and 14.

20. The difficulty with the lack of curriculum representation is the *ad hoc* nature by which schools take up the opportunity for their young people and release funding. Increasingly, better performing schools are integrating outdoor personal development into the curriculum whilst lower performers are not. The issue for government is to replicate best practice across all schools.

---

[1] *Outdoor Education Aspects of Good Practice*, September 2004, Reference HMI: 2151.

CONCLUSION

21. Out of school learning as represented by Outward Bound® has been shown to have a very positive effect on the individual and their ability to maximise the benefits from formal education. However, significant barriers to participation exist, these include availability of funding, the fear of accidents and litigation and teacher workload. To increase participation the government needs to consider increased entitlement to provision within the school curriculum and a more responsive funding regime.

October 2004

Memorandum submitted by the Real World Learning Campaign: A partnership of The Royal Society for the Protection of Birds (RSPB), The National Trust (NT), The Wildfowl and Wetland Trust (WWT), 3D Adventure (PGL Ltd) and the Field Studies Council (FSC)

BACKGROUND TO REAL WORLD LEARNING CAMPAIGN (RWL)

The Campaign was launched by the Chief Executive of the RSPB at the FSC's 60th anniversary conference in conjunction with the Royal Geographical Society at the RGS on 10 December 2003. The partners represent a membership of over 5 million people providing "Out-of-Classroom Learning" (OoCL) for over 1.25 million day visitor equivalents in both day and residential formats covering a range from outdoor adventurous activity to urban based museum and heritage sites plus a mix of reserves and day/residential "environmental" centres in suburban, agricultural and wildscape environments.

The proposition from the RWL partnership is that there is no substitute for learning in the real world outside the classroom for all young people, in all sectors of education. Our combined practical experience, evaluation and research suggests that young people of all ages derive enormous benefits from such experiences.

"There is substantial evidence that OoCL, properly conceived, adequately planned, well-taught and effectively followed-up offers learners opportunities to develop their knowledge and skills that adds value to their everyday experiences in the classroom." (Ref 4, 18, 19).[2]

Despite a number of innovative initiatives, the RWL believes that as a result of a combination of factors there has been a general decline in the number OoCL opportunities, including fewer and shorter residential experiences. This amounts to a huge missed opportunity for several generations of young people to develop their creativity and curiosity to learn about the world around them.

SUMMARY OF SUBMISSION

Despite being highly valued by teachers and students there is strong evidence of a continuing decline in provision of Out-of-Classroom Learning especially in secondary schools, post-16 institutions and universities, particularly in science/biology education. A number of critical factors have been identified including:

— changes in curricula and assessment;

— profile of outdoor education within schools and school inspection;

— cost;

— health and safety concerns, including the increased bureaucracy/form-filling associated with taking young people out of the classroom;

— fear of litigation;

— perceived lack of value of out-of-classroom learning.

The importance of each factor varies between subject, location and age group, but all will need to be considered to reverse the decline or even stabilise it.

The lack of out-of-classroom experiences amongst trainee and qualified teachers is also a major area of concern that needs to be addressed. To some degrees this is equivalent to the Red Book species scenario—fewer numbers, increasing age of population, low recruitment to the population, death of species—as "older" teachers suggest they have little confidence that the Out-of-Classroom Learning activities they now lead will continue with the new tranche of recruits to the teaching profession as they lack the competence and confidence to undertake this work despite Initial Teacher Education's (ITE) inclusion of Health and Safety matters, including risk assessment, in their curricula. (Ref 1).

---

[2] See Ev 6 and 7 for references.

INFLUENCES ON FIELDWORD

1. *Overall trends*

   (a) Most schools want to undertake OoCL at the same time of year, mainly due to "modularisation" of courses and the timing of SATs; a trend which is common across the whole sector. (Ref 2, 3).

   (b) There has been a 25% decline in biology groups coming to the FSC's centres over the past 20 years (Ref 2, 3).

   (c) There have been increasing numbers of geographers to centres, although these courses have also been shortening (Ref 5).

   (d) The dominant Key Stage group attending National Trust and RSPB properties is Key Stage 2. (Ref 4a and 4b). 3D Adventure have a similar profile with Key Stage 2 forming the dominant group though the museum sector has identified a growing proportion of Key Stage 3 visitors.

   (e) Fieldwork course have shortened in length across all sectors; schools, post 16 institutions and higher education, (Ref 6).

   (f) There is strong evidence throughout the UK that participants visit sites and centres that are more local to them, and are more likely to be non-residential at all levels, including university (Ref 6, 7).

   (g) There are now much tighter links to fieldwork/coursework and assessment in science/biology and geography (Ref 8).

   (h) There are now very few 11–16 year olds doing science fieldwork, with fewer than one in 20 pupils having a residential experience (Ref 3).

   (i) The FSC trends are also repeated elsewhere—verified through several independent surveys, which have also shown dramatic falls in university as well as school science fieldwork provision (numerous reports) (Ref 2).

   (j) Geographical Association biennial reports have identified a reduction in OoCL/fieldwork at the secondary level. It is unlikely that this position will improve in the immediate future considering the lowly position of Geography in primary education and the use of non-specialists at Key Stage 3. (Ref 20, 22)

2. *Financial influences*

   (a) Costs are known to be a major influence on present-day out-of-classroom provision, but this has also been true in historical surveys (Ref 3, 5, 10).

   (b) There is a heavy reliance on parental/guardian contributions, even in the most disadvantaged boroughs. (Ref 11).

   (c) There is some evidence that the decline in biology fieldwork has been more pronounced in the maintained compared to the independent sector (Ref 12).

   (d) Costs are not the exclusive, or even the most important barrier in past surveys of teachers' opinions though recently teachers are identifying spiraling transport costs as a barrier to half and one day, OoCL activities. (Ref 5).

   (e) There is concern within schools that financial support targeted through measures such as free school meals excludes a significant number of deserving pupils (Ref 11).

   (f) The increasing dependence on part-time jobs does affect fieldwork provision, particularly amongst A level and University students (Ref 3, 7)

3. *Curriculum influences*

   (a) The changing curriculum is a major critical factor for teachers in prioritising whether or not to engage in OoCl. (Ref 5).

   (b) The statutory requirement to carry out fieldwork in geography has a major positive impact on levels of fieldwork within the subject. (Ref 5)

   (c) Pre-16 geographers are 10 times more likely to undertake residential fieldwork than science students (Ref 5).

   (d) Curriculum 2000 and new AS/A2 level specifications, have had a major influence on the numbers and timing of field courses (Ref 3, 8)

   (e) A strong curricula requirement also affects the content of Ofsted inspections as a geography inspection is five times more likely to comment on out-of-classroom experience compared with a science inspection. This affects the profile of OoCL within schools; "if it isn't inspected it isn't important" (Ref 8, 13). *Estyn have indicated that out-of-classroom learning will from a part of future school inspections.*

(f) The Secretary of State continues to signal his personal support for OoCL and the residential experience plus the DfES's Growing Schools initiative which "aims to use the 'outdoor classroom' as a context for learning, both within and beyond the school grounds". (Ref 23).

(g) Out-of-classroom experiences represented by RWL can support teaching and learning across curriculum subjects and are not limited to science and geography. (Ref 25).

4. *Organisation and integration of fieldwork*

(a) There is substantial evidence that Out-of-Classroom Learning, properly conceived, adequately planned, well-taught and effectively followed-up offers learners opportunities to develop their knowledge and skills that adds value to their everyday experiences in the classroom

   (i) Specifically, OoCL can have a positive influence on long-term memory due to the memorable nature of the fieldwork setting. Effective fieldwork experience can lead to individual growth and improvements in social skills. More importantly, there can be reinforcement between affective and cognitive developments in young people, with each influencing the other and providing a bridge to higher order learning. (Refs. 17, 18).

(b) Where schools have an active policy for OoCL there is clear evidence of access and inclusion for all and progression in the nature of the activities from year to year and Key Stage to Key Stage. (Ref 9).

(c) "Outdoor education continues to thrive where headteachers and individual enthusiasts provide leadership and a vision that promotes a well-balanced PE curriculum and outdoors off-site, day or residential experience as part of curricular extension and enrichment. They recognize the importance of outdoor education experiences in giving depth to the curriculum and to the development of students' personal and social development." (Ref 19)

(d) The provision of OoCL/fieldwork is variable within A level subjects—students' descriptions ranging from "inspiring" to "tedious and dull": "just like work in the classroom". (Ref 12).

(e) In secondary science and geography fieldwork there is a very strong association with techniques, skills and coursework, and associated assessment. (Ref 8).

(f) The outdoor experience is sometimes poorly integrated into the whole school curriculum and is often lumped into the end-of-year "activity" period (Refs. 14).

(g) Initiatives such as the DfES/NOF Get Real programme indicate both the benefits and the challenges of one off residential programmes. (Ref 25).

5. *Qualification and motivation of teachers*

(a) Most A level biology and geography teachers and students maintain that OoCL is important (Refs. 3, 5, 12).

(b) Many teachers are not aware of the positive outputs and outcomes of Out-of-Classroom Learning—improvement in social and communication skills, increased motivation, positive changes in the relationship between pupils and accompanying teachers—with improved behaviour on the activity/course being transferred to the classroom. (Ref 14, 18).

(c) Some teachers celebrate the fact that courses/out-of-classroom activities "had enabled us to see a great potential in inner city kids which is often not so apparent in schools" and allow young people with learning difficulties to excel in a non-classroom environment. (Ref 14).

(d) There is strong evidence that many trainee teachers are entering the profession with little previous out-of-classroom experience: for example, nearly half of trainee biology teachers (all with good biological sciences degrees) in one leading PGCE course had less than two days fieldwork in total during their previous school and university experience (Ref 15).

(e) An FSC survey of students/teachers ability to recognise common plants has demonstrated that most participants will be able to name fewer than two out of 10 plants (Ref 16).

(f) Strengthening the amount and quality of initial teacher training and in-service support is seen as critical in many surveys (Ref 2, 8).

6. *Effect on teachers' workload*

(a) Negotiating timetable cover and paying for supply cover, are a major barrier cited by teachers who are trying to organise fieldwork. This appears to have become more of a problem as courses have become increasingly modularised, thus reducing flexibility (Ref 2, 5, 8).

(b) There is concern that the teachers workload agreement may adversely affect the provision of OoCL. (Ref 24).

7. *Fear of accidents (and Litigation)*

(a) Whilst fear of accidents is perceived as an important influence on OoCL provision, it is of lower importance than curriculum and cost (see above) in some recent surveys (Ref 5, 11).

(b) Within the workforce there is a perception that accidents or incidents will result in significant media exposure and litigation that may lead to civil or at worse, criminal, action. This perception still remains despite the Secretary of State's commitment to tackle the "compensation culture" (speech to the NASWUT at Llandudno conference) and the recent report of the Better Regulation Task Force indicating a significant reduction in the number of accident claims. (Ref 21)

(c) There is some evidence that LEA protocols for delivering out-of-school visits are dissuading rather than supporting OoCL provision. DfES, LEA and School policies have established robust systems but they have made the organisation more burdensome: ". . . there are just too many hoops to jump through these days!". Providing appropriate, certificated training for classroom assistants could assist in the sharing some of the administrative load.

8. *How UK Provision compares with that in other countries?*

(a) Until now there appears to have been no systematic collection of data by the government or its advisers to enable assessment or monitoring of Out-of-Classroom Learning activities in schools and colleges in the UK. This makes historical, geographical or subject comparisons of fieldwork provision within the UK, or comparisons with other countries, not feasible (Ref 2).

(b) In the past, several states and countries have attempted to implement what they interpreted as the UK model of OoCL provision.

(i) 1960–70s—FSC advice to the Toronto Education Board to establish an entitlement for Out-of-Classroom Learning for primary and secondary students. Creation of an Urban Centre in Toronto and the Shelburne Outdoor Education Centre in the wildscape of Ontario plus support, teacher advisers/mentors for schools undertaking local out-of-classroom activities.

(ii) 1996–2002 British Council supported FSC to provide advice and support for CSOD, Slovenia, a government supported organisation providing OoCL for all in a residential contexts. The initial four Centres have now been extended to over 20 with a widening of the initial sports/outdoor adventurous activity provision into the historical and environmental areas.

(iii) Provision within the EU varies from country to country with different countries having different emphases: eg The Forest School initiative is used by many Danish Nursery/Early Years learners with children exploring and learning woodland context for part of each day or week throughout the school year. (In the UK this approach to Out-of-Classroom Learning is being piloted in Sheffield and Derby with training provision for childcare and nursery staff. The approach has relevance to others ages and sectors of the student population with real benefits for adolescents with emotional behavioural problems through its emphasis on "hands on" activities. (Ref 9)

References

1. Personal communication. (2004) Teachers leading groups at FSC and 3D Adventure Centres during RWL MP visits to Centres.

2. Barker, S, Slingsby, D and Tilling, S. (2002). *Teaching Biology outside the classroom: is it heading for extinction?* Field Studies Council Occasional Publication, Shrewsbury.

3. Lock, R and Tilling, S. (2002). Ecology fieldwork in 16 to 19 biology. *School Science Review* 84 (307): 79–88.

4. (a) FDS International. (2003). *Teachers Needs and Wants: research for the National Trust:*

   (b) *Education Updates paper to RSPB Council*

5. Tilling, S. (2004). Fieldwork in UK secondary schools: influences and provision. *Journal of Biological Education 38:* 54-58.

6. Internal FSC data.

7. Smith, D. (2004). The University field trip: where is it heading? *Journal of Biological Education* (in press).

8. Field Studies Council/British Ecological Society (2004). *Creating the right balance: delivering fieldwork for effective 16–19 ecology teaching.* Field Studies Council Occasional Publication, Shrewsbury.

9. FSC Magazine, Summer. (2004) Case studies from the FSC 60th Anniversary Conference and the launch of the DEMOS/Green Alliance "A Child's Place".

10. Fido, H S and Gayford, C G (1982). Fieldwork and the biology teacher: a survey in secondary schools in England and Wales. *Journal of Biological Education 16:* 27–32.

11. Field Studies Council/DfES (2004). Unpublished surveys of London Challenge schools. Available from FSC.

12. Stagg, P *et al.* (2004). *Life Study: Biology A level in the 21st century.* Wellcome Trust.

13. Croft, P and Thomas, A. (2004). *Reviews of Ofsted inspections in selected boroughs.* FSC internal report. Available from FSC.

14. Amos, R and Reiss, M. (2004). Evaluation of London Challenge residential courses. Unpublished survey, available from FSC.

15. Harrison, C. (2004). Pers. Comm. Unpublished survey of King's College PGCE students.

16. Bebbington, A (2004). Wild flower survey. *Journal of Biological Education (in press).*

17. Nundy, S. (2001). *Raising achievement through the environment: a case for fieldwork and field centres.* National Association of Field Studies Officers.

18. Rickinson, M *et al.* (2004). *A review of research on outdoor learning.* National Foundation for Educational Research/King's College. FSC Occasional Publication.

19. HMCI. (2004). *Outdoor education: Aspects of good practice.*

20. GA Secondary School Committee report to Education Committee. (2001). *Review of Geographical teaching.*

21. Better Regulation Task Force. (2004). *Better routes to Redress.*

22. HMI Geography. (2004). *Position of Geography in the Primary School: presentation to Primary Geography Co-ordinators Conference.*

23. DfES. (2003). *Growing Schools.*

24. Conservative Party Conference: RSPB RWL Fringe. (2004). Pers.Comm—*contribution from the NUT member of the panel.*

25. The National Trust. (2004). *Learning Audit.*

26. NOF. (2004) *Get REAL pilot programme summer 2003: evaluation.*

Contact details (for unpublished reports): A D Thomas, Field Studies Council, Preston Montford, Montford Bridge, Shrewsbury, SY4 1 HW. adt@field-studies-council.org

October 2004

Memorandum submitted by the Royal Geographical Society

OVERVIEW

1. Fieldwork and outdoor education is not just an add-on, it is absolutely core for geography and for young people's learning in general. Learning outside the classroom provides a unique and important perspective to a young person's education in that it builds upon and engages young people's experiences, it challenges them in settings they are not accustomed to, it encourages team building skills and confidence building, and it helps to show the relevance and applicability of what they study in the classroom.

2. The Society believes that there has been a profound decline in the opportunities for fieldwork and outdoor educationin recent years. The issues that we believe most need to be addressed are: a fully trained EVC in every school; increased initial teacher training and continuing CPD for teachers in fieldwork knowledge, skills and safety issues; more time and resources dedicated to such specialist training and for the outdoor experiences themselves, both within geography and more widely in the curriculum; the perceptions of risk by teachers, media and parents and a willingness to seek to address risk positively as part of the educational process.

3. We further recommend that: the effect of the workforce agreement is carefully monitored in terms of potential negative effects for outdoor education; that good practice in managing fieldwork and outdoor education as part of the whole school OCL experience, and within school structures, is shared between schools.

ABOUT US

4. The Royal Geographical Society (with The Institute of British Geographers) is the learned society representing geography and geographers. It was founded in 1830 for the advancement of geographical science and has been among the most active of the learned societies ever since. The Society currently offers the following specific areas of support for fieldwork and Out-of-Classroom Learning (OCL):

— Training courses for anyone organising an off-site visit either in the UK or abroad, aimed at teachers, Educational Visits Co-ordinators (EVCs) and youth leaders. This year over 500 teachers and youth leaders received training from us. We also have courses and manuals covering different aspects of fieldwork methodologies such as Geographic Information Sciences, project design and implementation of people-oriented research and biological conservation projects.

— The Society provides funding for a range of desk and fieldwork based activities. In 2003, our Grants Programme supported projects which collectively involve more than 436 individuals, who will be visiting 47 countries worldwide. We also support a grants programme of new innovations for teachers that includes fieldwork projects.

— Provides advice through the Society's Expedition Advisory Centre, a world-leader in the provision of guidance and training for teachers and students planning fieldwork and expeditions with a learning purpose.

— The Society maintains a database of over 300 field centres anywhere in the world that offer education, training and research opportunities for individuals and teams. This is particularly useful for those teachers looking for a safe location to undertake field studies in both rural and urban environments in other countries.

— The Society provides professional accreditation, including a strand for teachers, in the form of Chartered Geographer, a key element of which is commitment to continuing professional development.

5. This response is based on consultations with our Education Committee (predominantly geography teachers), Expedition and Fieldwork Committee, the Society's Expedition Advisory Centre and other stakeholders.

COST AND FUNDING OF OUTDOOR ACTIVITIES

6. We do not believe that the costs of outdoor activities need be a serious barrier to access to experiences out of the classroom. Geography field visits, for example, do not have to be located in inaccessible locations that require substantial time and costs. Visits can benefit pupils, teachers and even the local community when conducted near the school, especially at the lower key stages. For example, a Qualifications and Curriculum Authority (QCA) focus group found that the teachers frequently used the local area as a focus for fieldwork at key stage 3 in most schools (Qualifications and Curriculum Authority, 2004). However, the teachers we have consulted believe that young people benefit substantially from out-of-classroom learning experiences in environments and socio-cultural areas different from where they live and that these should be an entitlement for all young people studying geography between the ages of 14 and 18.

7. There have been reports, however, that costs have become a barrier to poorer schools, which could result in children from lower socio-economic groups missing out on outdoor learning. There is also a very real concern that the National Agreement on Workforce Reform will in the future be a barrier to poorer schools as it will mean that schools will have to provide bought in cover for teachers absent on fieldwork rather than cover being provided by teaching colleagues.

8. There are also anecdotal reports that the costs of residential activities have become prohibitive and the majority of students are unable to take part in residential activities (Ofsted, 2004). According to OFSTED, the extra-curricular nature of the activity, its cost or limits on the numbers that can be taken, lead to a "first come, first served" basis for selection. This is regrettable, as some of the strongest and longest lasting positive educational and personal benefits occur with activities that are residential (National Foundation for Educational Research, 2004).

THE PLACE OF OUTDOOR LEARNING IN THE CURRICULUM

9. Education outside the classroom is absolutely core for geography and for young people's learning in general. Geography is fortunate in that there is substantial official recognition of the importance of fieldwork. Geography is the only subject that has statutory reference to the provision of fieldwork in school, and indeed the importance of fieldwork is also fully recognised in the benchmarking of geography in Higher Education (Quality Assurance Agency, 2000). Fieldwork has been fully recognised in the programmes of study for the National Curriculum, key stages 1, 2 and 3. For example, at key stage 3, students must 'carry out fieldwork investigations outside the classroom' (DfEE and QCA, 1999). The Qualifications and Curriculum Authority (QCA) subject criteria for geography GCSE and A levels also make fieldwork one of the "subject-specific essentials" (QCA, 2003). It is essential that fieldwork retains its status throughout the teaching of geography.

10. Outdoor education also has the potential to benefit other subjects in the curriculum or other Government initiatives. This is recognised in the DfES Growing Schools project, which has been designed to support teachers in using the "outdoor classroom" as a resource across the curriculum for pupils of all ages. We strongly endorse the Growing Schools project as a valuable resource for all schools.

11. OCL is also important for learning beyond the Curriculum. We fully endorse the statements made in the recently launched DfES Five Year Strategy on the benefits of education outside the classroom and recommend more initiatives to take forward this commitment. For instance:

> *"There is also not enough variety and choice within the curriculum or in opportunities outside the school day—for example, clubs and societies, trips, visitors or visits—to make sure that every young person is excited by school and builds the confidence and skills they need."* (Department for Education and Skills, 2004)

EXTERNAL ASSESSMENT OF PROVISION

12. The current system of safety checks, guidance and other external measures seems, for the most part, satisfactory. We believe that the key to safe, successful school trips is increased training and advice of teachers and others that deliver the outside education experience based on standards of good practice. Many schools across England already have staff trained as Educational Visits Co-ordinators (EVCs), who liaise with the outdoor education adviser in the local education authority, and help teachers to assess and manage the risks of a visit. We recommend that the EVC system is given extra support and that all schools, regardless of status, have a Co-ordinator. There should be a regular programme of CPD for EVCs and Group Leaders linked to professional accreditation either subject based or generic. We are concerned that the role of the LEA outdoor education advisor seems to be diminishing and that governors, particularly of independent and foundation schools, need to be made more aware of their responsibilities for setting school policy and training standards.

ORGANISATION AND INTEGRATION WITHIN EXISTING SCHOOL STRUCTURES
QUALIFICATION AND MOTIVATION OF TEACHERS AND THE EFFECT ON TEACHER WORKLOAD

13. These two items in the terms of reference are strongly related so we have responded to both of them together. The pressures of a busy curriculum mean that many teachers are reporting less interest in, and time for, outdoor education. However, some schools continue to build in substantial and effective OCL. It is important in our view to enable schools to understand and share the ways in which they cater for substantial out of class experiences. Furthermore, there needs to be increased time and resources dedicated to the specialist training and qualifications to ensure that teachers have the confidence and competence to lead or support school visits.

14. The current curriculum puts great pressures on the time necessary for training, preparation and provision of outdoor education. The curriculum flexibility introduced in September 2004 is a small but welcome step as it means that the number of compulsory subjects from the ages 14 to 16 has been reduced. The introduction of four statutory "entitlements": modern foreign languages, design and technology and the arts and humanities (which includes geography) could offer some opportunities for more outdoor education. The humanities entitlement requests that students develop a "range of skills in many different contexts, inside and outside the classroom. Courses should provide opportunities within and beyond school for first-hand experiences of places, environments, events and activities" (DfES, 2003). Schools are obliged to make these entitlements available. Pupils will not, however, be obliged to study these entitlements or experience education outside of the classroom after the age of 14, when geography ceases to be compulsory.

15. The National Agreement on Workforce Reform may also mean that teachers are less able to find support and cover while they conduct these outdoor activities. The current phase recommends a maximum of 38 hours a year that teachers can be expected to cover lessons for absent colleagues. This comes into effect now and teachers and heads have reported to us that this might limit outdoor learning, either through manpower reductions or the costs of providing teaching cover.

16. We also have concerns regarding the qualifications, training and experiences of students working for their PGCE in geography, Initial Teacher Training and the Newly Qualified Teachers. There is insufficient training in fieldwork at these early stages and we recommend that it is strengthened. This is often compounded by a lack of learning resources relating to fieldwork which the Society is keen to address. The current circumstances could undermine the provision of fieldwork for their future students. It is not just the pupils who will lose out; many geography teachers enjoy their fieldwork and list it as an important reason for taking up geography teaching in the first place.

THE FEAR OF ACCIDENTS AND THE POSSIBILITY OF LITIGATION

17. The perception of heightened risk and the consequences of accidents are a major barrier to OCL. Teachers express this as the perception of what might happen to them—such as losing their job. The National Association of Schoolmasters Union of Women Teachers (NASUWT) advice to its members against participating in school trips in February 2004 was another contributor to the decline in the willingness to participate in and to value fieldwork among some teachers.

18. Accidents are, however, rare. According to the Adventure Activities Licensing Authority there were 57 deaths on school trips, 19 of which occurred during adventure activities, between 1985 and 2004. Accidents and claims are not increasing but the perception and fear of litigation remains a serious concern

for teachers. Addressing the perceptions of teachers, and indeed of the media, is a much-needed action. Schools take increased care in the planning and risk assessment for all school visits; children are safer and more closely supervised on a school trip than ever before. According to the Better Regulation Task Force schools, rather than canceling trips and activities as the media would have us believe, have become much better at assessing and managing risks in recent years (Better Regulation Task Force, 2004).

19. Risk can never be completely avoided, however, and one of the benefits of outdoor education is that it offers a positive opportunity for students to examine and evaluate risk and thus to learn about risk management as a life skill. Schools already directly address issues of risk, choice and the implications of behaviour within established areas of the curriculum eg sex education/relationships and also drugs education. Why not therefore address risk positively in the case of outdoor education?

20. Fear of accidents and litigation must be ameliorated by further information and training. We have seen at first hand how the training run by the Society, such as the OCR-accredited Certificate in Off-site Safety Management course boosts confidence and a greater understanding of risk, as well as competence.

How Provision in the UK Compares With that of Other Countries

No comment.

References

Better Regulation Task Force (2004) *Better Routes to Redress.*

Department for Education and Employment/Qualifications and Curriculum Authority (1999) *Geography; National Curriculum for England.*

Department for Education and Skills (2004) *Five Year Strategy for Children and Learners.*

Department for Education and Skills (2003) *14–19: Opportunity and Excellence.*

National Foundation for Educational Research (2004) *A Review of Research on Outdoor Learning.*

Office for Standards in Education (2004) *The Outdoor Education, Aspects of Good Practice.*

Qualifications and Curriculum Authority (2004) *Geography 2002–03 annual report on curriculum and assessment.*

Qualifications and Curriculum Authority (2004) *Subject criteria for geography GCSE.*

Quality Assurance Agency, 2000 *Benchmark Statement for Geography in Higher Education.*

October 2004

Memorandum submitted by the Field Studies Council

Background to Field Studies Council (FSC)

Established in 1943, the FSC is an educational charity which has become the largest provider of secondary science and geography fieldwork in the UK. Each year, over 82,000 students from 2,300 schools visit its network of 17 residential and day centres It also attracts many primary and university groups, as well as adult learners—both amateur and professional—and is, therefore, uniquely able to detect trends in formal education, professional training and lifelong learning. The FSC is working with DfES London Challenge to co-ordinate the delivery of residential visits for all London Secondary schools. Dr Steve Tilling, the FSC's Director of Communication, is a biologist who has worked for the organisation for 22 years.

Summary of Content

Despite still being valued by teachers and students there is strong evidence of a continuing decline in provision of fieldwork in secondary schools and universities, particularly in science/biology education. This is now affecting human capacity in the environment sector. A number of critical factors have been identified including: changes in curriculum and assessment; profile of outdoor education within schools and school inspections; cost; and health and safety concerns. The importance of each varies between subject, location and age group, but all will need to be considered to reverse the decline. The lack of practical fieldwork experience amongst trainee and qualified teachers is also a major area of concern which needs to be addressed.

INFLUENCES ON FIELDWORK

1. *Overall trends:*

   (a) There has been a 25% decline in biology groups coming to the FSC's centres over the past 20 years (Ref. 1, 2).[3]

   (b) There have been increasing numbers of geographers to FSC centres, although these courses have also been shortening (Ref. 3).

   (c) Fieldwork course lengths in FSC centres, and in schools and colleges, have shortened (Ref. 4).

   (d) Most schools want to come at the same time of year, mainly due to "modularisation' of courses and the timing of SATs and end-of-year examinations; a trend which is being repeated outside the FSC (Ref. 1, 2).

   (e) There is strong evidence throughout the UK that courses are becoming more local, and more likely to be non-residential at all levels, including university (Ref. 5,6).

   (f) There are now much tighter links to coursework and assessment in science/biology (Ref. 7).

   (g) There are now very few 11–16 year olds doing science fieldwork, with fewer than one in 20 pupils having a residential experience (Ref. 3).

   (h) The FSC trends are also repeated elsewhere—verified through several independent surveys, which have also shown dramatic falls in university as well as school science fieldwork provision (numerous reports) (Ref. 2, 6).

   (i) There is now strong evidence that decline in fieldwork is affecting the numbers of potential candidates, and the quality of work, in the environment sector. Over 80% of environmental agencies and consultants have experienced difficulties in recruitment in the past five years; lack of field skills is a particular problem (Ref. 6, 8).

2. *Financial influences:*

   (a) Costs are known to be a major influence on present-day fieldwork provision, but this has also been true in historical surveys (Ref. 2, 3, 9).

   (b) There is a heavy reliance on parental/guardian contributions, even in the most disadvantaged boroughs (Ref. 10).

   (c) There is some evidence that the decline in biology fieldwork has been more pronounced in the maintained compared to the independent sector (Ref. 11).

   (d) Costs are not the exclusive, or even the most important, barrier in some teacher surveys (see curriculum influences below) (Ref.3).

   (e) Even with 100% funding many schools will not take up opportunities (Ref.10).

   (f) There is concern within schools that financial support targeted through measures such as free school meals excludes a significant number of deserving pupils (Ref. 10).

   (g) The increasing dependence on part-time jobs does affect fieldwork provision, particularly amongst A level and university students (Ref. 2, 6)

3. *Curriculum influences:*

   (a) The curriculum is the major critical factor amongst many teachers (Ref. 3)

   (b) The statutory requirement to carry out fieldwork has a major positive impact on levels of geography fieldwork (Ref. 3)

   (c) Pre-16 geographers are ten times more likely to do residential fieldwork than science students (Ref. 3)

   (d) Curriculum 2000, and new a level specifications, has had a major impact on the numbers and timing of field courses (Ref. 2, 7)

   (e) A strong curriculum requirement also affects content of Ofsted inspections—a geography inspection is five times more likely to comment on outdoor experience compared to a science inspection. This affects profile of outdoor learning within schools; "if it isn't inspected it isn't important" (Ref. 7, 12).

   (f) Nearly two thirds of biology teachers and A level students feel that there is insufficient time for fieldwork (Ref. 11).

4. *Organisation and integration of fieldwork:*

   (a) There is evidence that well planned and appropriately delivered fieldwork can add significantly to educational achievement (Refs. 16, 17).

   (b) The delivery of fieldwork is variable within A level biology—students' descriptions ranging from "inspiring' to "tedious and dull' (Ref. 11).

---

[3] See Ev 12 and 13 for references.

(c) There is a very strong association with techniques, skills and coursework—and associated assessment—in secondary science and geography fieldwork. This has been described as "unbalanced' in meeting of senior biology educators. (Ref. 7)

(d) The outdoor experience is sometimes poorly integrated into the school, and often lumped into the end-of-year "activity' period (Refs. 10, 13).

5. *Qualification and motivation of teachers:*

(a) Most A level biology teachers and students think that fieldwork is important (Refs. 2, 3, 11).

(b) There is strong evidence that many trainee teachers are entering the profession with little previous fieldwork experience: for example, nearly half of trainee biology teachers (all with good biological sciences degrees) in one leading PGCE course had less than two days fieldwork in total during their previous school and university experience (Ref. 14).

(c) An FSC survey of students'/teachers' ability to recognise common plants has demonstrated that most participants will be able to name fewer than two out of 10 plants (Ref. 13).

(d) Strengthening the provision of teacher training and in-service support is seen as critical in many surveys (Ref. 1, 7).

6. *Effect on teacher workload*

(a) Negotiating timetable cover, and paying for supply cover, is a major barrier cited by teachers who are trying to organise fieldwork. This appears to have become more of a problem as courses have become increasing modularised, thus reducing flexibility (Ref. 1, 3, 7).

(b) There is concern that the workload agreement may have an impact on fieldwork, particularly where there is a requirement to undertake such work.

7. *Fear of accidents:*

(a) Whilst fear of accidents is an important influence on field work provision, it is of lower importance than curriculum and cost (see above) in some recent surveys (Ref. 3, 10).

(b) There is some evidence that LEA protocols for delivering out-of-school visits are dissuading rather than supporting fieldwork provision; although they have introduced robust systems, they have also made organisation more burdensome; "there are just too many hoops to jump through these days".

8. *UK Provision:*

(a) Until now there appears to have been no official collection of data by the government or its advisers to enable assessment or monitoring of fieldwork in schools and colleges in the UK. This makes historical, geographical or subject comparisons of fieldwork provision within the UK, or comparisons with other countries, impossible. (Ref. 1).

REFERENCES

1. Barker, S., Slingsby, D. and Tilling, S. (2002). *Teaching Biology outside the classroom: is it heading for extinction?* Field Studies Council Occasional Publication, Shrewsbury.

2. Lock, R. and Tilling, S. (2002). Ecology fieldwork in 16 to 19 biology. *School Science Review 84* (307): 79–88.

3. Tilling, S. (2004). Fieldwork in UK secondary schools: influences and provision. *Journal of Biological Education* 38: 54–58.

4. Internal FSC data.

5. Smith, D. (2004). The University field trip: where is it heading? Journal of Biological Education (in press).

6. Davenport, J. (1998). *Marine Biology Field Teaching Forum.* Occasional Publication , University Marine Biological Station, Millport.

7. Field Studies Council/British Ecological Society (2004). *Creating the right balance: delivering fieldwork for effective 16–19 ecology teaching.* Field Studies Council Occasional Publication, Shrewsbury.

8. Hillcox, S. (2003). *The graduate ecologist's skills base.* Unpublished thesis. MSc Ecology and management of the Natural Environment, University of Bristol.

9. Fido, H.S. and Gayford, C.G. (1982). Fieldwork and the biology teacher: a survey in secondary schools in England and Wales. *Journal of Biological Education* 16: 27–32.

10. Field Studies Council/DfES (2004). Unpublished surveys of London Challenge schools. Available from FSC.

11. Stagg, P. et al. (2004). *Life Study: Biology A level in the 21st century.* Wellcome Trust.

12. Croft, P. and Thomas, A. (2004). *Reviews of Ofsted inspections in selected boroughs.* FSC internal report. Available from FSC.

13. Amos, R and Reiss, M. (2004). Evaluation of London Challenge residential courses. Unpublished survey, available from FSC.

14. Harrison, C. (2004). Pers. Comm. Unpublished survey of King's College PGCE students.

15. Bebbington, A. (2004). Wild flower survey. *Journal of Biological Education* (in press).

16. Nundy, S. (2001). *Raising achievement through the environment: a case for fieldwork and field centres.* National Association of Field Studies Officers.

17. Rickinson, M. et al. (2004). *A review of research on outdoor learning.* National Foundation for Educational Research/King's College. FSC Occasional Publication.

Contact details (for unpublished reports): Dr S.M. Tilling, Field Studies Council, Preston Montford, Montford Bridge, Shrewsbury, SY4 1 HW steve.tilling@field-studies-council.org

October 2004

Witnesses: **Ms Sarah Henwood,** Chief Executive, and **Mr William Ripley,** Operations Director, Outward Bound Trust UK; **Dr Anthony Thomas,** Chair, Real World Learning Steering Group; **Mr Andy Simpson,** Head of Education, RSPB/Real World Learning; **Dr Rita Gardner CBE,** Director, Royal Geographical Society (with the Institute of British Geographers); and **Dr Steve Tilling,** Director of Communications, Field Studies Council, examined.

Chairman: Can I welcome today's witnesses on this opening session of our new inquiry, and we are very grateful that so many talented people were able to give their time to the Committee today. Jonathan Shaw has a great interest in this but also some time ago this Committee went to Denmark to look at pre-school education, and we stumbled across forest schools and the whole concept of using the external environment to enhance the educational experience of very young children, and we have always since that time had at the back of our mind that rather than just mentioning it as a short part of that major inquiry we would come back to this and look at the value of the external experience in the broader sense to education. This is why we have been persuaded to embark on this inquiry, especially at a time when there have been what most members of this Committee view as a small number of tragic incidents that seem to have impacted on both the willingness of trade unions in the teaching profession to engage in outside activities, the insurance industry to ensure reasonable rates, and so on. So it seemed to us a very good topic for a brief inquiry to see if it can be helpful in evaluating the value of external experience, and if there are problems that have emerged in recent times whether there is anything we can do to aid the understanding. So let us get started and I am going to ask Helen to start the questioning.

Q1 Helen Jones: Thank you. We have received different sets of evidence on the value of education outside the classroom, and on the different experiences that it tries to give young people. I wonder if members of the panel could, first of all, try and tell the Committee what they think is the value of learning outside the classroom, particularly what young people can learn that they do not learn in lessons inside.

Chairman: And, as you respond, if you want to say something about your organisation and where you come from in two minutes that is allowable, and then slant back to the questioning you are answering.

Mr Ripley: Concerning the Outward Bound Trust, I have sent some notes along but we have been in the outdoors working with young people for sixty years and I think the answers I will give you I will slant a little bit towards the area I know about most, which is working in an adventurous environment. What Outward Bound adds to the classroom, I think, which is in a structured way, is the ability to do those practical hands-on things that are really right across the whole of the learning experience. What do I mean by that? We all know that when we work with people we want them to have skills, we want them to be able to communicate, we want them to have confidence, work hard, and problem solve. Those are all the kind of attributes we can put in a practical hands-on way in an out-of-class, out-of-school environment, and I think that where we work best is when we enhance what is happening in the school, so that links into particular areas of the curriculum and then the learning that we have got can feed back in. That is the real value to the work that we would concentrate on. So it is broadening the curriculum, and people's learning experience.

Q2 Chairman: Do you agree with that, Sarah?
Ms Henwood: Absolutely. I would sum it up in one of the Government's favourite phrases of "joined-up learning". What you can do in the classroom can be added to, supplemented and improved by the outdoors, so it is a symbiotic relationship.

Q3 Helen Jones: That is interesting and I have seen many young people who have benefited from Outward Bound courses, but what you outline to us is, if I may say so, what many teachers would say about their normal lessons—those are the skills and the values they try to inculcate—so what we are trying to get at really is what is the difference, what is the added value of outdoor activities? Does it benefit some children more than others? Is it a kind of learning that is appropriate to particular young people with particular skills, or can it be read across the board?

Mr Ripley: It would be crazy of me to say it applies to everybody. For some people it works brilliantly for but, as with any subject, there are some people who do not perform as well. We all have different learning styles and different ways of working but by and large it does have a great read-across and I think it is the practical hands-on that works so well. What kids really enjoy when they come to Outward Bound is that they have practical real life situations. Whether it is building a raft or canoeing across a lake or going climbing, they are practical things they can do, and so often in the classroom they do not see those practical elements. The other important factor is that it has such a long life. People will remember even now. I met somebody on the way here who said "Yes, I did my Outward Bound course when I was a cadet", and this guy must have been late 50s/60s, and he could remember the experience he had had, and we said to him "Did it help you?" and he said "Well, I guess it made me the person I am now"—he was slightly tongue in cheek but the fact that people go away and it is so memorable is so important as an element.

Mr Simpson: I am Head of Education for RSPB speaking on behalf of the Real World Learning Partnership which includes ourselves, the National Trust, the Field Studies Council, the Wildfowl and Wetland Trust and others. Our point is based on two very simple principles, and the first one is this: that something you find out for yourself is massively more impactive on you than something that is delivered as a piece of secondhand information. In other words, there is no substitute for experience. The second principle is a society-wide one which is that surely it is unreasonable for society to expect young people to value things of which they have had no experience. It is that combination of first-hand experience and being there and seeing it that leads to the lifetime kind of values, and I am not just talking environmentally but artistically, culturally—the whole gamut of what we call civilisation, and increasingly our research shows that less and less children are getting that.

Dr Thomas: Chief executive, FS Council, also speaking on behalf Real World Learning. We chose Real World Learning for that very point; we wanted youngsters to explore the real world. There is a slight tendency, and a very understandable one, that within the classroom and the laboratory to some degree you sanitise things to ensure you get a black and white outcome, because we have things to perform. We want youngsters to do a particular test; undertake a particular project, therefore we tend to simplify it. Once you go into the outdoors then you have to deal with a myriad of different conflicting issues and that is what real life is about. It is about making decisions in the real world which often do not give clear-cut answers, and if we keep on producing, whether they are scientists or humanities, graduates who see things in a black and white perspective we will not get that generation of what I would call concerned and aware citizens.

Another point that was raised by Will is that memories bridge. There is increasing research evidence which is showing that the fieldwork experience, the out-of-classroom experience, not just fieldwork but much broader out-of-classroom experience, actually generates memories, and we recall them and they act as a trigger to the cognitive area, and increasingly evidence is showing links between the effective and the cognitive domains which is suggesting that if you can visualise it because you have experienced it, there is a reasonable chance it acts as a trigger to greater understanding so, putting the two together, that is your added value—that experience in the real world, and the memorable experiences helping understanding.

Q4 Helen Jones: That is very interesting and I think any evidence that you could direct the Committee to from that would be very useful to our inquiry, but can I follow up from that? Presumably if outdoor education is to be effective then all the young people taking part have to have a quality experience and we have had some evidence given to us to say that some of the quality of outdoor education is not as good as it should be. There is clearly some which is very valuable indeed but Ofsted criticises some poor value outdoor education, as you will know; we have had evidence from the Field Studies Council to suggest that it is now becoming much more limited to many children to experiences within the school grounds; I wonder if any of our witnesses can tell us whether they believe the quality of what is on offer is deteriorating and, if so, what do you think the reasons are for that and what do you think ought to be done about it?

Dr Tilling: I think certainly the FSC can pinpoint trends which have been happening over a number of years. As you have seen from your evidence, we take something like 2,500 schools per year coming through our centres so we are obviously in a position to be able to see trends both in terms of course length, of where people are coming from, but also content, and a very strong trend which has emerged in the areas that we deal with, which is largely secondary biology, secondary science and secondary geography is a diminishing of course length, a contraction of the distance that people are travelling, which in itself obviously throws up various issues. But one of the things which has changed undoubtedly is a much closer, much more prescribed content than certainly was the situation ten years ago, and particularly links with coursework, for example, in both areas, both in geography and in science, which now has led to real concerns which have been shared by chief examiners, moderators for most bodies of the learning bodies, for example; that the whole curriculum since it has become imbalanced has become very driven by skills and techniques and things which are easily measurable, or measurable in a predictable and, some would say, sanitised way, and that we feel is an unbalanced provision in that part of the outdoor sector.

Dr Gardner: I am Director at the Royal Geographical Society which is the learning society and professional body for geography with a wide remit across geographical education, research and wider public understanding. From our experience in geography there are places where geography fieldwork is brilliantly taught and others where it is much less well taught, so it is a very patchy provision. This is despite the fact that the provision of fieldwork has, of all the disciplines, a statutory status within the geography curriculum so, for example, one young person from 5–14 might only have three lessons in the school playing ground. Now, there is nothing wrong with that and there is a brilliant DfES project Growing Schools but one questions is that enough in that period, and as they move on to GSCE it may be just one day, and possibly at A level two days. So there is patchy provision and the picture we are starting to see is one in which some argue it would be helpful to have some guidance on, if you like, statutory requirements as to the amount of fieldwork, and many of those that we have consulted suggest that there are issues in the professional training of teachers with limited capacity in very tight PGCE programmes to include training in fieldwork inquiry and skills, and even if a geographer has come through a graduate programme where they are taught fieldwork and taken in the field, that is very different from then taking a group of kids out in the field and teaching them inquiry learning and skills. So there is a need at PGCE; there is also a need for on-going continuing professional development in the training of teachers linked of course because of teachers' mobility around the country to very real resources on places and locations at which fieldwork may be undertaken, so we would say one element is the continuing professional development of teachers and their development from the various early stages right through their career.

Dr Thomas: On the quality, there is a statement that I think is from Stuart Mundy which is quoted in our evidence, and it is a part of the NFER research programme, that "out-of-classroom learning, properly conceived, adequately planned, well taught and effectively followed up offers learners opportunities to develop their knowledge and skills that add value". It is when you have the whole of that together. Where you have a snapshot where it is not particularly well planned, where it is seen as maybe a prize at the end of the year and there is some evidence of bunching of out-of-classroom learning at a particular time of year, if it ends towards the end of term you have then 5–6 weeks, what is basically gained in that experience, especially if it is a short-term experience. So it is where you have schools that are clearly identifying and developing a school policy towards out-of-classroom learning, and that it is progressive from year to year from key stage to key stage that you

are developing quality, and people can clearly see what is being delivered and can clearly see where it fits within the whole curriculum, rather than these one-off snapshots which can be very good in their own right but do not actually add the value that you are exploring.

Q5 Chairman: You have a lot of experience between you. Is there a guide? What is the guidance to schools and local education authorities about what is the best quality of experience meeting at your point, Anthony? Is there a model of what works best in terms of your approach, a continuous approach over time embedded in the curriculum? What sort of information do you give to schools in order to help them perform well?

Dr Thomas: I think that is a rather interesting question. There has been some excellent advice put forward by both of the geographical associations and also the Royal Geographical Society IBG. They have given a great deal of advice both in the management of groups, especially with health and safety, and also in the different approaches. It is interesting that if you look across the border to Wales, and I know this inquiry is not covering Wales, they felt it important to gather all the various groups together and they are producing a code of practice as a guidance document for out-of-classroom learning. If you look at some of the documentation from the Association of Heads of Outdoor Centres, from NAOE before it became the Institute for Learning, they have also produced guidance, as have NAFSO, and you spoke, Chair, at a number of NAFSO conferences in the past. They have also produced guidance and also offer a series of workshops to both members and interested participants. I would not necessarily say there is a definitive guidance: I think one of the pieces of comment that comes out of the research and also out of the chief inspectors' research is to identify more clearly what is the best practice and how that assists people in terms of identifying what they learn from different sorts of activities, and I think as a sector we have to explore that more ourselves.

Q6 Chairman: When there is a good experience what is the evidence? Where does it come from? Is it a committed head? Is it a good LEA? What marks off the good from the not-so-good? Where does the inspiration come from? Is it from the head?

Dr Gardner: Again, I can only talk from the point of view of our consultation with our committees and members and so on but it certainly requires a committed head; it certainly requires a passionate teacher; and one who is knowledgeable about the area in which they are undertaking that fieldwork. It also comes back to this idea of progression and continuity in fieldwork, not a one-off experience. It is part of a programme of development that is an educational development over a period of years, so I would say of those three embedded in the culture of the school and the curriculum, a passionate teacher and a really committed head who sees and understands the values, and can convince their governors too, of the values of out-of-classroom learning.

Q7 Chairman: Some evidence we have had suggests, and our experience going round schools is, that local educational authorities used in the past to own buildings, have centres, and so on. Has that gone into decline? In a sense you do need to have access to premises in the right location, do you not? Is that a problem?

Mr Ripley: That certainly is the case. The authorities where we have the greatest uptake from schools with Outward Bound are quite often those authorities where they have still got infrastructure, so it stems from the top of the education authority. There is a commitment to outdoor education and outdoor out of school learning, residentials and so forth, and that filters down. What an education authority by and large cannot do, and there are some very unusual exceptions, is provide that facility right across the piece but what they can provide is that leadership, and that is the key issue. It is about leadership, as Rita says, from the head teacher, from the teachers in schools. That is what really makes a high quality outdoor educational experience, and it is where it is integrated into the school. I have been into schools where they have integrated Outward Bound right across the school, and you would meet teachers who were completely over to one side from the residential experience but they will have seen the benefits of it because the young people would be going away getting those skills, and yet the maths teacher is telling me "Oh, yes, it is much better when the kids have come back from Outward Bound because they have some changes in attitude which they can experience in their maths lesson" whereas they would not naturally be the people leading that, so you have to have the leadership from the top of the school to make that into reality.

Q8 Chairman: Is this experience mainly for better-off kids? Have you done research on who gets the benefit? I am very concerned that many of my most impoverished constituents probably do not travel far from their homes in their lives, especially in their educational lives, and middle-class kids go to the seaside, get out-of-school experience and all the rest. Is it a posh club, external access to the environment in schools?

Ms Henwood: On behalf of the Trust only on this about 40% of 30,000-plus young people that come through our courses we financially support through fund-raising. That said, we are turning people away because we cannot fund them. The other problem that we are up against particularly is that when you are asking parents or schools to support funding of a course you are put in the same bracket as an activity holiday, and we are very keen to make sure that the understanding and commitment from the purchaser, be it the school or the parent, understands exactly what it is that they are getting,

some educational development. You could say that this is a club for posh kids but actually what you tend to find is that at some of the posh schools the parents have spent all their money on school fees and they cannot afford this either, so you have to be quite careful with your terms of inclusivity or exclusivity.

Dr Tilling: We have some evidence to support that. In the evidence that has been submitted to you, the FSC has been involved in the London Challenge project, and as part of that earlier this year we carried out a survey of London secondary schools which included interviews in thirty schools in five of the most disadvantaged boroughs in London. In total we had data from one in three secondary schools in London and the evidence we got from that was very interesting and surprised us, in that there appeared to be absolutely no pattern in terms of a third of schools. We were offering 100% funding to those schools, so fees, transport, supply cover was all covered, yet despite that a third of the schools did not take up the opportunity. We have never quite managed to find out why but we have managed to find out who was not coming, and there is no pattern in terms of value added tables, in terms of GCSE league tables, in terms of free school meals, in terms of any socio economic figuring—so it is not as simple as a straight financial need. There is something more fundamental in there.

Mr Simpson: I think it is probably important that the Committee recognise that we are talking about a huge spectrum of out-of-classroom learning as represented by a long list, from the residential through to ourselves and the National Trust who handle enormous numbers of children but almost exclusively on day visits. From the RSPB's point of view as a national organisation we know absolutely that if I compare the take-up between our reserve in Pulborough in West Sussex compared to Marsden Rock in South Tyneside, and the research we have done with teachers, cost is a major factor and there is a very pronounced link between those schools who I would argue need the experience most and, in our experience, some of the children least likely to get it.

Q9 Chairman: So should there be a right to a certain amount of out-of-school education that every child is given? The word "voucher" would never cross my mind but should there be some entitlement that every child should have, and we can find out if they have had it or not?

Dr Gardner: I would certainly agree there should be an entitlement. I wonder if there are mechanisms that might be explored a little bit like the e-learning credits, but that is on your side of the table rather than mine. I do feel very strongly that we also need to take note of the fact that some excellent fieldwork and out-of-school activities can be carried out locally in the environment. We have tended to concentrate here on young people experiencing new social and environmental circumstances. Do not forget that in geography at least a great majority of the fieldwork for those under the age of 14 is carried out within their local environment, and if that is a city environment then there are great challenges in local neighbourhoods and different neighbourhoods.

Chairman: Excellent. Well, it was Helen's job to warm you up, and now it is over to Andrew to ask you how this relates to the school curriculum.

Q10 Mr Turner: Dr Thomas has suggested in his paper that there should be a clear direction that it is important, and that out-of-classroom experience should be an integral part of every child's education. How strong a direction? Do you mean it should be part of the statutory curriculum?

Dr Thomas: Well, to some degree it is already. From 5–14 within geography there is a requirement to explore the outdoors and to undertake inquiry through fieldwork. Elsewhere, it is not, in a sense, a statutory requirement and there are options that even with an outdoor adventurous activity is not one that you have to opt for rather than it being in a sense an element that every candidate will be exposed to. Even within geography there is evidence from work I have done with a colleague on Ofsted reports that at key stage 3 in particular certain schools are not meeting their statutory requirement, so even when there is a statutory requirement there is a failure on delivery.

Q11 Mr Turner: So on the basis of that are you suggesting that the requirement should not go any further?

Dr Thomas: No, I would be saying probably the opposite; that at the very minimum there ought to be delivery under statutory. One might get the impression from some of our documentation that this is only about geography and science. It is about humanities; it is about the whole issue of citizenship and out-of-classroom learning are so integrated, so powerfully go together, and that was our evidence to Professor Crick when we put evidence to him when he was discussing the whole question of a citizenship curriculum. The Secretary of State uses the word "signalling". He says that he "signals" to the sector that this is important, and I believe personally he does believe it is important both for day and residential out-of-classroom activity. I think it needs more than signalling; it needs to be a statutory requirement in certain areas; where guidance is given that it is appropriate it needs to be backed up by helpful suggestions of how that guidance can be integrated. On occasions some of the schemes that work I think that have been developed are very good pieces of work; I would have liked to have seen more integration of the out-of-classroom learning opportunities within those schemes of work.

Q12 Mr Turner: I am very sympathetic to the objective but I am worried that when the national curriculum was introduced everyone wanted to hang the bauble on the Christmas tree and we have been trying to slim down the Christmas tree ever

since, and now we have people asking for out-of-classroom, we have community service, additional sport, competitive games, musical instruments—one could go on. Where does your objective and perhaps ours come in relation to those other objectives because, whether it is a signal or a statute, it has to form part of a priority list, has it not?

Dr Tilling: I think one of the things which will occur time and again over the next few minutes is you have just mentioned a whole list of things and various bodies making various recommendations. One of the strong points which emerges from all of the documents, both our reports and the evidence, is that we would see multi agency actions being necessary to support the provision of outdoor learning. For example, if there was a prescription for schools that have to deliver outdoor learning, with that obviously is a demand for CPD and teacher training because simply putting something on paper cannot be delivered. There would have to be, we feel, a building of critical mass in terms of being able to deliver this, and I think one of the other things which has come through from the Tomlinson Report is that within the sector there are lots of opportunities for more joined-up thinking, if you like, so perhaps PEs as exclusive from geography or from science—there are possibilities to deliver across the sector which does not mean that coming up with a long list of bullet points, if you like, means we have to choose one or two. It can be delivered coherently.

Q13 Mr Turner: Mr Ripley was saying that it does not apply to everyone, I think the phrase was. I am not quite sure what did not apply to everyone but --

Mr Ripley: I was kind of answering the specific relating to outdoor adventure rather than to out of class learning. That was really the point I was making.

Dr Tilling: Can I give you an example of what is happening on our courses? As people pointed out, we are traditionally a supplier of science or geography courses, and people to do either/or. What is happening now is there is a recognition within schools that they can achieve both at the same time. I know, for example, within outdoor and adventure sector there is now more attention being given to courses which combine curriculum areas and subject areas with outdoor activity, and the feedback we have from London Challenge courses is that that is absolutely spot on. They do like activities which deliver, for example, subject areas but also like other areas which are delivering more strongly in personal and social, the other development areas—PSE for example. You were asking about value: I think there are areas in which value has been developed all the time within the outdoor sector.

Mr Simpson: I think, Mr Turner, it is important to say we are not asking for extra bits to be thrown into an overcrowded curriculum. Quite the contrary. We are talking here about what we believe is more effective delivery of whatever curriculum DfES wants to us operate, and this is all about creating a climate where there is status and support for the kind of out-of-classroom learning where it is appropriate, not where it is ubiquitous, and certainly not where it is extra.

Q14 Mr Turner: So it is not extra but it is better of the same. In that case, is it not something which schools, if they assess their performance properly, effectively, would be able to judge for themselves, or should be able to, and which produces demonstrable benefits for their pupils and, therefore, should not need signals or guidance on statute?

Mr Simpson: Coming very quickly back on that, one of the perverse things we found with our research is that the schools where out-of-classroom learning is thriving are those where they are confident, they are successful, they are demonstrably succeeding. There seems to us to be a direct link between those schools who, if you like, are not quite as confident, who are not in their Ofsted inspections succeeding and being widely praised. They tend to retreat into the prescriptive curriculum more so I think it is human nature. That is what people would do.

Q15 Mr Turner: So prescriptive curriculum is a comfort blanket?

Mr Simpson: Yes.

Mr Ripley: The point I was trying to make in my notes was that the schools that are taking outdoor learning to its highest level are really the high-performing schools, and for them they will find a way round any of the problems and issues. For those schools that are not performing that do not have that level of confidence, if you like, they will say "Oh, no, this is something too difficult, let us get down to the basic minimum requirement". So we have schools that are taking their young Year 7 children out of school for a whole week of the curriculum at the beginning of their first year of secondary school. The benefits they see result in the fact that by the time they get to Christmas they are really adding value to those young people's education, yet poor performing schools are taking those kids in and it is beyond Easter before they have a coherent group of Year 7s. So it is not about building it into the curriculum; it is saying that by doing interventions like that, you can improve all of the other elements that are existing in there and that requires a degree of confidence, and it is about a message of value; this is a valuable thing to do; this is what high-performing schools are doing, this is what Ofsted sees as adding value. That is the kind of message that we are trying to get across, as it were.

Dr Tilling: Again, to give you an example of how that might work, in Birmingham schools some of the most imaginative outdoor learning goes on through flexi days where timetabling is completely thrown up in the air and everyone works together, so all the subject departments work together. In

that case a number of different targets can be reached within various departments, but it does need a whole school approach.

Ms Henwood: You do have to define what you expect the value output to be because it is very easy to tick a box that says "outdoor learning" and until you determine what the criteria are that you are expecting to be delivered against that then it is not going to add any value at all.

Q16 Mr Turner: That is rather the point I was going to challenge Rita Gardner on; that you asked for some fieldwork but there is such a wide range, is there not, for summer residential experiences which outside the home are unheard of, but for others it is frequent. It seems to me that you have a good product which you are not able to sell and I am rather concerned that you should rely on politicians to be able to sell it for you because politicians are notoriously badly trusted. So why do you think we, or the Secretary of State specifically, would be better than you at selling this, who know about the product and know about the benefits?

Dr Gardner: We do have a good product that is capable of being sold. I think it is not simply politicians selling that message for us, of course. We need to sell it ourselves in terms of good exemplars, drawing together good exemplars. What is the National College of School Leadership in a sense doing here? What roles could it play in facilitating amongst the heads of schools greater awareness and understanding of fieldwork and out-of-school activities? So I think there is a number of players. There are the teachers themselves; there are the subject bodies and other associations involved; we can provide continuing professional development; we can try and assist and work with teachers to raise standards overall in the provision of the delivery of the fieldwork experience; we can to some degree work with others to provide resources to support that, but if there is not a message coming in a sense from on high about the value of out-of-classroom learning in a curriculum that is very tight in a school timetable that is equally very tight, so, for example, many schools are finding that they can only put their fieldwork at certain times of the year because of the tightness of the curriculum, in a school where resources are very tight and when schools can sit behind, yes, a statutory requirement in geography but without any guidance as to the extent, so it can be those three hours over years 5–14—the point I am trying to make is it is a game that all of us have to play. I do not mean a game in a jovial sense but it is an issue we all need to contribute to from our areas of expertise if we believe in out-of-classroom learning, and one of those contributions should be, in my view, a stronger signal of the value of out-of-classroom learning from the politicians and through DfES as a partner in the whole.

Q17 Valerie Davey: Following on from that the educationalists presumably, on the basis of all that we have said so far, see this as added value. How could they better improve teacher training? We have mentioned PGCE courses but in all the teacher training what would you like to see there which would be better value for the outcome in the schools to which those teachers will go?

Dr Thomas: I think one of the interesting things about the guidance from TTA, rather like as has been suggested elsewhere for young people, is that the curriculum has been loosened up now and has been quite prescriptive. There have been challenges in terms of coverage. I think what we were hoping for was that as young people, and our belief is especially those within science and to a lesser degree within humanities, they have less experience both with their parents and also in school of out-of-classroom learning. They do not build up that background, and that has increased as you go into higher education. There is evidence within sciences that there is less and less out-of-classroom learning going on. In biology per se, and understandably because all the research money now is for biogenetics and biochemistry, there is little emphasis on ecology so therefore, because there is not, you do not go outside the classroom, you do not go beyond the laboratory. You then enter, if you are doing a PGCE course, with limited experience and probably get under the new guidance one day—and this is not anecdotal, this is personal communication with lecturers and institutes of teacher education. They can allow one day's dedicated learning within what they provide. There is the opportunity for voluntary weekends. So what would we like? We would like some experience. We would like to go beyond. Health and safety is important; risk assessment—very important. Yes, we see those as building blocks but they are in a sense the basic foundation skills which allow you to do the activity in a health and safety approach. What we also want to do is give people the confidence and the competence to work with young people out of doors. It is different, whether it is in the school grounds, the local community or some distance away, so it is getting that experience and giving them some opportunity of a little bit of contextualisation, and not just have the theory of working outside the classroom but putting it into practice. As we want our youngsters to have that put into practice, young teachers need that as well.

Mr Simpson: To take up on that, this is not a conspiracy. I do not think anybody ever set out to deny trainee teachers or even in-service teachers the capacity to do this sort of thing, but I do think it is a consequence of the way the whole thing was organised. When the national curriculum was instituted and the silos of the subjects were built, obviously that was what was concentrated on within training. What that has led to, certainly in primary sectors, and anybody who goes into schools will notice this now, is the demise of things like the nature table. I am not trying to look through rose-tinted spectacles but it is just kind of going out for a walk and collecting things and being curious about that sort of thing, and gradually less and less teachers are in a very rigid

training system which is as crowded as the curriculum itself and it is not becoming the norm any more. One of the problems with it is, and I would like to say this right at the very end of the education sector, is that although they are not here agencies like the Environment Agency will turn round to you now and say, "We have real problems recruiting people with the kind of taxonomic skills and the skills of going and recognising things that only come through experience that we need to take the environmental agenda which is ever more important forward", so there is a cost right at the end of the process.

Dr Tilling: Supporting what has just been said, one of the comments which often comes back from our colleagues working in universities who are delivering PGCE courses, for example, is that obviously there has been an increasing dependence on, if you like, in-school training, mentoring within schools, and even within the schools an age and cohort, if you like, perhaps of teachers who had these skills who are dropping out the other end, and we were joking earlier that we are actually a representation of that cohort, if you like. So if a new teacher comes into a school and is looking for that sort of support within the school, then the chances are it is no longer there so unless it is delivered through the college then it will not be delivered, and the stance that we have at our fingertips suggests it is also disappearing from college provision. One of the responses that we have made jointly with the British Ecological Society is to set up some sponsored training courses for PGCE students, and these are biologists and geographers, and again the take-up of those courses has been very good and the responses and evaluations to those courses has been very good. The interesting thing is that what seems to have happened is that we had to put a ceiling on those courses because of the amount of funding that was available or just putting two or three from any one institution, and what seems to happen subsequently is that a number of institutions are then coming afterwards so the students have gone back and said, "This is a very worthwhile experience; it has helped us in terms of our training" and then the following year a number of year groups from that institution actually came along, and what that suggests to us is that sort of thinking has dropped out of the system in terms of training, and this is beginning to feed it back in again but it does need a lot more support and a lot more impetus to really get it integrated.

Dr Gardner: I think it goes also beyond the formal sense of training in a number of areas. One is that much of the fieldwork inevitably will be based around local areas. Whether it is the local area you live in or a local area that you visit there is an enormous amount of government data available now on local areas from the Census, neighbourhood statistics and so on which, at the moment, is not as ready available to teachers as it might be, and this is something we are working on within the Society. So there is the knowledge resources and areas change and develop, and we have some of the data available to be able to illustrate that. That is the first point. Secondly, accreditation. The subject bodies or professional bodies through their disciplines can perhaps do more to ensure that in their teachers' plans of accreditation they can put an emphasis on CPD programmes that relate to fieldwork, for example. Lastly, we have talked about the teachers at the coalface but there is also the Educational Visits Co-ordinators, and we have been providing a substantial number of courses on risk assessment and management for Educational Visits Co-ordinators, including those who are taking overseas visits as well, and we feel very strongly that all schools should be encouraged to have an Educational Visits Co-ordinator to work alongside the teachers in the delivery of the out-of-classroom activities.

Q18 Valerie Davey: I think what is coming out of that discussion is that if there is added value for out-of-classroom then there ought to be added value for out-of-lecture room for all HE studies, whatever they may be, before they get to the add-on of the PGCE, and dare I say out-of-Parliament which is what we have just experienced! We reckon it is added value and, if it is, right the way through the system then how do we get parents on board, because if they knew that this added value of hands-on experience was valuable to their youngsters learning then perhaps a few more of them might do it. My train journey from Bristol to London has been transformed by a Dad with his four-year-old son who have talked non stop the whole of that journey pointing out a building without a roof and this station and that, and it has been brilliant, but how many parents do that? The added value of that for that youngster was just brilliant. It was demanding. I can remember those days when those children asked and asked but I have not had a journey like that on that train for a long time, so what are you doing to enable parents to recognise the value of what is happening in their schools but also what they could be doing by walking to school and observing and getting involved?

Mr Simpson: There is no easy answer to that. I would point you in the way of pester power being proven by our marketing colleagues to be a very significant motivator. Allied to that, I know we are talking about the formal sector. I think we need to recognise that there are two sides to the way that young people live—the school and the home. Yes, ideally I would love every child to have the kind of experiences you are talking about but I think we need to recognise that, for instance, the kind of experiential discovery play that used to be the norm is now no longer what children have, and at a time of material prosperity many children's physical world is shrinking. Obviously the education sector cannot make up for parenting but I would argue very strongly that, in the absence of things coming from home, the education sector has a duty to

allow children to experience that sort of thing and hopefully generate the enthusiasm that will make them go home and demand those kind of experiences more from their family. It sounds a bit trite but what we cannot do is, on the one hand, accept that parents do not allow children to play out any more and all of the things allied to that, and then have this formal education system wash its hands in it as well.

Q19 Chairman: What we are trying to get out of you, though, in terms of all of your experience is what the best way to provide that is. In a sense when we ask you questions within a category like the study of geography or the study of a specific subject as a film study linked, what I think Val was getting at in her way, and let me put it in mine, is how do you get a whole group of kids in school to start thinking about global warming, and how do you then take them out into the external environment to do that? It is not subject specific: it is what every child in this country should know about because it is going to influence their lives and the lives of their children. How do we do that better when it is not subject specific? How do we raise the consciousness, change the culture? How do we do that?

Ms Henwood: I cannot specifically talk about global warming but I can talk about how we try and encourage the parents and the kids and our teachers to come on our courses, and that is about going to the schools and talking to teachers and parents and children about what they are about to experience, and what they will get from that. There is nothing that makes up for it other than hitting the streets and doing it. For parents, or the units of the family, there is this, as we know, abrogation of responsibility to schools to engender, to take up responsibility for other areas and skills that they should be developing, so you are not necessarily talking to an easy audience and they will not always turn up and listen, but those that do are very persuaded and you carry on the communication so that when the young people come back from their experience they then present back about what they have learned and what they are going to do as a result of it and you carry on that as a continuum within the education environment they are in. But it is about creating profile and worth and value around the whole subject, and we can only do it from a very small percentage and we are relying on bigger agendas taking part.

Q20 Chairman: Whose? On Friday I will be presenting Computers for Schools in my local Tescos. Tescos takes one pound of every seven spent in the country, as I understand it, these days. Should large companies like that really be getting involved promoting the kind of programme we have been discussing here? Should the Bill Gates Foundation? Should it be coming from that sort of partnership at a very senior level?

Ms Henwood: We have a number of those for example, HSBC and Barclays Capital, who will support us over five years with a significant amount of funding to do that. Yes, they have an agenda that they want to fill on corporate social responsibility, which is absolutely fine because everybody is in a win–win situation, but, yes, we have to look at that sort of funding from those sorts of companies who can involve the level of people we want involved.

Dr Thomas: There are examples of large companies, and as Chair of the Welfare and Wellness Trust I can say that HSBC has been very generous to that particular Trust in terms of funding travel to centres, and as travel is an increasingly spiralling cost for many schools and youth groups, it has been a tremendous benefit to getting access. Trying to get to parents is very challenging. All the organisations linked to the Real World Learning campaign have family groups and specific initiatives for young people that they try to run and engage for youngsters and youngsters with parents and grandparents. On occasions grandparents and guardians are probably better people because they have a bit more time, so they say, to be with young people, so I think there has been a lot of initiatives from this sector to try and make their engagement but trying to get to individuals is quite charging. Parent/teacher organisations is another route that we are taking to convey the benefit, and also we are looking at after school clubs and things of that nature. RSPB has run after school clubs, Saturday clubs as another way of trying to engage people in out-of-classroom learning. You're right in a sense to point the finger: it is a responsibility of the sector to convey the benefits, and I am not about more prescription but I am about trying to, in a sense, redress the balance, because I think we have got a bit out of kilter and increasingly we have to get an engagement about a cost benefit analysis where people are more aware of what are the benefits in out-of-classroom learning. As you say yourself, it is not just teachers, not just heads, governors, but parents. You get that message across, and I think the media, which we have not talked about today, also has a role because some of the media is fast to make very negative judgments about when things do go wrong. There are not too many good news stories—and I know good news does not sell many papers but there is a need to try and get that balance, and that is what I mean by the signal—to try and have that positive engagement about having that fair cost benefit analysis, and how we do that is say "Yes, we are asking for a bit of guidance and support from politicians, but also we recognise we have a significant responsibility within the sector".

Mr Simpson: I have two very quick examples. We cannot solve this problem in one go but I would point you to the fact that in the RSPB we know there is a very clear linkage between children visiting our reserves with school parties during the week and then coming back with their parents at weekends. We statistically know that, and in some of our reserves it can be up to 70% of children returning. Equally, statistically we know there is a very clear linkage between children joining Wildlife Explorers, which is our junior branch as children, and then coming back and being environmentalists and joining the RSPB as adults when they grow up. The gap can be as long as 25 years but nevertheless in childhood the seeds that are sown are very important.

Dr Gardner: Let us perhaps not forget that parents do support out-of-classroom learning. They pay for it on a regular basis so although they may not be standing there waving banners saying "We support this", inherently they do support it and it would be very interesting to know and have a much better handle on the extent to which parents more generally support that area. One of the areas that we have touched on is risk and we have seen an increasing number of parents concerned about risks for their children on out-of-classroom activities, and it comes back partly to the media—and the individual cases are indeed very sad—raising awareness of the relatively low, in comparable terms, levels of risk. If I may just quote --

Chairman: Do you mind just holding on because we are going to come to that area in some detail. We do not want people's noses to be put out of joint because their questions have been stolen by another Member! Paul is going to ask you a couple of specifics.

Q21 Paul Holmes: It is partly in terms of the framework that has been put there to try and meet those risks, after one or two particular tragic incidents that we had. You now have the Government, the Department for Education and Skills issued guidance in 2001 as to what should be done to minimise that risk. You have local education authorities who are now supposed to have an outdoor education advisor in place. You have schools who are supposed to have the education events co-ordinator in place. You have a whole bureaucracy of paperwork which I remember well from filling in myself as a teacher not many years ago, to try and do the risk assessments and everything. Has all those layers of paperwork and guidance and coordinators, is that a good step forward or is it unnecessary bureaucracy?

Dr Thomas: I think there is some excellent guidance provided by the Department, by local authorities and by many, many schools. I think that where teachers follow them, then as far as one can, in a sense, be predictive and manage risks, then you create a situation which is reasonably positive. Having said that, I think what we are picking up is examples where teachers do feel now it has become excessive; the anecdotal comments that it takes me 16 forms to fill in to take a half a day trip to an RSPB reserve, which was used by colleague in a different context a day or two ago. If that is the case then do we have the right balance because that, in its is right, is becoming a barrier. Whilst we know that we have to demonstrate health care, the health, safety and welfare of young people, of teachers, classroom assistants, accompanying parents into consideration, as well as others they might come into contact with, if we become so, in a sense, bound by this, then I think you will just put people off. I think there is a genuine worry that there is the other element which is about the fear of litigation, which you might want to come on to in a moment or two, but it is out there. I know that the Regulation Task Group did this report that was quoted by the Chief Inspector recently in his outdoor education report. There has been a reduction of maybe 600,000 in terms of claims in the last year, a tremendous reduction, but there is still a real fear of litigation.

Q22 Chairman: We are coming to that in the next session. Okay. Anybody want to come back -- what about these events co-ordinators? How many schools have these?
Mr Ripley: Increasingly schools have their events co-ordinators. I think it just is increasingly hard for teachers to get out of the classroom. The challenge for us is always to make that as simple as possible.

Q23 Chairman: There has been a massive investment in teaching assistants to free up teachers to have more time to do other stuff. Is that true?
Ms Henwood: We have had two examples recently where courses have been cancelled because they could not get the cover for teachers.
Dr Thomas: It is an interesting opportunity to use classrooms assistants and if you provide them with training to take on some of this bureaucratic responsibility. I know the FSE is discussing this with Open University colleges to develop modules to prepare classroom assistants to take on some of that task. Personally, I think that is very positive.

Q24 Paul Holmes: Partly, again because you have the layers now of defensive paperwork and co-ordinators, and so forth, which obviously is very good from a safe point of view. Two questions: (1) is it possible to quantify in the last three or four years since this network has been set up, and has there, therefore, been a reduction in serious incidents and injuries and fatalities, or is it not possible to quantify, or is the level exactly the same and the Press was just hyping it up and it was all taken out of proportion?
Dr Thomas: Obviously, the source of the detailed information will be with AALA and with the Department, who would have a clear indication of those incidents and accidents that have taken place. Obviously, we are all aware of the very tragic accidents that occurred in the Leeds Group not too long ago and also in the Lake District. I think if you look -- and we were looking at the last 25 years of evidence -- and I think you are looking at probably something in the order of 30 fatalities over that period. My own view is that fatalities that occur, you have one or two sad rather high number

of fatality events and I have not necessarily seen a clear change. I think I will stop there. I have not necessarily seen a clear change.

Q25 Chairman: I just want to press you a bit on the availability of teachers to do this job. What is the myth and what is reality? Has anyone costed how much this work costs a school and would it be better if you just franchised it off? The information cannot be to look after outdoor education for kids. Are their commercial concerns that do that? If you want X amount of, if you take my model, every child has an entitlement of ten days a year. You have to deliver that or Ofsted is going to come and be rather nasty to you. Should it not be up to you to do it? You can hire someone to do it with the legal responsibility if you are too busy in the school or you can get parents to do it, but you make any arrangement you like, surely. Why are you making it such a fuss about this?
Dr Gardner: The experience has to be one, in my mind as a former field work teacher in higher education it has to be a learning experience. Now that we have all the improved risk assessment and so on in place, the quality of the experience we can now start to really build on. I do not personally believe that outsourcing that, taking the kids out for a few days and bringing them back, is necessarily a good idea. The Field Studies Council, of course, does a brilliant job on the sorts of courses that it does, but to outsource it generally means that you lose the opportunity, which is a very substantial opportunity, for the teacher and the class bonding, which is a key element we did not refer to earlier on. You lose the opportunity to bind that work effectively into ongoing classroom activities and learning. You also lose the opportunity to build your progression through fieldwork from 5 to 14, in some cases, because, again, you have lost your continuity. I really strongly feel that to outsource the learning base of out of classroom activities is losing an enormous amount of the potential value added, so we do need to release teachers into this.
Dr Tilling: You asked two points of evidence. One is what the actual costs are and we have very precise costs. For example, the London challenge where we have the funding to pay for transport and fees, and I do not have them at my fingertips, but I think that the figure that springs to mind is that a quarter of the costs ended up paying for those residential courses actually went towards supplying cover. Just to enable students to come out of the London schools and go on a residential field trip I think two thirds of the cost was actual fees, but the rest of the money was towards transport and supply cover. The other major barrier that was identified, and we have been talking about barriers at different levels within the school community, the major barrier that was identified at school level, so management level within the school in terms of the residentials, was actually the quality as well as the

level of supply cover. It is not simply having the money to buy someone in to cover the course. It was also the quality of the supply.

Q26 Jonathan Shaw: It is the bit that people have heard spoken about a little bit in terms of the barriers and the litigation and all the stuff that we get in the media. I enjoyed reading the Outward Bound magazine. There was not one young person there who had lost their sock and they were complaining; they all seemed smiling, happy people.
Mr Ripley: Of course.

Q27 Jonathan Shaw: Of course. Is it laziness? Are people scaredy cats? What is wrong with the perception within our society about Outward Bound activities? I am using "Outward Bound". I will get into trouble if I use that all the time.
Mr Ripley: I think we are talking here about the fear and risk of litigation and the accidents. When tragic accidents have happened, and they have happened, they go right to the top of the profile. I think that what happens then is that that spreads a fear and people are very, very concerned, parents are very concerned, teachers are very concerned, schools are very concerned to make sure that they have dotted every i and crossed every t.

Q28 Chairman: So we get 16 pages.
Mr Ripley: You have 16 pages. We have a licensing system and yet a school will apply to come and do a course with us and so there is a process that they go through whereby they will send us their Local Authority forms, "Will you fill these forms in". The first question is: do you have an adventures activities licence to which the answer is yes. Instead of saying: go to the bottom of the form, because we have had an external agency do all that work, it then says, "answer all the questions that you have already answered for the licensing authority", That is the kind of reaction and process that we are in amongst. When you then get to a situation where you are asking teachers to do that on their own back it is relatively easy for them when they ask an organisation like us to do that. They can cover, something Barry was saying, you can buy in some of that service, but when you are looking at trying to do that in the school as well it just compounds the issue. It just compounds the difficulty. I think it is a balance between perception and actual reality. I think when you look at that evidence on the ground there is a big gap between the two.
Dr Thomas: I think there is another issue as well, that if one of the leading trade unions actually gives you advice to its members.

Q29 Jonathan Shaw: My next question. Go on then, answer it.
Dr Thomas: I keep on digging a bigger trench for myself. If one of the unions gives you advice not to take your own groups out of the classroom then for many members that is going to be a negative thing. There you are, they are your union group, they

obviously offer to provide you with legal advice if you get into difficulties, et cetera. If they are saying, "our advice is that you should not take groups out", then I think that is quite challenging for a teacher who belongs to that union. You either move union or you say do I put it aside and all the risks that go with that or do I abide by that guidance. The sector has to engage with unions absolutely. I think it is critical that the sector does engage with all the unions and to discuss some of the issues that they are concerned about. The Real World Learning partnership has been doing that with a particular union that has these concerns. One of their leading people spoke at an RSPB fringe at both the Labour and the Liberal Democrat conferences. They basically said that many of their members do put their guidance aside, but they still feel obliged to give, because of the situation, because of the climate, because of what they regard as safe, and for legislative process, their view is that they will continue to give this advice to their members. That does not mean that they will not necessarily say if you go with that provider or that provider you will be reasonably okay because I know that they have made gestures in that direction.

Q30 Jonathan Shaw: You can answer my next question.
Mr Simpson: 16 pages of a form to visit an RSPB reserve, actually it was 16 different forms. Many of those forms were multi-paged. This was for the most hazardous activity involved: going pond dipping, not in itself recognised to be a particularly dangerous occupation. I think we have to recognise that teachers do have this fear. I think they feel that they are bottom of the food chain in this. What they feel is that everybody else, all the organisations and bureaucracies around them, are being very defensive and covering their own backs, but ultimately it is the teacher who feels exposed. I am afraid unless that culture is changed in some way and teachers are made to feel supported, valued and will be defended, of course nobody is talking about defending negligence, then it is a not unreasonable point of view for the teacher to say: it is easier not to go.[1]

Q31 Jonathan Shaw: Yes, but if you are filling in 16 pages to go and scoop up a few tadpoles it is no wonder that it creates and atmosphere when people are a little bit concerned.
Mr Simpson: The ridiculous nature of that is that it would be epitomised by the risk assessment. The RSPB is a professional organisation. We take risk assessment very seriously. We automatically send out risk assessments on our sites and for our activities when schools book with us. Sadly the teacher that I am referring to came back to me and said, "We would like to have used your risk assessment, but it is not in the format that my local authority wants, so I have to dismantle the whole thing and rebuild it". Can you blame her for not going?

[1]Also see Ev 31.

Q32 Jonathan Shaw: These are all the problems, are they not, and what we all want to do is if we agree out-of-classroom education is important. Are there some effective and simple steps that, as a Committee, we could recommend to the Department that we could improve the situation?

Mr Ripley: I think the reality is it is about trying to convince people that out-of-door learning is no more risky than in-school learning. I can use our own example for that. We look at all the incidents that happen in our centres, as you would imagine, throughout the year. Increasingly, the kinds of incidents that we get are the same kind of incidents you would get in school learning. They are to do with kids misbehaving and doing things that they would do in the school environment and I think the issue is to try and continually reinforce that whilst things do happen they are the same things that happen in the school environment. They are the same things that happen on the way to school, away from school, and it is the same things that would happen in the youth group. It is trying to get people to recognise that that is what happens in life.

Q33 Chairman: Why does your organisation not put out some data on that? Everybody knows that the most dangerous place for a child to be is with its parents at home, being driven, and all those things. Why on earth do you not get together and put out a hazard thing and explain to the parents that the most hazardous thing your child could do, and put them in a rank order of priority. It would be something that would be rather valuable.

Jonathan Shaw: Statistically, so we are told by our advisers, that a child is more in danger at home in bed than they are on a school trip.

Q34 Chairman: Or skinny dipping rather than pond dipping.

Dr Gardner: In fact, something like 500 young people die falling down stairs each year, whereas only three or four die on school trips. Yes, we would be doing more, but there is also perhaps a different way of looking at this, which is that we live our lives as citizens day-to-day confronting risk; that is what we all do all the time. There is a huge potential value in educating the young people themselves about risk in the real world. Why do we not use the opportunity of school trips to actually do that? Most of them will have to deal with their risks if they are protected from them on their school trips by the time they go off to, God knows where, on their gap year. I would like to see more inclusion of the students and pupils from the point of view of risk and using it as a learning process to deal with risk as we grow into being adults. You do not see that.

Ms Henwood: Can I just say that that is what we do on the Outward Bound courses. We teach people about risk and how to manage it rather than run away from it.

Q35 Jonathan Shaw: Do you have difficulty in recruiting people to work in your centres?

Ms Henwood: To be our instructors?

Q36 Jonathan Shaw: Yes, talking about the quality; do you have any difficulty?

Ms Henwood: No. To have Outward Bound I am very proud to say on your CV is a very big plus. The difficulty is retaining staff because we cannot pay them that well.

Q37 Jonathan Shaw: You have a high turnover do you?

Ms Henwood: Yes.

Q38 Jonathan Shaw: Does that affect quality, or you are not going to say that, are you?

Ms Henwood: We have very good training.

Q39 Jonathan Shaw: Could I come back to your point about what are the constructive things we could say. Very simply, for groups of activities we ought to have a template for risk assessment which is common to all rather than have a --

Dr Thomas: All the different ones. I am sure through the outdoor educational advisers, Committee, Working Group, that they are moving towards having a common template. To me, that would be eminently sensible. I think there are whole issues about trying to establish protocols for providers with the unions that the unions and the Department are content with to give reassurance to parents, to teachers, to head teachers, organisations, who are not covered by are la. This is one of the issues that when you get a risk assessment or the form to fill in and you say to someone, "We are not AALA, we do not hold an AALA licence", that can be the death for your organisation. You do not have an AALA licence because you are not within scope, therefore, you cannot be licensed. I think there are some interesting issues here about people. The general public sees out-of-classroom learning as one thing. It does not see all the myriad of contributions to it. I think we need something which helps us to give some recognition especially to unions and parents, and say these people are well recognised, whether it is a BAHA activity badge or someone else's where everybody has signed up to an agreed set of protocols and are implemented, independently inspected or at least reviewed so that that gives that reassurance.

Q40 Chairman: Better bureaucracy.

Dr Thomas: A very light touch, a lot of self-evaluation, but the fallback that anyone has the right at any time, ie, from an independent body, to go in and check, not that you are bureaucratising it but making it meaningful so that people know that there is something there uniform.

Q41 Chairman: Could we have data on that? It is slightly beyond familiarity. Okay. A note on that.

Dr Thomas: I will do one.[2]

Q42 Jonathan Shaw: Just about funding. Is outdoor education under funded and to what extent?
Mr Simpson: Just to give a very clear example. RSPB for a day visit we charge schools and we are not apologising for that because we believe we are providing a professional service depending on ratios. However, the cost benefit analysis shows that for every child who steps off a bus for a day visit to an RSPB reserve, my organisation is directly subsidising that visit to the tune of £10 per child per visit. What that means is that whilst we want to do more it is unreasonable of the NGL sector for us to be expected to be open ended in our commitment to do hundreds of thousands.

Q43 Jonathan Shaw: Did you not just tell us that the next day they brought their parents back, so they spent a whole load of money then?
Mr Simpson: I am afraid not. What they get is a personalised invitation inviting them to bring their parents back for a free visit. To do our job professionally as we want to and to offer the kind of professional education service, for instance on an RSPB reserve we operate on a ratio of one of our teachers to 15 children for the whole duration. It is not: there are your work sheets and off you go. It costs money. Whilst we want to do more we are very cognisant of fact that the money has to be raised from somewhere. If one was being critical of Government over the years, one would say that since local management of schools and the demise of many of the local authority field study centres which offered subsidised visits to children -- which is how I started -- Government has had pretty much of a free ride. It is the NGO sector and other providers that have stepped in to fill that vacuum. We want to do more. We would appreciate some help.
Mr Ripley: If I could make a point. There are three barriers we think. There is litigation; we have talked about that. There is the supply of teachers and teacher access. Then there is cost. For us we think the cost is really one of the biggest barriers. It is about being able to find the funding to access the training that we want, the teaching that people need to get the benefits of that. This is really about encouraging schools into freeing up cash within schools. If this is going to be more than a holiday, and what we have been saying here is that the learning that we have is a central part of the teaching, then it does not make sense that you then say to the parents: you have to pay for this, or at least if you are going to go down that route do not expect a high uptake of it because the cost of this experience.

Q44 Jonathan Shaw: Are more people coming to your centres or less?
Mr Ripley: More people are coming to our centres because we are able to subsidise it by getting cash from the charitable sector, basically from the corporate sector. We have had significant growth in young people coming to centres. That is because we have been able to offer bursaries and financial support for people to come and do the work that they are doing. Without that, we would be in decline.

Q45 Jonathan Shaw: We could say it is an argument in terms of the local taxation you set in terms of how much we spend on those kinds of things. If it is a bit lower then individuals and companies make their own choices.
Mr Ripley: There are a number of ways that you can get there, but I think cost is a major barrier. If you are looking at outdoor education in the round and saying outdoor education, education out of the classroom, it is more expensive. There is a number of ways that we can mitigate that expense.

Q46 Jonathan Shaw: More people are coming?
Mr Ripley: More people are coming because more funding is being found, but quite often their funding is of a short-term nature. I can give you some examples of that. We have had a number of different projects. We have talked about the London Challenge, Steve talked about that earlier. Get Real is an initiative that has been started by David Miliband. We have the U Project, which is at the end of three years. We have other programmes like this. Increasingly what happens is people think outdoor education access is a very important issue. How are we going to fund this? Let us send it off to the lottery: a new project, Get Real, let us go off to the lottery and find funding there. The lottery will then fund it in a very inefficient way for the length of the project -- two years, maybe three years -- and at the end of three years we have gone round a whole lottery funding cycle which is desperately inefficient, that does not necessarily hit the target. The funding comes to the end. Somebody says: ooh, we had better have outdoor education because we do not have any more of it. Let us go and find another funding source. You have this continual -- from a provider's perspective that can be great news because if you can get in at the right point you can end up delivering some work from a funding source, but in terms of straight efficiency and increasing accessibility, it is desperately, desperately inefficient. I think it is not so much there is not any funding; it is the funding is in the wrong place. It needs to creatively be put into the right place.
Dr Gardner: A couple of things. The first is picking up on the point about the continuity of commercial and other sources of funding. There is huge competition out there for all manner of trusts and foundation and commercial funding. That is not, to my mind, a solution for provision of substantially increased support over a medium term for education. It would help but it will not take its place. The other point is the National Agreement on Workforce Reform. I think a number of us raised this, but certainly those teachers that we talked to were very concerned that the Workforce Agreement would impact negatively on field work, particularly because of the difficulty of providing cover for

colleagues on field work and having to pay for that cover. That was one of the key issues that the head teachers we spoke to raised with us.

Mr Simpson: Some more information. We did not actually ask schools how effective additional funding would be to increase residentials. These were 11–14 year olds with learning skills again and mainly from disadvantaged boroughs. The information which came back was interesting in the sense that we knew from previous answers that most of the course fees were being paid for by parents anyway, even in those boroughs. About two thirds of the fees were paid for by parents, with another third or so coming from schools. There is a great deal of sensitivity in learning skills. If additional funding is available it should be sensitively targeted. By that we meant that we had agreed who were reasonably well in terms of parental contributions or carers' contributions were available so that they could go. Then we had other groups who were already being supported through various mechanisms—hardship funds, LEA funds or whatever—so they were also reasonably well endowed. Time and again when we asked the schools there were a big middle group who they thought were critical who were being missed. They were the ones who they felt really needed to be help through existing or additional funding.

Q47 Jonathan Shaw: Poorer children? These were the ones who just missed the boat.

Mr Simpson: Also, interestingly refugee groups and people who were not aware of the mechanisms which exited to support the groups. Time and again, and this really was a very, very strong response which came back from all the schools, was that they felt that first of all if funding became available it needed to be ring-fenced so it did not get absorbed into the school funding and end up doing something else. The other one was that the schools should have the flexibility to target the funding themselves because they were using all sorts of mechanisms to identify the children who were most likely or most needed residentials. This was, for example, things like exam results or it was attendance records or evidence of having done something positive through the year. Those were very, very strong pieces of feedback which came through. There is a group that would be helped I think.

Q48 Jonathan Shaw: You advocate allowing head teachers and governors to make this discretionary?

Mr Simpson: With strong guidelines.

Paul Holmes: Just coming back to something you said I think it was about ten minutes ago Rita was saying that we need to move away a little bit from the layers of bureaucracy and the cosseting of everything and trying to remove all risk and go to a system where we teach children to manage risk and assess risk themselves. Last week the Committee was in Finland and Norway. We were looking partly at prison education and partly at schools. One of the things we noticed in the schools was that you will see photographs of children from kindergarten age upwards out in two foot of snow with the teachers

with an open camp fire with a sausage on a stick cooking over it. We were saying: in England, snow, it is too cold you cannot take them out. Open camp fire: too dangerous, you cannot do that. Sausage on a stick: food hygiene regulations; cannot do that. Then on Friday morning we were at a kindergarten in Oslo. They had children from one to six. The teacher opened up a cupboard that had saws and tools in it and said: "At the age of three we get them to use these to cut wood up and make things. If one of them cuts themselves then that is part of the learning process." From your contacts with similar organisations in other countries, how typical is that? Are we so cosseted it is ridiculous? Do other countries do it better than us because they certainly to in Finland and Norway?

Q49 Chairman: When we looked at first schools, the low down was that there is no such thing as bad weather, just inappropriate clothing.

Dr Thomas: As Chair of the Forest Education Initiative—

Q50 Chairman: Tease you out a bit, Anthony.

Dr Thomas:—can I welcome that you did go and see it. If you had not seen it would you have believed it?

Q51 Chairman: No.

Dr Thomas: As a Doubting Thomas in this grouping I think it is really important that other people have that opportunity. It is not just youngsters. It is those young adolescents with behavioural and emotional difficulties. Those are the ones who are really benefiting from a lot of this experience, trust being developed. A lot of things at the Outward Bound we do with forest schools is about trust and opportunity. It is opportunity in a practical way. You asked a very good question. In 1935 a Justice said a quite sexist thing it would be regarded as these days: five little boys, cover them in cotton wool, one of them will suffocate. That is the reality. If you over protect then I think you are doing a disservice to young people. We are not preparing them. It was not too long ago that the head mistress of the Girls' Day Trust said quite clearly: we are molly coddling our youngsters. We need to give them the opportunity to develop in confidence and competence to go out into the wider world. We are protecting them to the age of 18 or 19 and then saying: go.

Chairman: We are getting a very good analysis of the problem from you chaps. What are you doing about coming up with the answers in the sense: what is your prescription for change? Should there be a right to so many days that every child has? How many days would you recommend? Should there be convened a meeting of all the players to find out if we can overcome these barriers of the resistance to risk? What are you saying about what the answers are to overcome the barriers? You have been brilliant in terms of analysing the problem. We are very grateful. What are the answers?

Q52 Paul Holmes: Added to that, coming back to my original question: are there good examples from other countries from sister organisations that you go and see in other countries where we can say they do it better than us and they do not have lots people having fatal accidents.

Mr Simpson: To answer that, I think there is a real danger that our system is increasingly being held up as being ridiculous; I use that word very carefully. Colleagues recently from South Africa had had the stories of the conker fiasco last week and the school banning daisy chains because daisies might have germs on them. It is not about them having examples of how they do it. We have gone way too far, absolutely way too far.

Q53 Chairman: You are still not giving us any answers.

Mr Ripley: To answer both your questions, I think we should be moving towards and looking towards being residential right for all young people when they are at school. That should be a practical thing that we should be looking for. That should be integrated, not within a particular curriculum area because that right can be delivered in a number of different fields. It can be delivered on a curriculum basis or it can be delivered on a non-curriculum basis. I do not think there is the requirement there, but it is saying that as part of your education at various stages there is a right to spend some time away from home, away from school because that still, for so many people, is an experience (A) they do not get and (B) having that experience with their school colleagues is a very central learning experience. We see that every day. On the issue of what is happening overseas. There are some good examples out and about. In Singapore there is a far greater integration between the economic well-being of the country and the economic benefits of Outward Bound and the schools and the whole education system. That is certainly something that stands out as an example. In terms of examples of us being more or less protective, if you go across to North America it is increasingly a more protected situation.

Dr Thomas: The work that has been done in central and Eastern Europe will demonstrate to us that we are over-protective. If you go to Slovenia, Slovakia, Hungary, Poland, while increasingly cautious about how they deal with health and safety and welfare then there are no (inaudible). I think there is a balance. I hope that they will be moving slightly towards us and we will be moving slightly towards them. There is a separate issue about the media. We have to and there is a responsibility on our side I recognise it to engage more with the media. When things do go wrong, as they will continue to go wrong, whatever are the systems things will happen. It is being able to put that into an appropriate context. Whether it is going on to look at a certain programme and putting your point of view forward, as Andy did last week, or whether it is telling the Editors of *The Mail, The Mirror, The Sun,* et cetera, and maybe one or two others to engage in some form

of discussion, without that you are not going to change this culture which I think it has become over-concerned.

Chairman: They are so interested in the threat to children in the environment that they are all here scribbling away today. I joke. Andrew, you wanted to say something.

Q54 Mr Turner: I was going to observe. William Ripley did not answer your question. You did not say how we can make it easier. It is no good giving people a right if the right is to be in a dormitory or rather in single cubicles because they are so unsavoury dormitories with central heating and food that is prepared for them and they go out in crocodiles holding hands. Could you answer the Chairman's question?

Dr Gardner: I think all young children should have a right to experience environments and societies outside their normal range of experience in their school; whether that is locally or in another part of the country really is immaterial to me, but we must not forget that in out-of-classroom learning we need to keep a local link as well as the more distant residential activities. That is the first. The second is that I think it would be helpful to have a dedicated funding strand although I realise the calls on DfES funding are enormous, that that dedicated funding strand should particularly perhaps support the residential based out-of-classroom experiences but with a light touch for the minister. I would like to see consolidated guidance from the DfES, not its 16 sets of different forms or whatever, have a look and see whether the guidance can be consolidated. That is something that our head teachers were concerned about. There is lots of it. Can it be trunked down and consolidated? I would like to see risk assessment brought into the curriculum in the way that I talked about previously. I think there is a great deal we can do with working with heads in terms of exemplars and disseminating those to raise awareness of whole school approaches to out-of-school learning, and again quite a considerable amount that could be done with and for and by teachers; again, in terms of exemplars of broad-based learning. There is quite a lot of practical aspects there, but I am talking very much from the non-adventure, from the discipline based approach.

Mr Simpson: Nearly every workshop that we have convened and brought together practitioners irrespective of where they have come from ultimately one of the things which always cropped up, obviously the top was teacher training and support for teachers, both continuing professional development of the teachers but also initial teacher training because I think we all recognise that whatever bureaucracy emerges or whatever curriculum changes emerges, what funding emerges, we have had to take the teaching profession with us so ultimately they would want to make the decisions.

Ms Henwood: Just one point. The key audience we are forgetting is young people. Until we make outdoor education sexy for young people we are never going to win this battle. At the moment hanging around coffees bars or doing whatever they do seems more of a turn on that going in the outdoors.

Mr Simpson: Positive things. Obviously, there is a lot of passion along this table. We are good at identifying the problems and perhaps not so good on the solutions. I think what we are trying to get is a level playing field. There is not one quick fix to this. The things that I would promote would be things around the status and support of out-of-classroom learning. On status, clear signals from the DfES that you cannot QCA, you cannot deliver the national curriculum exclusively in the classroom. Very simple things like questions in a standard Ofsted inspection about what have you done to broaden children's horizons beyond the confines of the school which currently are not there. There is a real willingness on everybody's part, both Government and the trade unions and the suppliers, to sit round a table and to produce some realistic solutions to the problems that the trade unions have correctly identified. In terms of support, it has already been referred to: increased in-service and pre-service training to give teachers the competence and confidence to want to do this sort of activity. Finally, a financial safety net to ensure equality of access for children that are demonstrably not getting these kind of experiences now.

Chairman: David, a bit of a mission creeping in.

Mr Chaytor: One of the difficulties I find with this whole discussion is we are talking about a hugely varied range of activities and experiences from cycling over the Andes to underpinning in the school playground. My impression is that in terms of the formal part of the curriculum the role of outdoor education has systematically been reduced. I think in your evidence you quote a 25% decline in biology groups visiting FSE centres, but in terms of the more ambitious residential activities of skiing in the Pyrenees and so on, that the numbers seem to be continually increasing. Ultimately, for older students going to university the gap year is now well established for a substantial majority of 18 year olds. My question is: do you think a common manifesto can apply to everything from pond dipping to skiing? Where should the priority be if Government is going to take this more seriously, should it be to ensure that all children have an entitlement to outdoor education as part of the formal part of the curriculum and not only in geography but in biology also and other areas, almost at the expense of the emphasis on the more informal benefits of residential activities? I can see we have a conflict of interest here between children going on the residential route and maybe the more pressing needs to get them 50 yards down the road and see what is happening in their own neighbourhood. I would be interested to see what you feel about priorities and is there a need to get more cmnd more youngsters to benefit from the more informal experience of the residential course, or is the priority to get more youngsters to have outdoor experience to supplement their geography, biology? That is the longest question of the afternoon, Chairman.

Q55 Chairman: I would like to see both.

Dr Thomas: What the research shows is that where you have evidence that there is a continuity, that can be residential, three, four, five nights. Outward Bound might be three weeks, et cetera. Where you have half days where they go together, that sort of experience brings real benefit and that can be both in terms of social skills, it can also be behavioural change. There is excellent research from the States which shows that juvenile criminals have benefited from this out-of-classroom experiences, out-of-school activities. What you do not expect is that for any activity you get a reasonably warm glow immediately after the activity, it plummets down after a week or fortnight, et cetera. With these particular groups there was quite a significant resurgence of interest and many of those stayed. There were some who, in a sense, did not come back to crime after that. I find it difficult to separate the two. What I would be saying is that I would be hoping that my advice, for what it is worth, is I would be looking forward—I do not want to be accused of yet further bureaucracy—but I would be looking for the schools developing their approach, their school approach to out-of-classroom learning. Obviously, it would deal with the formal. It will look at also those softer informal areas that you have also alluded to. It will be developed and if we do get to this discussion between key stage 2 and key stage 3 and we get that discussion going on, it will flow from pre-nursery and it will build up what youngsters in the particular area have experienced. I would hope in my, in a sense, aspiration of perfection, yes, there could be a residential or maybe next summer they will be able to go up Helvellyn or go abroad, but it is that range of opportunities. I do not say that one is better than the other. I am looking for a totality of experience.

Q56 Mr Chaytor: That is an interesting explanation. If there were a million pounds to spend would you put more of it into biology field trips or more of it in making residential trips cheaper?

Mr Simpson: I think I have semi-answered this earlier on. I did not articulate my answer particularly well. I would argue still that they are not mutually exclusive, which I think is what Tony was saying. One of the trends as we know it has been the decline not just in numbers of field trips but of course length. If you asked tutors and teachers who accompanied those groups what has actually gone missing as a result of that, it is the very intangibles. You are talking about personal development, a sense of place, all of those additional soft benefits: recruitment. All those things have gone adrift as it has become much more curriculum focused. Perhaps by extending the entitlement in science, geography or any curriculum subject we are also widening, if you like, the experience to bring in the other areas that you have mentioned. I am sure the same is true of outdoor and adventurous activity. As I said earlier on, people are exploring now the possibility, for example of bringing in stronger curriculum into the outdoor adventurous area. I would urge you to stay clear of the mutual exclusivity angle, if you like. I think there are real exciting opportunities to bring those things through. I think one of the things that is coming through, for example, through the Tomlinson report and anticipated through that report is the need for that perhaps to happen anyway and that it may be one outdoor experience to which different sectors will need to feed.

Q57 Mr Chaytor: I was just going to ask about Tomlinson because as we have been discussing the Secretary of State has been making his statement. The question is: have any of you made a submission or did any of your organisations make a submission to the Tomlinson Inquiry and what was the essence of your submission?
Dr Thomas: The essence of the submission was around out-of-classroom to which Mr Tomlinson very clearly said it was his belief that learning outside the classroom was essential. He gave a number of contexts within the community and that could be perceived in a number of ways; that could be local business, it could be environmental action within the local community if one was trying to engage people in local issues. He was also very clear in my mind that we wanted links with higher education and further education. It was all the time I think he was pushing the boundaries of whether he thought learning was going on. He also had a quite clear steer in terms of learning within the family he thought was equally important. How do you help the family to help the student learn? In terms of maybe more fieldwork or outdoor and adventurous activity he said he felt that all of them, even a physicist, he felt that all of them had significant contributions and there was a place but he did not specify what that place was. That is my recall of our discussion.

Q58 Mr Chaytor: You are not totally happy with the drift of the report that has come out today?
Dr Thomas: I do not think so. All that would reflect was a major sector of industry in terms of leisure, in terms of education, in terms of outdoor learning. There is a whole issue there about the practical and the applied and the Q levels 1 and 2 in terms of outdoor education. There is a lot of opportunity there to (inaudible) and that linkage that he has strongly made between the vocational and the academic I could see sitting cheek by jowl quite happily.

Q59 Chairman: What document would we look to which was the most coherent summary of your case for greater outdoor education? Where is the tablet of truth?
Dr Thomas: That is a quite challenging question, Chair, but I think the better analysis that has been undertaken by The National Foundation For Educational Research and King's College at least gives a ten-year overview of the benefits of a review of out-of-classroom learning. There is some clear identification of its strengths. There are equal identifications about the Chief Inspector's report of clear priorities for action and some of it is in a sense

for you as policy makers but also for us as sector in terms of providers. I would suggest that that document is a helpful review of the last ten years of research.

Q60 Chairman: Interestingly, is it not, that very often people come here and they have a pretty firm campaign behind them. The evidence you are giving to me today and giving to my colleagues, one of the things we might be able to do in this report is to focus on the priorities that you might then run as a national campaign, which is interesting because usually when people come in with a national campaign we reflect that. There is a bit of a lack of joined-upness. You are talking to a Committee that really by and large wants very much to attend to this deficiency in our education system. I suppose what I was looking for was whether -- I cannot remember my history well enough -- whether the chart was an 8 point or a 10 point demand.
Mr Chaytor: It is only six.

Q61 Chairman: Whatever number it was, there ought to be a focused campaign where you say this is what we want, this is the evidence. I just wonder whether there is out there anything like that.
Dr Thomas: The Real World Learning Campaign documentation has been sent to various parliamentarians. What I am hearing is there is a get out there and trigger your learning manifesto.

Q62 Chairman: That is exactly right. I do not know if it is my job as the Chairman to say that. That is what I am doing.
Dr Thomas: I think it is an idea that we have shared with one or two people and also with colleagues in the Department that maybe this is an area that needs to be discussed. As has been said before, for this very wide sector, and I think it is how we actually clarify that matter.

Q63 Chairman: We have kept you for quite some time. One thing that did not come up here: what are you hearing out there about insurance premiums? We hear on the grapevine that insurance premiums for insuring schools, insuring people have been soaring. Is that true and if so why?
Mr Simpson: It is true but we do not know why.
Dr Thomas: It is true the National Association have their own views.

Q64 Chairman: Is the insurance industry ripping us off because the risk does not seem to be there that we have been talking about? Why should premiums escalate beyond the reality of the risk?
Ms Henwood: Perception becomes reality I think.

Q65 Chairman: So the insurance industry is going to a world where it is not actuarial facts.
Ms Henwood: Of course, the insurance industry here is heavily led by the American insurance industry.

Q66 Chairman: Zurich?

Ms Henwood: If you talk about litigation in outdoor activities it is more led by America than anywhere else.

Dr Thomas: I think there is an interesting issue of whether it is the activity or whether it is the residential provision. I think there have been significant issues around residential provision and that can be in a whole series of context; whether that is the fear that is driving the insurance industry, the negativity about the potential in terms of residential activities that that can be given concern. Obviously, all the groups here their staff will be CIB checked, but it is a genuine concern that is out there in some quarters. That is my only reason that I can appreciate that the insurance industry might be going way beyond what I think is a reasonable increase in their costs.

Q67 Chairman: Is the Government not missing the issue in terms of the Government backing the schools?

Dr Thomas: It is interesting you suggest that. I think there has been a little bit of discussion, in a way it has taken us responsibility that the Government did in Northern Ireland under terrorism when it become a provider in its own right. You could get to the stage where the sector is under tremendous threat from that alone.

Q68 Mr Turner: Could I just make an observation on that? I am told that regattas and carnivals and so on are certainly not residential, but I wonder whether as a group you are better capable of negotiating insurance than as individuals. I do not know whether you do that. Secondly, the extent to which you shop around or if it is rather a sort of traditional insuring the particular companies.

Dr Thomas: Last year we came to the stage where only one organisation was prepared the Field Studies Council, so much so that there are now meetings of independent schools and also residential providers to look at coming together to either negotiate on a larger base, or the alternative, rather as some of the education authorities do and becoming in a sense their own insurer. These are things we are definitely investigating in the context of this particular item.

Mr Simpson: Chair, there is one other item on insurance which is the way that local authorities, certainly as far as our centres are concerned become increasingly defensive about insurance and demand that we carry more and more insurance. The figure often quoted at the moment is £15 million-worth of public liability single issue insurance, which when we go to our lawyers they tell us: short of an organised group of six golden eagles carrying a child off, which we say is unlikely, they could not conceive of any possible incidence that would get even remotely near to that on one of our reserves. It seems to act like: one local authority demands £10 million and the next one demands £15 million.

Mr Ripley: I think what happened two years ago with insurance was that the insurance companies just did not want to take on the risk. There was enough perceived risk, the outdoors is something odd and awkward, this is outdoors; and the insurers didn't want to touch that. In terms of that negotiation we were like the Field Studies Council left with the sole insurer that we had always insured with and they were questioning whether they would write this insurance for us again. It was not a matter of shopping around; it was a matter of pleading that they would insure us.

Q69 Chairman: When the private sector fails to provide, the public sector should provide. A dangerous thought.

Mr Ripley: It has made a substantial increase in cost. That was a step change the year before last. It has plateaued. It will be interesting to see whether it then becomes a competitive market when reality catches up with it. In the meantime it makes life very uncomfortable.

Q70 Chairman: You have been very good and very patient. You have given us some awfully good answers. Is there anything any of you want to say before we wind up the session, bearing in mind we would like to be in touch with you as we conduct this inquiry. We will appreciate your comments and communication with us on an ongoing basis, until we come to what we hope to a very good report. Anything you want to say before we finish?

Mr Ripley: The only offer I was going to make is if you want to do some outdoor learning we are out there and you would be more than welcome to come and visit us at Outward Bound.

Q71 Jonathan Shaw: In a canoe.

Mr Ripley: You do not have to go all the way to Denmark or Scandinavia.

Q72 Chairman: You could do team building?

Mr Ripley: We certainly can.

Q73 Chairman: That is the value of young people working as a team.

Mr Ripley: I tried to make that point right at the beginning.

Q74 Chairman: It is a very important point.

Mr Ripley: Absolutely.

Dr Thomas: I sense, Chair, that we are speaking to the converted but I would just in passing invite you all to reflect. I bet, for instance, you cannot remember what you did in maths when you were ten years old. I bet that every single one of you could remember your out-of-classroom experiences. Thank you for taking it seriously because it is very important to us that the next generation have the benefit of those. Thank you.

Chairman: It is very important for us. We are going to do it as in our usual style: vigorously. We hope to come up with a powerful report of which you will like the result, I hope.

Supplementary memorandum from the Real World Learning Campaign

During the oral evidence session on Monday 18 October, in the context of providing reassurance to parents, governors and headteachers, reference was made to AALA inspection and licensing of providers who offered activities "within the scope" of the Activity Centres (Young Persons Safety) Act 1995.

The abstract attached is from NAHT's leaflet. Section 5 identifies which activities fall within the scope of the Adventure Licensing Regulations (AALR).

Providers are regularly inspected by AALA (Adventure Activities Licensing Authority) to establish and maintain their licensed status. Such independent scrutiny based on sector standards should provide reassurance to parents Governors and headteachers.

Where activities fall "out of scope", ie not within the activities specified by the 1998 Act, providers have to attempt to satisfy potential users that their safety standards are appropriate".

Increasingly, groups such as BAHA and the Real World Learning Campaign partners are producing Health, Safety and Welfare Protocols/Codes of Practice inspected and verified by independent inspectors to reassure groups such as NASUWT and others, that providers are operating to appropriate sector standards.

Abstract from NAHT's Leaflet

5. *Licensed Activities*

5.1. The Activity Centres (young Persons Safety) Act 1995 and the associated Adventure Activities Licensing Regulations (1996) require certain activities to be licensed when commercial companies sell then or where Local Authorities provide them with or without charge. The activities that require a licence are:

— caving: the exploration of underground passages, disused mines or natural which requires the use of special equipment or expertise;

— climbing: climbing, sea-level traversing, abseiling or scrambling over natural terrain or certain man-made structures which requires the use of special rock-climbing equipment or expertise;

— trekking: going on foot, horse, pedal cycle, skis, skates or sledges over moorland, or on ground over 600 metres above sea level when it would take 30 minutes to reach an accessible road or refuge;

— watersports: this comprises sailing, canoeing, kayaking, rafting and windsurfing, on sea, tidal waters, inland waters at a location where any part of those waters is more than 50 metres from the nearest land and turbulent inland waters. Rowing is exempt.

5.2. A licence holder has demonstrated that the Licensing Authority is satisfied that appropriate safety measures have been taken for the provision of the activity licensed. The presence of a licence does not indicate any standard of accommodation or catering. Before undertaking an activity that falls into the licensing category, head teachers should ensure that the provider is licensed. The school staff (and designated volunteers) accompanying the activity retain overall responsibility for the pupils throughout the visit even when the pupils are being instructed by a member of the provider's staff.

5.3. The Licensing Authority is only required to license those activities that come under the auspices of the Act. Not holding a licence does not mean the activities offered by a provider are unsafe. However, where a provider is being used that does not require a licence, the school should be satisfied that the safety standards are appropriate and that where specialist staff are used they have appropriate experience and qualifications. In these circumstances, it is vital that pre-visit is made to ensure that the safety standards are appropriate.

5.4. Part two of the DIES HASPEV supplement contains detailed guidance on verifying competence and categorisations of Adventurous Activities.

October 2004

Memorandum from Andy Simpson is response to a supplementary question from Jonathan Shaw MP

In which area is the school is that had to fill in so many different forms for a visit to an RSPB reserve?

This story was told to me by one of our field teachers in Summer 2003. I am fairly sure that it was at Rye Meads, a reserve in South Hertfordshire, so the school would be from either Hertfordshire or North London. I am sorry but I can't identify the specific school and when you understand that we employ a 160 part-time field teachers you will see the difficulty of tracing this back to a precise source. The report came to me that the teacher in charge of that school party said "its a wonder I'm here at all—because there is so much bureaucracy that if I didn't really want to come it would have been far easier not to come." I think its important to state that my impression of the bureaucracy is that it was imposed primarily by the school. As I remember the teacher identified the following steps:

1. Form to Head seeking permission to visit.
2. Form to Governors seeking permission to visit
3. Form assessing transport needs.
4. Form on safety of transport booked (seat belts etc)
5. Form to parents on visit
6. Form seeking helpers
7. Forms on safety checks for helpers
8. Form on pre visit to site by teachers
9. Risk assessment of site
10. Risk assessment of activities
11. Special risk assessment on activities involving water
12. Form for medical needs of children
13. Emergency plan should accident occur

and there's three that I can't remember but the figure of 16 is vivid in my mind.

Obviously this is an extreme example and our feeling is that streamlining this process would have been helpful to the teacher. In his questioning Paul Holmes identified the bureaucracy he had to go through to walk his pupils to the library. The key point here is that the teachers perception was that all the agencies and management structure were adopting a defensive strategy which involved lots of work on the part of the teacher and still left that teacher feeling somewhat exposed.

From an RSPB perspective this in itself is not a critical barrier but put alongside the other barriers we identified in our evidence, this level of bureaucracy (and perceived bureaucracy!) is another reason for lack of engagement by schools.

I hope this clarifies the situation. It made me feel a bit uncomfortable hearing an MP talk about forms of 16 pages and would not want you to get the wrong impression.

9 December 2004

Monday 1 November 2004

Members present:

Mr Barry Sheerman, in the Chair

Mr David Chaytor	Mr Kerry Pollard
Valerie Davey	Jonathan Shaw
Paul Holmes	Mr Andrew Turner
Helen Jones	

Memorandum submitted by the Department for Education and Skills

BACKGROUND

1. The Department published its *Five Year Strategy for Children and Learners* in July 2004. It sets out an ambitious agenda for reform which will give high standards for all within a broad and rich curriculum. Out of classroom learning is an important contributor to an enriched curriculum.

2. Five key principles underpin our drive for a step change:

— greater personalisation and choice with the needs of children, parents and learners at the centre;

— opening up services to new and different providers and new ways of delivering services;

— freedom and independence for frontline headteachers, governors and managers with clear simple accountabilities and more secure streamlined funding arrangements;

— a major commitment to staff development with high quality support and training to improve assessment, care and teaching;

— partnerships with parents, employers, volunteers and voluntary organisations to maximise the life chances of children, young people and adults.

3. For schools this translates into more freedom to teach and to improve. We intend to strip out unnecessary bureaucracy, give teachers and headteachers more confidence, and treat different schools differently—challenging those that underperform, but being less directive with those that perform well. This means a single annual review (less often for high performing schools) conducted by a "school improvement partner"; a new inspection regime with shorter, sharper inspections and a stronger role for school self evaluation. We will help schools to engage more effectively with parents and the local community.

4. For pupils, at both primary and secondary schools this means a richer curriculum, with better teaching and more personalised support. Our focus on subject specialism will enable teachers to refresh and develop their subject knowledge and teaching skills. Our network of specialist schools will grow, until all secondary schools of sufficient standard are specialist by 2008, providing strong community links and centres of curriculum excellence.

5. The thrust of these reforms is to demand excellence and high standards for all within a framework of accountability, support and challenge. The majority of schools will have more freedom to determine their own direction in a way that meets the needs of their pupils and local communities. There will be support for staff development and to help schools work together in powerful networks.

6. Freedom from many existing constraints and burdens, coupled with added confidence and expertise, will encourage enriched teaching and learning. Teachers who are confident in their own ability and who are encouraged to broaden their range of teaching approaches, will be more willing to get out the classroom and to use the outdoors as a resource across the curriculum with pupils of all ages and abilities.

7. Our strategy makes two specific offers which will underpin the wider reforms in encouraging education outside the classroom:

8. Every school—not just extended schools—should do their utmost to serve the needs of the whole child. In particular, our aim is that every school should be a healthy school, giving good teaching and advice about nutrition and exercise backed up by its school lunches, by its PE and school sport, and by its playground activities. Through this work, we will tackle levels of obesity in children, aiming to halt the growth in obesity among under-11s by 2010.

9. Every school should also be an environmentally sustainable school, with a good plan for school transport that encourages walking and cycling, an active and effective recycling policy (moving from paper to electronic processes wherever possible) and a school garden or other opportunities for children to explore the natural world. Schools must teach our children by example as well as by instruction.

10. And, as part of our offer for secondary schools:

11. We will widen opportunities beyond the classroom. Often, these provide some of the most memorable experiences at school—the school trip, the drama production, or playing in the school team.

DEFINITIONS

For the purpose of this Inquiry, we are including the following within "Education outside the classroom":

For pupils aged three to five; five to 11; 11–16, using the outdoors as a context for learning. In the English National Curriculum, this encompasses study within most subjects, but particularly science, geography, citizenship, history and PE. It includes out-of-school sports, gardening, and other clubs.

Off-site day visits to field study centres; field studies in local area—eg street, shopping centre, ponds, rivers, woodland, coastline; outdoor museums and heritage sites; commercial and city farms, allotments, country estates; outdoor and adventure centres and swimming pools.

On-site—school grounds development, eg using D&T to design and make an artefact; science in wildlife area; sustainable development; PE and sport on playing fields/netball courts etc; art and drama in the outdoors.

Off site residential experiences—sporting, cultural, field study, DofE—to a variety of places in UK and abroad—eg campsites and youth hostels.

HOW DfES POLICIES ARE SUPPORTING AND PROMOTING EDUCATION OUTSIDE THE CLASSROOM

12. The policies set out below are already in place, or under development and help to support and encourage schools to use the outdoors as an integral part of teaching and learning. This is part of a thread running through mainstream policies to stimulate a broader and richer educational experience for pupils of all ages, exemplified, for example, through the publication of *Excellence and Enjoyment*, the Department's strategy for primary schools in summer 2003.

13. In our evidence to the Inquiry we seek to draw out how we are tackling the barriers identified by the Committee in its terms of reference:

— costs and funding of outdoor activities;

— the place of outdoor learning within the curriculum;

— external assessment of provision;

— organisation and integration within existing school structures;

— qualification and motivation of teachers and the effect on teacher workload;

— the fear of accidents and the possibility of litigation;

— how provision in the UK compares with that of other countries.

COSTS AND FUNDING OF OUTDOOR ACTIVITIES

School budgets

14. From 2006 we will provide guaranteed three-year budgets for every school, geared to pupil numbers, with every school also guaranteed a minimum per pupil increase every year. This will give unprecedented practical financial security and freedom to schools in their forward planning.

15. The new dedicated Schools Budget will enable us to give all schools guaranteed three-year budgets, aligned with the school year, not the financial year as now. Schools funding from Local Authorities will increase by more than 6% in 2005–06, and we plan that the dedicated Schools Budget will deliver increases at at least that rate in 2006–07 and 2007–08.

Paying for school activities

16. The law states that education provided during school hours must be free. This includes materials, equipment, and transport provided in school hours by the Local Education Authority (LEA) or by the school to carry pupils between the school and an activity. Schools can however ask parents for a voluntary contribution towards the costs.

17. Parents can only be charged for activities that happen outside school hours when these activities are not a necessary part of the National Curriculum or that form part of the school's basic curriculum for religious education. In addition, no charge can be made for activities that are an essential part of the syllabus for an approved examination. However, charges may be made for other activities that happen outside school hours if parents agree to pay.

18. Where schools are seeking voluntary contributions, it must be made clear that children of parents who do not contribute will not be treated any differently. If a particular activity cannot take place without some help from parents, it should be explained to them at the planning stage. Where there are not enough voluntary contributions to make the activity possible, and there is no way to make up the shortfall, ie from school funds, then it must be cancelled. The essential point is that no pupil may be left out of an activity because his or her parents cannot, or will not, make a contribution.

Costs of outdoor centres

19. Costs will vary according to whether the provider (for example, an outdoor centre) is commercial or wholly funded by the LEA. LEAs have discretion to delegate funds to schools for outdoor education and a power to retain it at LEA level if they so wish. Having granted this power, DfES recognises a few LEA centres have been closed in areas where the LEA has decided to send pupils to commercial or charitable trust centres. The DfES has no view on this so long as the opportunities for adventure are made available for those pupils who want them.

School Transport Bill

20. The School Transport Bill will enable a small number of Local Education Authorities to put forward innovative proposals that offer a range of good quality, cost effective alternatives to the family car on the school run. Schemes must reduce car dependency, focus on local priorities and consider the travel and transport needs of all pupils. We will welcome proposals that cater for pupils with specific needs, for example those who want to join in extra curricular or off-site activities.

21. The Bill will allow LEAs to charge affordable fares for home to school transport whilst guaranteeing that children eligible for free school meals will be protected, where transport or travel assistance is provided, whether or not they live beyond the statutory walking distances. "Pump-priming" money of up to £200,000 will be provided to LEAs who implement schemes we have approved.

Capital Funding for Schools

22. The Department allocates capital funding to Local Authorities (LAs) and schools, for the improvement of their school buildings estate. Decisions about how to spend capital funding on school grounds and facilities for outdoor learning are made locally at LA or school level. There are no barriers from DfES on the use of government capital for investment in school grounds, or in facilities for activities outside the classroom. We do not, except in very exceptional circumstances, fund the acquisition of land itself.

23. Our funding programmes include the standards focused Building Schools for the Future (BSF) initiative to re-build and/or re-furbish the secondary school estate over the next 10–15 years. Schools, LAs and their partners are encouraged to look as widely as possible at all educational needs, both inside and outside the classroom, as part of their overall capital strategy.

24. More specifically, we provide design guidance in the form of Building Bulletins:

— building Bulletins 71: "The Outdoor Classroom" (2nd edition 1999) and 85: "School Grounds" (1997), highlight the potential of school grounds as a valuable resource to support and enrich the whole curriculum and the education of all pupils;

— building Bulletin 95: "Schools for the Future" (2003), gives guidance on developing external areas in "schools for the 21st century";

— non-statutory area guidelines for outdoor areas have recently been updated and are available in Building Bulletin 98: "Briefing Framework for Secondary School Projects" and Building Bulletin 99: "Briefing Framework for Primary School Projects". For the first time, these now include specific recommendations for "habitat areas" developed for a wide range of activities (such as meadowland, wildlife habitats and gardens to support the curriculum and improve play and recreational spaces), as well as outdoor PE facilities and informal and social areas.

25. We commissioned 11 leading architectural practices to develop "exemplar" designs for primary and secondary schools. School grounds were included in the brief and several of the design teams considered the outdoor environment as a key part of their overall design. They proposed ambitious options as the basis of future development.

26. We fund a number of LEA-driven pilot projects for "Classrooms of the Future" to explore the potential of school grounds for enhancing pupils' learning, play and social experiences. For example:

— Sheffield, which concerns integrating the indoor and outdoor classroom;

— Bedfordshire, developed in partnership with the Science Museum, which includes the installation of external skill-based interactive displays, mixing play, exercise and social interchange;

— Bournemouth, which is the only field study centre in the initiative. It will be a sustainable centre of e-learning and environmental discovery at a Site of Special Scientific Interest, and will have electronic links to schools in the area and to remote centres worldwide.

27. We are developing joint working with other organisations, for example, Learning Through Landscapes (LtL). We are providing funding over three years (2002–05) to support school-based projects and guidance. The LtL "School Grounds of the Future" programme aims to demonstrate how school grounds can be transformed and managed as high quality curriculum environments for the benefit of children's learning and development and provide an asset for the whole school community (http://www.ltl.org.uk/). A School Grounds of the Future pilot phase with 20 schools is completed. This is being followed by a wider outreach phase, available to all LAs in England.

28. We also manage the process whereby LAs and schools cannot dispose or change the use of school playing fields without the Secretary of State's consent. When agreed, any proceeds must be used to improve schools sport and leisure facilities

THE PLACE OF OUTDOOR LEARNING WITHIN THE CURRICULUM

The Foundation Stage

29. *Birth To Three Matters* recognises the importance of outdoor play in child development. There are references to visits to parks, shops and libraries and children participating in outdoor activities. *Curriculum guidance for the foundation stage* makes clear that play, both indoors and outdoors, is an important way children learn with enjoyment and challenge.

30. We continue to work with Local Authorities, providing advice and support on planning and developing outdoor early learning environments. We continue to promote the importance of how outdoor play is crucial for children's growth and development. We encourage children's opportunities to explore the outdoor environments through a range of activities covering the six areas of learning in the Foundation Stage. We support early years settings to plan and use the outdoor space available for children's socio-emotional, cognitive and physical development.

31. We are tackling some of the barriers to outdoor learning by supporting the Learning through Landscapes voluntary organisation to provide a programme promoting and increasing equal access to quality outdoor play spaces for children from birth–five years old. In 2003–04 Learning through Landscapes developed; Early Years Outdoor support materials and resources, an Early Years toolkit and video, website, birth to three materials, and a training package.

32. The Early Years Outdoors training package offers training, support and motivates Early Years practitioners, childcare professionals, volunteers and all parents who have responsibility for helping children learn and develop physically, emotionally, socially and academically. The Foundation Stage Directors work closely with LtL and we continue to provide support through them.

33. The Sure Start guidance on the design of Children Centres emphasises the importance of a well designed and managed outdoor environment, to provide a range of opportunities and experiences that are essential to healthy growth and development and can never be replicated inside a building, however well designed or resourced. The guidance includes a case study on outdoor environment in an early years centre.

The Primary Strategy

34. The Primary Strategy is supporting outdoor learning by recognising it as part of a broad and rich curriculum and as an area that can be used to support literacy and numeracy as well as teaching other skills. For instance, the recently developed professional development materials for teachers—"Excellence and Enjoyment: learning and teaching in the primary years"—include a video about creating a learning culture which has a section based at an outdoor pursuits centre. This shows pupils experiencing various challenging outdoor activities, which help them to develop a wide range of physical and interpersonal skills, whilst also linking into a range of curriculum subjects.

35. We have recently produced a CD ROM for teachers showing good practice of ICT in teaching, which includes examples of outdoor work such as the use of digital cameras. We also propose to issue to schools later in the year a CD ROM, entitled "Making the curriculum your own" which will include examples of outdoor learning.

36. Through these materials we are:

— providing best practice examples to schools to demonstrate how outdoor learning can help schools meet the objectives of the Primary Strategy;

— boosting teacher confidence by providing support and guidance;

— cutting down the time needed to plan activities from scratch;

— ensuring that outdoor learning activities and resources link directly to the Primary Strategy and National Curriculum.

Key Stage 3 National Strategy

37. The strategy is improving the quality of teaching and learning in all secondary schools so that pupils are equipped with the skills and the learning experiences to become active independent learners for the future. Through the Key Stage 3 National Strategy we are helping teachers to tailor teaching, regularly assess progress and use a variety of learning opportunities, including outdoor learning, to meet the needs of individual pupils and thereby personalising their learning and school experience.

38. The Strategy is tackling some of the barriers to outdoor learning by providing resources for teachers to make lessons engaging, challenging and enjoyable, including the use of outdoor learning. For example, the Foundation Subjects strand of the KS3 National Strategy encourages beyond the classroom learning,

contextualising the subject in the wider context of its application in real life situations. In geography pupils investigate a wide range of environments and carry out geographical enquiry outside the classroom. Similarly the Science strand of the Strategy actively supports and promotes science professional organisations which are also committed to effective use of outdoor learning.

39. The Strategy also provides a £10k school development grant for each secondary school to spend on any purpose to support improvements in teaching and learning, which can be used by schools to undertake outdoor learning.

NATIONAL CURRICULUM SUBJECTS

Science

40. Within the context of the Government's 10 year investment framework for Science and Innovation we are ensuring that the science we teach in schools is relevant and accessible, enthusing students by encouraging exciting practical work, outdoor learning opportunities and use of cutting edge ICT equipment.

41. We are tackling some of the barriers to outdoor learning by:

— enhancing opportunities for continuing professional development for science teachers through the development of a £51 million network of science learning centres. We have funded the Association for Science Education (ASE) and the Geographical Association to develop training courses that will increase teacher skills and confidence in providing outdoor learning opportunities. These will be delivered through some of the science learning centres from 2005;

— training a new cadre of science-specialist Higher-Level Teaching Assistants to enable every secondary school in England to recruit at least one by 2007–08;

— expanding substantially the number of undergraduate volunteers supporting pupils learning science, by 2006–07;

— developing a flexible curriculum that encourages development of practical skills and encourages use of a range of teaching formats and techniques—QCA's new outline Science Programme of Study for Key Stage 4 is based around practical skills and knowledge of how science works; and knowledge and understanding in selected areas of science. Will be in schools from 2006;

— new GCSE for Science, *science in the 21st century*, piloted in 80 schools from September 2003 and new GCSE in Applied Science in schools from September 2002.

Geography

42. Geography is the only subject where outdoor learning is a statutory requirement for pupils aged 5–14. Fieldwork is an essential part of the subject because it enables pupils of all ages to experience places for themselves, enabling them to relate this first hand experience to what is learnt in the classroom. There are important personal and social benefits to the learner, as well as subject learning. Several recent research reviews supported by the Department clearly make the case for fieldwork as an integral part of geography pedagogy.

43. Recognising the barriers to outdoor learning, the Department is funding the Field Studies Council and the Geographical Association to develop a professional development unit in managing and leading fieldwork, a companion to that being developed via the science learning centres.

44. The Department has established a Geography Development Fund in 2004–05 in recognition of the need to improve the teaching, learning and status of the subject. This, combined with Humanities specialist schools; the new Secretary of State's Geography Focus Group; supporting work through the National Strategies and Stephen Twigg's announcement that the Department will be appointing a new Chief Adviser, are sending clear signals to the subject community and schools.

45. The Geography Development Fund (GDF) will support work in primary geography, the new GCSE, building subject networks, creating new materials for the QCA Innovating with Geography website and a scoping study into progression and teaching and learning 5–19. All strands of the GDF will support fieldwork. The Department works closely with the two main subject associations—the Royal Geographical Society and the Geography Association—which will be undertaking the GDF work.

46. The Focus Group, which brings together representatives from the subject bodies, teachers, Heads, higher education, business, international development and the media, met for the first time on 13 October, and identified the unique benefits of first hand experience through fieldwork as a key part of its future work programme.

47. The post of Geography Chief Adviser will be advertised shortly.

History and Art & Design

48. The National Curriculum Programme of Study for History at Key Stages 2 and 3 sets out that pupils should be taught historical enquiry skills through a range of sources. Artefacts and visits to historic buildings, sites and museums are all given as examples of sources. The Programme of Study for Art & Design sets out that pupils should investigate different kinds of art, craft and design. Visits to museums and sites are given as examples of ways they can do this. The Scheme of Work for Art & Design includes a unit on "Visiting a Museum, Gallery or Site". The 2002–03 Ofsted subject report on Art & Design in secondary schools said that the potential of these visits for many schools "remains untapped, despite the considerable impact such visits can have on pupils' understanding and appreciation of art".

Citizenship

49. The Programme of Study for citizenship includes that pupils be taught to negotiate, decide and take part responsibly in both school and community-based activities. Many schools provide opportunities for this through their involvement with, and pupils' interest in, volunteering and other forms of community service, for example, renovation of environmental and community outdoor areas.

50. We have successfully piloted Active Citizens in Schools, which extends the Millennium Volunteers principles to 11–15 year olds, providing opportunities for active citizenship lessons through engagement in schools. Guidance for schools has been produced and is being disseminated.

PE and School Sport

51. Outdoor learning is an integral part of Physical Education (PE) and school sport. The National Curriculum PE programme of study also encourages schools to choose Outdoor and Adventurous Activities as one of the six activities that should be taught to pupils. As a national curriculum subject, typically delivered outside of the classroom and even the school, PE is inspected by Ofsted.

52. Outdoor learning via PE and school sport is being transformed through delivery of the PE, School Sport and Club Links (PESSCL) strategy, which aims to increase the percentage of pupils who spend a minimum of two hours each week on high quality PE and sport within and beyond the curriculum to 75% by 2006 extending to 85% by 2008. Within the context of the five year strategy and New Relationship with Schools, the PESSCL strategy is supporting outdoor learning by encouraging partnership working, workforce reform and providing schools with greater choice through targeted funding for example.

53. The PESSCL strategy's major investment comes through the School Sport Partnerships programme—Partnerships of schools that come together to share best practice, expertise and resources. Each partnership receives a grant of up to £270,000 each year providing choice on how to deploy these resources and all schools will be in a partnership by 2006.

54. This high profile national strategy is tackling many of the barriers to outdoor learning by:

— implementing the national Professional Development programme for PE—to provide modules specifically advising teachers on delivering Outdoor and Adventurous Activities (on and off-site) and ensure that teachers who lack the confidence to deliver PE have the tools and expertise they need. This is available to all teachers in England, although primary teachers, who are often intimidated by PE for fear of accidents and litigation, are being given priority.

— funding the £10 million Sporting Playgrounds programme, which aims to enhance school playgrounds to increase physical activity and improve behaviour. 592 primary schools are benefiting from this programme and many encourage pupils to act as outdoor play leaders for younger children. Many of the playgrounds have facilities and innovative markings that allow a number of curriculum subjects to be delivered in what is now regarded by heads as an outdoor classroom.

55. We support all kinds of educational visit that have clear educational objectives and are properly risk-assessed and managed. We need to recognise that not all pupils wish to undertake high-hazard adventure activities. More and more schools and LEAs are using professional providers whose safety management is inspected and licensed on behalf of the Government. This makes sense for ensuring a high standard of pupil safety.

ACROSS THE CURRICULUM

Growing Schools

56. Growing Schools began in 2001, as a response to concerns that young people had become distanced from nature and that pupils of all ages needed to understand the connections between the food they saw in supermarkets and the land that produced it; to understand the interdependence between urban and rural environments, to learn about the countryside, and the wildlife and the people it sustains.

57. Growing Schools is for pupils of all ages and abilities and encourages teachers to see the outdoor classroom both within and beyond school grounds as a valuable learning resource. This is not about adding extra burdens, or something new into the curriculum, but underpinning personalised learning through a wider range of teaching approaches. More than 10,000 schools have signed up to participate in the Growing Schools programme which works in partnership with some 25 organisations from the outdoor sector.

58. Growing Schools began by consulting teachers and practitioners from the NGO sector. Two things emerged: first hand, active learning was an invaluable, part of the learning process; but while many schools were keen to use the outdoor classroom, there were significant barriers—either real or perceived. These included lack of funding (either to develop school grounds or make out-of-school visits), health and safety issues, lack of training and confidence among teachers and no time to plan creative outdoor lessons; difficulty in accessing information.

59. Five flagship projects were set up to provide a sample of replicable best practice—training modules, lesson plans, schemes of work, case studies, activity packs—all focusing on one or more of the identified barriers. More than 30 partner organisations and 350 schools were involved, with pupils aged three to 19 participating.

60. Some schools focused on growing within their school grounds, with pupils growing vegetables and fruit, then preparing and eating them. Others shared a community allotment with local groups or established links with local commercial and city farms, regularly visiting to study the animals and crops. Some worked with land-based colleges, for example, having an incubator on loan until the chicks hatched, then following the chicks' growth and life via a web cam as part of science and maths. At field study centres, schools joined in growing and composting on day or residential visits, and then explored healthy eating, recycling, food miles and global issues.

61. In 2002 Growing Schools exhibited work from schools in their own grounds at the Hampton Court Palace Flower Show. The garden has since been relocated to Greenwich Environmental Curriculum Centre in East London and provides CPD and inspiration for teachers. Over 15,000 schools have requested the Growing Schools teacher resource pack.

62. Growing Schools supports key policies:

— *Foundation Stage Curriculum*—encouraging Early Years Settings to make the most of their outdoor areas in delivering the six key areas of learning. Learning through Landscapes has established projects in Yorkshire with support from Growing Schools. This has continued to expand over the past year with further support from Sure Start.

— *Excellence and Enjoyment: A Strategy for Primary Schools*—providing a broad, balanced, rich and exciting curriculum which retains the literacy and numeracy focus while providing varied teaching and learning to stimulate and motivate pupils. Growing Schools offers teachers access to tried and tested schemes of work, lesson plans, and activity packs.

— *Field Studies*—promoting the importance of learning off site, particularly as part of Geography and Science. Growing Schools encourages and supports schools making off-site visits.

— *Healthy Schools and the Healthy Living Blueprint*—Growing Schools supports teaching about food, where it comes from, how it was produced, and the importance of a healthy and active lifestyle.

— *14–19 Education and Training*—supporting young people to choose careers in the land based sector, through "Growing Lives", linked to a careers and course database.

63. The website is a micro-site within teachernet at www.teachernet.gov.uk/growingschools. It provides access to health & safety guidance, funding sources, research, training (ITT & CPD) for both teachers and providers. There is a database of resource materials (case studies, schemes of work, lesson plans). Schools can register, join the e-discussion group, receive regular new letters and exchange ideas. It provides access to over 1,000 places to visit, enabling teachers to find, for example, farms, field study centres, forest schools and outdoor museums.

64. Pilot area partnerships in the North East and London bring together support and CPD opportunities for schools locally and regionally. Hampshire LEA offers a similar Outdoor Learning Trailblazer network. Others being developed will build on work already undertaken, for example Gloucester University supported by Growing Schools to develop a local network, website and Citizenship ITT and CPD training modules.

65. Growing Schools supports Access to Farms which has developed an accreditation scheme to help providers improve the quality of what is offered to visiting schools. Further work is planned with other providers, for example, estates, field study centres, woodlands/forests and gardens. Support is also offered to schools with their own farms, through the Schools Farm Network.

66. Growing Schools is developing a Local Schools Support Network. Schools will register their needs through the website, eg how to grow seasonal vegetables, manpower to build a wildlife pond, help maintaining the school grounds during holidays—which will then be passed on to associate organisations

and groups (including The Royal Horticultural Society), who in turn will disseminate these needs to their membership base around the country. Members will then be encouraged to share their expertise and time with the registered schools—either on a regular basis or for a specific project.

67. At the National Advisory Group meeting on 20 September, the Music Manifesto was presented to the group. The music manifesto is about creating more music for more people. It offers a strategy and set of priorities for the next three to five years, focusing on children and young people. Developed by a 60-strong coalition of musicians, composers, educators, music industry representatives and policy makers, the music manifesto has been designed to be a living, interactive resource, owned by all those who sign up to it. Using this site, organisations and individuals can sign up to the manifesto on-line and showcase their own contributions by pledging tangible programmes and resources to help make it a reality. Growing Schools NAG members agreed there was considerable potential for a similar approach for outdoor learning.

THE BUILT ENVIRONMENT

68. In 2003 DCMS and DfES Ministers appointed the Joint Advisory Committee on Built Environment Education (JACBEE) to examine the potential for the contemporary and historic built environment to be utilised more effectively as a learning resource, particularly by schools. Recommendations were submitted to Ministers in September 2004 and were approved in principle. The recommendations included that CABE, English Heritage and interested parties should work together to produce a proposal for the creation of a "one stop shop" for built environment education that would provide a comprehensive resource of tools, advice, best practice and contacts for schools and the general public.

69. Implementation of the recommendations will be considered by a post-JACBEE steering group in the next few months. A summary report of the Committee's findings will be published by DCMS and DfES early in 2005 with the aim of raising awareness with teachers, other educators and the public about the educational value of buildings, places and spaces.

Outdoor museums

70. Between 1999 and 2006 DfES will have contributed £12 million to museum and gallery education, to assist museums and galleries to support projects with schools. Outdoor museums will have been among the museums benefiting from this funding.

71. As part of the Renaissance in the Regions programme to regenerate regional museums, DCMS has ring-fenced £10 million (to 2006) for delivering education programmes to school children. DfES has contributed an additional £2.2 million to this education fund.

72. In 2003–04 DfES contributed £1.25 million to the DfES/DCMS National/Regional Partnership projects fund (DCMS contributed a further £1.35), whereby National museums formed partnerships with one or more smaller regional institutions to deliver education projects to schools.

73. The DfES Museums & Galleries Education Programme (MGEP) ran from 1999 to March 2004 and saw a total investment of £4 million in schools-focused museum and gallery education projects. The programme used the collections and exhibitions of museums and galleries to enrich the National Curriculum. There were 118 projects in 130 museums and galleries and at least 20,000 school pupils took part. The evaluation of the 2nd phase of this programme was published on 30 September 2004 and was positive about both pupil and teacher learning outcomes (the full report and Executive Summary are available at www.teachernet.gov.uk/mgep2).

74. In April 2004, DCMS and DfES announced joint funding of £7 million over two years (2004–06) for museum and gallery education. This will be directed towards national and regional museums and galleries to enable them to work more closely with schools. DCMS and DfES are due to be publishing a Museums and Galleries Education Strategy later this year.

SPECIALIST SCHOOLS—THE RURAL DIMENSION

75. Since October 2003, all schools aspiring for specialist status have been able to develop a "rural dimension" in their application. Schools with a rural dimension can provide opportunities for their pupils to increase their understanding of aspects of life in the countryside. These include courses in land management (farming, animal health and welfare, forestry, fisheries, building, leisure), environmental stewardship (eg biodiversity, recycling, pollution), rural business and livelihoods (eg leisure & tourism, sports & recreation, rural crafts, farming) and natural and cultural heritage. There are currently five schools with a rural dimension.

76. The rural dimension is relevant to all schools, not just those located in a rural area. These schools will provide a balance between opportunities for learning first hand using the outdoor classroom as a context for learning—eg farms, parks, school grounds; and using rural issues or themes as learning contexts and/or applications within the core specialism subjects.

77. Schools will be expected to: encourage the use of school grounds, allotments and horticulture as contexts for teaching & learning; provide opportunities that relate to living things in their environment, both natural and managed; support the development of social economic and environmental responsibility and citizenship; emphasise healthy eating and lifestyle; develop business education links, work based and work related learning—in a rural context; raise achievement through preferred learning styles such a naturalistic learning, practical learning and spatial/visual development.

The World of Work

78. All young people have an opportunity for work experience. From September 2004, there is a statutory requirement that schools include work-related learning within the curriculum for all students at Key Stage 4. Work-related learning involves using the context of work to develop knowledge, skills and understanding useful in employment.

— The Increased Flexibility for 14–16 Year Olds programme, began in September 2002 providing enhanced vocational and work-related learning opportunities for 14–16 year olds. Young people generally spend one or two days a week in an FE college, others visit a sixth form college, private training provider or learn with an employer.

— The Young Apprenticeship programme is a new opportunity for 14–16 year olds to combine the practical application of skills and knowledge in a vocational context with the pursuit of qualifications that related to particular occupational sectors. Wherever possible, the study will be practical and applied to work experience, working alongside full-time employees and full-time apprentices—for up to two days a week throughout the duration of Key Stage 4.

79. The opportunities available depend on the labour market and businesses in the area where they live. In areas where outdoor occupations, such as farming and forestry are strong, many young people will be able to experience the outdoors as part of their work experience.

Study Support (Out of School Hours Learning)

80. Study support provision includes a wide range of learning activities including education outside the classroom. Young people participate voluntarily in study support and the learning activities take place outside normal lesson time. Study support helps to improve pupils' motivation, build self-esteem and help them to become more effective learners. This has a positive effect on their achievements in school and on their employability when they leave school.

81. The Ofsted report *Learning Out of Hours: The Quality and Management of Study Support in Secondary Schools* (October 2002) reinforces the positive effect of study support activities in improving attendance and attitudes.

82. A report produced by MORI/BMRB in August 2000, *Out of School Hours Learning Activities: Surveys of Schools, Pupils and Parents*, showed that in a survey of 204 schools, 97% offered some form of study support activity. A follow up survey of 850 schools (findings to be announced on 28 October 2004) found that 90% of primary schools and 98% of secondary are providing study support.

83. The Department has worked with the Teacher Training Agency to promote the benefits of study support to teachers and to embed the concept within initial teacher training and continuing professional development opportunities. Teachers frequently report that engagement in study support provides opportunities to be creative and experiment with a range of learning techniques which can be transferred into the classroom, and that it encourages more relaxed, informal relationships with pupils.

Get REAL

84. A new initiative is being piloted in the UK. Get REAL is a pilot programme, currently in its second year of development, which is being funded by the Big Lottery Fund. In 2003 Get REAL created opportunities for almost 2,000 11–17 year olds to take part in exciting residential programmes during the summer school holidays. The overall aim of the initiative is to give young people from all walks of life the chance to have time filled with adventure and fun in a safe environment, enjoying new and challenging experiences. The residential experience should provide young people with the opportunity to increase their awareness of their own learning skills and have a memorable experience through active adventure.

85. As set out in the 14–19 green paper, the government is committed to making sure that all young people should be encouraged to engage in active citizenship, work-related learning and wider activities such as art, music and sport. Access the DfES website; http://www.dfes.gov.uk/14-19greenpaper/ for a full copy of the green paper 14–19: extending opportunities, rising standards. The aim of Get REAL is to engage young people into learning through a range of wider activities which are not school-based.

86. The aims and desired outcomes and benefits to young people are:

— that they learn through active "adventure" to create a memorable experience that broadens horizons and enables them to:

— increase their awareness of their own learning skills;

— improve their life-skills and take them back to the classroom.

— that the programme content is not an extension of the school curriculum, but designed to increase awareness of learning and life-skills;

— to give young people from all walks of life the chance to enjoy a residential experience;

— to support development of community and social values, increase connections across socio-economic groups and promote citizenship.

ACADEMIES

87. We expect, as more of them open, that many Academies will be at the forefront of the provision of outdoor education. As independent institutions, they have the flexibility to raise standards by introducing innovative approaches to their management, governance, teaching and curriculum. Many Academies will have specialisms which focus on outdoor activities, from the more traditional activities such as sport, to newer innovative specialisms like design and the build environment and environmental science. Academies are also central to the significant capital investment we are making in the schools building stock. Their buildings and the surrounding grounds and playing fields are designed with the delivery of the curriculum in mind. Central to the programme is Academies commitment to sharing their expertise and first rate facilities with their local family of schools and the local community.

EXTERNAL ASSESSMENT OF PROVISION

88. Ofsted remains committed to inspecting any aspects of a school's provision, including "out of the classroom" learning that has a significant effect on the achievement, personal development, attitudes or behaviour of pupils. Arrangements under both the current and future inspection frameworks have the scope to cover these aspects of a school's work, although the extent of this will vary depending on the context of the school.

89. Ofsted has reported on this area as a part of its thematic work, such as in the publication *Learning out of hours: the quality and management of study support in secondary schools*—Ofsted (October 2002). Ofsted published its report *Outdoor Education—Aspects of Good Practice* on 28 September 2004. There are also draft plans for an Ofsted survey in 2004–05 on *The impact of geography field work on pupils' attitude and motivation.*

90. Current inspection guidance contains specific references to "off-site study" and flexible curriculum arrangements (for example in pages 59, 61, 98, 99, 105 of the *Handbook for inspecting secondary schools*). Inspectors are required to consider these and the effects they may have on the standards pupils achieve and their personal development, including their attendance and attitudes to study.

91. The same approach will apply under the new proposals. If "out of the classroom" learning, is identified by the school in its self-evaluation as an area of significance or is regarded by the lead inspector during the pre-inspection as an area to pursue, then it will be pursued. A number of the questions in the proposed SEF (self-evaluation form) from September 2005 require schools to give details of any such provision and the effect the school feels it may have.

92. Safety of provision: The Department sponsors and funds the Adventure Activities Licensing Authority (AALA). This public authority inspects the safety of commercial, charitable and LEA providers of high hazard adventure (that is, climbing, caving, trekking and waterborne activities) to under 18s on behalf of the Government. Holding a licence means a provider's safety management meets the AALA's rigorous standards. In this way we ensure that those pupils who wish to can experience exciting and stimulating activities outside the classroom without being exposed to avoidable risk of death or disabling injury. There are currently just over 1,000 licences in place. Our review of the Licensing Regime elicited strong support for the improvement and continuance of statutory safety inspections.

93. While continuing to fund and support the AALA, DfES is now exploring the possibilities of alternative means of regulation other than "classic regulation". With the support of the Health and Safety Executive and the Better Regulation Task Force, we are working with the outdoor sector to consider whether some form of self-regulation would be viable, initially for activities or providers complementary to those covered by the AALA.

ORGANISATION AND INTEGRATION WITHIN EXISTING SCHOOL STRUCTURES

Education Visits Co-ordinators

94. The Educational Visits Co-ordinator (EVC) role, monitoring and checking on the safety of visits, was developed in 2002 and funding of £3.5 million enabled LEAs to send delegates to training-the-trainer seminars delivered by the Outdoor Education Advisers Panel. All LEAs in England are signed up to the programme and some LEAs already have an EVC in every one of their schools.

95. The principal function of the EVC is to liaise with the LEA's outdoor education adviser and to ensure that school staff taking pupils on any kind of educational visit are competent to do so and trained as necessary in pupil safety outdoors. The Independent Schools Adventure Activities Association (ISAAA) holds training courses for independent school staff in all kinds of visit.

96. Risk assessment will disclose that school staff leading a visit normally need to hold an appropriate level of accreditation from the relevant National Governing Body. This is important since school staff leading their own pupils are not safety-inspected by the AALA. This is because outdoor education is not a school's prime function and it would be difficult to license a whole school for its incidental off-premises activities. It is more effective to try to ensure the relevant staff are accredited.

97. The Health and Safety Executive enforces the safety regulations that control adventure and the more general health and safety regulations that cover all other activities. Local authorities enforce safety law on commercial firms.

QUALIFICATION AMD MOTIVATION OF TEACHERS AND THE EFFECT ON TEACHER WORKLOAD

Initial Teacher Training

98. We are tackling lack of teacher confidence, expertise and experience in outdoor learning by recognising that valuable pupil learning can take place in a wide range of out-of-school contexts, and by recognising that teachers need to be able to plan to make the best use of such opportunities.

99. To this end, it is a requirement that, as relevant to the age range they are trained to teach, those awarded qualified teacher status (QTS) must demonstrate that they are able to plan opportunities for pupils to learn in out-of-school contexts, such as school visits, museums, theatres, field-work and employment-based settings, with the help of other staff where appropriate.

100. This requirement is specified in *Qualifying to teach*, which sets out the standards for QTS and requirements for initial teacher training. These standards came into force in September 2002 following extensive consultation, and describe the minimum amount that trainee teachers must know, understand and be able to do before they are awarded QTS.

101. *Qualifying to teach* is supported by non-statutory guidance in the form of a detailed handbook. It is in this handbook that the standards are unpacked and the implications of a range of issues for teaching and teacher training explored. Both these documents can be viewed on the Teacher Training Agency's website, www.tta.gov.uk.

Continuing Professional development

102. Central to improvements in teaching and learning is excellent professional development for all teachers—with more emphasis on classroom observation, practice, training, coaching and mentoring. We are building up teachers' demand for high quality training and development, by linking participation in professional development with career progression.

School Workforce Reform

103. Teachers must be given better support so they can focus more of their time on their professional role of teaching and on activities which directly improve pupil attainment. The workforce reform agenda provides an opportunity for teachers and support staff to focus on individual pupils in a way that the profession has long campaigned for. The limits on cover introduced in September and the commitment to guaranteed planning, preparation and assessment (PPA) time from next September, together with enhanced roles for support staff, present real opportunities to make a difference to each pupil's learning.

104. Educational visits are planned activities. Where teachers are absent due to participating in such activities, the absence is most appropriately covered by supply teachers or by using cover supervision. If a teacher at the school is used to cover for such an absence the amount of cover will count towards the annual limit of 38 hours. Where a teacher acquires non contact time in the timetable as a result of a class or group being absent on an educational visit, then the guidance for gained time should apply.

105. The guidance (see paragraphs 46–78 of School Teachers' Pay and Conditions Document 2004 & Guidance on School Teachers' Pay and Conditions) states that activities to be undertaken by teachers in such gained time must be planned well in advance of the visit. It also contains a list of activities that teachers can be asked to do during gained time, eg teach booster classes. It may be possible, in some circumstances, to re-timetable in advance of trips so that those teachers left behind are able to do productive work with students, and not just "cover". For a large trip, this could involve providing in-school activities for the rest of the year group outside their normal timetable.

Support Staff

106. Since DfES published *Health and Safety of Pupils on Educational Visits: A Good Practice Guide* in 1998 the Department has developed its policy on support staff in the light of the National Agreement on raising standards and tackling workload.

107. A key development is the introduction of The Education (Specified Work and Registration) (England) Regulations 2003 which came into force on 1 August 2003. These regulations set out the conditions under which support staff in schools may undertake specified teaching activities. Only well-trained support staff—normally having attained higher level teaching assistant (HLTA) status—will be leading classes, and then only under the direction and supervision of a teacher. There is no assumption that the teacher will always be physically present when a member of support staff is carrying out specified work.

108. It may be the case that support staff have the experience or skills to organise outdoor activities or will be able to provide cover for a teacher who may be out on visits. The Department envisages a number of ways in which support staff may help teachers, including acting as: Educational Visits Co-ordinator; or Group Leader; or Supervisor. Head teachers will decide the precise duties of support staff, based on the skills and experience of individuals. A range of advice and publications in this area are being revised and will be available in due course.

The Fear of Accidents and the Possibility of Litigation

109. We believe that school staff following the good practice guidance (see paragraph 107) should have nothing to fear from unfair accusation. We are pleased that Her Majesty's Chief Inspector shares this view. The recent Ofsted report on outdoor education focuses on the mainstreaming of outdoor education but reports that some teachers nonetheless do fear litigation where things go wrong. (They also fear the risks themselves, which is where the good practice guidance mentioned above serves a useful purpose in helping teachers in the skill of good risk assessment and risk management).

110. The Secretary of State said earlier this year that he would look into teacher union concerns about the implications for their members leading school visits if a child is injured. The Department believes there might be room for an improvement in the local management of injury cases and is looking into next steps along with teacher unions. On the litigation point, the Better Regulation Task Force has indicated that the number of civil claims actually decreased in 2003–04 by 60,000 across all sectors. Compensation amounts, in a smaller number of cases, have risen for reasons linked to medical costs and longer expectancy of life.

111. We recently supplemented our 1998 good practice guide, Health and Safety of Pupils on Educational Visits (known as HASPEV) with new material based on three levels of risk assessment and approval by EVC or LEA. The new titles are Standards for LEAs in Overseeing Educational Visits, Standards for Adventure and A Handbook for Group Leaders (all 2002) and Group Safety at Water Margins (published in 2003 with the Central Council for Physical Recreation. This is used as course material for the EVC INSET training currently being rolled out at LEA/school level. To avoid unnecessary burdens we do not send our good practice literature automatically to every school; however over 100,000 copies of HASPEV and some 50,000 copies of the supplementary leaflets have been sent out on request.

Research

112. The Department has commissioned the Duke of Edinburgh's Awards and the Scouts to carry out a map of Residential Experience opportunities for young people. It will help us to look at how residential opportunities can contribute to more young people taking advantage of extra curricular activities. The work is due to be completed by the end of December.

113. A literary review of the research into using food, farming and the countryside as a context for learning (UK and abroad) was funded by Growing Schools in partnership with CA & FACE (published report available at www.dfes.gov.uk/research).

114. Growing Schools is funding further action research by NfER/King's College/CREE. It includes in-depth case study research at a selection of outdoor sites; investigating teaching & learning processes; learning outcomes and wider benefits; and curriculum links. The study is also conducting action research through a group of teachers, field centre staff and farm educators, to devise and trial teaching and/or evaluation strategies. Focus groups are exploring the views of providers and key stakeholders to inform the design of the project, get feedback on emerging findings and act as a dissemination channel. The project is due to report in April 2005.

115. The Department part-funded the Field Studies Council led literature review into outdoor learning which was published earlier this year. The review examined 150 pieces of research, covering three types of learning—fieldwork & outdoor visits; outdoor adventure education; school grounds/community projects. The study found:

— substantial evidence that fieldwork, properly conceived, adequately planned, well taught and effectively followed up offers learners opportunities to develop their knowledge and skills in ways that add value to their everyday experience in the classroom;

— strong evidence of the positive benefits of outdoor adventure education, both short and long term, particularly for interpersonal/social outcomes;

— important impacts, including greater confidence, pride in community, stronger motivation towards learning, greater sense of belonging and responsibility.

116. This study is very helpful in building the case for the positive benefits of outdoor learning.

Annex A

INTERNATIONAL COMPARISONS

The Department has not recently undertaken a systematic comparison of provision in other countries. However, for the purposes of this Inquiry, we have sourced some examples from around the world—from Denmark, Italy, Ireland, Sweden, Netherlands, Germany, Japan, Singapore and New Zealand.

DENMARK

Children in Denmark start compulsory schooling at age seven. Children between the ages of three and six attend kindergarten, and the majority of children age six to seven are in pre-school classes.

Kindergartens

Childcare facilities are obliged to draw up learning plans for the children covering six areas. One of these is nature, and it is clear from Ministry guidance that first hand experience of nature is essential. It is normal practice for children in kindergartens to spend a fair proportion each day in the playground/outdoor area attached to the kindergarten, and in addition to play activities such areas may have small allotments for plants, vegetables, and others may have an area with animals (rabbits, goats or sheep). All kindergartens and nurseries take the children for walks, and arrange regular trips to the local library, farms, forests, the zoo, a museum, etc. Many kindergartens have an annual trip with a couple of overnight stays either at a seaside cottage, or a cottage in the woods. Some kindergartens are situated in the woods, and children in these spend practically the entire day in the forest.

Schools

The central administration of the Folkeskole (curriculum) is in the hands of the Ministry of Education. The Danish Parliament takes the decisions governing the overall aims of the education, and the Minister of Education sets the targets for each subject. But the municipalities and schools decide how to reach these targets.

The Ministry of Education publishes curriculum guidelines for the individual subjects, but these are seen purely as recommendations and as such are not mandatory for local school administrators. Schools are permitted to draw up their own curricula as long as they are in accordance with the aims and proficiency areas laid down by the Minister of Education. However, nearly all schools choose to confirm the centrally prepared guidelines as their binding curricula.

Guidelines for specific subjects state an expectation for teachers to undertake education outside the classroom in science and geography, and many teachers do so. It will however vary from teacher to teacher how often it is done. The exact wording in the Order setting out aims etc for science and geography can be found on http://eng.uvm.dk/publications/laws/Aims.htm?menuid=1515.

Although, it may not refer to activities outside the classroom in the guidelines for all subjects, many teachers will arrange such activities. Examples of these are: weekly trips to swimming-pools (at least one year during the school years as part of PE), field studies in local area—lakes, forests etc, an annual sporting day, outdoor sport activities from Easter to mid-October, visits to museums of all kinds (art, natural science, history—indoor and outdoor), theatre and cinema visits, etc.

Most activities are organised by the teachers themselves, but there are some providers of outdoor activities. These include farmers who open their doors to school classes, Learn about Forests arrangements (funded by money from ministries, local authorities, organisations and private funds), private companies who organise tree climbing or other special sporting activities (these are mainly used by after school care clubs), and organisers of events for school classes to forests, lakes, etc. The latter are "Nature Schools" (often situated in a forest) are funded by local municipalities jointly with the state forest district administration. The heads of the "Nature Schools" are specially educated staff (biologists etc). There are 100 schools spread out over Denmark, and they have 1/2 million visitors a year.

Most museums have dedicated staff dealing with school class visits.

The providers are not inspected, but do of course have to comply with legislation in any given area to ensure for instance that play areas are constructed in a safe manner, and teachers and providers have to ensure that the safety of the children taking part in such activities is considered as far as this is possible.

Generally, schools/local government fund outdoor activities, but parents may be asked to contribute a small sum of money for instance to a theatre trip.

Outdoor activities are left to the teachers to organise, sometimes in conjunction with a specific provider/museum etc. (see above)

The teachers/leaders involved in providing outdoor learning are not required to have special qualifications or training.

ITALY

The law of 15 March 1997 granted autonomy to schools in didactic management, financial administration, research activities, experimentation and development. Schools organise lessons to best suit individual school needs, respecting certain parameters. School autonomy allows individual schools to increase the educational offer with optional subjects and activities taking into consideration local cultural, social and economic factors.

The head teacher manages the school in collaboration with the school council. Various stakeholders are involved in the internal decision making process; school authorities, educational staff, social partners and families. Each school is obliged to prepare and follow a school plan or "POF", piano dell' offerta formativa. The curriculum is set down at a national level.

Education outside the school is not mandatory and is left up to the discretion of individual schools. Italian schools do not have a strong history of outdoor learning within the curriculum, but that does not mean that it is not done. Indeed the Ministry of Education states that individualplans "may include" school activities which are organised for a group of pupils of the same class, or of different classes, with the aim of carrying out activities related to the needs of pupils.

The teacher's council within the second month of the school year must present a plan setting down all planned activities. Having said this, teachers are not forbidden in taking a class to a nearby park as they see fit for an outdoor lesson.

Generally parents must make a financial contribution and must give their permission for any school trips. These trips are covered by the school's insurance.

Traditionally overnight trips are organised for students in lower secondary school. Once again, parents' consent must be provided and they must also subsidise the trips.

IRELAND

The provision of "outdoor learning" occurs mostly in secondary schools only. In the first three years of secondary school, referred to as the junior cycle (age 12–15), fieldwork is an integral part of the Geography syllabus. There is an option for pupils to submit a fieldstudy assignment as part of the Junior Certificate examination. The exam papers contain a special section with questions designed to test some of the skills which pupils develop through fieldstudy; this section is intended for those who do not take up the option of submitting a fieldstudy assignment. This is an optional unit and is only taken by a small percentage of students. Within the Science curriculum, field study is optional.

Physical Education in the Junior Cycle includes adventure activities, aquatics, athletics, dance, net and field games etc. Physical education teachers have the relevant national teaching qualification and if the outdoor learning activity involves a specialised skill such as adventure sports there will be a qualified instructor present. Outdoor activities which take place outside the school grounds would generally take place in approved centres. However these centres are not approved by the schools or the Department of Education, but are approved by the Government or a National body.

In the Senior Cycle (16–18 yrs), the Geography syllabus consists of a range of core, elective and optional units for study. A geographical investigation, to be completed individually by each candidate, forms a compulsory element of the syllabus. The report on the geographical investigation is submitted in advance of the final written examination.

Students also have an option to pursue an outdoors education module which is assessed as part of the overall course.

Developing appropriate linkages between school and the workplace is a growing feature of the senior cycle. Students are involved in organising visits to local business and community enterprises; meet and interview enterprising people on—site and in the classroom; plan and undertake interesting activities that will build self—confidence, creativity, initiative and develop teamwork, communication and computer skills.

Generally, all outdoor school activities are co-funded by parents and schools and organised by the schools themselves—there is no local/national body involved.

SWEDEN

Provision of education in Sweden is highly de-centralised. Framework legislation issued at the National level states what targets to reach but leaves great scope for local authorities in deciding how this is to be done. Sweden's 290 municipalities are responsible for provision of childcare, compulsory and upper secondary schooling. Most of the funding for education comes from locally raised income tax.

The only subject where outdoor/outside the classroom activities are required according to the syllabus is Physical Education (PE). The requirement is not explicit but the syllabus states that the aim of PE is partly to encourage pupils to spend time in nature and to be able to find their way around in nature (demands knowledge of how to use a compass and a map). PE also requires pupils to be able to swim and to have practised life-saving measures around water before leaving compulsory school. Swimming and life-saving around water is usually practised at an in-door swimming pool.

Other activities may include visits to museums, libraries, zoos, the cinema, the theatre etc. All of this is at the discretion of individual schools and teachers. There is no requirement for visits like these to be carried out.

There are no separate inspections of outdoor/outside the classroom activities. Schools are however responsible for the supervision of children during school hours and can be held responsible for any accident that occurs throughout the school day. This means that schools must ensure that there are proper routines in place eg regarding any outdoor activities or visits that are carried out. Many municipalities also take out insurance to cover children while at school.

Education and activities carried out within the framework of pre-school and compulsory school should on principle be free of charge. There is anecdotal evidence of schools in certain areas asking parents to pay for certain activities, such as visits, where parents are able to afford this.

Any activities taking place within the framework of the curriculum are arranged by the school itself. Teachers who include out-of-the-classroom visits or projects in the teaching of their subjects do not require special training.

In addition to the outside-the-classroom activities mentioned above, it is common for Swedish children below the age of 10 to attend after-school childcare. These facilities are often located on school premises or in connection with school premises. Municipalities are responsible for ensuring that staff have the proper training to take care of and understand the needs of children at this age. Municipalities must also ensure that the premises used for after-school childcare are appropriate for that purpose and that the sizes of groups are manageable.

NETHERLANDS

Dutch schools are not required to offer pupils education outside the classroom, but most schools offer out of school experiences such as excursions, visits etc. Most municipalities offer school-garden clubs for 10 year olds. The central government offers school vouchers for cultural activities (actor in classroom, visiting a theatre or a studio etc).

In addition, out-of-school care is available for schoolchildren aged between four and 13. These centres are open before and after school (and sometimes at lunchtimes), on afternoons or days when there is no school, and during the school holidays. These centres offer leisure activities and facilities for doing homework.

GERMANY

In Germany responsibility for school education lies with the 16 Laender or regions. This means that in practice there are 16 different school systems which have their own set of rules and regulations on education outside the classroom. It is not possible therefore to give a full picture for the whole of Germany, but the information that follows applies to the situation applying in most Laender.

There are no out-of-school activities which are compulsory for particular subjects. Class trips, excursions etc take place at the discretion of the school or the individual teachers. Physical education is compulsory in primary as well as secondary school in most Laender.

All school pupils are automatically covered by accident insurance (provided by the local authorities) during lessons, on the way to and from school and during all school functions or out-of-school activities for which the school is responsible and is providing supervision. This also includes school trips outside Germany.

Parents have to cover the costs of their children's school excursions (travel, accommodation etc). Accompanying teachers get reimbursed for their expenses by their school or local/Land education authorities. However, due to budgetary constraints several Laender ask their teachers to cover at least part of their expenses.

All Laender have their own set of rules and regulations for education outside the classroom. North Rhine Westphalia (Germany's largest Land), for example, issued detailed guidelines for school excursions in 1997. The most important elements of these guidelines are as follows:

— class trips are integral part of school education;

— excursions have to be embedded into the curriculum and have to be prepared in class and assessed afterwards;

— schools have overall organisational responsibility and decide whether or not to make use of excursions;

— the school conference (in which teachers, parents and pupils are represented) decides on the overall framework for excursions, including on the length and maximum costs. Parents, teachers and pupils have to be given the opportunity to discuss any proposals before the school conference takes a decision;

— costs have to be kept at a minimum so that they do not prevent any pupils from taking part;

— if class trips exceed two weeks, the extra time has to fall into school holidays;

— class teachers make suggestions for the programme, the length of time and the objectives of an excursion. Parents are asked for their opinion and the head teacher decides whether the plans are in line with the school's educational objectives and with the guidelines produced by the school conference. The head teacher also has to check whether there is sufficient funding;

— any service contracts with transport, catering or hospitality companies are signed by the school, not by individual teachers;

— parents have to produce written confirmation that they will cover the costs of class trips which are taking place over several days, even if their children are 18 years or older;

— in order to provide sufficient supervision with larger groups, parents or pupils over the age of 18 may take the place of additional supervisory teachers;

— private transport for class trips is not allowed for safety reasons;

— there are additional health and safety guidelines for excursions which involve swimming or other activities in water, mountaineering or skiing.

JAPAN

Out-of-classroom activities are considered an important part of a child's education in Japan. Such activities are conducted by schools mainly through: (1) "tokubetsu katsudo" or "Special Activities" within the school curriculum; (2) sports and cultural clubs carried out at the school; and (3) as part of subject teaching in the school curriculum. Learning opportunities may also be provided independent of schools by local boards of education and private organisations.

Special Activities

In the elementary and lower secondary curriculum (age 6–15), 35 hours a year (one hour a week) are allocated to "tokubetsu katsudo" or "Special Activities". Special Activities consist of: ceremonies (entrance, graduation, etc), arts/cultural events (cultural festival, etc), physical/health activities (sports festival, etc); outings (school excursions, field trips, longer school trips, etc); and work and volunteer activities.

Schools are free to devise their own plan according to the available resources although schools will have to work within the regulations and guidelines of the respective local board of education. A board of education, for example, may have a restriction concerning the ages of students allowed to participate in trips involving overnight stays. Before the beginning of the school year, schools have to submit annual plans to their local boards of education, which will include details of their special activities, for approval.

Parents in Japan are expected to pay for the cost for out-of-school activities such as school trips. Some schools have a monthly payment system for parents to cover such costs. In cases of financial hardship, boards of education can provide financial support to families through special funds for those families on low incomes.

Evaluation of activities is carried out within school and schools are monitored by their local board of education, which has a supervisory role over the schools in its area.

Sports and Cultural Clubs

Club activities are an area of great importance in Japanese education. In addition to developing students' interest and skills, club activities give students the opportunity to learn how to act as part of a group and are crucial in developing interpersonal skills, perseverance as well as leadership qualities.

In elementary education, club activities are limited to students from the 4th to 6th grades (age 9–11). Club activities are not compulsory but students are encouraged to take part in one of the sport or cultural clubs at the school after classes. At the junior high level, some sports clubs meet 4–5 times a week and practices or games may take place at the weekends or in the school holidays. Clubs are supervised by teachers and most teachers are responsible for one of the sports or cultural clubs at their schools. Teachers receive a small allowance for supervising a school club. Some clubs, though, can involve considerable extra work for teachers.

Subject Teaching

In the Course of Study (national guidelines) for each subject, teachers are encouraged to provide students with experiential learning activities as part of their subject teaching which may occur outside the classroom. The School Education Law in Japan has been revised in recent years to include a stipulation that schools, in carrying out their subject teaching, should seek to cooperate with social education-related organisations to expand and improve experiential learning activities for students.

Although such activities will vary according to the teacher and the school, out-of-classroom activities may include growing plants at school as part of a science project or looking after a class animal as part of moral education and out-of-school activities may include museum or library trips as part of social science education, field trips to local parks or woodlands as part of science education, and visits to local companies as part of a Period for Integrated Study project.

Local Boards of Education and Private Organisations

In addition to schools, boards of education and private organisations play a role in providing students with learning activities outside the classroom utilising skilled local people and local facilities. Such learning activities are considered as part of lifelong education in Japan. One example may be an English class offered at the local public hall on Saturdays to students at schools in the area. Another example may be a cultural festival in the local library. Although not directly involved, schools may play a role in promoting such events and cooperating with local organisations.

On a national level, through a cross-party initiative and with the cooperation of the private sector, the Children's Dream Fund ("Kodomo Yume Kikin") was established to provide grants for children's experiential activities, contributing to the healthy development of young people. Examples of activities include: activities to experience nature such as summer camps; activities to experience community service such as caring for the elderly; and also activities to promote and support children's reading. Again, schools may play a role in promoting and cooperating with the organisations providing these learning opportunities in the local community.

SINGAPORE

Apart from the formal school curriculum, pupils participate in co-curricular activities (CCAs) which are intended to provide healthy recreation, and instil self-discipline, teamwork and confidence in the pupils. The Ministry of Education, Singapore established The Outdoor Education team in 1999 to provide assistance and guidance to Singapore schools in the planning and implementation of their outdoor education and adventure programmes.

There is a wide range of CCAs available in schools. Pupils may choose from a variety of sports and games such as track and field events, basketball, tennis or uniformed organisations such as the Red Cross Society and National Police Cadet Corps. They can, alternatively, opt for a cultural activity such as the Military Band, the ethnic dance group or the drama club. Students can also participate in clubs and societies like the Photographic Society, the Computer Club and the Gardening Club.

Pupils are introduced to CCAs at Primary Four (age 10) and participation is voluntary. At secondary level, they must participate in at least one core CCA.

Schools compete in a number of co-curricular events at the zonal and national level each year. These include sports events such as track and field, swimming and cross-country. The Singapore Youth Festival is an annual event which showcases the creativity and talent of Singapore students through drama presentations, choral singing, an art and craft exhibition, uniformed group events and sports events.

New Zealand

Education Outside the Classroom (EOTC) in New Zealand is defined as any curriculum-based activity that takes place outside the school, including museum visits, sport trips, field trips and outdoor education camps

There is a strong history and culture of outdoor education in New Zealand, with education documents over the past century recognising the educational value of EOTC. By the 1960s most schools offered field trips to students, which increased in frequency throughout the 1980s and into the 1990s. However, it has been suggested that there has been a small decline in EOTC in recent years, due to the decentralisation of education in the late 1980s, increasing compliance costs and concerns about liability for student injuries/ deaths.

Schools are not required to offer EOTC, but as a general rule all schools do. The provision of EOTC varies from school to school, and often depends on the teachers' enthusiasm for EOTC.

EOTC is offered to students of all ages, from early childhood through to secondary school level. Different approaches to EOTC are appropriate for children of different ages—the following is a guideline of the types of EOTC activities that may be offered:

Ages 3–5: In early childhood centres, the specific EOTC focus is on fieldtrips, which are generally short and frequent with a high ratio of adults to children.

Years 1–4: EOTC is primarily about exploring the local community within walking distance from the school or accessible by local car, bus or train ride.

Years 5–6: In addition to the above, EOTC is more likely to involve exploring rural or city environments and possibly involving staying overnight.

Years 7–8: In addition to the above, exploring bush and water environments within a few hours' walk from a road end or accessible by vehicle.

Years 9–10: In addition to the above, exploring other towns and cities in New Zealand, back-country areas that take a day or more to get to, using marked tracks and involving staying a few nights.

Years 11–13: In addition to the above, possibly involving more remote back-country environments or overseas visits.

At most intermediate (Years 7–8) and secondary schools (Years 9–13), in addition to curriculum extension activities and opportunities for personal development, EOTC includes camping and outdoor pursuits such as canoeing and abseiling, which require tutors with specific skills.

Witnesses: **Ms Helen Williams**, Director, School Standards Group, and **Mr Stephen Crowne**, Director, School Resources Group, Department for Education and Skills, examined.

Q75 Chairman: Can I welcome Helen Williams and Stephen Crowe from the Department for Education and Skills who have kindly agreed to be here to answer some questions on what we have called an inquiry into the benefit of outdoor learning. This is an inquiry that we certainly take very seriously since three years ago some of us went to look at the Forest Schools Initiative in Denmark and saw the way in which even at pre-school the outside environment was used very positively as part of the educational experience of young children. There has been a whole number of issues that seemed to suggest that not only was it a time of change in outdoor learning but there were certain barriers to either its development or continuation. Stephen Crowne and Helen Williams, is there anything you would like to say about your responsibilities? Interestingly enough, when we looked at your background in the department it did not really point up the reference and the relevance of outdoor learning to your particular remit, so perhaps you could illuminate us on that.
Ms Williams: I am a Director within the Schools Standards Group within the DfES. I am responsible, among other things, for policy on the national curriculum and on support for all subjects and themes within the national curriculum, including

outdoor education as a context for teaching and learning across the curriculum. That is how I come to be here today. The Department does see outdoor education as being a very important part of what schools should offer pupils to support a broad and rich curriculum. We know that some schools do use outdoor education pretty well but that there are other schools which, for whatever reason, are not fully exploiting the potential of outdoor learning. The department's policy is to work with a very wide range of partners to promote good practice in outdoor education and also to develop teachers' confidence and knowhow in planning and delivering outdoor education. We think it is absolutely key to getting outdoor education fully into the system to convince heads and their staff that outdoor education has a contribution to make to pupil achievement and development so that they can build it in at the start into the curriculum and timetabling.
Mr Crowne: I am Director of the School Resources Group which is responsible for school funding, capital investment, school organisation, school admissions, transport and safety, the last of which is essentially the reason I am here. My particular interest, as Helen says, is in working with partners to identify what are the obstacles to outdoor education which can range across issues of safety but also

funding, transport and so on, to see whether there is more we can do in partnership to help give a greater sense of confidence amongst all schools that outdoor education is a central part of the offer and that there are ways of delivering that offer consistently and with high quality in all schools.

Q76 Chairman: Thank you. This is a department that believes in evidence-based policy. Have you got any evidence that opportunities for outdoor learning are of any value at all?
Ms Williams: There is a considerable amount of evidence, some of which we refer to in the memorandum that we sent you. I have not got chapter and verse at my fingertips but I am sure we can produce a lot of evidence showing that outdoor education has a contribution to make, for example, in science and geography and giving pupils first-hand practical experience of doing things in the wild, as it were, adventure activities in terms of developing pupils' skills, extending their horizons. There is quite a body of evidence. Outdoor learning is a very wide topic. Perhaps that is a point that ought to be made at the outset. It covers a great variety of things from field work in geography and biology through to trips to museums or places of cultural interest through to the Outward Bound activities.
Mr Pollard: And Parliament?
Ms Williams: Indeed, Parliament, and also we included in outdoor learning community-based activities, for example, volunteering which we encourage through the citizenship curriculum. We think that in all of those various areas there is evidence that, properly planned, outdoor learning can make a contribution to outcomes, to pupil achievement, but the emphasis is there on proper planning. It needs to be integrated into the whole curriculum offer for pupils rather than just being something done as an optional extra.

Q77 Chairman: Is that one of the problems, that it is too diverse, that you start looking at this subject and, as you said, it includes a whole range of activities for a variety of ages? Where does your responsibility in terms of age begin?
Ms Williams: I do not think it is a problem that it is a very rich and diverse field. I think that is just a fact. My interests in outdoor education span the full range of the curriculum from the foundation stage through to Key Stage 4 in a whole variety of subjects.
Mr Crowne: From our perspective the key thing is that the school needs to be very clear about how particular activities form part of a rich curriculum for the pupils involved. In a way it should not be for us to try and lay down how each style or activity contributes; rather to ensure that the school is very clear, learning from what works in other schools and in other contexts and drawing together the best practice. When we are talking about removing the barriers we are also talking about encouraging the spread of understanding of how particular activities support particular curriculum objectives or social objectives, pastoral objectives and so on, in the school. To repeat the point, there is a tremendously

wide range of activity here and one where we essentially need to work with a broad range of partners to ensure that distinctive contributions of each kind of activity are recognised and integrated in the school's overall offer.

Q78 Chairman: What I am trying to get at is that if we do not have a pretty clear focus on what the value is and what the variety of contribution can be it is quite difficult for the Department to prompt schools to achieve high levels of added value for all the age ranges. Is that not the case?
Mr Crowne: I am very wary of the Department seeking to distil out as it were, in a kind of salami-slice way, what distinctively each area contributes because in the end it is about how the school looks at the curriculum as a whole and plays to its local circumstances, the particular contexts it has to work with and feeds those into its overall view of the curriculum. I think there is a balance in this and where we ought to be putting our effort is in encouraging and promoting what the wide variety of partners believe to be the best practice and giving schools a menu of opportunities from which they can then select and mould and adapt in the light of their own particular circumstances.

Q79 Chairman: Should it not be the Department's job to persuade by the evidence, by good practice, teachers in training, that this is a priority, that it is something that adds value to the life of the school and the life of the individual student? Is that not the level at which you should be taking a particular interest?
Mr Crowne: It is a very good point and clearly this process has to start with initial training. The amount of time available for initial teacher trainees is limited and all we can expect is to give some basic tools around planning these kinds of activities. The real value added has to come during the early period of professional development in post when we should encourage all teachers to work together to see the benefits that can accrue from different types of activity and ensure that they are confident, through continuing professional development, in taking those kinds of activities forward. It is building the confidence and the understanding of the potential benefits where you get the real gains. You have to see it as a seamless development rather than focus specifically on the initial end.

Q80 Chairman: How many people in the Department will be working on this area?
Ms Williams: In our curriculum area, for which I am responsible, we have a small team of four or five people which covers two or three subjects in the national curriculum—geography, design and technology, ICT—as subjects within the national curriculum and that team is also the focus for work on outdoor education. They are focused and mobilise other people in other subject teams. For example, people who work in science have an interest in outdoor education, as do people who work on citizenship. It is quite difficult to give you a figure but there is a significant staff effort in the

Department going into working with partners on outdoor education. Following on from what Stephen was saying about what we are doing, the Department is doing quite a lot to promote, publicise and disseminate guidance about outdoor education. I will not take the Committee's time up with reading off a lot of detail but there is guidance on the foundation stage curriculum which talks about the role of outdoor learning to develop young children. There is stuff in the primary national strategy materials on outdoor education. There is some material in the Key Stage 3 strategy. We also have supported the Growing Schools programme which is an alliance that brings together some 25 organisations which are interested in outdoor education. That Growing Schools programme we support in various ways but in particular we have supported them to undertake research on identifying good practice. There is a Growing Schools web site which has an enormous amount of material on it about what works in outdoor learning at different stages in different subjects, what advice is available to teachers, and that web site is a very well visited web site.

Q81 Chairman: Do you think there is a problem that too often we discuss this, and perhaps even the Department may look at this, as beneficial to a particular subject, like geography or one of the science subjects, as a practical aspect of getting out there and looking at real plants and so on rather than looking at it as a beneficial exercise for the ethos of the school, for the team building of the kids? Is it the less focused bit of it the bit that you are least comfortable with? You tend to come back to curriculum-related issues rather than the other thing that we are trying to tease out.
Ms Williams: That is a very interesting question. My instinctive response would be that we value both the specific curricular contribution of outdoor education but also its contribution to the less tangible things like team building and developing pupils' horizons and experience. I very much hope that is reflected in the guidance and materials we put out. I am sure it is although I cannot quote chapter and verse.

Q82 Helen Jones: I want to take up what you said about continuing professional development. How many teachers are undertaking or have undertaken continuing professional development which relates specifically to outdoor education?
Mr Crowne: I do not think we can answer that.[1]

Q83 Helen Jones: That is exactly my point.
Mr Crowne: If I could say a little more about this, there is a lot of continuing professional development which is highly relevant to this which covers different subject areas and covers the way school activities are organised. The key thing is that the school itself should have a clear overall view of how it wants to use outdoor education across a broad range of its curricular areas and the other aspects of the life of

the school and it should ensure that the professional development necessary to realise that particular vision is in place. Often when it is said, "How do we ensure there is enough training?", you do that by being very clear at the school level about what you want to deliver and how you are going to deliver it. We could of course seek to collect more and more information about this. I am not quite sure that we could come up with a methodology for doing it that would fully illuminate the picture that you want, but I do not think we have that data at the moment.

Q84 Helen Jones: That is my point really, that you cannot be sure because you say to us, quite rightly, that schools should do this. Do you have any information as a department on how many schools actually do it?
Ms Williams: It depends what you mean by "do it".

Q85 Helen Jones: I am taking up Mr Crowne's point. Tell me what schools should do. I would like to know if you know whether they are doing it.
Ms Williams: We know that 10,000 schools registered last year in the Growing Schools programme. Growing Schools is an alliance which is promoting the use of the outdoors as a learning resource. It does not follow from that that in each of those 10,000 schools all the teachers have necessarily been very energetic in following up and getting relevant CPD but it is of some significance that that number of schools, which is more than 50% of the total number, is positively participating in that programme.

Q86 Helen Jones: I just want to be clear. You are not telling the Committee that that necessarily means that their teachers have undertaken continuous professional development work in that area, are you?
Ms Williams: No.

Q87 Mr Chaytor: Can I ask about the impact of the Workforce Reform programme on the amount of electorate taking place? In your submission it says that the limits on cover introduced in September, the commitment to guaranteed planning, preparation and assessment times, together with enhanced roles for support staff, present real opportunities to make a difference. It does not say "a difference to outdoor learning". I thought it did. It says, "a difference to each pupil's learning". In fact, I am not sure why it is here because it does not say anything about outdoor learning at all. I will revise my question. Why is this paragraph in because it does not seem relevant to the inquiry? Previous witnesses have flagged up school Workforce Reform as an obstacle to the expansion of outdoor learning. The implication of this paragraph being here in this submission, even though it does not mention outdoor learning, is that school Workforce Reform could provide an incentive to outdoor learning. What is your view on the pros and considerations of the Workforce Reform agreement?

---

[1] Ev 62.

Mr Crowne: We are aware of concerns that there maybe an obstacle here but we are very clear—and this is working with our partners on the Workforce Reform agreement—that there are real opportunities. One of the issues for us is to ensure that the advice and briefing going to schools about the opportunities with Workforce Reform cover this and other areas. What we see as the opportunity essentially is that there is now a broader range of ways of organising and covering for activities of this kind. We are not and should not be wholly reliant on supply cover; there are different ways that we can use the evolving school workforce to help manage these kinds of activities. The first point is that we need to be clear in our guidance to schools in order to build their confidence about how it can be done. The other opportunity there is about what happens in the school while these trips and other activities are going on because that does open up opportunities for different kinds of provision with the groups of children that are left, and again, with a more flexible workforce, teachers and others, it should be possible to devise stimulating, interesting and different kinds of activity back in the school as well. I do see it as an opportunity but I recognise that there is a real job to be done to identify the practices that work and help and help all schools to understand what they can do to access the opportunities.

Q88 Mr Chaytor: What you are saying is that the opportunities really are that teaching assistants and other support staff take on many of the functions of organising these activities?
Mr Crowne: Absolutely.

Q89 Mr Chaytor: But are you not then getting the worst of both worlds in your relations with the NUT and the NASUWT, because the NASUWT is saying to teachers, "Do not get involved in these activities at all", and the NUT was opposed to teaching assistants in the first place? How are you going to get out of all that?
Mr Crowne: If I can answer that more generally, we recognise that there are various kinds of concern. Certainly in relation to the NASUWT concerns, and we have been working very closely with NASUWT to see how we can take those matters forward, there are plenty of practices now in schools about the way different groups have started to contribute to these activities. All we are saying with Workforce Reform is that there is now a wider range of opportunities because we have a stronger cadre of non-teaching staff available and we just want to build on the experience of using the whole school staff to support these kinds of activities.

Q90 Mr Chaytor: Leaving aside the impact of the administrative tasks and the use of non-teaching assistants, if a teacher is taken out of the classroom for a given period of time the Workforce Agreement means that supply cover will kick in earlier than it would have done before 1 September, so there is going to be an additional pressure in terms of supply cover that was not there previously, is there not?

Mr Crowne: That is only if you assume that that is the only way you can deal with the teacher absence.

Q91 Mr Chaytor: The non-teaching assistants will be covering for absent teachers in addition to organising the trip in the first place?
Mr Crowne: What I am saying is that because we are now developing the notion of high level teaching assistants there are different ways of providing for teacher absences. As I said before, those provide some opportunities back at the school to do some different things as well. I am not laying down the law on this. The way we have to proceed is looking with our partners at examples of where the different approaches work well and share those quite widely. In the end it does not matter what we say. It is the confidence that schools have in their ability to organise and deliver these things that matters. That above all is the obstacle to progress. It is about delivering that confidence and sharing the practice that seems to work.

Q92 Mr Chaytor: There is not a specific funding stream directly to schools for outdoor learning, or is there? There has never been a strand of the standards funds?
Mr Crowne: I could not say never.

Q93 Chairman: Helen Williams, for the record, is shaking her head.
Ms Williams: Within living memory we are not aware of there having been a specific strand.

Q94 Mr Chaytor: If the Department is so confident that this has advantages for pupils and their learning is there not a case for having a ring-fenced funding stream as there is for certain other parts of the curriculum?
Mr Crowne: As you will know, within our overall strategy we are trying to get away from the ring-fencing of specific sums for specific purposes. That builds on the very solid consensus across all of our education partners that a much more effective approach is to give maximum flexibility at local level and encourage schools to be very clear about what their priorities are and then to use their budgets flexibly to deliver those. The challenge for the Department is, rather than using a directed approach through ring-fenced finding, finding a style of leadership which encourages schools to want to take up these opportunities and to prioritise them within their overall budgets, and then we come in to provide guidance and support and access to best practice which will influence behaviour locally. It is getting away from what I call the regulatory ring-fencing approach which we have found over time has rather diminishing returns in terms of leading the system. It is a deliberate attempt to move away from that but we recognise nevertheless that there are some challenges in how you influence and provide the kind of leadership where it is clear that we want more schools to be able to benefit from these kinds of activities.

Q95 Mr Chaytor: Finally, can I ask about academies? In your submission it says, "We expect as more of them open that many academies will be at the forefront of the provision of outdoor education". Is there any evidence that the first wave of academies have put particular emphasis on outdoor education?

Ms Williams: I am not personally aware of the evidence but we can certainly let you have whatever evidence there is.

Q96 Mr Chaytor: Has there yet been the review? I think when the Secretary of State was here last time he said there was going to be an internal review of the first year of academies to be published, as I recall, at the end of September.

Ms Williams: We do not know about that but we can put in a note about that.

Q97 Chairman: How would you take the notion that there should be a dedicated part of the budget to a school? There are two ways of looking at this, are there not? One is that every school spend X amount of its budget on outdoor education, or there can be an entitlement for every student to have so many hours per term in outdoor education. Which of those would you favour, or none?

Ms Williams: Shall I comment on the idea of some kind of entitlement in terms of hours? We would be rather inclined against an entitlement expressed in terms of hours per pupil because that does not offer any assurance about the quality or the relevance of the experience. It is an input measure. The important thing, as Stephen has said and as I have said already, is to create the demand in schools to convince heads and their staff that outdoor education is something that can make a contribution. You have to create that sense of ownership and buy-in within the profession. Simply having a statutory entitlement for pupils to have so many hours per week or per month of outdoor education does not in itself carry the profession with you. Our instinct would be to stick with the approach of promoting the benefits of outdoor education to schools, to building up the capacity and confidence of staff through CPD and through information and by signposting the opportunities that already exist for schools to take advantage of that.

Q98 Chairman: I would say that sounds a bit weak and waffly in the sense that if you were going to look for an energiser in the past you would look at the local education authority. A good LEA was at the heart of providing good outdoor education. Of course, the government has given LEAs relatively a weaker role in most of these things, or at least that is the view that some of us on this committee have. Is it all going to be done from Sanctuary House that you are going to encourage people or is there a mechanism? I gave you two possibilities, a certain amount of time that students should expect of outdoor education or a special budget like the e-learning budget. What about making Ofsted take it

much more seriously? I am looking for ways in which you are going to convince me that the department takes it seriously.

Ms Williams: Perhaps I can suggest a third possibility.

Q99 Chairman: Do you not mean the fourth? I have given you three now.

Ms Williams: This is something we have already talked to partners about, the possibility of developing with partners, including local authority organisations, including teacher union organisations as well as professional organisations, the idea of agreeing some kind of manifesto for outdoor learning on the lines of the manifesto that has recently been agreed among partners on school music. The idea of having such a manifesto would be that it would identify what the partners saw as the contribution of outdoor education within the curriculum to teaching and learning. It could identify some agreed key issues. It could set out a set of priorities and this would be a kind of agreed framework not just for the partners but also for local authorities, non-government bodies. Everyone who has a stake in this field could work together to promote outdoor education.

Q100 Chairman: Who came up with the notion of calling it a manifesto?

Ms Williams: The music manifesto? I suspect David Miliband may have been the author of the term "manifesto".

Jonathan Shaw: He does write them, you know.

Chairman: It is a very interesting use of the word "manifesto". I thought manifestos led to mandates and were used in a rather different context. We will come back to that. Let us carry on and look at the litigation and bureaucracy that allegedly dogs this whole subject.

Q101 Paul Holmes: There is a well known phenomenon now in terms of European legislation whereby Europe passes some regulations and then the relevant body in Britain gold-plates it, makes it belt and braces, makes it really complicated and poor old Europe gets the blame. It seems, looking at this, that there is a similar process going on in that for example the DfES issue Health and Safety of Pupils on Educational Visits guidelines and then the LEAs add their bit to it, except that each LEA adds a different slant so you are not getting any consistency, and then the school governors add their slant and the poor old classroom teacher looks at all this stuff and says, "I don't think I'll bother organising that trip after all". Do you think that is a fair assessment?

Mr Crowne: There is always a risk that we will end up with more complicated arrangements than we need as a result of that kind of process. What we are concerned to do, as in the other areas we have been talking about, is to build confidence at school level so that they know the best way to approach in particular the risk assessment side of this which drives a lot of the bureaucracy. What we have been doing is focusing the guidance that is prepared at national level on practical steps that can be taken. In fact, it has had pretty good feedback from the users. We have to recognise that at the end of the day it is the employers of the teachers and those with responsibility for the children who bear most of the legal responsibilities here, so there is always a risk that, with that responsibility and the onerous legal burden that places on you, you will want perhaps to go a little further than you might in protecting against risk. What we have to do is work with local authorities to ensure that that is not happening. We can use Ofsted, which will comment on these things in inspecting LEAs, and we need to ensure that where there is evidence local authorities may be going a little too far we can encourage them to look at best practice elsewhere. We have to have sympathy for those at the front line here because in the end it is the risk assessment that you do locally that is key to this. That determines how much effort, what kinds of resources, what kind of expertise you need to apply and everything that we do at local authority government level needs to support that. I am confident, as I say, that our guidance has been helpful but we are not complacent about this and I recognise that it is a big issue for schools and we need to continue to work to build that sense of confidence in how to approach the issues sensibly.[2]

Q102 Paul Holmes: You said though that you needed to try to work with local education authorities, for example, and heads and governors on this issue. Since you issue the initial advice through the Health and Safety of Pupils on Educational Visits guidance could you not also take a more proactive role in issuing the standard assessment forms to use? We heard from the Royal Society for the Protection of Birds an example where they had prepared material to fill in these risk assessment forms but different schools coming from different LEAs had to have the information in all sorts of different formats because there was no standard process and that just creates more work for everybody. Why not produce with your initial guidance some standard forms as well?
Mr Crowne: That is an idea we could well follow up. If the committee felt that was a fruitful avenue to go down we would be very happy to do that. I would be the first to recognise that there are almost inevitably going to be some inconsistencies of practice here across local authorities and we do need to make sure we are focused on what the best practice is, and if there is anything we can do to help that process I am sure we would be willing to consider it.

Q103 Paul Holmes: We also had the suggestion from previous evidence that where you have adventure activity licensing authority licences issued to certain centres why then would schools which are using those already accredited and licensed centres have to go through the same hoops of risk assessment when those centres have already gone through a very rigorous process?

Mr Crowne: The process of risk assessment is all about making a judgment from the point of view of the people who are actually responsible for the safety of the children as to what they should do. Obviously, if you are working with a licensed centre that will change the nature of your risk assessment because you know you have a quality assurance there in place. If you are working in some other context you will perhaps come to a different conclusion. I think you still have to go through the process of risk assessment. What I do not think you need to assume is that it is at the same level of detail in every case. I would hope that if you are working with a licensed adventure provider you will not have to go through the same degree of risk assessment as if you are working with a different kind of provider who does not have that kind of background.[3]

Q104 Paul Holmes: You said you would hope that and that would be the commonsense approach, but again are you aware whether that hope is realised?
Mr Crowne: I am only saying "hope" because if we accept that there is a variation in practice there are bound to be some examples of where that is not the case and our job is to work with local authorities to make sure there is consistency based on best practice.

Q105 Paul Holmes: In general terms do you think we need to step back and look at this whole area anyway, not just the specific examples I have been giving? We keep reading these examples of schools that ban playing conkers because it is dangerous, which sounds ludicrous. I can think back to four years ago almost exactly to this week when I was still teaching and I was taking my year seven form down to the local library to familiarise them with the library in case they had not been. These kids every morning walked up from the town centre to the school on their own and every night walked back and yet we had to fill in pages and pages of risk assessments to walk these kids eight minutes down the road from the school to the library. We have got stopping conkers, stopping playing contact sports, rugby, whatever, and doing risk assessments to walk down to the local library. Is it not all going a bit far?
Mr Crowne: I am certainly not complacent about the need to continue to work on this because I think there are pressures in the system which tend to encourage people to err on the side of ultra caution, and you can understand that, given that we are talking about safety. We have to continue to work to get common sense applied at every level in this and we recognise that we have a role in doing that as well. The first thing we should do is make sure our guidance is clear and based on best practice and is encouraging straightforward common sense approaches and then we have to try and work with local authorities to make sure we are not overlaying that with more complexity than we need. It is just

---

[2]Also see Ev 61.

[3]Also see Ev 61.

working away at the common sense approaches in partnership on a continuing basis. It is not a job that has been done fully yet.[4]

Q106 Paul Holmes: You keep saying this will be the logical thing to do and then you say it has not been done fully yet, so how proactively is the department doing this or planning to do it in the near future?

Mr Crowne: We have worked on our guidance, we have produced updates, we work with local authority folk in their efforts to work with local schools co-ordinators' activities. We are encouraging professional development in areas like risk assessment. I would want to avoid us taking an overly prescriptive approach here. What we are interested in doing is making sure the best practice is identified and that we are working with our partners to ensure that that is fed down through the system, but when you have 24,000-odd schools that is a lot of partners to work with. We have to be sensitive to local circumstances and avoid being overly prescriptive where that might not fit the bill. At the same time we need, as I say, to drive through the common sense approach to make sure that people locally feel confident about the processes. It is not just about the schools, of course. The parents have to feel confident in these processes as well. Often I suspect we get these extreme cases because the school is bending over backwards to show to parents that they have taken this very seriously, that they are doing everything in the best interests of the child, so I think it is building confidence throughout: parents, pupils and the staff, that the approaches we want are the right ones.

Q107 Paul Holmes: I have two final questions, both relating to the fact that you are at the centre of the whole process. You initiate it by issuing the regulations to start with; other people then respond to it and build on it. Are you aware from your central position of any hard facts about how far litigation arising out of activities of this kind are rising or falling or not? Again, we hear that schools ban conkers because they do not want to be sued because a kid gets injured playing with conkers. We hear of local authorities chopping down horse-chestnut trees so that kids are not putting sticks up to knock the conkers down. We hear of one of the major teachers' unions saying to teachers, "Do not get involved in this at all because of the dangers of litigation". From your central position does anybody collate figures on this? Is there really an increase in litigation or is it an urban myth?

Mr Crowne: It is rather hard to answer those questions. We do not have detailed information covering all those different examples.[5]

Q108 Jonathan Shaw: Not every conker?

Mr Crowne: Not every conker, no. What you can say is the amount of civil litigation in this general area does not seem to be going up. That tends to cover more serious cases though, so I would not like to speculate on whether the number of examples of conker banning, for example, is going up or down. I think we tend to see those as one-off reports in the press and it is difficult to get a sense of scale there. Again, I come back to the key point which is that for us it is about making sure that at every level of the system people are feeling confident that they know what is the right thing to do. If there was evidence that suggested there were particular areas of problem we would certainly be prepared to respond to those but I am not aware of evidence that shows that any particular area is becoming more of a problem than it has been.

Q109 Paul Holmes: If you were aware of a particular problem then it would be your role to do something about it. Some of the evidence we have heard so far suggests that it is now becoming very difficult to get insurance policies in this area. Would you agree with that from your central position and should the government do something about that since they are issuing the requirements that are leading to the lack of insurance companies willing to do this? Should you do something about providing the insurance cover?

Mr Crowne: I agree: I think there is an issue there. It is frankly part of a wider issue to do with school insurance where we have a current position which is of concern, that it is difficult and expensive to get insurance cover for a wide range of school activities and so we are working across government and also commissioning some studies on possible options for the future. As I say, it goes wider than this area because it is about the overall cost to schools of insurance which is becoming higher for a number of different reasons and it is about the availability of alternatives in the market places which again, for various reasons, has been rather restricted. We are looking actively at that. We have a study in progress now which we hope by the end of this year will illuminate some of the options that might be available.[6]

Q110 Paul Holmes: What possible options are you considering?

Mr Crowne: There is a range of things, is there not? There are market development options using private sector employers, but there are also options around developing local authorities' capacity to insure for themselves. There are examples in larger authorities where these things happen. Of course, in some of the areas we are talking about, third party liability and so on, you would expect a market solution, so we want to look very carefully at the possibilities there.

Q111 Valerie Davey: We seem to have come full circle. It seems to me that the insurance is based on the risk assessment; the risk assessment ought to be based on some factors which apparently we do not know. In other words, how many accidents on overseas, local, regional trips are there? What is the risk of taking a child on different types of trip? If we have not got that how on earth do we do a general risk assessment and does that not affect the insurance?[7]

Mr Crowne: The kinds of cases I suspect you are thinking about are the more serious ones where you are expecting a civil case or whatever to flow. We do have evidence in the sense that we do not see the overall numbers of those cases rising. What we have seen, of course, is a rising cost of the awards that are made where the cases have been successful and that tends to follow from the cost of medical treatment going up faster than inflation and some other factors. I do not think we should assume that the cost of premiums is necessarily only affected by the assessment of risk in the particular cases. There are other factors that tend to influence what the private sector charges for insurance. There is no doubt that, for a number of reasons, the private sector has not seen this market as a particularly attractive one, which tends to be why you get the higher premiums. I do not think that is driven only by an assessment of the particular risks and the costs to insurance.

Q112 Chairman: Is it not the fact that it is a kind of fashion thing? Evidence to this committee is that the most dangerous place for your child to be is home with the parents, the stats show that, or being driven by the parents on the roads and all that, and children's likelihood of having an accident at home is far higher than at school. Though they are tragic when they happen these are very unusual accidents that happen when a school is in charge. Does the department not have a responsibility both to parents and to the public and to trade unions to come out with the statistics, to say, "Look: this is a very rare occurrence", and the nonsense you get in the tabloids you very rarely have in these sorts of committees because we use long words, so we do not get them here; we do not ever have a dialogue with those sorts of journalists. There is no counterbalance to the nonsense they publish when there is a tragic accident, as though this was something that was likely to happen every other weekend.

Mr Crowne: I do agree. I think the Department has got an important role to play in explaining what the situation is, what the facts are where we have them. The fact is that any serious incident involving children's safety is a serious matter and one should never denigrate that but there is no sign that there are increasing problems here. In fact, for the most serious incidents there are encouraging signs that the numbers of cases are going down. The various steps that have been taken, certainly working with trips co-ordinators and the rest, show that the system as a whole is taking this area very seriously and there are very few cases which reveal serious failures in the system. I do not want to sound complacent but I am responding to your point about the need to get the balance right. Of course, we will strive to ensure that we get a balanced view here in the interests of balance but also in the interests of encouraging the practice in the system that we want to see because it is often fear of repercussions and the way cases

are treated that is deterring some of the schools and teachers from undertaking these important activities.

Q113 Helen Jones: Can I ask you to clarify something for the committee please? You referred to having no evidence of the number of cases going up. Are you referring to cases that actually proceed to court, not to cases that are settled before they get to that stage and is there a fear amongst schools of what are often very minor claims which are often settled very early on, because, frankly, people do not want the bother of the litigation; it costs more than settling the thing?

Mr Crowne: That is a good question. I was referring to the number of cases that proceed. I do not think we could estimate the numbers that are settled before but that is a good point.[8]

Q114 Mr Turner: Could I come back to a question that you answered earlier? You said something about the need to convince heads and staff of the value of outdoor education but you do not seem able to express it yourself.

Ms Williams: There is a lot of material that the Department has put out which defines the value that outdoor education can add in a number of subject areas generally.

Q115 Mr Turner: As the Chairman said, it is very waffly. I do not argue with the idea that it might be a good thing but there does not seem to be any evidence that it is a good thing.

Ms Williams: I think there is a lot of evidence. Maybe we have not done justice to the evidence in the memorandum that we gave the Committee. We can certainly have a go at distilling some of the key facts from the evidence about what outdoor education can provide. I am quite confident that we have got that evidence base. If we could pull it out and present it in a summary perhaps the committee would find that helpful.

Q116 Mr Turner: You rejected the Chairman's proposal for a guaranteed number of hours because it did not offer any assurance about quality or relevance. Do you have evidence that what is offered is of good quality or poor quality, and relevant to what?

Ms Williams: We rely on Ofsted's report on the quality of the provision made in schools, including provision made for outdoor education where that is part of the curriculum. Ofsted, under the current inspection arrangements, does look at outdoor learning when it goes to schools. Under the new inspection arrangements, which are going to be based more on school self-evaluation, the self-evaluation form which schools have to complete includes questions which invite the head to consider the contribution that outdoor education is making to the whole school offer. We should be able to rely on Ofsted to monitor this aspect of schools' provision. It would also be open to us to ask Ofsted at some point to do a special survey of outdoor education in schools.

Q117 Mr Turner: But the fact is that you have not asked them and you are spending £35 million as far as I can judge from your report—maybe there is more—and most of that is coming from DCMS. It does not sound as if you regard this as a very high priority.
Ms Williams: Outdoor education is one of a large number of priorities for the department. We do accord it a reasonable measure of priority and we have been extremely active with partners over the last two or three years in commissioning research, commissioning surveys, identifying what works. We have commissioned, for example, the Association for Science Education and the Geographical Association to produce CPD modules for field work for geography teachers, science teachers. We are supporting bringing money into Growing Schools which also enables them to have this much-visited website. I can point to quite a long catalogue of things that we are doing to promote outdoor education.

Q118 Mr Turner: Mr Crowne, if you were in the position where, for example, one of those advocates of abolishing the DfES and giving the money to the schools was saying to you, "Look: you are allowed to keep a small amount of money", how would you justify spending that money on outdoor education rather than one of the other myriad of priorities which the department appears to have?
Mr Crowne: Do you mean if I was able to retain it in the budget centrally?

Q119 Mr Turner: A small budget for one aspect.
Mr Crowne: Our basic strategy is, as I was describing earlier, to provide a maximum amount of flexibility to schools to apply their overall budget in support of their priorities. The key thing for the Department in areas like this where we are trying to signal a degree of priority is to provide some incentive and some encouragement for schools to prioritise locally and we are trying to move away from doing that by ring-fencing sums of money or defining the inputs, as Helen was saying. If I had a small central budget to do this, the way we would do it is the way we are doing it, which is to identify, working with partners, what activities are beneficial, how we can promote the capacity of the system to make best use of them and how we encourage those responsible for defining school level priorities to make this a priority. The way you do that for schools is to point out the benefits, to draw attention to other schools who are getting the most out of them. That is the way we try to approach these things. I am the first to admit that it is the more indirect way than some of the approaches we have used in the past, which tended to involve identifying a sum of money for a particular purpose and limiting it to that purpose.

Q120 Mr Turner: You appear to think that the LEAs cannot do it. Otherwise you would not be doing it.

Mr Crowne: No, I do not think that is true. What we are saying is that we each have distinctive roles in this. The Department has an important role in articulating the national sense of priority on what can be done. Local authorities are responsible in two senses: one, in working with their schools to help support them in providing the opportunities; two, very importantly on the health and safety side, as we have seen as an employer, but we also work with a wide range of other partners, a lot of voluntary organisations, subject associations. Each in its own way has a contribution to make. I would describe our role as articulating that activity and giving it a sense of purpose and direction to influence priority decisions that are made at school level.
Mr Turner: I think my problem is this. You are doing a fair number of things. The DCMS has clearly influenced one significant area, because they have put something like, as I said, not £35, £20 million into museums and galleries. I cannot quite see how much you have spent in any other area. I am wondering how we assess, which is one of our responsibilities, the value for money, albeit the relatively small amount of money, that you are spending on this and judge whether it would have been better if you had not got that money but somebody else had?

Q121 Chairman: What have you to say to that?
Mr Crowne: I think that is a very hard question to answer. We have something like £30 billion going into school budgets. The Department is committed to increasing the proportion of the overall resources going to schools, increasing the proportion that goes into school budgets as opposed to other levels of the system, so I think we are increasingly scrutinising the way we look at the need to retain money, whether it is at local authority level or, indeed, at national level, and I think our focus for money that we retain at national level is around three things: first, it is about promoting innovation and development in the system, second, building the capacity, trying to build the capacity of the system itself to take some of these things forward, and I think probably the third is to make sure we have got the right framework of incentives and accountability in there to move the system in the right direction. I think those are the kinds of tests you have to apply to any centrally retained expenditure. Of course there are lots of organisations who would like additional resources from us, but we have to be very careful about going down the road of what I describe as supporting the supply side in this, because in the end the test has to be whether these opportunities are ones that schools think are in the best interests of the children and they are prepared to support them from the £30-odd billion budget that is delegated through the system. So I think we have to be very wary of precisely how we use those centrally retained funds. I think I am rather supporting the point you are making about value for money. It is a real test whether we have got the right engagement and we are using that money for the right things.

Q122 Chairman: Could I ask one other question? Hampshire County Council tells us that it has moved outdoor education facilities to a department outside the education department in order to protect it from "pressures created by the increasing devolution funding directly to schools". Clearly it is your policy to do the opposite, and you say so in paragraph 19. What will be the effect on schools of having more money delegated to them rather than having the LEA decide where that money will be spent on their behalf?

Mr Crowne: I think one of the effects will be that we will have a much richer discussion between the school and the LEA about the benefits of delegating the money or retaining it centrally. As you will know, we set up schools forums which bring together all the local stakeholders to talk about school funding, and one of the big issues that every schools forum will be discussing is what is the case for devolving these resources to schools as opposed to retaining it centrally in the local authority to provide a service for schools as a whole. That is very important discussion, and, of course, it is entirely within the local authority's discretion working with its schools forums to decide to retain the resources if that is what the schools want, and what better test can you have of the need for service than if the main clients of that service want it. So that would be my answer. I think over the next few years, as schools forums become stronger and more confident, we will see more of those discussions going on and the level of retention and what it is retained for will be based on a really clear understanding between the LEA and schools about what the schools actually want and need. I think that is an important step.

Q123 Chairman: Do you think there should be more of a champion, either at ministerial level or within the Department, for external implication. If there was someone really banging the drum for the . . . And I am surprised, because you have been a little bit reluctant to give us evidence, but we have heard some convincing evidence from a range of experts and also from Ofsted in written evidence on the value of outside education. This is a world where for most of us who have experience of a large town or city many children do not travel much outside the community in which they live, especially if they have come from an economically deprived background. If you then look at the work we have done on school meals and the Heath Committee has done on obesity, it all seems to be arguing that there is a champion needed here, because a lot of the activities that traditionally have been done as out of school activities are beneficial on a range of different criteria. Do you think there is a need? Do you think you have that ministerial spark there to guide you?

Ms Williams: At ministerial level within the DfES Steven Twigg is the Minister who has responsibility for outdoor education within his portfolio, and he is very positive on the benefits of outdoor education. The Department's five-year strategy that was published in July also contains some warm words about the importance of the value of wider activities.

Q124 Chairman: That is the problem, is it not, "Warm words"? Tomlinson on 14–19 has warm words, but they are not very focused words, are they?

Ms Williams: No. They were a carefully selected positive endorsement of the value of outdoor activities to enrich and to develop the curriculum both at primary and secondary level. It is not just warm words because there are a whole range of things that we are doing from the Department to build on those warm words.

Q125 Chairman: If we have not seen the manifesto yet, can we have a look? We are interested in manifestos in this Committee. Could we have a look at the manifesto?

Ms Williams: The manifesto for outdoor education is at the concept stage; we have not got one yet. I was suggesting this would be something we might work up as a shared agenda among departments.

Q126 Chairman: I see. Okay.

Ms Williams: What we could do is show you the music manifesto as an example of what we mean by this.

Q127 Chairman: Music to our ears. Thank you very much for your attendance, Stephen Crowne and Helen Williams, and thank you for your time.

Supplementary evidence from the Department for Education and Skills

STANDARD RISK ASSESSMENT AND PROCEDURES

DfES guidance contains model assessment forms for risk assessment, which take up just two sides of A4. It is up to LEAs and schools whether they use our forms. Activity providers can, if they wish, encourage schools to use standard forms. The main point is to assess and manage the risks. Forms are useful for structuring and recording, but the doing is more important than the recording.

Additional information in response to points raised during oral evidence sessions is attached at Annex A.

ACADEMIES

Evaluation: The evaluation of the Academies programme is a five-year longitudinal study. The first annual report is due to be delivered in December. There are no plans to publish the findings at the end of the first year as these would be based on a very small number of schools over a very short timescale.

However, preliminary, indicative findings of the study are that "Academies do seem to have made a strong impact on the educational aspirations of large numbers of children from disadvantaged areas and their families." We also have provisional 5+ A*–C GCSE results for Academies which again show an overall increase to 30% (compared to 16% in the predecessor schools of the first wave Academies).

But the Academies policy is a long term strategy and we do not expect all Academies to be an immediate success. They are a radical solution to the most intractable problems of poor performance.

Outdoor education: Most of the outdoor education proposals from Academies are still in the very early stages, and as many of the Academies themselves are still in the planning stages, the information provided below could change. Most of the information refers to plans rather than outdoor education which is currently provided by Academies.

Bexley Business Academy

The Academy is planning to provide an outdoor learning area and have taken advice from the Department's "Growing Schools" programme. One of the guiding principles behind the approach is that it is sustainable. The Academy has been advised on sources of funding from the voluntary sector.

Grace Academy

Whitesmore school, the predecessor school for the Grace Academy which is due to open in September 2006 has an impressive market garden which is built into the vocational curriculum for KS4 pupils.

Macmillan College

At Macmillan CTC, which is due to open as an Academy in 2005, all pupils have a module of outdoor education as part of their core curriculum. The school works with Mobex which provides outdoor education activities, equipment and minibuses. Planning for this area of work is in the very early stages.

Academy of St Francis Assisi in Liverpool

The Academy, which is due to open in 2005, has a planned specialism of the Environment and Sustainability. Each Year 7 class will have its own garden and the produce will be used in the canteen or sold to the public. There are also plans to work with local conservationists to restore a local park.

The Waltham Forest Academy of Design

This Academy is in the early planning stages but has part of its vision that each student should embrace the richness of the world beyond the local community. Students will be encouraged to understand the land and learn through doing, in particular by growing their own food, preparing, cooking, and sharing it with their families and friends. There are also plans to convert some adjacent ground into a meadow for use by students and the local community.

WHAT IS THE EVIDENCE BASE SHOWING THAT LEARNING IN THE OUTDOORS IS VALUABLE?

In the last three years, the Department has initiated and part-funded several studies. This year, through the Growing Schools programme we are funding Action Research by NfER/King's College/CREE with teachers and outdoor providers and scoping further studies into Initial Teacher Training and practice in a sample of LEAs. The Department commissioned Ofsted to report on outdoor education, which was published in September. The Department is also funding a survey into residential experiences with the Duke of Edinburgh/Scouts Association.

The literature review of the research into using food, farming and the countryside as a context for learning (UK and abroad) was funded by Growing Schools in partnership with CA & FACE (published report available at www.dfes.gov.uk/research). Among the main findings, the study found current evidence highlights the potential of:

— school visits to farms—which offer a wide range of learning opportunities in the affective and cognitive domains;

— other out of school learning associated with fieldwork, after school programmes, camps, outdoor centres and supermarket visits.

The Department part-funded the Field Studies Council led literature review into outdoor learning which was published earlier this year. The study examined 150 pieces of research published in English between 1993 and 2003. The literature covered three main types of outdoor learning with primary and secondary pupils and undergraduates: fieldwork and outdoor visits; outdoor adventure education; school grounds/community projects. The study found strong evidence of the benefits of all three. The executive summary reports:

— substantial evidence to indicate that fieldwork, properly conceived, adequately planned, well taught and effectively followed up, offers learners opportunities to develop their knowledge and skills that add value to their everyday experiences in the classroom;

— substantial evidence of how outdoor and adventurous education can impact positively on attitudes, beliefs and self perception; and on their interpersonal and social skills;

— significant evidence that social development and greater community involvement can result from engagement in school grounds projects. Students develop more positive relationships with each other, with teachers and with the wider community.

The Growing Schools Action Research is due to report Spring 2005. The research has three strands:

Strand 1: The research team has undertaken in-depth qualitative investigations into the processes and impacts of outdoor learning activities in the three research contexts (school grounds and gardens, farms and city farms, field study/nature centres and parks). The aim is to carry out research with pupils, teachers and other educators both during and after outdoor learning activities in order to generate grounded understandings of outdoor learning across a range of age levels.

Strand 2: Involves a small group of teachers, field study centre staff and farm educators carrying out small-scale investigations in their own outdoor settings. With support and training from the research team, these have focused on: (a) trialling and evaluating teaching and/or evaluation strategies, or (b) exploring ways of planning outdoor experiences into schemes of work.

Strand 3: designed to explore individuals' and organisations' different perspectives on the benefits (academic, social or personal), planning, management and evaluation of purposeful and/or successful outdoor learning provision in relation to curriculum requirements, alongside other possible constraints and barriers.

The Ofsted report into outdoor education concentrates on the opportunities provided for students of age 9–16 years in outdoor education, linked to the National Curriculum in physical education (PE). Among the main findings, Ofsted report:

— outdoor education gives depth to the curriculum and makes an important contribution to student physical, personal and social education

The Department has commissioned the Duke of Edinburgh's Awards and the Scouts to carry out a map of Residential Experience opportunities for young people. It will help us to look at how residential opportunities can contribute to more young people taking advantage of extra curricular activities. The work is due to be completed by the end of December.

Annex A

Q101, Q179. LEAs and schools, by adding to DfES guidance, deter teachers?

We have had good feedback on our safety guidance from the education sector. Our guidance says upfront (page 1, para 2) that we do not intend it to replace LEA guidance where that already covers the same topics. We would be interested to hear first-hand from any teacher who has decided not to organise an outdoor activity because of LEAs and schools asking them to follow two lots of local safety guidance, and DfES guidance on top of that. So far we have only heard third-hand, that someone thinks they heard of someone else who might have felt deterred. Our first-hand evidence is that most LEAs tell us outdoor activity in their schools is stable or increasing.

Q103. Is there no need for schools to assess aspects of a centre which AALA have already safety-inspected?

DfES agrees. DfES wrote to all AALA licence-holders and every LEA in England in May 2004, to remind them that there is no need for schools to duplicate AALA safety inspections at AALA-inspected centres.

Q105. What about schools which banned playing conkers because they believed it was dangerous?

DfES is not aware of any school in England banning playing conkers for safety reasons. We read in the press of one school that was happy for children to play conkers, and gave them safety-goggles in case splinters went in their eyes. In response to press coverage of that isolated case, the HSE stated that wearing safety goggles while playing conkers is the sort of thing that gives sensible health and safety a bad name.

Q107, Q113. Is DfES aware of claims rising or falling in this area, litigated in court or settled out of court?

Published Government figures show that public liability claims overall fell by 16.7% last year (including both claims that went to court, and claims where the insurer settled without going to court), as mentioned by Lawrie Quinn MP during the debate on the Promotion of Volunteering Bill [*Hansard* col 1672–3, 16 July 2004]. We have not found any insurance company that separately records personal injury claims against schools, which in itself might suggest that claims against schools are not a significant proportion of claims overall.

Q109. Government has issued requirements that lead to a lack of insurers willing to insure school activities?

We would be surprised if the requirements of the Health and Safety at Work Act, or the recommendations of DfES guidance, in any way deterred insurers from insuring school activities. On the contrary they should, by reducing the likelihood of injuries, have a positive effect. If a school can demonstrate its good practice on safety, that should help it to find insurance on reasonable terms. The Government has recommended that the insurance industry should take full account of a school's safety practice when it costs the risk of insuring an educational activity, and is working with the industry to that end.

Q111, 179. How many accidents on different types of visit? When a pupil is injured where staff leading the activity had followed guidance from eg the employing authority, should that authority (and not the staff) be answerable?

In the last eight years, DfES is aware of 26 fatal accidents to pupils from England on educational activities, of which nine so far have led to prosecutions. Of those, four were overseas—hence our 2002 Guidance on LEA oversight and on adventure standards; and six involved water—hence our water margins guidance in 2003. Courts found that an employer in the case of four fatalities, and an employee in five, had neglected health and safety law or their duty of care. In cases where the court found that the employer was at fault and not the staff, the court did hold only the employer responsible, fining one LEA £30,000 plus £50,000 costs over two drownings, and another LEA £120,000 plus £11,000 costs over one drowning, and not penalising staff in either case.

Q173. Should outdoor centres provide generic risk assessments?

Centres inspected by AALA have done such assessments in order to pass their AALA safety inspection—schools can rely on this (see *Q103* above). School staff should still discuss the assessment with the centre: the centre knows the activity, but only the school knows its pupils. For school-led provision, generic risk assessments are discussed at paragraphs 17–36 of the Department's "Standards for LEAs in Overseeing Educational Visits" (2002). Generic assessments for activities regardless of venue are usually prepared by the LEA; we do recommend sharing these with others, to reduce duplication and spread good practice. Venue- or group-specific assessments were seen by our drafting group of outdoor experts as best carried out by the in-school EVC on the basis of knowledge of the group's needs in the venue. But there is nothing hard and fast about this. EVCs and outdoor education advisers can come to their own mutually helpful arrangements.

Q82. Continuing professional development

We do not have statistics on the volume of Continuing Professional Development (CPD) in outdoor learning. This is because the majority of CPD is carried out at school or LEA level.

Central to improvements in teaching and learning is excellent professional development for all teachers—with more emphasis on classroom observation, practice, training, coaching and mentoring. We are building up teachers' demand for high quality training and development, by linking participation in professional development with career progression.

There is no evidence of lack of opportunities. The Growing Schools web service regularly updates training and development opportunities available. For example, in October and November alone 44 are listed, ranging from Mountain Leader awards and managing coastal zones, through to bird identification, first aid and garden design. Many LEAS run their own courses for teachers as well.

We do know, however, that many more teachers than before are being trained in the practicalities of outdoor supervision. This results directly from the DfES establishment of the Educational Visits Co-ordinator or EVC programme. Training the trainer sessions were begun in 2001–02 at local authority level and the Department distributed £3.5 million to LEAs in England to help them send delegates. All LEAs are signed up to the programme and at least two local authorities in England already have an EVC in every one of their schools. The second phase training for teachers will soon begin.

The aim of the EVC programme is to ensure that school staff are competent—and therefore more confident and ready—to lead pupils off-site to the benefits of learning beyond the classroom. The EVC function is not a new idea—it formalises what exists in some degree in most schools. The programme encourages co-operation between schools and LEAs over such matters as visits-approval and monitoring. For the high-risk kind of exercise—where the overcoming of natural hazards is the whole educational objective—we continue to encourage those teachers who lead pupils and who are properly experienced and qualified.

At the same time we have recently renewed our commitment, by means of a revised Statutory Instrument, to the operation of the Adventure Activities Licensing Authority; this means that schools wishing to contract with a licensed provider—one inspected on the government's behalf and declared to be safe—can continue do so. Some 1,030 providers hold licences to provide outdoor activities to schools and youth-groups, a good sign of a booming market.

15 November 2004

Memorandum submitted by the National Union of Teachers

INTRODUCTION

1. The National Union of Teachers represents 240,000 teachers in England and Wales. The NUT has members from all sectors of the education system from nursery to post-16, including special education.

2. The National Union of Teachers is committed to a balanced, broadly based curriculum as an entitlement for all children and young people. Such an education must provide young people, not just with the ability to gain the qualifications they need to get a job or go on to the next stage of education, but with a foundation which they will continue to build upon and benefit from throughout their adult lives.

3. Educational visits is an area on which NUT members regularly seek advice from their Union. It is an issue about which they have many concerns, and rightly so. Any teacher who undertakes an educational visit takes on a heavy burden of responsibility. The NUT has its own guidelines on educational visits which are available from the NUT website at www.teachers.org.uk.

4. The NUT's submission to this inquiry will examine both the importance of education outside the classroom as part of the curriculum, as well as important conditions of service and health and safety issues for teachers. It will cover the following areas:

— the Educational Value of Fieldwork and Residential Trips;
— supporting creativity in the Curriculum;
— school sport;
— the "Growing Schools" Initiative;
— NUT policy on school visits;
— DfES Guidelines;
— staffing and supervision—general;
— staffing and supervision for visits including pupils with special needs;
— external assessment of provision;
— teacher workload;
— fear of accidents and possible litigation;
— role of the NUT safety representative; and
— costs and funding of education outside the classroom.

FIELDWORK AND RESIDENTIAL TRIPS

5. The NUT believes that it is important that young people experience activity-based fieldwork and residential trips. Nevertheless teachers face, day-to-day, the pressures of meeting the demands of the National Curriculum. The teaching of science and geography can be greatly enhanced, however, by undertaking work in the field. In particular to develop an enquiry-based approach to the subject. Such fieldwork can also help to reinforce cross-curricular themes in the National Curriculum, for example, some pupils' social and cultural development, or education for sustainable development.

6. Her Majesty Inspectors (HMI) and additional inspectors (AI) from the Office of Standards in Education (Ofsted) were commissioned by the DfES to undertake an evaluation of the personal aspects of outdoor education, with specific focus on the work of outdoor education centres ("Outdoor Education—Aspects of Good Practice", September 2004). The NUT supports the findings of the report, which found that students generally made good progress in outdoor education both at school and at outdoor centres, because they developed their physical skills in new and challenging situations as well as exercising important cross-curricular skills such as teamwork and leadership.

7. The report highlighted the fact that outdoor activities and residential trips were particularly helpful for the least able students who had become disaffected due mainly to an academically bound curriculum:

"By the end of the week, the students had made considerable progress. For example, their greater confidence and team spirit had an unexpectedly positive impact at the school". (Paragraph 36)

8. Members have also expressed a concern that there is a bureaucratic burden associated with co-ordinating field trips and outdoor school activities which could be a barrier to taking such projects forward.

9. The NUT recognises the importance of outdoor education experiences as giving greater depth to the school curriculum as well as contributing to the development of students' personalised social development. NUT members have reported that students' participation in a range of activities enables them to develop cross-curricular skills, including the ability to work independently, to form social relationships, to take on new challenges and to focus on aspects of personal development and citizenship. The wider skills that young people acquire when taking part in schools visits is beneficial to them in all areas of the curriculum.

10. A review, "Research on Outdoor Education" (March 2004), highlighted the fact that students taking residential fieldwork developed the wider skills of co-operation, leadership, perseverance, reliability and self-motivation.

SUPPORTING CREATIVITY IN THE CURRICULUM

11. The National Union of Teachers believes that a creative environment is an essential component of learning—an environment where schools and teachers feel able to innovate, to teach creatively, to be creative in seeking solutions which work, in terms for example, of curriculum design, classroom organisation or meeting the needs of specific groups of children.

12. One of the main barriers to developing creativity in the curriculum, however, is an overemphasis on testing and on over-assessment, which leaves little time for wider creative activities. This narrows the curriculum by closing down opportunities for students to experience drama, music, theatre, dance, artists in residence, etc. Specific resources in terms of time and teachers therefore need to be invested in order to give students the opportunity of visiting theatres and art galleries during the school day.

13. The NUT believes that the issue of integrating academic and vocational elements, such as work experience and life skills, should be an essential part of the 14–19 curriculum. Initiatives for work-related learning, involving the co-ordination of schools, colleges and workplaces should be available to all students. Such opportunities will provide progression in the 14–19 curriculum.

14. The NUT welcomes the six objectives set out by the Department for Culture, Media and Sport. They are set out below.

— all public libraries should have internet access by the end of 2002;

— at least 12 Creative Partnerships should be introduced by March 2004, targeted at deprived areas, ensuring that every school child in the Partnership has access to an innovative programme of cultural and creative opportunities;

— the average time spent on sport and physical activity by those aged five to 16 should be raised, significantly, year on year;

— the numbers of children attending museums and galleries should increase by a third by 2004;

— the number of people experiencing the arts should be increased by 500,000 in 2004.

15. Creative Partnerships have been developed to provide a template for schools and cultural organisations, to enable every pupil to have a chance to work with creative professionals and organisations to develop creative skills, for example, to:

— dance, sing, learn a musical instrument, act, paint, sculpt, make crafts, design and create television, radio and internet content, write scripts, stage manage, choreograph, direct and produce, put on a performance, visit theatres and galleries, and develop understanding and critical appreciations through regular experiences.

16. Creative Partnerships encompass a broad range of creative and cultural activities that include art galleries, theatres, museums, cinemas, art centres, libraries, historic buildings, dance studios, orchestras, and recording studios. The organisations involved are determined by local consultation and differ in each partnership area. They give arts and cultural organisations the opportunity to develop sustainable work with schools in their local region. In any newly appointed region, creative directors are responsible for brokering the link between the schools and artists. Schools are working with architects, web and fashion designers, filmmakers and DJs as well as musicians, actors and visual artists.

17. The NUT believes that Creative Partnerships should be rolled out nationally because they offer children and teachers a range of enhanced and sustained opportunities customised to their needs in order that they can work directly with, and experience the work of artists, and of culture and creative organisations. These opportunities will build on and enrich the entitlement delivered by the National Curriculum and out-of-school activities.

18. The NUT welcomes also the acknowledgement by the Government that museums and galleries can make a valuable contribution to the social and cultural identity of the nation through education.

19. In 1999, a £500,000 DCMS/Resource Museums Education Challenge Fund was launched by the Museums and Galleries Commission. Channelled through the area Arts Councils, this spend has contributed to funding of 400 collaborative projects between schools and museums all over England. One of the key findings of the evaluation of these projects was that access to collections could bring history to life and encourage learning in other subject areas as well as helping children to build confidence and develop skills. Using museum objects of teaching seems, from the evidence, to really switch children on to learning.

20. The NUT has recognised consistently the importance of wider activities other than those which contribute to formal qualifications. That the 14–19 Working Group is now proposing to integrate "wider activities" into the 14–19 curriculum is a positive step forward.

21. The NUT supports and endorses the views of the National Advisory Committee in Creativity and Cultural Education in February 1998. The Committee, headed by Professor Ken Robinson of Warwick University, highlighted the need to give children the chance to express themselves in schools. The report emphasised that creative and cultural education were not new subjects in the curriculum, they were general functions of education. Promoting them effectively, therefore, called for a systematic strategy that addressed the school curriculum, teaching methods, assessment, inspection, how schools connect with other people, resourcing issues and the training and development of teachers and others. The Committee's recommendations emphasised the importance of creative and cultural education being explicitly recognised and provided for in schools' policies on the whole curriculum.

PE and School Sport

22. Physical education and school sport have an important place in this curriculum. The NUT supports a guaranteed entitlement to all pupils to at least 90 minutes of physical activity per week *within timetabled curriculum time*. This differs with, but is not necessarily in conflict with, the Government's own aspiration that there should be a minimum of two hours PE and school sport (PESS) a week, since the Government's target relates to extra curricular activities also. The NUT believes that only when physical education and school sport are timetabled during the normal school day can they be truly defined as an entitlement for all young people.

23. The NUT was one of the signatories of the *Charter for School Sport* published by the Central Council for Physical Recreation in 2000. Among the recommendations were that all teachers with a responsibility for teaching PESS should receive appropriate training (which might include areas such as conducting appropriate risk assessments as well as subject and pedagogical expertise), with appropriate funding made available for professional development.

24. The Charter's recommendations also included a focus on swimming. Ofsted has identified a small minority of schools where children in Key Stages 1 and 2 showed "a limited knowledge of water safety". It is vital that schools are supported in ensuring that children meet the National Curriculum requirements in swimming by the age of 11. Currently, they are hampered by transport costs and pool closures in particular.

25. A further recommendation was the importance of recognising all the contributions made by teachers to school sport as professional work.

Growing Schools

26. The NUT also welcomes initiatives such as "Growing Schools" which began in September 2001 to try and develop young people's understanding of the interdependence between urban and rural environments, along with learning about the countryside, wildlife and the people it sustains. Barriers identified to taking this initiative forward were a lack of funding, health and safety issues connected with working outside the classroom, a lack of training and confidence among teachers and little time to plan to creative outdoor lessons in place of standard classroom learning. Projects were set up to provide a sample of best practice, with some schools focusing on horticulture within their school grounds, enabling pupils to study a community allotment with local groups or established links with local commercial and city farms.

NUT Policy on School Visits

27. The NUT has always given the highest priority to the health and safety of teachers and pupils. We also recognise the enormous value to pupils of education beyond the classroom. The NUT does not advise members to refuse to be involved in school visits. Most visits are, however, voluntary and teachers who are already stressed by a heavy workload would be advised not to take on the additional burden of organising a school trip.

28. Teachers who are willing to organise school trips must be given the maximum support from their employer in terms of up-to-date procedures to follow, training and, of course, sufficient time to plan the visit.

DfES Guidelines

29. In 1998, the DfES published "Educational Visits: A Good Practice Guide". This was followed in late 2001/early 2002 by three supplementary documents covering specific aspects of organising and supervising school journeys. The NUT was consulted on the content of these guidance documents and is broadly supportive of them. There are, however, a few areas where we believe the guidance could be improved. One such area is that of staffing ratios.

Staffing and Supervision—General

30. The DfES recommends the following staffing ratios as a general guide for visits to local historical sites and museums or for local walks:

— one adult for every 6 pupils in school years 1–3 (under 5s reception classes should have a higher ratio);

— one adult for every 10–15 pupils in school years 4–6; and

— one adult for every 15–20 pupils in school year 7 onwards.

31. The DfES recognises that higher ratios may be appropriate in particular cases, such as for higher risk activities, for particular groups of pupils or for all trips abroad. The DfES also prescribes higher ratios for swimming activities.

32. The NUT's advice on this issue goes further:

— the DfES ratios should be regarded as the minimum appropriate staffing ratios for school journeys;

— these ratios should preferably be interpreted as referring to the number of staff needed to supervise the party. Voluntary helpers may be involved in assisting teachers with the organisation and supervision of visits but teachers will retain primary responsibility for supervising the party at all times;

— a minimum of two teachers should be involved in every school journey, regardless of how many other adults are helping. Given the possibility of members of the group needing to be taken home or back to school or to hospital, at least two teachers are needed in order that one teacher may remain in charge where another is called away;

— with a mixed party it is obviously desirable that there should be teachers of each sex accompanying the group;

— supervision arrangements for swimming activities should also include provision for supervision by qualified lifesavers;

— at least one member of staff should be a qualified first aider and aware of the special medical needs of any member of the party;

— newly qualified teachers should not lead school parties in their first year of teaching.

Staffing and Supervision for Visits Including Pupils with Special Needs

33. The NUT is concerned that there is insufficient guidance available for teachers who take pupils with special needs on educational visits. The tragic death of a pupil at Hay Lane Special School in the London Borough of Brent served to highlight this lack of guidance. Following this tragic incident the NUT recognised that its own guidance needed strengthening. Our guidance document now includes, at Appendix 1, factors to be considered when assessing staffing levels for an educational visit. We would urge the Education and Skills Select Committee to put pressure on the DfES to extend its own guidelines to cover this area more fully. The lack of such guidance constitutes, in our view, one of the "barriers to the expansion and development of out-of-classroom learning" which the Select Committee wishes to examine.

External Assessment of Provision

34. Since the introduction of the Adventure Activities Licensing Regulations 1996, which the NUT was instrumental in bringing about through its support of David Jamieson's Private Members' Bill, the NUT has remained concerned that the regulations do not cover schools offering activities to their own pupils. Recent tragedies demonstrate that it is often these activities which are particularly hazardous. Bringing schools within the scope of the regulations would ensure that schools only use staff with the training experience, qualifications and personal qualities to enable them to assess risks and institute the necessary safety precautions.

TEACHER WORKLOAD

35. Teachers should also have the benefit of a reasonable "work/life" balance. If teachers are already pressured and stressed by a heavy workload the further pressures of organising and supervising school visits may be the cause of unacceptable safety lapses. Teachers who do not choose to take on these burdens are entitled to decline to be involved in voluntary visits and will be supported by the NUT in doing so. The NUT will also support teachers who have a responsibility for curriculum based visits in demands for the highest safety standards and for acknowledgement of the workload involved.

36. Some teachers have also expressed a concern that there is a bureaucratic burden associated with co-ordinating fieldtrips and outdoor school activities which could be a barrier in taking such projects forward.

FEAR OF ACCIDENTS AND POSSIBLE LITIGATION

37. Accidents and litigation are undoubtedly foremost in teachers' minds when organising school visits.

38. Teachers involved in school visits must be fully aware of the standards of care demanded of them by the law. These form an objective standard of what can reasonably be expected from teachers generally, applying skill and awareness of children's problems, needs and susceptibilities. The law expects that a teacher will do that which a parent with care and concern for the safety and welfare of his or her own child would do, bearing in mind that being responsible for up to 20 pupils can be very different from looking after a family. The legal duty of care expected of an individual teacher is, therefore, that which a caring teaching profession would in any case expect of itself.

39. This means in practice that a teacher must:

— ensure supervision of the pupils throughout the journey or visit according to professional standards and common sense; and

— take reasonable steps to avoid exposing pupils to dangers which are foreseeable and beyond those with which the particular pupils can reasonably be expected to cope.

40. This does not imply constant 24 hour direct supervision. The need for direct supervision has to be judged by reference to the risks involved in activities being undertaken.

41. It is important for teachers to realise that the mere fact that an accident has taken place does not mean that they are automatically negligent. It is also important for society in general to accept the concept of a genuine accident.

42. If teachers are properly supported by their school and LEA, however, incidents and resulting claims of negligence are less likely to occur.

ROLE OF THE UNION SAFETY REPRESENTATIVES

43. One of the best ways of ensuring high health and safety standards in schools, including out-of-school activities, is for employers to support the valuable work of trade union appointed safety representatives. Such safety representatives do not only undertake inspections of the premises, they inspect and comment on policies and procedures, including policies on educational visits. They also investigate complaints by employees, make representations to the employer and examine the causes of accidents and near misses at the workplace.

44. Schools with active union safety representatives, whose work is supported by management, are likely to have a better safety culture which will extend into education beyond the classroom. The NUT would, therefore, urge the Education and Skills Select Committee to recommend that the Government actively promotes their valuable contribution to health and safety in schools.

COST AND FUNDING OF EDUCATION OUTSIDE THE CLASSROOM

45. The NUT shares the concern raised by Ofsted that for many schools and pupils, the opportunities to participate in activities outside the classroom are perceived as prohibitively expensive. The report *Outdoor Education—Aspects of Good Practice* published in September 2004 states:

> Often, the extra-curricular nature of the activity, its costs or limits on the numbers that can be taken, lead to a "first come, first served" basis for selection. This means that even in those schools that do want to promote outdoor education, many students who would like to take part are not able to participate. (paragraph 40)

If insurance premiums continue to rise as a result of the real or perceived fear of litigation, then outdoor education centres will be less likely to be able to subsidise the cost of places and schools will be even more reluctant to participate in activities outside the classroom. Similarly there is a danger that rising insurance premiums could have a detrimental impact on work placements, 14–19 vocational education and the extended use of school buildings. The cost effectiveness of school visits is likely to be a particular issue for small rural primary and secondary schools who may also be faced with increased transport costs.

CONCLUSION

46. The National Union of Teachers has maintained consistently that young people should have an entitlement to important experiential areas across a range of "disciplines", including arts, humanities, languages and technology. Such an approach would have been more preferable to simply increasing the numbers of subjects which young people choose not to continue to study post-14. The National Advisory Committee on Creative and Cultural Education was emphatic that creative and cultural education is being poorly served by the National Curriculum:

> "Little will change without a new balance in the structure and hierarchy of the National Curriculum that gives a genuine parity to English, mathematics, the sciences, arts and humanities, technological education and physical education".

47. The NUT is equally concerned that the entitlement of young people to a creative curriculum should be accompanied by the highest possible health and safety standards and levels of support for teachers.

Memorandum submitted by the Secondary Heads Association

1. The Secondary Heads Association represents over 11,000 members of leadership teams in maintained and independent schools and colleges throughout the UK. This is an area that is of great interest to many of our members both in relation to the operation of their own schools and colleges and out of their concern for the education system as a whole.

EDUCATION OUTSIDE THE CLASSROOM

2. Educational trips and visits may be more or less extended, and require planning long in advance or might ideally be close to *ad hoc* in response to an event or a point raised by a learner. Visits to a law court, a local firm, a museum, or a local cultural event are all examples of such visits that have real value. Students involved in virtually all types of course and stages of education can benefit from such visits. These are generally half or full day visits that do not require overnight stays.

3. Fieldwork is required for some examination courses and can add an important dimension to many others. Geography and biology use fieldwork most commonly, but other subjects may do so to good effect. These experiences may be in the locality, the best examples often involve an extended stay in some otherwise unfamiliar area. The experience of being away in a group is itself valuable.

4. Foreign exchanges clearly have the value of introducing young people to other cultures and teaching them something of how to travel abroad. Likewise, inviting a "foreigner" into the home is not an experience a great many young people would otherwise have, and from which they and their families benefit. This can lead to important social learning.

5. Sport will generally take place outside the classroom, though not necessarily outside the building. The value of sport in encouraging teamwork, and its direct benefit to the participant in terms of fitness and wellbeing are well rehearsed. Familiarising young people with sports that they can continue in adult life and developing good habits of exercise, is important to their future health.

6. Outdoor education in the sense of fell-walking, orienteering, climbing, canoeing etc, has many of the virtues of sport, and teaches self-reliance and useful skills.

7. The Duke of Edinburgh Award scheme has elements of outdoor education and elements of community service, both of which need to take place outside the classroom.

8. Community service has often to take place away from school, it has obvious benefits to the young people engaged in it as well as via the service they provide. The young people learn the value of service, and as many opportunities involve interacting with others they may learn greater respect for the elderly, the young, the disadvantaged etc.

9. Work experience is a requirement for year ten pupils in school and for many students enrolled in vocational courses. It can mean an afternoon a week, a block of two weeks close to home, or for older students an extended stay away from home.

WHY IT IS OF VALUE

10. Direct experience is needed for certain aspects of personal development. Children can be challenged via such experiences to behave in a more adult way, gaining useful experience and setting habits of mind.

11. Education outside the classroom has direct benefits in teaching and learning in providing pupils with experiences more vivid and memorable than even the best teacher can arrange in the classroom setting. Just a change of routine marks out the experience as special and helps to fix it in mind.

12. Teachers who have taken groups on residential visits of any kind almost always report an improvement in relationships between the young people, and between them and their teachers. Working well together is a critically important skill in its own right as well as improving children's performance in their studies.

13. Getting outside the classroom can be important to enable children to understand the wider society in which they live. As such it is a key preparation for citizenship and work.

14. At a time when there is widespread concern over obese children, opportunities to engage them in enjoyable exercise are of great value. Especially if that engagement will be (in at least some cases) carried forward into habits of exercise.

RISK

15. The examples mentioned above carry more or less risk. None are risk-free, no human activity can be. Most activities carry risks that would not be encountered in the classroom: travel, accident related to the activity, exposure to less well vetted adults, other children creating danger from their carelessness or inexperience, the "message" being less well controlled than in the classroom.

16. Such risks need to be carefully considered and managed, but if they are, they are generally felt to be risks worth taking for the benefits of the experiences gained.

17. There is also a value of risk in itself. Children grow up protected, rightly so and increasingly so, but as they enter adulthood they have to learn to manage risks—and the only way to do that is to take some.

A CULTURAL TREND

18. It is widely thought that we are living in an increasingly litigious culture. Citizens are tending to greater dependence, and to lesser acceptance of their own responsibilities. So that if something goes wrong they look for someone to do something about it, and perhaps look for someone to blame. This has certainly been noticeable in the education world, with much more challenge and many more court cases than would have been the case in an earlier generation.

19. It is right of course that schools, colleges, teachers and education leaders should take care of young people. Reasonable steps should always be taken to protect children, and thought should always be given to keeping risk to a reasonable level.

20. Not everyone agrees about what is reasonable though, and there is a need for a new consensus. With the benefit of hindsight an injured person or the parents of an injured child, will often take a different line from that which they would have taken before the event. This, the cultural change mentioned above, and in some cases greed, have all contributed to an increase in legal action against schools, colleges and individuals.

21. The desire to attribute blame has also in some cases led to schools or individuals being hounded by the press and media. Some of these cases have been very widely reported and have caused alarm amongst teachers and school leaders.

22. Some official bodies, in an excess of zeal, have taken a similar line and persecuted individuals for faults that were either non-existent or those of a system rather than an individual.

THE REAL DANGER

23. These valuable activities are in decline because the governments, both national and local, LEAs, governors, school leaders, and teachers are all tending to play safe. Despite all precautions accidents will continue to happen, and other things will continue to go wrong, but naturally no one wants to be the one held responsible for them. So there is buck-passing up and down the chain and a marked tendency always to favour the most restrictive "safest" option.

24. The bureaucracy is generally not helpful. Guidelines issued may be unworkable in practice, leaving those who wrote them safe, but those closer to the young people faced with a choice of giving up on a valuable activity or taking a risk to their own career.

25. At present there is real uncertainty about what qualifications a teacher should have to drive a minibus. One interpretation is that teachers should have a licence to drive a passenger-carrying vehicle. Few do, so that much of the activity mentioned above would cease—yet there is no reason to suppose that the accidents that have taken place when teachers have been driving minibuses are attributable to their lack of driving skills, still less to the lack of such a licence.

CONCLUSION

26. All this has already led to a reduction in education outside the classroom, and the danger is that it will decline still further.

27. The effect is damaging to all children by denying them opportunities for growth, and opportunities to learn important skills, facts, and habits.

28. Schools and colleges are happy to take responsibility for their actions, and do not expect immunity. But a lot that is of real value will be lost if the balance is not redressed so that individual teachers, their leaders and their institutions can make reasonable arrangements for education outside the classroom with confidence.

29. Despite every obstacle, and although it has reduced, much very good work continues in schools and colleges.

October 2004

Memorandum submitted by the National Association of Head Teachers

INTRODUCTION

The National Association of Head Teachers welcomes the opportunity to present evidence to the Committee on this important matter. Staff, pupils, parents—indeed the whole school community can benefit from increased opportunity for learning that such activities can supply. However, there needs to be an awareness of the implications for the school that the organising and running of out-of-school activities can have.

COSTS AND FUNDING OF OUTDOOR ACTIVITIES

The increased demands on school budgets means that priorities for allocation are contentious and budget allocation hard-won. Any activity organised by the school must be able to demonstrate a favourable cost-benefit analysis. This applies to any out-of-school activity as much as in-school curriculum enrichment opportunities. There is no doubt that out-of-school activities can incur substantial costs in time, financial and human resources. Schools need to budget carefully for these and consider the "value for money" aspect.

Just to arrange a one-off, off-site visit for a day has implications for transport costs, staff cover costs, preparation time and debrief time. A residential visit has the potential to increase these costs exponentially and also residential costs must be incorporated. There is no opportunity for schools to recoup these costs other than through voluntary contributions from parents. Needless to say, these may or may not be forthcoming! Where they are not forthcoming, the school can only resort to placing the whole trip in jeopardy.

Staffing costs for out-of-school visits can vary hugely, but it is fair to say that there is always an expense over and above that normally incurred if the pupils were to remain in the classroom. In ensuring that the degree of extra risk inevitably associated with off-site visits is kept within acceptable limits, the adult : pupil ratio is generally higher. Where pupils with special needs are involved, this can also lead to additional costs to cater for the pupils' needs. All of these costs have to be met from the school budget and/or voluntary contributions. This can produce an unacceptable drain on already stretched budgets.

THE PLACE OF OUTDOOR LEARNING WITHIN THE CURRICULUM

There is an expectation that learning objectives will be specified for any educational provision: for education outside the classroom the imperative is to specify clearly what is to be learnt, and how, and to indicate why such learning needs to happen outside of the classroom environment. The value of such activities in terms of character-forming exercises, team-building, development of leadership qualities cannot be overestimated. However, consideration of such benefits must also be weighed against the costs and the fact that, in general, they not central to the school's curriculum and learning objectives.

Examples of activities that have historically formed part of the off-site provision are:
— science and geography field trips;
— PE/games activities off-site, like orienteering, horse-riding etc;
— historical activities, such as museum visits;
— visits to places of worship as part of religious education;
— theatre trips;
— visits abroad, to support modern foreign languages;

— exhibitions, art and music events.

In general, many of these experiences could not be replicated adequately in classrooms. They should be considered as essential off-site activities and should be funded as such.

External Assessment of Provision

The adequacy and quality of specialist outdoor provision is the responsibility of the employer—the LEA for community and voluntary schools, the governing body for foundation and voluntary aided schools. Obtaining information about providers is not always straightforward but is necessary. Some routes are reasonably easy, such as those providers that are covered by the Adventure Activities Licensing Scheme. Others are less so, though equally important.

External accreditation of providers should be more widespread. Staff involved in organising off-site activities should be expected to undertake appropriate training.

Organisation and Integration within Existing School Structures

Planning for even the most straightforward of off-site visits can be extensive. If the off-site visit starts and/or finishes outside the normal times of the school day, for example, this may mean arrangements for delivery and collection of pupils, checking on availability of parents/carers to meet the timings, additional opening hours of the school grounds. Work experience placements can provide their own challenges.

Where not all children from a particular class participates in an activity, this can add pressure to the resources of the school. Any children left on the premises must be catered for. This can happen on a regular basis for sporting activities off-site, for example, but is not confined to such activities.

Though the setting may be different, the management, control and authority issues with regard to the pupils still remain the same as on-site. In some cases, they become more acute. Sufficient staff must be present, emergency procedures should be in place and well communicated to all participants, medical needs must be catered for, playtime must be arranged etc. Managing these out of the pupils' usual environment can present additional challenges.

Qualification and Motivation of Teachers and the Effect on Teacher Workload

Training is available for leaders of off-site activities, for example, OCR's training course, "Off-site Safety Management Scheme" is aimed at those who organise off-site visits of any nature and covers all aspects of planning, including risk assessments, pre-planning etc. Any staff members organising and planning off-site visits should be expected to undertake such training, as this will better prepare them for the task they are undertaking.

Although staff are generally motivated to plan and undertake off-site visits, it is true to say that this is not as widespread as it was. Teachers undoubtedly have concerns about the possibility of litigation. These may be unfounded but they are very real. The idea that, if an accident occurs, then someone must be to blame and that person, in the eyes of the parents, must be the teacher, does nothing to assist with willingness to organise off-site visits. Lack of clarity with regard to what can be expected in terms of right to participate for children with special educational needs can also cloud the issue.

Workload issues must be taken into consideration when looking at the additional burden put on all staff. Planning and organisation is in addition to the normal work undertaken by staff. Where an educational visit is arranged over an extended period, for example, staff may be considered to be "on duty" for the whole period, day and night, as they continue to be responsible for the pupils in their care. Organising off-site visits is potentially a great drain on the staff concerned.

In the context of workload issues, it is not unreasonable to mention work experience. The organisation, monitoring, assessment, on-site visits to pupils, can reach nightmare proportions, and not always to great effect. The value of such placements should be balanced against the huge effort required to set these up.

The Fear of Accidents and the Possibility of Litigation

There is no doubt that there is ever-present concern with regard to both accidents and the possible litigation that may arise. It is also true that the compensation culture mentality does nothing to encourage schools to undertake the additional workload that off-site visits require. Although the vast majority of activities take place successfully and without incident, the tiny minority where problems occur are reported so widely that the effect is greatly skewed.

Training of staff will help to minimise the likelihood of things going wrong. Some form of protective insurance would assist in reassuring understandably nervous staff that they will not be made the scapegoat for any potential untoward incident. It might also be helpful if a positive publicity campaign were to be mounted to demonstrate the value of education outside the classroom and also how successful and safe almost all activities can be. The current advice document, *Health and Safety of Pupils on Educational Visits*, is seen as very helpful and should be commended to all those involved with the planning and running of school visits.

How Provision in the UK Compares with that of Other Countries

We have no comment to make in this area.

Conclusion

We would not wish to see education outside the classroom diminish. Its value both in supporting the curriculum and in character development is immense. However, unless adequate training, sufficient funding and explicit protection/insurance can be identified, it seems unlikely that schools will be able to maintain the current provision, let alone increase it. An accreditation scheme for specialist providers should be more widespread.

October 2004

Memorandum submitted by the NASUWT

1. NASUWT is the largest union representing teachers and headteachers in all sectors of education throughout the United Kingdom. The Union is pleased to have the opportunity to submit evidence to inform the Education and Skills Select Committee Inquiry. This submission draws upon the extensive knowledge the Union has gained from feedback from members undertaking these activities outside the classroom and from the representational casework in which the Union has been involved.

2. The submission focuses in particular on educational visits, including academic fieldwork but also makes reference to the other activities highlighted within the Committee's terms of reference.

3. NASUWT recognises that education outside the classroom can provide valuable educational experience and curriculum enrichment, providing it is planned, properly resourced, linked to the curriculum and has clearly identified intended learning outcomes. However, NASUWT is not convinced that that is the basis on which all such activities are planned and there are a number of issues of concern which the NASUWT would like to draw to the attention of the Committee.

Educational Visits

4. The NASUWT's position on teachers accompanying educational visits has been well publicised. The Union strongly advises members not to participate. This advice is rooted in extensive experience of supporting members who have been involved in high profile incidents which have resulted in serious injury or death of teachers and pupils. A copy of the NASUWT advice is attached to this submission. It details the Union's position but also provides information for those teachers who may, despite advice, choose to accompany a visit.

5. The concerns of the NASUWT are as follows:
— the possibility of litigation;
— vulnerability of staff accompanying visits to false and malicious allegations;
— the workload of teachers;
— the lack of consistency of the role of LEAs in planning, monitoring validating and risk assessing activities; and
— the quality of staff training.

The Possibility of Litigation

6. Society is increasingly litigious and no longer appears to accept the concept of a genuine accident. It also fails either to understand that perfect judgement, total attentiveness and faultless foresight are beyond normal human capacity or to accept that in the best ordered of activities things will occasionally go wrong. Schools, therefore, find themselves increasingly vulnerable to the growing compensation culture.

7. Claims against schools are not, of course, confined to incidents which occur on educational visits but there is an increased risk involved in activities off-site.

8. NASUWT has witnessed, at first hand, the personal and professional devastation experienced by teachers who have volunteered to conduct an educational visit, have followed local and national guidelines and then, following an accident during the visit, have faced months of internal and external investigation as a result of being cited in legal action instigated by parents or carers.

9. To add to their trauma teachers in this position find that their employer will decline to support them citing "conflict of interest" between the employee and the pupil.

THE VULNERABILITY OF TEACHERS TO FALSE AND MALICIOUS ALLEGATIONS

10. NASUWT has for a number of years been campaigning for recognition that teachers are vulnerable to false, malicious or exaggerated allegations by pupils. Vulnerability is increased when teachers are away from the school environment, particularly when they are in residential situations. A number of NASUWT members accompanying residential visits have been victims of false allegations of abuse.

THE WORKLOAD OF TEACHERS

11. The National Agreement, "Raising Standards and Tackling Workload", has introduced contractual changes which are the much needed drivers for remodelling of the school workforce to reduce teacher workload and to free teachers to focus on teaching and learning. The Agreement provides for enhanced roles for support staff, recognising the valuable contribution they can make in supporting teaching and learning.

12. The remodelling agenda is bringing about a number of changes in relation educational visits and other types of education outside the classroom. The traditional assumptions that only teachers can organise and supervise these activities are being abandoned. There are now numerous examples of appropriately qualified support staff organising and co-ordinating and, in some cases, supervising these activities. This has removed from teachers many of the time consuming administrative tasks often associated with these activities.

13. Unfortunately there are still too many schools who have not explored the full potential of remodelling and much of the existing guidance produced by the DfES and LEAs still places the responsibility for all aspects of these activities on teachers.

14. Despite the success of the remodelling agenda in alleviating the workload burdens on teachers, NASUWT believes that the best solution for schools is to use professional providers of educational visits if such activities are thought to be essential in meeting the school's curriculum objectives.

15. As a result of the National Agreement on Raising Standards and Tackling Workload the teacher's contract was changed in September 2003 to ensure that they were no longer required to be involved in any administrative and clerical task which did not require the professional skills and judgement of a qualified teacher. The administration of work experience was one of the examples specifically cited in the Annex to the School Teachers' Pay and Conditions Document as a task which could be transferred to appropriately qualified and trained support staff. There is evidence that an increasing number of schools are now doing this.

16. Whether teachers or support staff undertake this role, there is no doubt that the provision of high quality work experience places considerable burdens upon schools.

17. Time is needed to source appropriate placements, make site visits both before and during the placement and conduct risk assessments. Members have raised with NASUWT the problems of finding appropriate placements and their concern about the expectation that they will conduct the necessary risk assessments.

18. It is also important to recognise that remodelling and transferring responsibilities to support staff does not address the issues and difficulties NASUWT has identified elsewhere in this submission as the risks for support staff would be exactly the same as for teachers.

THE ROLE OF LEAs

19. NASUWT believes that there is inconsistency in the way in which LEAs support schools with regard to educational visits. The National Outdoor Education Advisers' Panel has recognised this and has made consistency of practice a key aim over the next two years.

20. The DfES does advise schools and LEAs to consider the educational value of any visit which is organised. Despite this there are still significant numbers of schools which conduct visits to venues of dubious educational value and which bear little relationship if any with the school curriculum.

21. There also appears to be an increasing tendency for some schools to consider distant, exotic locations for visits increasing cost, risk and difficulty.

22. NASUWT believes there should be clear educational justification in every visit and a relationship to the school curriculum. However, there is a tendency to define educational benefit so widely that any activities, even visits to fun fairs can come within the definition. NASUWT believes that the question schools and LEAs should pose is not: "Can the pupil gain *any* benefit from this activity?" "Rather, "Is this an activity

the school should be organising for this pupil rather than it being provided by a parent, voluntary organisation or specialist centre?" A visit to a fun fair is of course interesting and enjoyable for most children but the question is not whether these activities are "educational" in the broadest sense but whether it should be schools and teachers who take the responsibility for organising and supervising them.

23. NASUWT welcomes the DfES "Standards for LEAs in Overseeing Educational Visits" and believes that all maintained schools in an LEA area should be subject to these standards and not just those for whom the LEA is the employing authority. The DfES supplement to the Standards says that *the LEA will need to monitor and where necessary challenge the educational objectives that schools have stated for a visit.* NASUWT has no evidence to demonstrate that this responsibility is being carried out with any rigour.

24. NASUWT has argued consistently for LEAs to identify and conduct generic risk assessments of sites and venues which have a clear educational benefit and to recommend these to schools. This would address the problem of teachers, often untrained, feeling obliged to conduct their own risk assessments.

25. NASUWT has provided specific advice to its members on the particular risks involved in accompanying pupils with disabilities on educational visits. The health, safety and welfare of these and all other pupils and staff should be paramount. Proper risk assessments by appropriately trained staff should be undertaken prior to the activity to identify what reasonable adjustments may be required for particular pupils, including whether additional staff above the recommended ratios are needed.

THE QUALITY OF STAFF TRAINING

26. The main "training" for staff appears to be "on-task training" as they organise and supervise these activities. There is training available for educational visit co-ordinators but there is no requirement for this to be undertaken before an activity is organised. Given the potential risks to all those involved, the lack of attention to this important issue is of serious concern.

WORK IN PROGRESS TO ADDRESS THE CONCERNS

27. The Government is very keen to ensure that all pupils have the opportunity to have a residential experience and participate in activities which enrich and enhance curriculum provision. The Government has also recognised the validity of the NASUWT's concerns. At the NASUWT's Annual Conference in April 2004 the Secretary of State for Education and Skills, Charles Clarke, gave a commitment to work with the Union to address these.

28. Since that time NASUWT has engaged in discussions with senior DfES Officials and the following are currently under consideration:

— strategies to ensure that LEAs undertake more consistent monitoring of activities and take seriously the role of outdoor education advisers. The role of Ofsted is being considered in this context;

— the production of a checklist to assess the educational value of visits and discourage more dubious outings;

— the review of all DfES guidance to take account of workforce remodelling, particularly highlighting the role support staff can play in co-ordinating visits;

— more emphasis on the generic assessments already recommended by the DfES in its "Standards for LEAs in overseeing educational visits";

— further guidance from the DfES on the indemnification of staff who accompany visits and the on the role of LEAs in providing legal support for employees.

29. With regard to the vulnerability of teachers to false and malicious allegations, in response to the NASUWT Campaign the DfES has engaged in discussions with the Union to develop proposals to which will seek to address the concerns. The proposals will be published for consultation in the next few weeks.

COSTS AND FUNDING OF OUTDOOR ACTIVITIES

30. NASUWT believes that a strong case can be made for the review of the charging policies of schools in relation to these activities. Many are now funded by parents being asked to make a "voluntary" contribution. Many activities are costly, particularly the residential activities in outdoor pursuits centres or abroad.

31. Parents are advised that their contribution is voluntary but can be told in the information about the visit that failure to contribute may mean that it cannot proceed. This places unacceptable pressure on parents, particularly those from low income families, who may already be feeling concerned that they are not be able to afford to pay for their own child to go and then face the additional burden of responsibility for whether other children are able to participate.

32. Ofsted's recent report on Outdoor Education highlighted cost as an issue as it prevented some pupils accessing these activities.

33. The costs to parents has to be considered in the context of other "voluntary" financial contributions parents may be being asked to make eg school fund, music tuition and special events.

CONCLUSION

34. The timescale for submissions has prevented the inclusion of information on how provision in the UK compares with that of other countries. As a member of Education International NASUWT has access to a wealth of information on education systems throughout the world, in particular Europe, and would be able to submit information at a later date.

35. NASUWT will be pleased to expand on the points in this submission and other related issues at the oral evidence session on 1 November 2004.

Annex

EDUCATIONAL VISITS

A CHECKLIST FOR MEMBERS

An educational visit is defined as any excursion with children outside the perimeter of the school.

NASUWT advises members to carefully consider whether they should be involved in educational visits at all. When something goes wrong on a visit the leader bears a legal responsibility and so the finger of blame will almost certainly point at the teachers.

In recent high-profile cases teachers have been heavily penalised. Some have lost their jobs as a result of alleged misjudgements.

If you decide against NASUWT advice to take part in such a visit either as a leader, or an accompanying professional, you must follow the relevant advice and guidance set out below.

In particular, you must follow exactly your LEA guidance on educational visits, and NASUWT strongly recommends that you check the activities against the other checklists provided in this leaflet.

ESSENTIAL INFORMATION

1. LEA advice on educational visits.
2. Health and Safety of Pupils on Educational Visits (HASPEV) (DfES).
3. Standards for Adventure (DfES).
4. Standards for LEAs in Overseeing Educational Visits (DfES).
5. Handbook for Group Leaders (DfES).
6. Group Safety at Water Margins (DfES).

2–6 above are all available at www.teachernet.gov.uk/management/healthandsafety/visits/

CHECKLIST FOR GROUP LEADERS

A group leader is responsible for the health, safety and wellbeing of the group under common law. If you are a group leader use this checklist to ensure you have taken proper care in organising your visit.

1. Obtained appropriate experience, qualifications and training.
2. Carried out a pre-visit and liaised with the Educational Visits Co-ordinator.
3. Carried out appropriate risk assessments and are aware of health and safety issues regarding both staff and pupils, eg use of seat belts in a coach or minibus.
4. Gained approval from the employer for the visit and ensured there is adequate insurance coverage.
5. Arranged appropriate supervisory duties and ensured effective communication between adults on the visit, the children, their parents and the base school.
6. Ensured other adults are appropriate in terms of maturity, experience and police checks.
7. Ensured the visit has a clear educational purpose.
8. Have a clear plan of the activities to be undertaken and their educational objectives.
9. Have a clear understanding of emergency procedures and ensured there will be a qualified first aid person available at all times.

10. Ensured all staff on the visit are given a list of group members and that they check pupils' presence at regular intervals.

11. Have detailed clearly by letter to parents the activities on the visit and enlisted their support regarding acceptable behaviour and obtained their written consent.

12. Have a reasonable prior knowledge of the group, including any special educational or medical needs or disabilities.

13. Ensured the exclusion from the visit of pupils whose behaviour may put others in the party at risk.

14. Ensured that all monies have been collected and accounted for by school administrative/clerical staff. (Also see 36 below.)

CHECKLIST FOR ACCOMPANYING TEACHERS AND OTHER EDUCATION WORKERS

15. You should be familiar with the LEA guidelines on educational visits.

16. You should have been actively involved in the planning of the visit.

17. You should be supportive of the group leader and be prepared to act on his/her instructions.

18. You should carry a list naming all the pupils and adults on the visit.

19. You should be aware which pupils have special educational or medical needs or disabilities.

20. You should be fully aware of the nature of the activities that the group is going to be involved in.

CHECKLIST FOR HEADTEACHERS

If the headteacher has delegated responsibility for a visit to a suitable group leader then s/he should have ensured they are satisfied:

21. All LEA visits guidelines have been followed.

22. The visit is educationally justifiable and will not affect the efficient running of the school.

23. The group leader is suitably trained, qualified or experienced.

24. The LEA and Governing Body have been notified and have authorised the visit.

25. Child protection measures are in place.

26. A school contact has been nominated and there is a contingency plan for delays including a late return back to school.

27. Full and comprehensive information has been provided to parents including details of costings, modes of transport and the precise nature of activities the pupils will be involved in.

28. Parental consent has been obtained in writing with specific consent for activities such as swimming, along with relevant pupil medical information.

29. Supervision of the group is appropriate in relation to gender, experience and police checks.

30. The mode of transport is suitable and all safety measures will be taken.

31. Detailed costings of the visit have been approved.

32. Appropriate cover for teachers on the visit has been organised.

33. An emergency procedure has been planned with well-established lines of communication should the need arise, including the provision of a mobile telephone if requested.

OTHER CONSIDERATIONS

34. Since the Children Act was introduced NASUWT has dealt with many more allegations of abuse by teachers. Members are therefore advised:

— not to give a child/children a lift in your own vehicle;

— not to place yourself in a one-to-one situation;

— not to administer any medication.

35. NASUWT strongly advises any member contemplating driving a minibus in the course of an educational visit or journey to reconsider and instead enlist the services of a specially trained driver.

36. In order to ensure the avoidance of personal liability as the "provider" of the visit, NASUWT recommends that the group leader should:

— only act on behalf of the employer as the employer's agent;

— take professional advice on the level and type of insurance required for the visit;

— use a tour operator that has an externally verified safety management system rather than making arrangements on a "diy" basis.

37. A visit involving outdoor activities should engage the services of a specialist provider (for example, an LEA-run centre or a commercial organisation licensed by the Adventure Activities Licensing Authority) where pupils can be placed in the care of qualified instructors.

October 2004

Witnesses: **Mr Steve Sinnott**, General Secretary, National Union of Teachers, **Dr Fiona Hammans**, Head of Banbury School, Oxfordshire and a Member of the Secondary Heads Association, **Ms Kathryn James**, Senior Assistant Secretary, Professional Advice Department, National Association of Head Teachers, and **Ms Chris Keates**, General Secretary, NASUWT, examined.

Q128 Chairman: It is my great pleasure to welcome Steve Sinnott, the General Secretary of the NUT. This is your first appearance, is it not, Steve?
Mr Sinnott: As General Secretary of the NUT it is.

Q129 Chairman: Welcome indeed. Then we have Dr Fiona Hammans. Is that the right pronunciation?
Dr Hammans: Yes, it is.

Q130 Chairman: Who is here from Banbury School in Oxfordshire and a member of SHA, Ms Kathryn James, who is Senior Assistant Secretary to the Professional Advice Department, NAHT, and we have Chris Keates, who is General Secretary of NASUWT. Welcome all of you. You will have had the benefit of experience of listening to the Committee's questions so far. The bad news is we have got an entirely different set of questions for you. It is good to have you all here. Jonathan wants to lead the questioning, but before you start does anybody want to say anything? I cannot have all four of you saying something. Are we going to give pride of place to Steve Sinnott, only because it is his first appearance, or does Chris Keates, because she has been before us and has great experience, want to go first?
Ms Keates: It is also my first appearance, Chairman.

Q131 Chairman: I am sorry, Chris, I thought you had been here before.
Ms Keates: I have been here before, but not as General Secretary.

Q132 Chairman: I see. Who would like to kick off?
Mr Sinnott: I would like to kick off by congratulating Chris Keates on being General Secretary. I look forward to working with Chris for a long, long time; so congratulations to Chris.
Ms Keates: Thank you.

Q133 Chairman: I think that is totally out of order, but we will let you!
Ms Keates: I think we will go straight into questions.

Q134 Chairman: Okay. The opener is: did you find it rather a surprise that we were looking at this subject? Is it on the periphery of your interest and you thought, "What on earth is the Select Committee doing dabbling around with this bit of peripheral stuff"?
Mr Sinnott: I do not think it is peripheral at all, Chair, I think it is central to what goes on in education. As well as congratulating Chris and surprising everyone by congratulating Chris, can I praise the Government? One of the good things that the Government has done is to emphasise the relationship—

Q135 Mr Pollard: Can you speak a bit more slowly; I want to get all this?
Mr Sinnott: —is to emphasise the relationship between social class and education, and David Miliband, I think, has done a terrific job in raising the relationship, the achievement of youngsters and their social class, and there is no doubt in my mind that what teachers want to do, and what the Government and the local authorities should be encouraging to be done, is to ensure that youngsters have a rich experience of their time at school, and that will include giving an entitlement to children to go the theatre, to be involved in drama, to be involved in sporting activities, to visit a foreign country, to be involved in an outdoor activity of one form or another, to be involved in a residential activity—all of those activities—and there is real evidence of the way in which youngsters from economically deprived backgrounds benefit from them. The recent experience of September 2004— Ofsted said exactly what I have just said. At the same time we do know that all youngsters, whether they are gifted or talented or whether they are struggling at school, benefit from those activities and schools benefit from having improved relationships between the youngsters and the teachers following residential activity. So the benefits are clear and real, and I congratulate the Committee for picking up this issue?

Q136 Jonathan Shaw: A question to Chris Keates. In your evidence to the Committee you say that there is a significant number of schools that conduct visits to venues of dubious educational value. How many of your members take children to schools of dubious economic value?
Ms Keates: Educational value.

Q137 Jonathan Shaw: Educational value; thank you.
Ms Keates: We think there is less than when we first started to raise issues about educational visits, the conduct of them and the risk that we felt needed to be minimised as far as possible because, we accept, there is no activity that is actually completely risk-free, but we have for some time been identifying a number of issues and one of the issues we have raised about minimising risks is about making sure that there is a clear educational value to the trips that are being taken. It has been our experience that quite a lot of schools are engaged, particularly in the summer term, although, as I say, our information

back from our members is it is less now than when we first started to raise this issue, where you would get the annual trip to the Blackpool pleasure beach or Alton Towers—things that we would say might be an interesting experience for the pupils, might be something they had not done before, but whether it should be the kind of visit that is conducted by a school and what curriculum relationship it has, we would have doubts about that.

Q138 Jonathan Shaw: What I am slightly concerned about is the broad brushes that you are using, Chris, in your evidence, both written and what you have just said. "Quite a lot", "significant amounts". What we are trying to do is to drill down in this issue and to get to the heart of the matter. When you say "of dubious value educationally"—you have decided that it is so important that you want to put it in the evidence to the Select Committee—what are we talking about? What are the numbers? Does your union know?

Ms Keates: If you are asking me for statistical evidence to back up for a percentage of schools, I cannot give you that. What I can give you is the issues that have been raised with us from our members are on a large-scale across the country and we judge the impact of an issue by the response we get from members through our union's casework, and, since we have been raising the issue of educational visits, we have had, on a regular basis, from members in schools right across the country, the issues of concerns they have expressed to us about some of the educational visits; and so, if you are asking me for a percentage, I cannot do that. I think that it is perfectly legitimate for me to say that our casework evidence is demonstrating that this is a concern to some teachers, particularly arising from the risks with visits. They have been looking much more closely at the kinds of activities that a school should be involved in conducting.

Q139 Jonathan Shaw: How many of your members, how many of the NASUWT members have been the subject of false allegations on residential trips?

Ms Keates: Of the tracking that we have done, I think we have had in the last . . . The percentage of false allegations on visits, I would say, probably is about 5% of the numbers that we have, and we have been tracking educational visits now—I am sorry, false allegations now since 1991.

Q140 Jonathan Shaw: On residential?

Ms Keates: On residential things in terms of false allegations that have arisen, and there can be a variety. It is not just sexual abuse of people, which is what people immediately think of, it is actually physical abuse and a number of other things.

Q141 Jonathan Shaw: You could provide us with a number of incidences?

Ms Keates: I can provide you with the statistics we have on false allegations and the number of incidents on that, yes.[9]

Q142 Jonathan Shaw: Has that gone up?

Ms Keates: Over the time that we have been tracking that, I would say that the proportion has probably stayed the same of those, but the whole issue for us, of course, of false allegations, is much wider than the visits.

Q143 Jonathan Shaw: So you are not sure that the proportion has gone up; it has stayed about the same, despite your press release, which says, "Society is increasingly litigious and no longer appears to accept the concept of general accident." Therefore, you are advising your members not to go on these trips. So it is not going up, but it is increasing, the problem is increasing. My concern is are you, is your union, actually trying to find the solution to the problem or are you the problem? You do these press releases prior to coming before the Committee, you do not have the statistics to back them up and then we see headlines like this from your press release. Are you the problem?

Ms Keates: No, we are not the problem. In fact, we have been raising these issues for a number of years. That is not the first time there has been press coverage of that. I am sorry if that has caused you concern. In our evidence, in section 28, we actually list the work that we have now been doing with the DfES on the issue of trying to find solutions to some of the issues we have identified, and the issue of false allegations is not the major issue in terms of the advice we are giving to members, as we detail in our evidence. In fact, last April the Government recognised the validity of some of our concerns and, as we detail in our evidence, we have been working constructively with DfES officials to look at a range of processes that might actually start to minimise the risks and address some of the concerns that we have about protecting staff that go on educational visits. So we are not at all the problem, but we have a responsibility to our members to give them clear advice about the risks they might face. We also have an equal responsibility to try and raise and put forward constructive suggestions as to how they can be addressed, and we have certainly done that with the Government and we have listed the areas that at the moment are in progress with the DfES on the areas of concern that we have listed.

Q144 Jonathan Shaw: The final question for you, Chris. What is your union's assessment of the main findings of the Ofsted report *Outdoor Education: Aspects of Good Practice?* What is your assessment of the main findings?

Ms Keates: As we said at the time that was published, we recognise the value of outdoor education and some of the activities that are taking place. The questions that we pose are: are all of those activities ones that schools and teachers and sports staff should be conducting, and, in that context, there are still the risks posed that we have been raising. We are not a union that is opposing educational visits—that has never been our position and our evidence makes that quite clear—but we have a responsibility to our members to point out concerns and we have a responsibility to make sure that we have put forward constructive suggestions to government as to how to address that; and we believe we have done that.

Q145 Jonathan Shaw: There was very little in your evidence to suggest that you embraced outdoor education. It was mainly about the concerns about litigation and workforce. I have to say, that is in stark contrast with the other trade unions that talked about the benefits of outdoor education. As I say, in your evidence there is a lot that talks about increasing numbers and broad brush statements, and, when we ask you about the specifics, the numbers are not going up?
Ms Keates: I did not realise that what the Committee was inquiring into was for us to tell you the benefits of outdoor education. I thought what you wanted us to do was to highlight things that you might want to take on board in your inquiry in terms of some of the issues that are facing teachers that conduct these issues. I could have written several pages about the benefits, but there is plenty of research and well-documented evidence. My concern was to put to you issues that you might want to consider and also to show the progress that we were making on addressing some of those very taxing issues for schools, for teachers and for our head teacher members.

Q146 Chairman: Can I just intervene. You would not be surprised that this Committee is particularly interested in your decision as a union to advise your members not to participate?
Ms Keates: I understand that.

Q147 Chairman: That is very important. In many ways it is quite a shocking decision. When was it made?
Ms Keates: It was made over four years go, and we have reviewed it on an annual basis and raised it with the Government on an annual basis, and it has arisen out of casework, an increasing amount of casework that we were experiencing, some with some very tragic incidents. Some of the very high profile cases that have been in the press have involved NASUWT members and we reviewed the advice and we included that as an annex,[10] which shows that we give that strong advice but we also do provide a check-list for people who may say, "Despite that advice, we actually want to accompany these trips." We respect the position of people who do that, and that is why we have not been sitting back and saying we are not interested in educational visits, that is why we have been trying to engage the Government in looking at some of the things that we think can make sure that some of these valuable activities can go ahead but also minimise the risk to the staff that get involved in those. I think that is a perfectly legitimate position for us as a union to take.

Q148 Helen Jones: Can I ask you to clarify one thing in the written evidence you have given us? You say in, I think, point six that society is increasingly

litigious. We understand that. It says, "It also fails either to understand that perfect judgment, total attentiveness and faultless foresight are beyond normal human capacity or to accept that in the best ordered of activities things will occasionally go wrong. Schools, therefore, find themselves increasingly vulnerable to the growing compensation culture." I am not quite sure where you are coming from here, because that is not what the law says. The law does not expect perfect judgment, total attentiveness and faultless foresight; it expects people to take the precautions that a reasonable person would take. So how are you getting from one of those statements to the other: because that seems to me to be legally faulty— untrue, shall I say?
Ms Keates: No, it is not untrue.

Q149 Helen Jones: It is. That is not what the law on negligence is?
Ms Keates: I am not arguing here the law on negligence, I am arguing on the feedback we get in terms of the casework that we have, reports that we get from our head teacher members and reports from teachers about what they are finding in terms of any accident, and, through your previous questions to the DfES officials, you were raising the issue of the growing litigious nature of the accident culture, and educational visits are part of that. The feedback we get regularly from our members and from local casework is that accidents, whether they are on school trips, or in the school playgrounds, or in the classroom can often at the very first stages, simply things that we would probably at school ourselves have brushed off, a trip in the playground now can result in a solicitor's letter because there are people who are always looking for something to blame. That does not mean that all of them go as far as proceedings, but it is a symptom of a compensation culture that there is not a genuine accident any more.

Q150 Helen Jones: I could write you a solicitor's letter today, but just because you get one does not mean people have to pay compensation. It might not be worth the paper it is written on, frankly. So is not your dispute rather with schools and LEAs who settle claims which have no real basis in law at all rather than with the law as it stands?
Ms Keates: The issue . . . That is a different point than whether we have—

Q151 Helen Jones: It is not?
Ms Keates: No; it is a different point than whether we have evidence to sustain that there is a growing compensation culture. The fact that letters are now sent for things that at one time would have been dismissed as a childish accident in a playground is evidence of the compensation culture. The fact that people pay out, we are concerned and have raised it where we have come across it with schools or local authorities who, to avoid lengthy exchanges with solicitors, actually will settle because that does actually fuel the compensation culture.

Q152 Helen Jones: But that does not mean your members are being taken to court, does it?

Ms Keates: Our members quite often are enjoined in the first stages of litigation. Whether they end up in the full proceedings is an entirely different matter.

Q153 Helen Jones: If these are cases that are being settled then your members are not being taken to court, are they?

Ms Keates: It depends how the investigation is conducted by the local authority, whether the police are involved or where the people making the claims have gone to. There is a whole variety of circumstances in which that can happen. We do not make those kinds of comments lightly, and this has been generally accepted as a problem, hence the Government is actually working with us on some of these issues because they have had reports from schools, and I am sure my colleagues here can say about the pressure that many head teachers come under from solicitors who are writing letters at the drop of a hat that cause problems for schools. The other issue that we have, of course, is that our members may not be subject to criminal proceedings but can be subject to disciplinary investigations, which can be extremely stressful.

Q154 Helen Jones: Have you any figures for us again on the number of these cases where people are writing to schools or sending them solicitor's letters after school trips or any other sort of outdoor education and the numbers that are settled, as opposed to the numbers that are totally spurious and do not even get this couple of hundred pounds pay out?

Ms Keates: If I can say to you, I think it would be very unusual for a school nowadays not to have received at least one of these letters after some sort of accident. That would be extremely unusual. What the figures are in terms of settling, of course, that depends on a school and local authority policy. Some local authorities will not settle on these and they will take them forward. Only if our members are involved would we have any details of that case, but my colleagues in other unions have expressed the same concerns in meetings. They may take different advice in terms of what they ask their members to do, but the issue of teachers and other workers in schools and head teachers becoming increasingly vulnerable to legal action is a huge concern throughout the profession.

Q155 Helen Jones: So how many of these cases have involved your members recently?

Ms Keates: I have not got those figures. I will provide the figures for you.[11]

Q156 Chairman: The reason we are pushing you on this, it is fundamentally important to our inquiry, but on the one hand you said no cooperation. If all your members took your advice, basically out of school activity would cease, would they not, more or less? If they took your advice.

Ms Keates: Yes, and, of course, one of the things I think we all regret is the fact that the number of visits for some of the things that are curriculum related and have an educational validity, there is more concern and caution about taking those now. That is why we think it is important that you do have this inquiry, because one of the things we propose is supporting schools through local authorities with a check-list that can look at making sure that the risks are minimised by the trips that have been taken have got that direct curriculum—

Q157 Chairman: Let us continue. What would make you as a union change your mind in terms of what assurances the Government could give or LEAs could give, or a combination of factors? This is a four-year policy. We have had it for a long time, although it comes as a surprise, I see from the *Daily Express.* You have never had it!

Ms Keates: Indeed.

Q158 Chairman: They are not that clever at the *Daily Express,* obviously, because they blame the Government for this policy, but, tell us, we are trying to find out what would change your mind and make you cooperate?

Ms Keates: All of the items we have listed in section 28 of our evidence. The consistent monitoring of the visits, the support from their employer for teachers who actually take these visits, because they are actually abandoned when litigation starts or there is a particular problem. We would like a much firmer application of the Government guidance on monitoring of the educational validity, because again there is a lack of consistency.

Q159 Chairman: There is a difficulty there, Chris, is there not, because evidence that this Committee has had said there is nothing like the joy of seeing a child who has seen the sea for the first time, and you might say that for a child from a deprived background a visit to the Blackpool pleasure beach is wonderful.

Q160 Jonathan Shaw: Dubious?

Ms Keates: Or exotic!

Q161 Chairman: I know for the first time when I was a shadow minister for that sort of area that going to the Blackpool pleasure beach was a wonderful learning experience, but would not people think you were being a bit Stalinist if you did only the things that NASUWT thought were of value?

Ms Keates: I did not say only the things that NASUWT thought were of value; I said what we would get is a check-list against which schools could do that measurement themselves.

Q162 Chairman: But would a child's first visit to the seaside be educational or not?

Ms Keates: It is very easy to put a circumstance like that. What I would say to you is of course it is important for children to have that kind of experience. I would not disagree with this. I think it is borne out of this premise that somehow we are anti-educational visits, which I have tried to explain is not the case.

Q163 Jonathan Shaw: You are.
Ms Keates: No.

Q164 Chairman: Jonathan, I will be handing back to you in a minute. What we are trying to push is it was you that mentioned Alton Towers, not us?
Ms Keates: That is absolutely right. I am not sure.

Q165 Chairman: You have got to make a list.
Ms Keates: Yes, I am not sure—as I often have on these things—I am not sure that that is something I would say should be conducted by a school. The other point I would—

Q166 Chairman: So a visit to Scarborough is on the list or not?
Ms Keates: I would say, depending what they are doing at Scarborough. If they are going looking at coastline features and various other things to do with a field trip, then that might be.

Q167 Chairman: Not to have a paddle and see the sea for the first time?
Ms Keates: Of course you want children to have those particular experience, but, I have to say, I also think that you need to do some investigation into how many of the trips that are run actually get to the children that you are identifying, because there are a number of trips that take place that actually parents cannot afford for those children to go and they are often the ones that you want to have that first experience. My view is that the more that a trip is related to the curriculum the more opportunity pupils will have to go, because you cannot charge for trips that are necessary as part of the curriculum. Too many of the visits that go rely on voluntary contributions, and some of them are horrendously expensive, and parents get into the position of either they cannot afford for their own child to feel guilty or the voluntary contribution letter says, "If you do not make a voluntary contribution then other people may not be able to go either", which is a double whammy for some parents who have poor economic circumstances. So whilst I would never disagree that for a child to see the sea for the first time is a wonderful experience, I do not think we should get carried away on that wave of emotion that that is somehow what is happening in all these visits that take place and the bad old NASUWT is stopping these wonderful children having these wonderful experiences because that is not true; but I think I have a responsibility to draw to the attention of this Committee the real concerns that my members in schools face around these issues.

Q168 Chairman: But it is our job also to assess the evidence from NASUWT. A policy, on the one hand, that would stop all schools trips but, on the other, you seem to be in favour of school trips and out of school education. A lot of people that we represent—as elected politicians we have got to

explain a policy and that is our difficulty with your position, is it not? On the one hand the logic of your four-year policy would be the end of all out-of-door education for schools?
Ms Keates: It would until the issues were addressed that we have listed in our evidence that are currently being considered by the Government, because they had clearly thought there was validity to the arguments we put; otherwise I do not think Charles Clarke would have made a public statement at our annual conference that he recognised the validity of them, and he immediately set up meetings with senior officials to look at all of those issues and we are making really good progress because we want to be in a position to say that the risks have been minimised.

Q169 Chairman: That is excellent, Chris. So you are saying that the Government is putting in place a dialogue that could change—
Ms Keates: Absolutely; and that is what we say in paragraph 28 of our evidence.

Q170 Jonathan Shaw: Let me ask Steve Sinnott about the Workforce Agreement. Do you think that these have made school trips more expensive?
Mr Sinnott: More expensive?

Q171 Jonathan Shaw: Yes, given that they have placed a financial burden on schools and perhaps having to pay for supply teachers to take them out?
Mr Sinnott: I have no evidence of whether the Workforce Agreement has made the school trips more expensive or, indeed, less expensive. I have no evidence at all, Jonathan, in relation to that.

Q172 Jonathan Shaw: What about classrooms assistants? Could they be trained to undertake the risk assessments?
Mr Sinnott: They could. I think all sorts of people could be trained to undertake risk assessments, but to some extent I think, Jonathan, you are asking the wrong question. I think the right question—

Q173 Jonathan Shaw: Help me; you are a teacher!
Mr Sinnott: If you will permit me. The right question is to ask some of the centres that offer outdoor activities for them, for example, to provide generic risk assessments, and they would be of great assistance to schools and in that way reducing the burden, the bureaucratic burden, and, indeed, the work load on teachers, on head teachers and on appropriate support staff. So we think that could be done. Indeed, in activities that the NUT nationally has organised jointly with the NASUWT nationally to support the global campaign for education, we have used and we have undertaken joint risk. We have paid for joint risk assessments to be carried out and provided them with schools who have been sending them on activities that the NUT and the NASUWT have jointly organised?
Ms James: In terms of risk assessment, I think it is quite important to remember the involvement of local authorities carrying out risk assessments, though, again, I would strongly support the notion

of teachers receiving training and all staff receiving training in terms of actually running, planning and moving forward with any outdoor education activity. I think that is absolutely essential. We mention in our evidence the OCR training course, which is actually very valuable, and I think the more people that undertake this the better, or something similar.

Dr Hammans: In terms of risk assessments, I do not think that there is any need to explain to school and college leaders the importance of them, and most schools already have a bank of their own generic risk assessments which then link with LEA activity centre and association risk assessments, and they are used within schools all the time.

Q174 Jonathan Shaw: Can I ask you, Kathryn James, do your members have concerns about dubious trips?

Ms James: You will see in our evidence that we talk about the necessity for learning objectives, and that is for any lesson, and that would also include the necessity for the learning objectives for outdoor education. We think this is an essential part of the planning system. In terms of whether dubious activities, I think any activity that takes place within or without a school needs to have to a strong basis upon which the learning is to be forthcoming. By that I am not just tying it directly to curriculum learning, because you talked about the social aspect and the education of children in terms of their growing up, and particularly children from deprived areas need that rich experience that actually can only come from activities that take place out of school, and this is why we are very much in support of outdoor activities. Chris and I, I think, probably sit on different sides of the same line in terms of where we are coming from because we too see the necessity to make sure that there is adequate safety; that people are secure in what they are doing. We have talked about the concerns about litigation and they may be unfounded, but these concerns are still very real, and that can be off-putting for teachers and for support staff when they are looking at planning these particular activities.

Q175 Chairman: Dr Hammans, who are these people in schools, heads or governors, or whoever, who are they, who are planning ridiculous excursions to things that have no value? Who are these people?

Dr Hammans: I genuinely do not think, Chair, that there are any dubious excursions or planned trips; because the bureaucracy and the risk, whether it is real or not, associated with those in people's minds who are organising the trips and taking the students out is so great that there has to be a genuine agreed set of objectives for it. For instance, if it is Alton Towers, it may be a trip to reward students who have done particularly well, or it may be an entitlement for every Year 7 student to go to do some practical physics which is then built on throughout the whole of their visits curriculum in school, but the amount of work that needs to be done in advance has to be quite clearly worth it, otherwise what is the point?

We do not go on trips that take hours of planning with the risk associated just in case something goes wrong for just a jolly; it does not happen like that any more. It is not like that in schools and colleges.

Q176 Chairman: So these unnecessary value trips are a sort of urban myth?

Dr Hammans: Our impression certainly would be that they do not occur these days. They may have happened 10, 15, 20 years ago where teachers decided, "It is summer term, let's take the students out for a walk down the river bank", but these days with the pressure from national curriculum, the wider agenda for personal development for students, team-building, leadership skills, there is no spare time. Teachers do not have the time, students do not have the time to waste and parents certainly would not support us.

Q177 Chairman: Kathryn, is that your take on it?

Ms James: I would agree. I do not think that you ought to underestimate the actual planning time and the commitment that all of the staff need to give to make an outdoor activity valuable for all concerned. When Stephen Crowne and Helen Williams were here before, they commented about strengthening relationships with the school. Actually outdoor activities can even work in terms of strengthening relationships with the community, and, particularly in the more deprived areas, again, that can be a very, very strong element in terms of how schools function within their community; but that takes time, it takes effort, it takes a lot of resources, and I think the staff who give their time for this want to see that they are valuable and that the activity is valuable and that it is of value to the pupils who undertake them.

Q178 Chairman: You both say then that the concern that NASUWT has that is really central to their objection, one of the central concerns, does not exist. It is figment of someone's imagination?

Ms James: I think that there have been problems. Chris herself has said that in fact the dubious nature of school trips—I think she herself said that they think that this has decreased in NAS terms. From our perspective, we would say that the learning objects which are central to any activity actually mean that this has to now be defined before anything can go forward. So, yes, I would say that in fact they have been minimised, if not wiped out.

Dr Hammans: Could I add something there. I agree very much with what Kathryn says, but it is that fear of litigation, particularly for our members. So in terms of calls to the Secondary Heads Association hotline, the HQ, then there will be calls each week from members who have received a solicitor's letter or are outraged or intimidated either by the receipt of those, or disciplinary action from their own governing body or through the LEA or even the Health and Safety Executive. So whether it is real or not, whether it gets to a court of law or not, it is something additional on our members which needs to be borne in mind.

Q179 Chairman: So what is it, Dr Hammans? I am going to ask Chris Keates. What is it that would put your members' minds at rest? What kind of support do they want which would mean that they felt better about participation in out of school activities? You heard the civil servants talking about the manifesto, and so on. What should be in that manifesto that would put your minds at rest and lead to a greater level of cooperation?
Dr Hammans: There needs to be something which is definitive. So if you are looking at the bureaucracy that everybody has to fill in there is the DfES guidelines which need to be met, there is then the local authority set of guidelines which, as has been indicated earlier on, will change and will change somewhat, then you have got again school's interpretations, plus whichever group you may be going with, whichever partner you will be working with—so you have got a huge amount of bureaucracy—but even when you have dotted the "I"s, crossed the "T"s and something might have gone wrong, the view is somebody has to be responsible for what has happened to my child or that child; and it does not matter what you have done, the sense is that you as an individual, if you have been involved in that school party, or myself as head of a school, is the one who will be in court. Real or not, that is the fear. So something where the bureaucracy—if you want the guidelines, the safety, the nets, everything is filled in, that is the end of it and an individual is not identified but the authorities who have been giving you the guidance are the people who then are answerable.

Q180 Chairman: Would you favour getting rid of this responsibility? A specialist organisation in the private sector could take this all over and take the load totally out of schools?
Dr Hammans: Our view is very much that it is about holistic education of youngsters and it is not about, "We will deliver national curriculum plus a couple of options." It is about seeing a youngster when they arrive at 11 at our schools through to when they finish at 19 even, their complete growth from the eleven year old through to the 19 year old; and if we start parcelling it up so that behaviour is to do with one group of people, outdoor education someone else, classrooms to do with this, I think we lose sight of what is unique about the UK education system.

Q181 Chairman: What is your view on that, Steve?
Mr Sinnott: I think a lot of commonsense has just been spoken, and what I think we have started to see is considerable agreement on those people who represent teachers on this issue. The fear is a real fear. The fear of litigation is not something that Chris Keates is inventing; it is a real fear in the part of schools. So I share what my colleagues have said about that fear. I also say that that places an enormous responsibility—because you are asking the questions and we are answering them—it places a considerable responsibility on the Committee here in its report to do something about assuaging the fear that is out there on the part of parents and others. By asking the questions you really are

placing a tremendous responsibility on yourselves. The way in which we do it, I think, is by a good report from you, about all the teacher organisations.
Helen Jones: All our reports are good!

Q182 Mr Turner: Another good report!
Mr Sinnott: I would only say it because I have got absolute confidence in the type of reports that you produce.

Q183 Chairman: It is very nice of you to say things like this, Steve, but our reports have a curt reputation for being quite good?
Mr Sinnott: They have.

Q184 Chairman: I say that reasonably modestly, and our reports absolutely reflect the quality of evidence that we are given. We have been given good evidence today. Some unions sometimes have been relatively reluctant even to come to see the Committee, but that is not the situation today and the quality of evidence we get we can pick up the resonance, and what we are being given today is a very interesting amount of evidence; it is very positive; so do not worry about it.
Mr Sinnott: Can I steer you in a particular direction?

Q185 Chairman: It depends upon which direction!
Mr Sinnott: The direction is to . . . This is in terms of looking at the value of the types of activities that you are looking at, and it is to look at what was developed in Birmingham LEA and in terms of their secondary guarantees and primary guarantees in which they outlined specific guarantees or entitlements on children at different ages and the way in which all youngsters would benefit from having those guarantees met; and they relate to a whole range of activities, as I have mentioned, from artistic to sporting, residential or foreign visits. For youngsters whose parents cannot afford to do those things or whose parents are not interested in providing those things for their children, it is schools who decide to pick up those pieces. No private sector agency can do that in relation to your question earlier, but it has to be the schools and the teachers who make professional judgments about what is best in the interests of their school and in the interests of those children. What Birmingham did there, I believe, should have been taken up more nationally. It is tremendous evidence and I think there is evidence of youngsters, in particular from the economically deprived backgrounds, who have benefited from that. But there are a range of measures that may take place in the future that will make it for difficult for youngsters to go on some trips. It may be that some of the developments in relation to the Gershin review and the Lyons review may impact on staffing in some libraries or museums, and it may be that at the same time some of the pressures that will flow from the Lyons review in terms of local authority staffing, but local authority resources and local authority sites and local authority amenities, there may be pressure on

them getting rid of sites and amenities that benefit youngsters. So that is an area in which you might want to have a look too, Chair.

Q186 Chairman: If you could write to us about the implications of the Lyons review, because that is a relatively new one for us.
Mr Sinnott: We will do?

Q187 Chairman: We spent a week not very long ago in Birmingham, so some of the questions I was asking civil servants really come from that experience in Birmingham. Can I bring all of you back quickly, before we move on to education events coordinators. What is your general view of this as an initiative that will . . . When I was asking the civil servants should there be a champion in the Department or a champion minister, what about champions in schools or someone who has a specific role in seeing if the school is really up to good practice on these issues and energise them? Let us start with Dr Hammans and move across.
Dr Hammans: From our point of view, and I am speaking now as the head of a school, it has been a very useful addition to us being able to persuade staff that they are safe; because it is the fear of litigation, not necessarily the reality, which is the real concern. So we have our education visits coordinator. I will say that we would not let staff go unless we were fully convinced we were complying with everything such that if there were an incident it would not be the individual, it would be me that ended up in court. So the EVC, which is somebody who is nominated, trained, etc, is another layer to reassure those staff who do want to take students out on trips for good and valid educational reasons.

Q188 Chairman: Chris, does that help you in terms of having that?
Ms Keates: We have actually identified some very good practice that has come out of the national agreements, and the DfES is currently circulating to schools a video, which one of the examples they give from a Pathfinder school is an Educational Visits Coordinator, that is a highly qualified member of sports staff who has actually taken a huge burden off teachers in term of planning, coordination, identifying if risk assessments have been done, liaising with the local authority outdoor educational advisers, and we think that is very good practice to look at that, because teachers, quite frankly, with a full teaching load, one of their concerns is having the time to do those kinds of things properly, and we are very pleased in the way the remodelling of the school workforce is bringing on board other staff who are qualified to do those kinds of things and relieving that kind of administrative and coordination burden from teachers.

Q189 Chairman: So if there were not any of your members, if someone else was doing the job, you would be happier, would you?
Ms Keates: We think that it is better that there is somebody, given the issues that have to be addressed in the planning of these kinds of activities because, I

think my colleagues have emphasised, a great deal of the time and effort needs to go into these if they are going to be done properly. We do not think that it is appropriate to do something that a teacher can do on top of a full teaching commitment and that they are better focused on concentrating on the teaching and learning, look at the curriculum needs in terms of what kind of visit might support some of the curriculum and having somebody on the school staff who can devote some time to that. Certainly the feedback that we are getting is that where people have looked at remodelling of the workforce seriously, that is one of the issues they have looked at and staff are reporting that it has taken quite a considerable burden off them in that respect.

Q190 Chairman: Would you not miss out that sort of bonding that students get with staff when they do things outside the school?
Ms Keates: We are not taking it. I am talking about somebody who is doing all the preparatory work, providing all the information, making sure risk assessments are done. That is not necessarily, in fact quite often is not, the person who will conduct the visit. That can either be teachers or support staff.

Q191 Chairman: You still prefer your members to go on visits?
Ms Keates: I think if they are totally curriculum related and things like field work, and so on, you have to have a qualified teacher who is relating that back to the classroom issues. Some of the other visits that might not be quite such a subject based link, it might not be necessary for it always to be teachers. What we have said is in terms of teacher workload the big issue of administration, risk assessment and various other things, there are other people who can do that and have the time to do that. In terms of conducting the visits, we think there has to be an appropriate mix of people. What we do not support is the automatic assumption that every aspect of a school visit must be done by a teacher.

Q192 Valerie Davey: I think in this session I need to register my continued membership of the NUT. A slight change. In terms of the Government and its involvement, I would like to ask the two head teacher representatives, first of all, whether they feel that the recent Government initiatives, and particularly, I guess, the Growing Schools initiative, has been successful in highlighting the value of outdoor activities and, indeed, promoting them?
Ms James: Do I think it has been successful? I think it has been partially successful. I think it has been part of a growing move on the part of the Government in that there are lots of conversations taking place, if I can phrase it in that way, in terms of seeing how outdoor activities can benefit education and can be promoted. We talked before about the holistic nature of education and the use of outdoor activities within it, and I think we need to continue to see that being promoted so that all staff and parents and the general school community can

see the value of the outdoor activities and, therefore, again positive promotion, I think, is an important aspect.

Dr Hammans: I would agree with that. Anything which comes from any central source which says that this aspect is part and parcel of education, it is not just about sitting in the class room and doing your book work or doing some work on the inter-active white board, it is about a whole range of experiences which have educational outcomes, and I think anything is going to be positive.

Q193 Valerie Davey: So if the school were going to take this forward, do you think the decision to expand outdoor activities is more likely to happen if it has got the head teacher's backing, if it has got the LEA's backing, if it has got Ofsted's backing or the Government's backing. Where is the pressure going to come from that would be most effective in recharging the batteries in terms of outdoor school activities?

Dr Hammans: I think it needs the head teacher's backing, because that is the person who is likely to end up in court. So if we are talking about that fear, if the head is going say quite clearly, "These are valuable educational activities which we will run at minimum risk for the very best interests educationally of our students", then you are going to take your staff with you. You inevitably will have the backing of your governors anyway for that. If the LEA supports it, plus there are national initiatives and agendas to support it as well, then it is a winning situation, but I think it has to start with the school, much as the evidence from the DfES officials earlier on saying that it is for the school to determine its priorities locally, but, if it can link in with other national priorities, including Ofsted, then that is a stronger argument.

Q194 Valerie Davey: Would you agree with that?

Ms James: I would in the main, yes, though, again, we keep going back and I know we keep returning to this fear of litigation, but until we start to unpin that and actually almost start to try to remove some of that fear . . . Fiona referred before to the fact that the head is always the one that fears that they are going to land up in court. That is still there. If we want to promote a positive attitude towards outdoor activities being wrapped up within education, absolutely essential, then I think head teachers must be secure in saying, "Yes, I know that I can promote this, I know that this is safe, I know that this secure and I am going to be the one that ends up in court if anything goes wrong, but I know that I am secure in saying this", and I think that really needs to be—

Q195 Valerie Davey: It is really rather ironic, is it not, that we are using the word "fear" and yet many of these outdoor activities are there to help children overcome fear of climbing, or all the other things. It has to happen. We have to overcome it. I would like to come back very specifically because I know Banbury from old. There is a lot of overseas work, indeed, international European visits?

Dr Hammans: There is less now. We no longer do European work experience on the advice of the Education Authority. We do a number of overseas trips, which are the day trip to France or the Christmas shopping trip to Germany, which is two or three days, or a week in France residential, or Spain, including expeditions to more exotic places in the summer holidays for a month, but we are very clear that one of the things we offer as a very large school, which makes us distinct from other schools in the area, are staff who are keen and interested in running those sorts of activities, plus it is something value-added for education at our school. So we are fully committed to it as a school anyway, but that is a different starting point, I think, to other schools.

Q196 Valerie Davey: But clearly that is potentially the largest risk when you are taking children abroad and you are committed still, even if perhaps to a lesser degree you are still committed, to that work and you have overcome personally, as you must have done, the fear which says this is more important than me sitting here worrying that the world will collapse?

Dr Hammans: If I am honest, the fear is still there sometimes. Certainly when you are getting to the end of a month's expedition in Madagascar, for instance, and you get a phone call at 3.30 in the morning and they are saying, "Actually things are okay; we had forgotten the time difference", there is always a moment of panic then, but it is about as a school we do believe we should be doing it. It is about something special and distinct that we can offer our students. There is a risk there, but our parents have opted into the fact that we will do everything we can and more to minimise that risk, but there is no learning without some risk.

Q197 Chairman: Steve Sinnott wants to come in on that question, but can I push you on what do you give up on the advice of the Educational Authority?

Dr Hammans: We gave up European work experience.

Q198 Chairman: Why is that?

Dr Hammans: We were effectively sending students solo to places that we had not visited ourselves, were not able to risk assess in advance, had not met the adults, were not aware of the work situation. So in terms of the tick-list that we had to fill in, there were too many blanks and we were being too trusting, so we were not up for that.

Q199 Chairman: Steve Sinnott?

Mr Sinnott: Thank you. I wanted just start by correcting Valerie in terms of the way in which she viewed her union. The NUT is a head teachers' organisation and we claim to have the second highest number of head teachers in all the teachers' organisations, and I think I am speaking for Chris Keates here, because she cannot speak for herself this afternoon, as you will have noticed, so I will say they also have head teachers members in the NASUWT. So we are head teacher organisations as well.

Valerie Davey: I take rebuke from the leader of my union!

Q200 Chairman: Have you received her membership?
Mr Sinnott: She has paid her membership, Chair; she has done that! The Growing Schools initiative, which I think Valerie was referring to, they identified the range of barriers to schools becoming involved or taking forward that particular initiative, and a range of them were specified, and I do not think it included fee litigation, but they did specify a range of others, including lack of resources, lack of training, lack of confidence amongst teachers, I think also head teachers, in the way in which they were looking at this particular activity. Similar programmes where schools have specified an interest in the past but have seen—and I do not know whether you have looked at this as well—other barriers to schools becoming involved in this type of activity, one of them being the pressures of the national curriculum and national curriculum assessment and testing and, in particular, the way in which it impacts at Key Stage 2 in youngsters being involved in a variety of activities, because schools really do feel the pressure of wanting to have a good place in any published league table locally or nationally. So that is an area where I have not heard it specified as a barrier this afternoon, this evening, but I think we needed to draw your attention to, Chairman.
Chairman: That is a very good point.

Q201 Mr Pollard: We have been talking all afternoon about risk. Have we got a duty to prepare children for risk in the world, because, after all, the real word is full of risk each and every day? I give two quick examples. We were in Norway a week or two ago and we were told there children could be sent outside to play as long as the temperature did not go below minus 15 degrees centigrade! There are fairly clear guidelines. There is no way we would allow them out at those temperatures. The other thing that excited me was that this kindergarten that we were in was using very sophisticated tools: hammers and nails, for example, three-year old kids, sharp chisels and proper saws, and I was quite excited by that. I thought, "God almighty", this filled me with dread thinking, "What were these kids going to get up to." But apparently, as long as they are told properly how to use it and are supervised, they turn out some top quality toys. I was very impressed with that. Getting back to where I started from, we have a duty, do we not, to prepare kids for the world outside and to show them that you try and minimise risk, you try and do the very best you can. Is that not the right approach?
Ms Keates: From our point of view, I think I said very early on, there is no activity really that is without risk. I think the issue is the context in which schools are working, and there has been a lot made in the papers, for example, about schools actually stopping pupils playing conkers, that sort of thing. On the surface of it, that seems ridiculous—we would all say that—but in the context of what we

have been saying about the fear that schools have of the solicitor's letter and the litigation, that is the concern that schools have got. So in terms of letting children have a variety of experience, and so on, I think schools would be the first to say, "Yes, that is correct", but from the point of view that we come from as well, which is obviously about the concerns our members have, both head teachers and teachers, then we have to point out that at the moment we have that huge fear of potential litigation. So I think it is a balance there. We would certainly like to be in a position where children running across a playground and tripping up did not become the subject of a solicitor's letter. We certainly would like to be in the position where schools are not having to provide goggles to anybody who is playing conkers, or even banning it altogether. Our members would say that, but the fact is that is the climate that they are working, as you have heard from everybody giving evidence here.

Q202 Chairman: Is that really the climate, or are you just playing to the tabloid agenda?
Ms Keates: Not at all.
Chairman: You keep coming back to these examples that seem to most of us really—
Mr Pollard: Barmy?

Q203 Chairman: —only the sort of things that the *Daily Express* and other tabloids produce.
Ms Keates: Everyone who has given evidence here today has raised with you the concern of the fear of litigation. You have heard SHA saying—

Q204 Helen Jones: Give us one example?
Ms Keates: Fear of litigation is not the same as somebody being sued. It is about the issue—

Q205 Helen Jones: It should be based on fact?
Ms Keates: The fact—

Q206 Chairman: You just talk to the Chairman. I have asked you a question. I will bring Helen in if she wants.
Ms Keates: The fact is, as all of us have said in one way or another, that for things that we would all in a sensible world simply dismiss as being a genuine accident that has occurred schools are now getting solicitor's letters as a minimum and then finding they are subject to some sort of investigation, and so on, leading up to potential litigation as the end point on that. We have had people who have undergone, and I can give you an example from Wales, which is one we have publicised, raised with the Government and provided the details of, a teacher on an educational visit walking across a room in a residential place, the pupils were eating food, she walked across with some orange juice that spilt on the head of a child. There was a six-month police investigation in Wales for that of assault. Clearly that is the sort of thing that is totally ridiculous that anybody goes through, and there must be a process whereby at a very early stage and very quickly, the fear can be reduced by somebody saying this is clearly a totally frivolous action that has been brought here.

Q207 Chairman: Whilst the Committee is learning from these anecdotes and illustrations, we do get the feeling that you have a rather different attitude to what is going on than some of your colleagues here today. It seems to me some of your colleagues know that that goes on in some schools, but seem to put it in a better sense of proportion than you do. I get the feeling from listening to Fiona and Kathryn and Steve that, yes, they know that is going on but they do not really put it to such a high level of prominence in terms of the way that you see the changes.

Ms Keates: I can only speak for my union's experience and my union's view. Other people will express it as they feel from the point of view of their union. Perhaps if you examine details of casework, the level of casework that is involved with teachers and that perhaps we have been involved, in these issues may vary. I do not know. I cannot speak for others on that. The point that has been made about head teachers, our experience is even having head teachers in membership, they are not the ones that conduct the trips, take the trips away and so are not the ones who are the subject to these investigations, so there may be different perspective from that. I can only tell you as we find and why we have found the need to give the advice; and all I can say is that fortunately the Government recognises there is some validity, having talked to teachers themselves, having got reports from NUT, and they are working with us to address our concerns; and I am hopeful we can move forward in a way that produces much better procedures and gets rid of some of the nonsense that schools are having to face and the time and effort that goes in from a head teacher having to deal with a solicitor's letter that comes in. That is not a simple issue; it involves time and effort and liaison with the local authority, liaison with solicitors, investigations at the school. These are huge issues. The Government is actually looking now at something that at a very early stage might be able to identify something that could be dismissed as a frivolous claim without everybody having to go through that difficulty.

Q208 Mr Chaytor: I am surprised any NASUWT members turn up for work: they are either frightened about being poked in the eye with a conker or having a glass of orange juice poured over their head! I really wanted to ask about the three-day Christmas shopping trip to Germany to see if there are any places left on this year's trip! What are the specific learning objects behind that?

Dr Hammans: Students taking GSCE German are invited in Year 9—so they have already made their option selection for Key Stage 4—are invited in Year 9 to do it and it is sold to the children. The parents want them to go, but they do not want to go to Germany, they do not want to talk in German because it might be embarrassing, but when you say, "Actually, you are going to the Christmas markets. It will be great. You will be staying with your friends and then you will learn German as well. You will be able to practice and improve your German"—and that is how we sell it to the students.

Q209 Mr Chaytor: Can I link that with the point that Steve Sinnott made earlier, and this relates to the NUT's submission, because there is this paragraph—all the unions continuously refer to this—about the pressures of meeting the demands of the national curriculum and the pressures of assessment and testing, and so on, but the NUT's submission then goes on to spell out the benefits of outdoor education. It seems to me that none of the associations are linking these two together. Surely if you are convinced of the benefits in terms of the motivation of pupils and the development of confidence, maturity, team work and leadership, this will have a spill over in the class room which will reduce the pressure that you say your members are under because it will make teaching an easy job to do. No-one seems to be making that connection because you are so defensive or paranoid about being hit over the head with a conker. Am I missing something or is there not an obvious point to be made there, that if you can get the benefits of more outdoor learning, then this will reduce the pressures in the class room by producing better motivated pupils?

Mr Sinnott: David, I thought we were making exactly the same points as yours. If we have not expressed it in that way—the point you are making—then we should do. Do you know what would happen? If the Government issued guidance which said, "We advise all schools not to undertake outdoor visits and outdoor activities", if the Government issued that advice, schools would still do them. They would still do them. The reason why is because the teachers make a professional judgment that it is worthwhile. It is a worthwhile activity for the youngsters in their care. That is the professional judgment of teachers, and it is hard-pressed teachers who are still organising these activities because they believe that they are valuable, but we know that there would be more and there would be better activities taking place if we did more to reduce the work load on teachers and, if we freed up curriculum time to do it and if we had a less prescriptive national curriculum and we addressed issues to do with assessment and testing, we would have much better organised and more valuable activities taking place.

Dr Hammans: I was just going to say, that is essentially what the Secondary Heads Association submission said, that it is valuable and therefore we continue do it despite fears or worries or concerns.

Q210 Mr Turner: I was going to ask a similar question actually, because someone implied that schools, I think it was Chris, should be doing things which have curricular value as compared presumably with things which do not, and Kathryn said that the learning objectives have to be defined before anything goes forward. It is pretty sad, is it not, that schools are limited to those things?

Ms James: Can I take that one. Actually I do not agree with you. I do not think it is sad at all, because I think you are actually enabling people to plan and to put in place an holistic view of education by building those activities within the whole teaching and the whole education system. Picking up David's point before about seeing the benefits of outdoor activities, actually I would pick up your point about not supporting outdoor activities as seeing the spill over into the classroom. I think we do. That is why we are so—we would wish to see them continue, we would wish to see them grow and to see those benefits actually underlined.

Q211 Mr Turner: Steve was nodding when you said that, but when I made my initial remark I got the faintest glimmer of a nod from Dr Hammans. Did you agree with me or do you agree with Kathryn?
Dr Hammans: Tricky. I would be really nervous about setting up additional bureaucracy for any trips or anything which is not classroom based that said, "Tick off your learning objectives first", because we lose some of the creativity, some of the by-chance, the what-ifs that happen in class but also would happen outside class that we then say, "Sorry, that was not in the objective. We cannot follow that." It might be really naive but we are not able to pursue it because we planned it to meet these objectives. So I think too much prescription is entirely wrong, but being aware of what the students may benefit from that trip at the outset I think is very important, but please do not put tick boxes in and say, "You must do this. What is the personal development target for this trip? What is the curriculum link for this trip?"

Q212 Mr Turner: Is there some additional value in Dr Hammans opinion, because of all the teachers in this room, as far as I know, she is the only one who is teaching?
Ms Keates: I would be happy to answer that. I do not think that is the case at all. Who SHA chose to send to represent them is up to SHA, and I think that is absolutely fine, but the fact is we are accountable, elected people to our members and we do not make assertions or give evidence or develop policies without our members actually being included in that process. I think we are entirely representative and have hands-on experience from people right across the country in schools throughout the country.

Q213 Chairman: Before we finish, one last thing. We have had a very good session and we have gone on a little longer, and thank you for your perseverance, but much of what we have said has been couched today, the second session particularly, in terms of the 11–16 age group. Our inquiry covers really the early years as well, early years, pre-school and through. Would anybody like to mention how important this sort of activity is at the earlier stages of education.
Ms James: What I would say is that everything we have said this afternoon applies across the board as to how vital outdoor activities are. You only need to experience it from Key Stage 1 visiting, I do not know, a museum, or a farm, or whatever, and it is the

most incredible experience both for those who are accompanying and for the children themselves, and it is a vital and valuable piece of education.

Q214 Chairman: Thank you for that.
Ms Keates: Quite often in the early years, of course, they are less dubious and less exotic than some of the things they do with older pupils, and so the concerns we have apply right across the board in terms of where teachers are taking these, but some of the issues around the primary sector is often that context, that curriculum context, because of the more flexibility within the primary curriculum than there is with some of the secondary more special list based issues.

Q215 Chairman: It is interesting, Chris, you have again used the vocabulary "dubious and exotic", whereas Fiona Hammans and Steve and Kathryn all said to your original assertion that they do not know any dubious or exotic out of school activities from 11–16.
Ms Keates: Just because my colleagues and I differ on an issue does not mean to say that NASUWT will change its views, and I am not sure you would not want us to; you would want us to come here and be as honest as possible.

Q216 Chairman: We are still worrying about your "dubious" and "exotic" and trying to find out whether it exists!
Mr Sinnott: I have been scrupulous in not criticising colleagues in NASUWT. I do not want to do that. I have got a good relationship with the colleagues in NASUWT. The way you introduced this particular question, Chair, was to talk about 11–16, and an important point I want the National Union of Teachers to make is that some of the real benefits from Tomlinson and 14–19 education may be put at risk if we do not deal with some of the barriers that are clearly there that are part of your particular study. I think that is extremely important. At Key Stage 2, and this relates to David's earlier question, I know primary schools who, early in the school year of Year 6, undertake a residential activity, and they do it deliberately because they know that at that particular age youngsters will benefit from being on a residence activity with the youngsters, the youngsters are interacting together in a residential activity, because the relationship between the teachers and the support staff but also the relationship between the teacher and the youngsters really does benefit from that residential activity and that they believe that is the best way of setting them up for Key Stage 3 is to have that type of residential—

Q217 Jonathan Shaw: Early on?
Mr Sinnott: Early on in Year 6. So the benefits are clearly there.

Q218 Chairman: Steve, as you said that, memories of St Margaret's Bay and the Romney Hythe and Dymchurch Railway came flooding back! We finish on that note. Thank you.

Supplementary memorandum from Chris Keates, General Secretary, NASUWT

You have requested figures for the number of NASUWT members participating in school trips who have experienced difficulties.

As I sought to explain to the Select Committee, the Union has a regular number of referrals of cases of teachers who are subject to investigation as a result of an incident on a school trip. These statistics are not collated nationally, as it would simply be impossible to maintain such a database. The Union only maintains at national level a database of those cases where we need to engage legal support because of civil or criminal proceedings. In the last three years NASUWT has done this on 20 occasions and compared with statistics going back further than that this demonstrates a significant increase since the mid 90s. This figure of 20 represents only the tip of the iceberg, a point which has been accepted by the former Secretary of State for Education, Charles Clarke, hence the work he commissioned between the DfES and NASUWT, work which is currently ongoing and scheduled to reach a conclusion around Easter.

20 January 2005

Wednesday 3 November 2004

Members present:

Mr Barry Sheerman, in the Chair

Mr David Chaytor   Mr Kerry Pollard
Valerie Davey   Mr Andrew Turner
Paul Holmes

Witnesses: **Mr David Bell,** Her Majesty's Chief Inspector of Schools, **Mrs Miriam Rosen,** Director, Education, Ofsted, **Mr Robert Green,** Director, Corporate Services, Ofsted, **Mr Maurice Smith,** Early Years Directorate, Ofsted and **Mr Jonathan Thompson,** Director, Finance, Ofsted, examined.

Chairman: We appreciate that you have conducted an inquiry into education outside the classroom but on a rather more restricted remit than our present inquiry and we do have one or two questions for you. Who would like to lead on that? Kerry Pollard?

Q219 Mr Pollard: We visited Norway recently and went to a kindergarten that takes children from one year to seven when they start school. We were very impressed with the value they place on outside activity. A huge amount of time was spent outside the classroom: woodland trails, visiting museums and a whole range of activities. Have we got the balance right here, particularly in early years?
Mr Bell: This gives me the opportunity to bring Mr Smith in on early years. Before he comes in can I comment more generally? We published our report and I made the point that our evidence suggested that some teachers were concerned about what they saw as the risks of litigation in all of that. My view—and it was not universally welcomed, it has to be said—was that actually life is risky and one of the ways in which you help children and young people to manage and deal with risk is, in a sense, to put them in a place where they have to make difficult decisions and learn about things. Actually, the encouraging thing about our report on outdoor education was just how many schools are continuing to do it. Talking to people who are doing it in schools, teachers have a fairly robust view about it and say, if we take sensible precautions, do sensible preparation, behave reasonably when we are there, this is still eminently do-able. I think it would be a terrible, terrible shame if we lost these opportunities because they are so valuable not just in their own right—they are great opportunities for young people to have if they are in outdoor education—but actually it contributes, as our report suggested, to their learning in the classroom. They are ways in which you can enhance learning by being outside. Perhaps I could ask Maurice to say something on the early years' dimension of this.
Mr Smith: Briefly on the early years' side we do make judgments under the National Standard Three of care, learning and play. When we look at learning we look at outdoor learning as well as indoor learning and we look at outdoor play as well as indoor play. In the early years sector, as we see it from Ofsted's point of view, most group day care—that is playgroups and nurseries—have designated and specific outdoor play areas and usually of a very

high standard. It is not an absolute requirement and the reason for that is that there are one or two (and they are small in number) where the physical premises would not allow there to be any outdoor play and it seemed to be inappropriate to close that provision down because it does not have outdoor play. In those circumstances we would evaluate what use the group day care provision makes of its community: does it take children in small groups to the library, to the shops? They are very imaginative and very good at it. In fact, care learning and play is the standard where we are most praising. The only other thing I would say, I think, is that a significant number of children are cared for by childminders. Childminding in some ways is more geared to that day-to-day learning that we might think we were more familiar with ourselves as children. For example, childminders have to go to the shops so they take the children to the shops; childminders have to go to the park, so they take the children to the park, et cetera, et cetera. That type of domestic outdoor world is very suited, I think, to the childminder model. As the Committee knows, we now inspect all 70,000 childminders in this country.

Q220 Mr Pollard: Does the decline of education outside the classroom in some schools endanger the success of vocational education, particularly bearing in mind what you said about real life experience?
Mr Bell: I must confess I had not really thought of that connection before. We know that more and more young people—particularly fourteen-plus—are moving around, as it were. They are going to local further education colleges; they are going to the work place and so on. Again, one would say is that it is entirely right that a school or receiving college or whatever takes sensible precautions. It would be a tremendous shame if we said that these opportunities are too risky for young people. In many ways we might say that it needs to happen more and we need to simulate the work place more through centres where youngsters are using more advanced equipment, machinery and so on. Arguably you might say there is a greater risk but I hope that that would not prevent that happening because I am convinced that for young people the more opportunities that are world of work like will be beneficial for them. At the moment we have no evidence that that is putting youngsters or schools off moving youngsters around to benefit from a range of vocational opportunities.

Q221 Chairman: Going back to what Maurice Smith was mentioning in terms of the early years, what has impressed this Committee when we have been in other countries—certainly Norway and Denmark—has been the high quality of the training of the people in early years. We have found already in our inquiry into education outside the classroom that when it is done well it is done well by highly trained people who know how to use the environment. It is just not good enough to say that there is an educational experience outside the classroom, but going down to the shops with your childminder or going to the park is how you use that experience and how you use going to the shops or going to the park. We are still, surely, Maurice, dogged by low paid people working in pre-school settings, lucky to be on the national minimum wage and with very little training. There are few trained teachers in this area. It is of great concern to this Committee, the low level of training and pay in early years. Surely that must be a worry to you.

Mr Smith: Yes, it is a worry and I do not think that we would disagree with your conclusion or with the Committee's view. The National Standards do require certain levels of training in both group day care and with childminders. Some commentators might consider those to be modest. There are concerns particularly as the sector expands—and it has expanded quickly—about the quality of training and experience and maturity of the staff employed in the sector. I think it is worth pointing out that this is quite a different sector from the maintained schools sector in that over 95% of what we inspect in this sector is independently owned.

Q222 Chairman: Yes, but still, Maurice, the fact of the matter is that in other countries where it is seen that this early years stimulation of the child is so crucial—we have talked about this in numeracy and literacy and everything else,—and yet at this most important stage we have the least qualified and least trained people, whether they are in the private sector or the public.

Mr Smith: Yes, that is true.

Q223 Chairman: What are you saying to the Department about the problem?

Mr Smith: We are saying exactly what you are saying, which is that we have—particularly in group day care—staff who are young, inexperienced and not well-qualified.

Q224 Mr Pollard: One final question, have we an obligation to a society—as parents, as teachers and yourselves—to prepare children and students for the real world outside, including risk? I think you were getting into that. We must have an obligation to do that and you cannot insulate children. Walking to school, for example, at an early age has great advantages.

Mr Bell: One of the points we were at pains to stress in our report on outdoor education is that this is not just about teachers and schools; this is about what parents are prepared to accept. Parents, I think, have to do exactly as you are suggesting, Mr Pollard; they have to say, "It is important for my child or my children to experience outdoor opportunities". There is, with that, an element of risk. I do think, for the reasons you suggest, there are so many great advantages in having those opportunities. But we all have to be bold and say that it is worth taking a risk because if you learn to take a risk you actually become a more mature person. You can evaluate and you can cope with additional risks that might fall in the future.

Q225 Chairman: One of our teachers' unions—the NASUWT—gave evidence on Monday on this because that, combined with some of the tabloid coverage, seems to be very great pressure on using the external environment for education.

Mr Bell: I have the utmost respect for the new general secretary of the NASUWT but I disagree with her on this and I disagree with the advice that she has given her members. Our evidence suggested that the teachers—and it was the teachers and the outdoor instructors who were doing this—said that it is still do-able and you do not have to tie yourselves up into hundreds of pages of risk assessment forms before you can go anywhere. It can be done. I just worry a bit about that advice being given because are we not just fuelling precisely that risk averseness that Mr Pollard has been talking about?

Chairman: Val, do you have a question?

Valerie Davey: Chairman, you have brought out the exact statement I wanted from the Chief Inspector which I hope will go out to schools and parents in making that risk assessment as to whether or not they do the kind of outdoor activity which you have endorsed.

Chairman: Chief Inspector, that brings us to the end in perfect timing I would say for Prime Minister's Questions. It has been an excellent session as usual. We hope you do not think we have let you off too easily on this occasion; we try not to. Thank you for your attendance and for all the contributions that your team has made today.

Wednesday 8 December 2004

Members present:

Mr Barry Sheerman, in the Chair

Valerie Davey   Helen Jones
Jeff Ennis   Mr Kerry Pollard
Mr Nick Gibb   Jonathan Shaw
Paul Holmes   Mr Andrew Turner

Witnesses: **Mr Stephen Twigg,** a Member of the House, Parliamentary Under-Secretary of State for Schools, **Mr Andrew McCully,** Director of School Standards Group, and **Dr Kevan Collins,** National Director, Primary National Strategy, Department for Education and Skills, examined.

Chairman: We are going back to our report on Education Outside The Classroom. We are very grateful, Minister, for getting such good value for a number of inquiries. We might even drag you into prison education just to really upset you. Kerry, you were going to open up the questions.

Q226 Mr Pollard: This is a much lighter part of the proceedings. The evidence suggests, Minister, that education outside the classroom can raise achievement, not only by enriching the curriculum but by improving self-confidence, team work and, critically, inquisitiveness. Are you doing enough to promote outside-the-classroom teaching and are you committed to it?
Mr Twigg: I am passionately committed to it and I think it is absolutely right that you express it in the way that you have done, which is clearly there are areas of the curriculum where fieldwork and work outside the classroom is an element—geography, science, physical education—but in a sense the case is a bigger one than that. It is actually about the self-esteem that young people have, their confidence about themselves, it is about life skills and about citizenship at its deepest. I do not think we are doing as much as we need to do. I think there is a load of good stuff going on and we can no doubt go into some of it now. Growing Schools, for example, is a really, really powerful instrument of improvement but I think there is scope for us to do a lot more, which is why, like you, we are focusing on this at the moment.

Q227 Mr Pollard: What should schools be doing themselves?
Mr Twigg: What is very important about this is that we do not hand down a one-size-fits-all approach for every school. Clearly the circumstances of a school are going to determine what they do with respect to outside the classroom. An inner city school is going to have a different approach to a rural school at the most obvious. We want schools to make the very, very best use of the various opportunities that are available and what we know is a lot of schools do but a lot of schools do not. What that says is there is the potential within the framework we have got at the moment to get there. Our role needs to be to see what can be done to encourage all schools to take up the opportunities that are available to them.

Mr Pollard: Your colleague, David Miliband, found £30 million to promote music. Do we need to do the same for outdoor activities? Do we need to have a champion perhaps?

Q228 Chairman: Do we have a minister with a partner who is very keen on outdoor activities?
Mr Twigg: I will ask around—the other Ministers rather than potential partners! I think it is important that this is championed. I think it is a bit different to music, partly in a sense for what you and I have just said which is that this is not just about part of the curriculum, this is something that runs right the way through the whole of the curriculum and citizenship and the ethos of schools. One of the things we have been doing, as the Committee will know, since Charles Clarke became Secretary of State is to have a much stronger focus on subject specialism in all schools and we are looking to have a geography champion. There is a big concern about geography, particularly in primary schools, and geography is clearly a major component of what we are looking at here. We have recently established a focus group on geography, bringing together the Royal Geographical Society, the Geographical Association and others to look at some of these issues. We will have a champion for geography as a subject and we have citizenship advisers and we have a champion for citizenship. It will probably have to make do with me as the champion of this but I will do my best.

Q229 Mr Pollard: A brilliant champion! Should Ofsted say a bit more about this outside-of-school activity?
Mr Twigg: I think they should. What is interesting as the Ofsted framework moves forward with the much greater emphasis on self-evaluation by schools is that there is that flexibility according to the circumstances of each school. The Committee will know that we asked Ofsted to do the piece of work which you have probably seen on outdoor education, which is looking particularly at the centres so it is obviously only one aspect of your inquiry but an important aspect. That was a particular inquiry. I would certainly like to see Ofsted taking this seriously as an element of the inspections that they do of individual schools. I think we have to look further at whether there is

scope to go beyond the inquiry they did earlier this year to look at some of the broader issues beyond the classroom, and not only of the various field centres.

Chairman: Jonathan is the inspiration for the Committee on this subject. He is our champion!

Jonathan Shaw: Perception and reality, Minister. There is a perception that it is high risk taking kids outside the classroom. The HSE says no it is not. That is the reality. There is a perception that there is lots of red tape. The reality is that there is tonnes of the stuff. One school from which we heard evidence had to fill in 16 different forms for a half-day visit. You will tell the Committee that there is a two-pager from the DfES so did that school not know about it? The perception is that insurance is sky high. In some cases it is. Some LEAs are obviously in the grip of fear from the NASUWT and are requiring that there is cover of between £10 million and £15 million. So what are you doing about all those perceptions.

Chairman: I think there were a lot of questions there.

Q230 Jonathan Shaw: One question.

Mr Twigg: What are we doing about it? The central one in terms of perception and risk is your first one, Jonathan, which is about the sense of what the risk is for the kids who go on these journeys and therefore the fear that some teachers have as reflected in the evidence that the NASUWT gave. The Committee will know the figures about how safe trips are. We have seen fatalities and any fatality is horrific but the numbers are very, very small.

Q231 Jonathan Shaw: Why do you not take on the union, the NASUWT because they came to this Committee with very broad brushes saying people are concerned, there are lots of worry. I suggested to them that they were the problem rather than the solution. Why do you not take them on?

Mr Twigg: We want to persuade them and we think we can persuade them. We are in discussions with them right now on this issue. The Committee will be aware that the Secretary of State made a major speech about a whole range of issues to do with pupil behaviour but he also addressed this issue in that speech, and we are very much led by the Secretary of State on this aspect of what the Committee is looking at, looking at all of the things that you have mentioned, talking about the NASUWT to try to bring them on board in terms of these issues which I think would be the best approach to take. We are talking to the insurance industry about the premiums because that is a serious issue—

Q232 Jonathan Shaw: What are the insurance companies saying to you? They are under pressure these days. Perhaps this is easy pickings for them.

Mr Twigg: They are not saying that but—

Q233 Jonathan Shaw: They would not say that, would they, but that might be a perspective?

Mr Twigg: We are at quite an early stage of our discussions with them but I think we have good evidence to present to them in terms of the levels of

risk on the basis of the statistics that the Committee will be aware of in terms of the very, very small numbers of accidents that do happen.

Q234 Jonathan Shaw: You send out lots—and I know you are trying to cut it down—of bits of paper to head teachers. Could you not say, if an LEA is saying 16 pages for a half-day trip, ignore that and ring the DfES and get a two-pager? Have you done that?

Mr Twigg: I am not aware that we have done that. It is a very good idea.

Q235 Jonathan Shaw: That is a good start.

Mr Twigg: We produced the two-pager for a reason. The two-pager is there because it has got the—

Q236 Jonathan Shaw: Why not give it to a headteachers then? That would be a good thing to do, would it not?

Mr Twigg: We are trying to reduce the amount of paperwork we send to head teachers but it might be in that particular case it would be a good—

Q237 Jonathan Shaw: You produced a report and then you are saying you want to enable, that you do not want to see one-size-fits-all and take a centralist approach, but this is one of the issues and it results in quite a lottery for kids across the country. If the LEA are in the grip of fear from the NASUWT then they are unlikely to get a trip because they have not got £10 million to £15 million worth of cover. If they are in a more sensible authority they will fill in your two-pager and the kids can have a great time in the way that Kerry Pollard referred to earlier.

Mr Twigg: I think it is certainly important that we do all we can to support schools to limit the amount of paperwork and bureaucracy they are getting.

Q238 Jonathan Shaw: You would say that, of course you would.

Mr Twigg: Then if there is evidence that there are LEAs who are providing that sort of length of form then we can do something about that and I will take that away to do it, Jonathan.

Q239 Jonathan Shaw: The number of outside-the-classroom experiences for kids is going down.

Mr Twigg: I do not know that we know that. The evidence is mixed between different parts of the country.

Chairman: The evidence to this Committee would suggest that.

Jonathan Shaw: We have not heard anything to say that it is going up or it is staying the same, we have only heard evidence to say it is going down.

Q240 Chairman: Only since you became a Minister!

Mr Twigg: Rising until then. Then I apologise to the Committee.

Q241 Jonathan Shaw: We want you to be the reigning champion not the future champion.

Mr Twigg: Thank you very much. I think it varies massively from one community to another and where the local education authority has taken a decision that this is a big priority and that they are going to push on it then I think we are seeing the number of visits rising. There are examples of authorities that have really embraced this.

Q242 Jonathan Shaw: Maybe something the Department could consider is to ask local education authorities how much they are charging. Those in the grip of fear are charging for between £10 and £15 million of insurance cover. How does that co-relate to the number of visits and experiences outside the classroom that the kids get in their LEAs compared to those who are taking a more pragmatic line and filling in your two-pager? Because then you can have some answers to this and whether it is, as I am suggesting, grip of fear that is actually seeing the downward trend.
Mr Twigg: As I say, I am not absolutely convinced that we can say there is a downward trend nationally. I think it varies from one community to another.

Q243 Jonathan Shaw: Let us find out if it is the £10 or £15 million people or the two-pager people.
Mr Twigg: That is exactly what I was going to say. We then need to identify—and this is the work we are doing right now as a consequence of the Secretary of State's speech—what is the key element. Is it the fear factor or lack of confidence or is it issues to do with insurance or teachers not willing to take the trips, and that will be available school-by-school and community-by-community.

Q244 Chairman: Minister, we have taken quite a bit of evidence about this and the evidence does suggest that the number of activities outside is declining. It may not be a steep decline but it is a steady decline. One of the things that seems to give it a bad name is the poor quality of provision in many schools, in other words it seems from the evidence suggested to us by the unions and other people that there is a ritual. The kids have got to go and see Shakespeare, the kids have got to go and see the sea, or whatever. It is badly organised by teachers not particularly trained for that role and it all looks rather amateur, where if the Government really took this seriously we would be training a cadre of teachers so that in every school there was a real focus on this, that people believed it was not just going through the motions of keeping the kids quiet and taking them down the road for a bit of Shakespeare but it was really designed to use the external environment to stimulate the learning process.
Mr Twigg: That is exactly why we said we want every school to have a visits co-ordinator. In some authorities they are in a position now where every single school has its visits co-ordinator. It is the case in County Durham and it is the case in Worcestershire, to have a champion, if you like, in the school who has the responsibility and takes that lead. If that can be done in every school in Durham and it can be done in every school in Worcestershire

then I think it can be done in every school in the country. That then does get that variety and quality available to children so they are not just doing the same things year in year out, and schools are looking at the evidence of what is available. As part of the London Challenge we have developed a student charter which is very much about the sorts of thing that every young person in London should have the right to go to, be it the theatre or be it an outdoor adventurous activity as well.

Q245 Chairman: How much does the TTA do in this? How much is the training of teachers taking this seriously? In any other subject, whether it is languages or whether it is IT, you would have a real focus on producing some really good teachers who have that experience. None of the evidence we have had is that the TTA takes it seriously or anybody else in your Department.
Mr Twigg: It is an element within initial teacher training. I would not want to overstate how big that element is. The concern you have expressed is one that the organisations have raised recently with the Secretary of State, and I understand the meetings are due with Ralph Tabberer at the TTA to look at this. I would not put all my eggs in the ITT basket, I think we have got to look at the continuing professional development opportunities that are available alongside the initial teacher training that is available. I think there is a multitude—if you look at the Growing Schools web site—of opportunities for teachers with respect to their professional development in the whole range of things that are available for outdoor learning.
Chairman: You are getting a reputation for visiting a lot of schools. In fact, I do not know how—
Jonathan Shaw: Champion visitor!

Q246 Chairman: —I do not know how they can continue to teach with the number of visits you are making! The truth is that you must meet teachers so what is the role model, what kind of qualities and training does the teacher have that would make them good co-ordinators or champions? What are you looking for when you go to a school?
Mr Twigg: I think it is having the passion and the confidence. One of the issues which you might come to is about the curriculum and confidence that schools, particularly primary schools have got, about going beyond what they perceive to be the constraints of the national curriculum. I have been to a number of schools that have really embraced this Growing Schools approach, and that are passionately committed right the way through the school and whoever it is—and sometimes it is the headteacher, sometimes it is not the headteacher—it is having that confidence that this is something that is beneficial to the children in the school, and the confidence to go out there and make links with relevant organisations in the local community. I have seen some brilliant examples on my visits to schools across London but also in other parts of the country where this is happening.

Q247 Chairman: Is that not the problem? You can be lucky and find that passionate person, that leadership that knows about it and does it well, but it is more likely to be Buggins' turn and someone has said, "Sorry, you got the short end here. You are going to be in charge of out-of-school activities," but you have not got, Minister, a system that would change across the piece so that there was something that energises this across the piece. You just hope it will happen. That is what you are saying.
Mr Twigg: It is a little bit more than hope. If we look at Growing Schools—

Q248 Chairman: —but you have not got a systemic answer to it, have you?
Mr Twigg: We have got 10,000 schools signed up to Growing Schools. Almost half the schools are already part of this. What that means in practice in most schools is going to vary. They are not all at the excellent end of the spectrum but it is pretty impressive to have that number of schools already part of a network. In the end we have got to win their hearts and minds. If they are going to do this stuff they are not going to do it because of a diktat. That is where we will get into Buggins' turn. They will do it because there are people with the passion to do this. In most schools there are those people who if they are given the support and the confidence to do it, they will do it.
Dr Collins: Stephen is absolutely right, it is about the passion and the organisational skills and all the rest of it to do this kind of work, but in primary we have been sharing with schools the links between different areas of learning so you are not just going for geography or for history. You are going because a really well organised experience can lead to improved learning right across the curriculum and how you integrate it in a broader curriculum experience. We have just shared with schools—and the vast majority of schools (90-odd per cent) have taken this offer up—some materials which demonstrate how you make those links and how outdoor education and outdoor experiences are critical to improving and raising standards right across the curriculum. It is not only the individual's passion but it is the understanding that it impacts across the curriculum which is critical as well.
Mr McCully: Equally on your questions about quality, we share with schools a code of practice on study support which certainly goes beyond some of the specifics of the outdoor education we have been talking about to encapsulate a whole range of other experiences outside the classroom. The key part of that code of practice brings it back all the time to reviewing the impact on the learning of the children, how it links into the wider curriculum experience and what teachers and the headteacher in both primary and in secondary schools need to do to improve the quality approach and the passion that you have been talking about back into the organisation within the school. So a combination of some of the CPD that Kevan has been talking about, the quality framework for the whole range of better

support, plus the specific activities around your particular interest on outdoor learning are part of the piece.

Q249 Chairman: I understand that one of the great things about the new digital channel Teachers' TV when it is launched in February is that it will spread good practice. I know they have filmed in 250 schools. Has any of this been on out of school learning?
Mr Twigg: I do not know the answer to that, to be honest.

Q250 Chairman: The officials behind you are nodding.
Mr Twigg: Excellent, and they will know, so yes!

Q251 Paul Holmes: Obviously a lot of the talk is about outdoor education centres and going away from the school to further afield experiences, but quite a lot can also be done within school grounds. There is a lot in junior schools obviously but I have seen science teachers in secondary schools do a lot within the school grounds. Learning Through Landscapes submitted evidence to us and they have suggested that some of the new schools, particularly some of the new academies are coming on stream with school grounds that are substantially below the standard that would be expected of a modern educational establishment and they suggest that the public/private partnership consortia often appears to have a poor understanding of the teaching and learning potential of school grounds. There is a tendency to design expensive, aesthetic landscapes of little educational value. Have you any thoughts on that?
Mr Twigg: Firstly to say we work with Learning Through Landscapes a lot and they are a fine organisation. We clearly want to get new schools, be they academies or other new schools, to have the very, very best facilities and I have certainly visited schools where that is the case so clearly the picture is a mixed one. I think that having an effective outdoor classroom is absolutely critical and certainly some of the academy projects that we are looking at that are in their earlier stages will have a particular focus on the environment and some of the issues that relate to the outdoor classroom. I would have to study the evidence that they have given to the Committee in more detail to then see whether there is a basis for what they are saying and whether something can be done about it in terms of the guidance we give for the development of new schools. Certainly for academies which are directly our responsibility as a Department I think it is critically important that they do include those opportunities, particularly as these are schools focused in areas of great need and generally areas of educational under-performance and under-achievement.

Q252 Paul Holmes: Local education authorities do and certainly used to play quite a large part in outdoor education. When I taught in Derbyshire we used facilities at Leigh Green and White Hall for example. In the last ten years, 20 local education authority outdoor education centres have closed down and the trend seems to be accelerating. Your Department's new five year strategy envisages more and more money going straight to the schools and the LEAs being cut out almost completely. Does that mean that local authorities no longer have a role to play in providing outdoor education?

Mr Twigg: No it does not and I think this is an area where local authorities have a very important role to play, be it in providing centres (and clearly decisions will be made at a local level depending on the resources that available at the local level) or in a more co-ordinated fashion. I gave the examples earlier on of those authorities that have really taken the agenda of the visits co-ordinators very seriously, the two examples I gave where every school has that. The LEA and local authority more generally will continue to have an important role. Arguably, they will have an even more important role with some of the other aspects of what we are talking about in the five years, for example extended schools because clearly the extended schools programme gives all sorts of obvious opportunities for facilities to be even more widely available not only to kids but to the wider community as well.

Q253 Paul Holmes: Finally, it has also been suggested that there are unforeseen consequences that arise from one particular action, in this case the teachers workload, and that makes it a lot more expensive to provide outdoor trips because you have to provide qualified classroom cover back in school. This is a new issue particularly for primary schools.

Mr Twigg: I read the exchange that happened when the officials Stephen Crowne and Helen Williams came from the Department. I think the reality is that it is probably a mixed picture on workforce reform. There is the protection that is given in terms of the maximum contact time so that could a negative effect, but, on the other hand, part of the reason that workforce reform can happen is that there are all these other adults working in schools or with schools that were not there ten years ago, and that clearly does give opportunities both in terms of people to cover when trips are happening but also for those people to help with the organisation of the trips. I think workplace reform, in all honesty, will have a mixed impact, in some places positive, in some places it could have the negative effect you have described.

Q254 Valerie Davey: First of all, I want to say thank you for the evidence you have given to the Committee from the Department, which I think is very exciting. I think all the work that is encapsulated here—and quite a lot of it I have to admit I did not know about until this report came through—is genuinely encouraging. The one concern I have got is that outdoor education has to start by you starting from school. If you are not careful, the pendulum swings so that it is believed that you start in school and then go outside rather than recognising the role of parents because the child is more out of school than in school and therefore how is that experience encapsulated and brought

back into school. One brilliant example is the youngsters from Asian communities who find themselves out of school for eight or ten weeks when they go back to India or Pakistan. Until recently there has been a groan about this and then we learnt of a school which sent that child and their family back with a camera. "You are going to be out of school. Take a camera. Report back what you have done." How are parents encouraged to realise that education is going on all around them, whatever they are doing with their children? If you sit on a bus and a child and an adult sit there glumly then nothing happens whereas there is that experience that says, "Look, look, look. What is happening?" How do we get parents to get involved to realise that outside education is not what staff have to do by taking their children from school outside?

Mr Twigg: In the end that does come back to some of what we were discussing earlier on about the ethos of a school that does that and engages with parents. I gave the examples having visited just this week two schools where I could make that comparison with my own eyes. Some of the materials that Kevan was talking about earlier on with respect to general work in primary schools will have an impact there. Clearly from what you said, Val, you were not aware of a lot of this. I think we have to look at our own communications strategy about this work both with the general public but also specifically with parents so that parents can engage with Growing Schools and all of the other aspects of outdoor education. I think schools that are really opening their doors to parents and giving parents a direct opportunity to get involved will be able to engage parents in some of these particular projects and programmes that we are talking about in this evidence as well as engaging the parents with their children's own education on literacy and numeracy and all of the other areas, too.

Q255 Valerie Davey: Can I follow that up by saying that last Saturday I went to see the outcome of probably the best £1,750 the Government has invested in young people which was 150 to 180 youngsters, girls and boys, playing football on a Saturday morning regularly. This is Rockleaze Rangers in Bristol. I looked round these playing fields and all the coaches, all the umpires, all the people around were parents. They have got some sponsorship from another local company and it has been matched by the Government and every Saturday morning all these youngsters play football. They are finding it very difficult to get facilities. They have now got facilities thanks to Bristol University but schools, for goodness sake, are not available to this kind of parent-led club. It seems to me there is a diversity. We have to go into school and get this professional, insurance based, highly negative union impact and yet these parents, if they could be given these facilities more openly, are actually doing it.

Mr Twigg: That is a lot of what extended schools are about. Extended schools have got to be able to provide the opportunity for those sort of things to happen and for parents and community groups or whatever they might be. You see it occasionally but it is occasional and we need to get to a position where more schools are doing that. There is a broader issue about sport. One of the programmes that I am proudest of is Playing for Success and the impact that Playing for Success has had. That is education outside of the classroom. It may be in another classroom but if that classroom is at Highbury or Old Trafford, or wherever it might be, it has an incredible motivating effect on the kids and the evidence suggests a really positive effect on attainment as well.

Q256 Chairman: Before we get a warm feeling emanating from Bristol, the truth is that it is all a bit patchy, is it not? That is the problem; it is patchy. We would like you to come back to this question of how you train teachers. When you are training as a teacher, can you have this as a specialism that can grow? It cannot be taken for granted. I agree with you entirely that it is nice to have someone with passion about their job but they also need the training. They need to know how to do it properly. Is that not the case, Minister?

Mr Twigg: Yes, and I think I have said already there is scope to look further at this with respect to initial teacher training. My understanding is that there are requirements in terms of planning out-of-school activities which are a core element of the initial teacher training that is provided but I do not think it is area that can be specialised in, unless heads are now shaking behind me. I do not think it is an area in which a trainee teacher can specialise.

Q257 Chairman: There ought to be the opportunity. Recently in our report on retention and recruitment we said that we would like to see a cadre of teachers trained to work in challenging schools and almost have another cadre wearing different coloured berets perhaps doing this sort of job. Seriously—

Mr Twigg: —No, it is serious.

Q258 Chairman: —this Committee does believe that you are a bit complacent, Minister, not you personally but the Department and that you really should take this seriously. For example, we had the head of Banbury School who if she is not on an advisory committee giving advice on this she should be, and to take Val's Bristol experience, there ought to be group of advisers with the knowledge and with the experience telling you what to do.

Mr Twigg: We do have an advisory group working with us on Growing Schools and Growing Schools is clearly a central element of this work. That includes practitioners as well as people from organisations like Learning Through Landscape and the Geographical Association, so we do have that advisory support with respect to activities.

Q259 Chairman: I hope there are some lively people on it, not the Bugginses of this world.

Mr Twigg: No Bugginses, I promise.

Q260 Chairman: If the NASUWT does not like this really and it is very patchy, why do you not privatise it or outsource it? There are loads of both private companies and NGOs out there which are really good at this. Why do you not give all schools a budget and say outsource it?

Mr Twigg: I think a lot of schools and communities are using a whole range of different agencies and providers. The voluntary sector in particular is especially important in achieving, for example, Growing Schools so I think it is a mixed picture. There are places where it is directly done through an LEA and through schools in what you might call a traditional way and it works really well, so I would not want to force these schools and authorities to move away from that approach, but I think the voluntary and private sectors do have an important role to play.

Q261 Mr Turner: Can I just quote you some statistics which I only heard properly for the first time yesterday. Within five years of a child's birth only 8% of married couples have split up compared with 52% of cohabitees and 25% of those who marry after birth. Children from separated families are twice as likely to have behavioural problems and perform less well in school. How are you tackling that from both the effect end and the cause end?

Mr Twigg: I think it is important that we have proper sex and relationships education available in schools—and we have talked briefly about this when I have appeared before the Committee before and I think, Andrew, you have raised this on the floor of the House—that respects different relationships but has at its heart marriage and that is very much the guidance that was issued in 2000 around sex and relationships education. I am not familiar with the particular piece of research that you have cited today. I am happy to take a look at it to see what its implications are.

Supplementary memorandum from the Real World Learning Campaign

Written evidence in the light of the Minister of State, Mr Stephen Twigg, oral evidence to the Education and Skills Select Committee inquiry on "Education Outside the Classroom" with specific reference to the "Growing Schools Initiative".

Q226 Pollard quote from NFER research.

Mr Twigg:

"passionately committed . . . ."

"I think there is a load of good stuff going on and we can no doubt go into some of it now. Growing Schools, for example is a really, really powerful instrument for improvement: scope to do more and this is what we are focusing upon at the moment".

GROWING SCHOOLS—A POSITIVE MECHANISM FOR IMPROVEMENT?

Context: What will Growing Schools achieve?

— Growing schools aims to encourage and inspire all schools (nursery, primary, secondary and special) to use the 'outdoor classroom' as a context for learning, both within and beyond the school grounds.

— Growing schools aims to enable pupils to gain knowledge and understanding of the outdoor environment through first hand experience of growing, farming and the countryside.

— Growing Schools aims to raise awareness of food and where it comes from, of healthy lifestyle choices and to encourage a greater sense of responsibility for the environment.

DfES Growing Schools, March 2003

Comment 1: the above clearly indicates the aims/objectives of the Growing Schools Initiative. In both its timing and objectives the initiative appears to have been driven by the Government's concern that there was a widening understanding gap between the food on young peoples' plate and its source.

Issue of defining what is the "Outdoor Classroom"—What happens when other aspects of farming are hardly outdoors will not be especially germane to the aims of Growing Schools. Where do such locations as (battlefields sites, open air concert venues, industrial museums, town trails, athletic meetings) fit into this spectrum?

Growing Schools—The Innovation Fund—an external evaluation, March 2004

THE OUTDOOR CLASSROOM

There are also many organisations around the country, providing a wide range of opportunities for pupils to learn about food, farming and the countryside. These offer an invaluable service to schools and Growing Schools seeks to give them every encouragement.

DfES Growing Schools, March 2003

Comment 2: Out of Classroom learning is qualified to some degree within the Growing Schools initiative by having a focus on "growing, farming and the countryside". This is a laudable objective but it does not mean that the Growing Schools Initiative necessarily represent the broader church encompassed by "Out of Classroom Learning" as represented by the RWL partners and its supporters.

Getting out of the classroom poses difficulties for many schools, for a variety of reasons. But with the claim that significant numbers of pupils don't know that milk comes from cows, or that carrots grow in the ground, the need to reconnect them with nature is unquestionable.

DfES Growing Schools Initiative, March 2003

Comment 3: Therefore as a "positive mechanism" Growing Schools objectives suggest that the outputs and outcomes would be tied to out of classroom education through the first hand activity of growing plants, and developing the knowledge and understanding of farming and the countryside.

Q245 Chairman: How much does the TTA do in this? How much is the training of teachers taken seriously?

Mr Twigg ... need to look at CPD alongside ITT . . . . A multitude of opportunities—if you look at the Growing Schools web site—of opportunities for teachers with respect to their professional development in the whole range of things that are available for outdoor learning"

Q246 Chairman What kind of qualities and training does the teacher have that would make them good co-ordinators or champions?

Mr Twigg ". . . have passion and confidence. Seen many Primary Schools going beyond what they perceive to be the constraints of the national curriculum.

I have been to a number of schools that have embraced this Growing Schools approach—passionately committed right the way through the school."

—confidence to go out there and make links with relevant organisations in the local community.

Q247–8 Chairman   What if you do not get the passionate person in the role?

Mr Twigg   We have got 10,000 schools signed up on Growing Schools. Almost half the schools are already part of this. What that means in practice in most schools is going to vary. They are not all at the excellent end of the spectrum but it is pretty impressive to have that number of schools already part of a network. In the end we have got to win their hearts and minds. If they are going to do this stuff they are not going to do it because of a diktat.

Q245–246 "Training the teachers of today and tomorrow"

One of the four Innovation Fund projects was to look at the issue of Teacher Training. Key aims of that project were:

— To help teachers grow in confidence and competence, so that they are able and willing to use farming and growing as a context for learning.

— To develop best practice in the training of teachers in these new skills, both in teacher training colleges and within schools.

— To share best practice locally and nationally.

— To provide progression in teaching and learning between KS2 & 3.

Pg 9, Teacher Training, Growing Schools, March 2003

Q245–246 ". . . if you look at the Growing Schools web site"

Comment 4: The Growing School website is a rich resource covering a vast array of material and the current (17 December 2004) materials reflect the Initiative's aims and objectives.

Training:

— Outdoor Education.

— Horticulture.

— Garden construction.

— Health and Safety.

— Animal husbandry.

— How to secure funding?

Specific examples of the courses for teachers under the heading listed include:

— Managing wetlands for wildlife

— Identifying Mosses and Liverworts for Biological Survey and Recording (FSC FM)

— Freshwater Biological Monitoring Working Party (FSC PM)

— First Aid for Animals

— Training for Global Perspective in Schools

— Organic Gardening

— Lawn Care

— A weekend on Badgers

— Mountain Leader Award (Summer) (FSC CH)

— Animal Days for 12–14 yr olds (Harbury College, Gloucester)

— First Aid for Remote Places (FSC CH)

— Keeping Chickens in Your Gardens (Robaston College, Staffordshire)

— Setting up a Smallholding (BCA, Burchettes Green, Maidenhead)

— Digital Photography (FSC FM)

— Cooking and Quaffing (Hammersmith and West London College)

The major training initiative is the Countryside Educational Visits Accreditation Scheme that has secured funding to train 500 farmers to take educational visits.

The Evaluation Study identified that the; Base level of knowledge and confidence of teachers involved has been found considerably lower than expected and further funding dedicated to teacher training is needed.

Is there no teacher professional development involved here? Moreover why hasn't experience of similar past projects led to innovation in this one?

There is a requirement for some type of professional development training prior to involvement to introduce and aid the development of this type of project plan.

Note: how little some programmes spent on teacher time and professional development in an Initiative that had a remit to develop knowledge and understanding of farming and growing amongst teachers.

Growing Schools—The Innovation Fund Projects (2002–03)

Comment 5: The Evaluation Report identified that in the Innovation Fund work there was an obvious need for greater investment in teacher training. If one presumes that those involved in these original four projects were the "enthusiasts/committed" then there is an even greater need for training amongst the greater body of teachers.

In his evidence to the Select Committee, the Minister made reference to the "whole range of things that are available for outdoor learning' on the Growing Schools" website.

Comment 6: The image on the first page of Teaching resources element of the Growing Schools' website is one of three plates of vegetables; carrots, lettuce and, beetroot and radishes.

The web based Teaching Resources were interrogated using a number of key words under the heading "Science",

eg one Schemes of work:

— Key Stage 2.
— Biodiversity: the outcome was "not known" which is understandable but when the age was changed to Post 16, the outcome was still not known.

eg two Schemes of work and Lesson plan:

— Key Stage 3.
— Interdependence.
— Not known.

eg three Schemes of work:

— Key Stage 3–4.
— Food web.
— Not known.

eg four Lesson plan:

— Key Stage 2.
— Adaptation.
— Not known.

Comment 7: As mentioned earlier the Growing Schools' website does have an interesting series of resources and the web managers have encouraged the sector to provide information for inclusion on the website. The current site is a reflection of those engaged with the Initiative but there are a number of areas, at least within Science, that still appear to need addressing if the Initiative is to progress beyond an agenda of food and farming.

The News Page that Lists the Current Projects and Events Reinforces the Above.

News Page:

— Putting the "0001" Back into Food.
— National School Grounds resource pack.
— The Healthy Living Blueprint—launched 6 September 2004.
— More CEVAS (Farmer training) courses available.
— Blue Peter Turns Green.
— The National Farms Attraction Network.
— Seasonal Growing Calendar.
— FACE—Buzz Biodiversity Game—importance of biodiversity on farms.
— Greener, Safer, Healthier Routes to School.
— The Farms for Schools (FFS) Annual Conference.
— National Association of Field Study Officers National Conference.

Q257–258

Chairman   " . . . create a cadre of teachers to work in challenging schools, another to do "this sort of job".

—There ought to be a group of advisers with the knowledge and with the experience telling you what to do.

Mr Twigg	We do have an advisory group working with us on Growing Schools and Growing Schools is clearly a central element of this work. That includes practitioners as well as people from organisations like Learning Through Landscapes and the Geographical Association, so we do have that advisory support with respect to activities.
Q259 Chairman	I hope you have some lively people on it, not the Bugginses of this world.
Twigg:	No Bugginses, I promise.

Comment 8: The minutes of the meetings indicate that a number of issues from the original innovation projects, to the dissemination process, evaluation and research, and a sustainable development framework have been explored.

The reflections of Angela Overington (DfES Music) on the development of the Music Manifesto allowed the group to "refocus" on the generic objective of the Initiative. Whether they are or they are not "Bugginses" might be regarded as immaterial, as there appears to be a growing consensus the Growing Schools initiative should fully embrace the wider agenda espoused in its first objective,

"Growing schools aims to encourage and inspire all schools (nursery, primary, secondary and special) to use the 'outdoor classroom' as a context for learning, both within and beyond the school grounds".

Or accept that it is shackled if not dominated by a food and farming agenda and therefore should cease trying to be the sole voice of the Out-of-Classroom Learning sector.

The willingness of the Growing Schools Initiative to be one of the driving forces behind the development of a "Manifesto for Outdoor Learning" and its delivery will be crucial in ensuring that the Minister's aspirations are realised and his commitment produces tangible outcomes. It will also important that a much wider grouping than that represented on the Growing Schools Advisory Group has the opportunity to be engaged in the process of developing the Manifesto and monitoring its implementation.

Comment 9. In answering the Chairman's initial question, RWL partners believe that there is not a cadre of teachers who have the COMPETENCE, CONFIDENCE and therefore COMMITMENT to lead out of classroom learning. We agree with the Chairman and members of the Select Committee that good practice in Out of Classroom Learning does exist: Durham and Worcestershire are good examples, but the overall picture is very patchy! In the 21st century no young person in England should be denied the opportunity to learn outside the classroom.

Q254 Valerie Davey	How do we get parents to get involved to realise that outside education is not what staff have to do by taking their children from school outside?
Mr Twigg	I think we have to look at our own communication strategy about this work both with the general pubic but also specifically with parents so that parents can engage with Growing Schools and all of the other aspects of outdoor education . . . schools open their doors and engage parents in some of these particular projects and programmes that we are talking about in this evidence.
Q 260 Chairman:	If the NASUWT do not like this really and it is very patchy, why do we not privatise it or outsource it . . . to private companies and NGOs?
Mr Twigg:	I think lots of schools and communities are using a whole range of different agencies and providers. The Voluntary sector in particular is especially important in achieving, for example, Growing Schools so I think it is a mixed picture.

Comment 10: The Real World Learning partners believe that parents need to be aware of, and wherever possible, involved with the "out-of-classroom"/outdoor activities of their children.

We also believe that the Voluntary and Commercial sectors such as those represented by the Real World Learning partners and their supporters do provide that "mixed picture" the Minister comments upon. We believe that with encouragement and support that provision can be greatly extended.

We recognise that those Out of Classroom Learning providers operating outside the scope of the AALA licensing scheme need to give reassurance to parents, headteachers and governors, and teaching unions that there operations achieve appropriate standards. To that end the RWL partners have circulated to the unions a joint Health and Safety Protocol and produced a "Quality Organisation" checklist. (attached). Similar "quality assurance" documentation such as the Field Studies Council protocol for London Challenge residential providers, can also be provided.

Anthony Thomas
on behalf of the Real World Learning Campaign
Chair of the RWL Steering Group

21 December 2004

REAL WORLD LEARNING—DRAFT QUALITY Checklist

WHAT IS A "QUALITY PROVIDER"?

Logistics

Quality providers:

— Understand that effective OOCL depends on establishing a contract between provider and visiting school. There should be communication before, during (and ideally) after the visit to agree and ensure that the expectations, roles and responsibilities of each side are met. The contract covers both logistical considerations (such as responsibility for discipline, contact time with providers) and learning ones (such as agreed learning outcomes).

— Have efficient booking systems and procedures with clear lines of communication. Know exactly who the organiser/group leader is.

— State terms and conditions on advance literature and/or web pages.

— Have a child safety and welfare policy.

— Provide risk assessments of the site and all learning programmes upon request.

— Have staff that are inducted and trained in health and safety, customer care, disability/gender/race awareness etc.

— Ensure all staff and volunteers are CRB checked.

— Provide trained first-aiders on-site.

— Have systems and procedures for incidents including accidents and emergencies.

— Have adequate public liability insurance.

— Are aware of, and act upon, LEA-recommended staff:student ratios for different Key Stages.

— Ensure safe access at arrival and departure points.

— Identify and aim to minimise barriers to access for different audiences (e.g. financial, mobility/transport, socio-cultural).

— Ensure that site infrastructure is adequate to cover needs of visiting schools. This includes the availability of facilities like toilets, hand-washing facilities , shelter from extreme weather and storage (lunches, bags, clothing).

— Ensure that site access conforms to the Disability Discrimination Act (DDA) as far as possible.

— Ensure quality equipment provision and maintenance.

— Aspire to "practicing what we preach", avoid mixed messages and lead by example in terms of environmentally sensitive working activities.

— Aim towards Total Quality Management (TQM) including Quality Assurance. Evaluation through monitoring and feedback should be an integral part of the process.

— Encourage visits during shoulder periods (avoiding the (often) over-subscribed summer term).

Learning

Quality providers:

— Understand about learning. Learning is individual, often builds on previous learning/experience, and frequently occurs in a social context. A "good learn" includes varying combinations of knowledge and understanding; skills; creativity, inspiration, enjoyment/fun; behavioural change and progression; attitudes and values. What you feel and do is as important as what you know.

— Have a written learning policy. Multi-site organisations will have a corporate learning policy customised to individual sites.

— Work in partnership with teachers (the contract) to agree on generic and specific learning objectives, outputs and outcomes for the visit. They recognise that visits do not happen in isolation—there are generally pre-visit, on-site, and post-visit components of a learning experience. All components need planning to be effectively implemented.

— Encourage teachers to make free preliminary planning visits to sites.

— Provide appropriate support material for pre-, on-site, and post-visit components. They work with teachers to 'extend the visit' as part of integrated work programmes.

— Support and encourage INSET , CPD and pre-service teacher training about OOCL .

— Ensure quality of delivery through appropriate training and continued development of all learning staff and volunteers. This includes monitoring and appraisal against a system of professional learning standards. Staff and volunteers should be trained to deal with different KS audiences (NB this paper confines itself to schools only).

— Evaluate, evaluate, evaluate—both teachers and students.

— Use a diversity of approaches and methods based on a variety of learning styles. Differentiate and provide layered provision for different audiences. Emphasise approaches that are child-centred, based on active (doing/practical/exploratory) learning, and start with the learner's agenda.

— Recognise they offer a unique experience, not to be found in the classroom.

— Absolutely capitalise on the uniqueness of their site/resources. Maximise the amount of time spent out of the classroom. Going from school to an OOCL provider should NOT be about going from classroom to classroom.

— Bring out the wonder of a site. Encourage a sense of place.

— Facilitate 'experience' and the ability of learners to make informed choices.

— Allow time and space for children to explore and experience. Do not fill the day with conventional structured learning. Offer "light and shade"—"wow" factors interspersed with space/time for solitude and reflection.

— Manage the energy of a group.

— Give context to the day. Relate agreed learning outcomes to wider issues.

— Tailor programmes to appropriate curricula (esp NC) and syllabi.

— Play to their strengths. Don't try to do everything and are honest about what they can and cannot provide.

Written evidence

Memorandum submitted by World Challenge Expeditions Limited

This evidence is submitted by World Challenge Expeditions Limited (WCE) which is an outsourcing company for adventurous school expeditions in the UK and abroad. WCE is the market leader amongst private sector outsourcers, carrying over 90% of outsourced trips, but probably also handles the majority (70%+) of all school expeditions to developing countries and a very high proportion (95%) of expeditions from schools in the maintained sector.

The company has 750 Secondary schools in its customer base, 15 Education Action Zones, Manchester and Birmingham City Councils, Southwark, Islington, Tower Hamlets, Waltham Forest, Hackney and the DfES.

In 2004 WCE **organised expeditions for 40,000 young people in the 9–18 age group.**

WCE is a good example of the commercial sector in provision, and has experienced the kind of high-profile incident which has attracted recent publicity (Amy Ransom fatal accident, Vietnam 2001).

Our summarised submission is that **expeditions for schoolchildren make a huge contribution to education, but are widely inaccessible due to restrictive practice and public sector bureaucracy rather than issues of funding.**

We submit evidence under the following headings:

1. FUNCTION OF EXPEDITIONS IN EDUCATION

Expeditions for young people have always been recognised as the key to inspirational and motivational development (Brighouse pledge; Milliband GetReal; Blunkett Activities for Young People; Graham Lane "Don't tell anyone I was a Cadet"; Duke of Edinburgh Award contains an expedition at every level). Expeditions represent a journey of mind and body with a real sense of purpose which microcosms life and teaches the art of the possible. In a modern society **individuals need to practise skills such as initiative, teamwork, planning, decision-making and caring for others,** but this cannot be taught in a classroom, and so needs to be done on an expedition at some time in a child's life. A study by the Church Schools Company found that employers value life skills as much as academic or vocational qualifications.

2. MEASUREMENT OF OUTPUT IN RELATION TO CURRICULAR AND IN-SCHOOL PROVISION

One barrier to provision is that its impact cannot be measured in the way that can be done with GCSE and other measurables. WCE commissioned a study by the University of Lancaster which established (in Education Action Zones) that attendance and GCSE grades A-C rose amongst a control group who went on one of our expeditions. However, this may have been a coincidence, and therefore the study carries no weight in a school budget aimed at targeted measurables. We submit that the **developmental expedition should be a measurable in itself** because it teaches (through experiential learning) specific essential skills which are not yet in the curriculum, and further raises levels of motivation and self-esteem (especially amongst non-sport/drama/music pupils) which in return raise attendance and passes at GCSE A–C.

3. FUNDING

We believe that lack of funding is an excuse, not a reason for lack of adequate provision. In 2004 over 50% of our Challengers raised more than 75% of their expedition fee, the majority in maintained comprehensive schools, some with over 20% of students on free school meals. Supervised "Money Management" (which used to be known as Bob-a-Job) can deliver to the majority, and those in genuine deprivation have access to endless funds which can subsidise the cost of the expedition. **The biggest challenge for provision is not the cost: it is allowing youngsters to know that they can do something which is attractive, rather than labelling them as "at risk".** For this to be possible the opportunity has to be available to all (as with Milliband's GetReal). Such volumes would generate huge economies of scale which is currently obscured by the tendering process (see below on Restrictive Practice). **The real cost of giving every child in the UK who wanted one a life-changing experience is probably no more than £50 million per annum.** At this scale all the results could be measured in respect of both life skills learned, and attendance or GCSE results improved.

4. REGULATION

Regulation of UK outdoor education is excellent by AALA, but no regulation of any kind exists in overseas expeditions, which is a disgrace and inhibits the proper expansion of opportunity, as well as confusing teachers who wish to provide. **We call on the DfES to work to develop a self-regulating inspection scheme within the overseas industry.** The risk-aversity of LEAs has increasingly stifled opportunity for pupils, and their advisory role needs re-defining. Much LEA advice to schools is inaccurate and delivered or received as regulation. HASPEV DfES guidance on school trips can allow a teacher or Head to believe that they are personally liable for any incident, and fails to recognise that much provision, and much of the liability, can be outsourced—as with school transport. If the industry was properly self-regulated, much confusion and fear would evaporate. We welcome messages coming from the DfES in this area recently, but await action.

5. Restrictive Practice

Outdoor education has traditionally been delivered in partnership with LEAs, and **many LEAs still operate extensive provision.** They also carry responsibility for advising schools on the value of various opportunity, accompanied by the self-appointed regulatory warnings on health and safety, and of course they employ the school Heads and teachers. Some LEA Outdoor Advisers have commercial interest in provision. **This is a conflict of interest.** WCE has evidence of situations where LEA advice on best value or educational benefit is delivered with the impression that it has health and safety implications.

Further difficulties arise over the allocation of funding, where **the tendering process for numerous central government initiatives obscures any reasonable chance of a level playing field.** Funds are distributed by Connexions partnerships heavily weighted towards local relationships, with no obligation to assess the quality of provision, innovation or particularly the ability of the provider to recruit children. As a result vast sums of money go unspent, except on a limited range of local opportunity—and at much higher cost to the taxpayer because the public sector adds in administration fees, whereas the private sector bid with a fixed inclusive price. The result, apart from being chaotic, also heavily penalises innovation or private-sector involvement.

6. Impact on Teaching Staff

Given 1–6 above, **which teacher would bother with arranging expeditions?** If the whole process was clear and simple, and allowed teachers, Heads and parents to make their own choices, the demand, and with it provision, would rise hugely.

7. Press and Public Support

Given that going on an expedition is safer than staying at home, and considerably better for you, it would be desirable to generate favourable positive publicity and encouragement across the board to engage in school trips, rather than fear the repercussions of an incident. **We urge the DfES to promote outdoor education.**

October 2004

Memorandum submitted by Hampshire Outdoor Service

1. Hampshire County Council (HCC) has had a long and continuing commitment to outdoor learning in all its forms. For many years HCC has maintained a network of outdoor centres offering opportunities to school children and other young people to take part in outdoor educational activities—from mountain walking to fieldwork. During the 1980s and 1990s Hampshire bucked the trend of LEAs that sold off or privatised their outdoor centres in the face of budget pressures and protected its centres from changes to educational funding arrangements by moving its centres into a department outside of education. Thus protected from pressures created by the increasing devolution of funding directly to schools, the county was able to grow and develop its outdoor learning opportunities. Additionally, a dedicated staff of experienced professional instructors and teachers have developed at each centre, able to fully support teachers working in the outdoors. A centrally based Outdoor Activities Officer is also employed to ensure consistency of service, operation and risk management across the centres.

2. In parallel with this, Hampshire opted to maintain a dedicated Inspector for Outdoor Education at a time when such responsibilities were being devolved to other inspectoral or advisor staff, in geography or PE sections. This permitted Hampshire to constantly maintain a clear focus on risk management in the outdoors, developing policies, structures, training and other support mechanisms to support teachers working in the outdoors and removing the feeling of isolation and lack of experience often felt by teachers wishing to work out of the classroom.

3. In 2001 the Outdoor Activities Officer and the Inspector for Outdoor Education developed a cross departmental partnership to create the Hampshire Outdoor Service. This structure allowed the development of a common view of the value and place of outdoor learning within Hampshire, and permitted the promotion of a focused strategy for outdoor learning within the county.

4. Outcomes from this partnerships are:

— The development of "Trailblazer", an accreditation scheme for schools, students, youth workers and young people that recognises activity and work in the outdoors and credits young people for their involvement. The scheme started in 2002 and now operates across nearly 200 schools in Hampshire.

— The further development of good practice systems of risk management in outdoor learning. Hampshire is recognised nationally for the depth of its risk management systems, and the Outdoor Service worked with the DfES to support the development of the 2002 DfES supplementary guidance to schools with respect to educational visits.

— A comprehensive training programme, linked to the risk management systems, which allows teachers to build skills and confidence when working in the outdoors. The "Open Country Leadership Award" was the first of its type nationally when introduced in 1985. It has grown and developed and now represents the top of best practice in the country.

— Consistent and continuing investment in outdoor learning. In the past 12 months the County Council has invested or agreed to invest over £2 million in new outdoor facilities and buildings, creating additional capacity and opportunity. In September 2004 we opened a new 40 bed unit at Tile Barn Outdoor Centre to go alongside the extensive heavyweight camping that we have done for many years. This is because camping is seasonal, and we are increasingly being asked by schools and youth groups for accommodation at the centre between November and March, when we have traditionally not taken residential groups. The cost of this was over £400,000. The County Council have just agreed the building of a new 60 bed block at Calshot Activities Centre, cost £1.2 million. Building will start in November. This is to extend both quality and provision. In Wales we are looking to expand the accommodation further, but no decision as yet.

— We have just started discussion with Rushmore District Council with a view to a partnership to develop a brand new Outdoor centre in the north of Hampshire. Estimated cost will be approx £1.5 million, but this is very much at the discussion stage. Nevertheless there is great support and demand for it from our northern schools and youth groups.

— A rapid growth in numbers of students engaged in outdoor learning. Last year (2003–04) some 120,000 HCC students were involved in off site learning of one form or another, lead by some 9,000 teachers/youth leaders. This was a 10% increase on the previous. This is also evidenced by the fact that Calshot Activities centre (our biggest centre) ran a record 16,000 "bednights" of outdoor education—the largest they ever have in one academic year. There is a similar pattern at all our centres. To deal with this we have increased staffing at Calshot by an additional three tutors (in a total pool now of 33 teachers/staff), and made all seasonal staff full time. At our Tile Barn centre we have made all seasonal staff full time and taken on an additional one staff (total now five). In Wales, we have again employed an additional teacher (total now four), and anticipate doing the same at our Beaulieu centre in January.

— An engagement with the raising achievement and school improvement agenda. We are engaged in outdoor learning research in conjunction with King's College, London to evaluate the impact of the Trailblazer scheme. We are engaged with the University of the First Age, developing ways to support teachers working in the outdoors with innovative ways of teaching and learning.

5. In short, outdoor learning in Hampshire is highly successful and developing. Barriers to teachers becoming involved in outdoor learning have been addressed by the development of a well resourced and professional infrastructure which ensures that teachers feel well supported, confident and trained. Specialist staff in centres are able to challenge pupils to their maximum potential, and schools have confidence in the systems in place. Teachers, schools and others clearly understand the potential and benefits of outdoor education, and political support is highly positive and committed.

6. The lesson we draw from this is that the role of the Local Authority/LEA is central to developing and maintaining the provision and impact of outdoor learning.

October 2004

Memorandum submitted by Roger Lock, School of Education, University of Birmingham

1. From the seven indicators available that could identify trends in fieldwork over the last 40 years, four suggest that there has been a decline in fieldwork over this period with two, teachers not doing fieldwork and the FSC database, giving indications of this being a continuing trend. Other indicators suggest there is stability in the number of habitats studied and that a range of locations continue to be visited.

2. Six key factors impact negatively on the number of teachers who are actively engaged in fieldwork; time, cost, the curriculum, its assessment, teacher enthusiasm and expertise.

3. The data on residential study give no clear indication as to whether opportunity for 16–19 year olds has changed in the last 40 years. Long term trends from the Field Studies Council's database suggest a different pattern . . . What the evidence does strongly suggest, however, is that residential biology fieldwork taught by "external specialists" has significantly reduced over the last 30 years.

4. The evidence base from ULK based research papers published between 1960 and 2003 tends to support the statements made by the HOC Select Committee, the BES and FSC namely that fieldwork provision is declining.

(Evidence from Lock (2004) Fieldwork at key Stages 3 and 4; Practices and Actions for Development. In Gujral, A. (ed) Science Education—Aspirations and Inspirations for Science Teachers. ATSE Conference Proceedings 2003. St Martin's College. Lancaster.)

1. Schools don't do fieldwork.

2. Schools don't follow the QCA scheme of work (and so not doing fieldwork is implied).

3. Schools do follow the QCA scheme of work BUT don't have a school field (or any facilities near to hand).

4. Schools do follow the QCA scheme of work but the ecology unit is at the wrong time of the year.

5. Schools have fieldwork in their scheme of work but pupil behaviour is an issue so it isn't always carried out.

6. There were some schools who followed the QCA scheme of work but felt that it offered a range of teaching and learning activities on fieldwork that could be carried out in the laboratory.

7. Schools may use model habitats, paper based habitats and virtual activities instead of work out of doors.

8. In some schools science work outside the lab is more associated with physical science than biology.

9. Physics and chemistry teachers are more reluctant to be involved in fieldwork. Where science is taught by a single teacher this means that field work may be avoided.

10. The author of the school scheme of work (if not a biologist) can exclude fieldwork.

11. At KS4 teacher confidence can be an issue. In the KS4 years, headteachers can inhibit work in the field by discouraging such activities in favour of a focus on improving GCSE grades.

12. GCSE boards can have a negative effect by discouraging fieldwork at Standardisation meetings.

13. A publication by a GCSE board discourages by stating that " . . . ecological investigations can be difficult to organise".

14. Teachers thought that a variety of aspects were needed to support their work. Those that were most frequently mentioned included:

— Picture matching keys specific to the school field and local site.

— Picture keys that permitted identification of herbs, shrubs and trees from vegetative structures only.

— Detailed lesson plans that were exemplary of fieldwork activity.

— Worksheets specific to fieldwork activity.

— Resources that showed Sc1 approaches to fieldwork.

15. There were a number of concrete suggestions made by teachers of ways in which examination boards could encourage fieldwork These included:

— Making fieldwork explicit and required (statutory) within programmes of study, schemes of work and specifications.

— Having it included as "exemplary" or "advisory" materials was seen as inadequate.

— Schemes of work should focus on the scientific rigour involved in ecological studies and help support biologists in dispelling the perception that ecology was a "glorified form of nature study".

— Coursework guidance materials provided by examination boards for teachers should include examples of how to attain high levels in ecological investigations.

— Including questions on ecology in examination papers would help to develop the profile.

— Relocating ecology study from Year 11 to Year 10 would enhance opportunities for carrying out such work, as it could be located at times when the weather was more appropriate.

— Improving moderator training with respect to their views on fieldwork.

— Recruiting more biologists as moderators.

— Reducing the syllabus content at Key Stage 4 whilst retaining an environmental/ecological focus.

October 2004

Memorandum submitted by Farming and Countryside Education (FACE)

DETAILS OF THE ORGANISATION

1. Farming and Countryside Education (FACE) aims to help young people learn more about food and farming in a sustainable countryside. It is a non-political organisation established by the National Farmers Union and the Royal Agricultural Society of England with 50 members representing the full spectrum of views across the sector. Members include Soil Association, National Farmers Union, National Trust, Farms for Schools and Federation of City Farms and Community Gardens. FACE was commended in the Report of the Policy Commission on the Future of Farming and Food, January 2002, as a "... more effective way of getting messages across". There are four key areas of activity: the school curriculum; access to the countryside; research and working in partnership. Further details can be found at www.face-online.org.uk

THE ROLE OF FACE WITHIN EDUCATION OUTSIDE THE CLASSROOM

2. FACE is committed to working with farmers and growers to increase the number of visits to such locations and improve the quality of the educational experiences offered to schools. With farmers and growers managing the overwhelming majority of the countryside, they have a key role to play in providing access and promoting understanding. FACE works with a continuum of outdoor learning providers which includes school farms, open farms who charge for visits and working farms funded through the Educational Access option of the Countryside Stewardship scheme. These range from those who employ a full-time education officer to farmers who take only a handful of visits from the local community.

THE OBSTACLES TO EDUCATION OUTSIDE THE CLASSROOM

3. Feedback from both the providers of outdoor experiences and schools has identified a number of key barriers. These consist of:

— Health and safety concerns;

— Financial constraints both for school and farm;

— Teacher workload;

— Low awareness of opportunities;

— Not meeting curriculum needs;

— Inappropriate location;

— Teacher union guidelines; and

— Lack of confidence and expertise.

Further confirmation of these barriers was reported in a scoping study on the feasibility of an accreditation scheme commissioned by the Countryside Agency and NFU in January 2003.

MAKING THE EDUCATIONAL CASE FOR COUNTRYSIDE VISITS

4. The countryside offers the starting point for learning which encompasses a wide range of opportunities in areas such as food production, environmental care, heritage and leisure. We believe that the countryside has five distinctive educational assets. It:

— Provides a stimulus for active engagement of young people;

— Facilitates the naturalistic learning style as espoused by advocates of multiple intelligence;

— Offers a variety of contexts and specialisms for the underpinning of learning;

— Motivates personal and social development; and

— Contributes to health and well being.

5. FACE believes that a credible educational case can only be made by underpinning assertions about the value of education outside the classroom through research evidence. FACE has instigated a research plan and by working in partnership with the DfES and the Countryside Agency has commissioned two substantial pieces of work. The first was a Literature review carried out by King's College London and NFER published in May 2003 which has helped inform planning by providing insights into, for example, teacher attitudes to the outdoors. It also found that poor evaluation is taking place and there are numerous gaps in knowledge. The second is research into the educational value of countryside visits by University of Bath, King's College London and NFER. This is assessing personal, social and curricular benefits of visits, conducting action research to trial activities and evaluation techniques and will result in the production of a toolkit for schools. An interim report raises a number of key points which comprise valuable evidence for the present enquiry.

6. At present FACE is discussing the possibilities of research into the confidence and competencies of initial teacher trainees and the quality of guidance provided by Initial Teacher Training institutions. Hopefully, this will result in ITT teaching guidance for fieldwork.

IMPROVING ON PREVIOUS BEST

7. There is an enormous amount of goodwill within the agricultural sector to encourage and support educational visits to the countryside. Much has already been achieved and could provide possible models for other sectors.

8. FACE works with farmers and growers providing help and assistance on an individual basis. It works closely with the Countryside Stewardship team at Defra offering advice on the existing educational access option which funds farmers to host educational visits and on the new Higher Level Entry Scheme. As part of this partnership, FACE has produced a CD package of templates and exemplar material on, eg health and safety to ensure that farmers produce a teachers' pack of appropriate quality.

9. FACE believes that countryside venues must be in tune with the current curriculum needs of schools and that schools should keep up to date with ways in which outdoor experiences can raise standards. FACE continuously updates schools and farmers by providing accurate curriculum information, training sessions and pupil activities. For example, FACE has developed an initiative called Biodiversity c/o British Farming which offers schools supported fieldwork visits to study wildlife habitats on farmed land. In response to the Healthy Living Blueprint, FACE is working with the agricultural industry to identify the opportunities of visiting the countryside to address issues of health and well being.

10. FACE is part of a consortium known as Access To Farms, all of whose members have an interest in outdoor learning. Members include for example, Defra, DfES, National Trust and Federation of City Farms and Community Gardens. All members have pooled their information about farms to visit to populate a comprehensive database, hosted by Teachernet, where schools can get the help they need from one source.

11. A scoping study on the feasibility of an accreditation scheme was commissioned by the Countryside Agency and NFU in January 2003. A clear desire was identified to establish a formal accreditation system with significant support from both schools and participating farms. The aim was to instil confidence that educational visits are carried out safely and to a high standard. The main benefits would be improved teacher confidence and improved farm standards with a need to provide assurance regarding safety of visits and good quality educational content. Two strands were identified for development:

— An accreditation framework with a focus on the farm premises involving self-evaluation and independent on-site verification.

— Accredited training for farmers wishing to host school visits.

12. FACE piloted the accreditation training with 110 farmers across England. The three days' training involved preparing the farm for educational visits; food, farming and the countryside in the national curriculum; and effective communication with teachers and pupils. It is worth noting that the Health and Safety Executive participated in the delivery of the training. Results of the pilot were highly encouraging with 97% of the farmers achieving certification by the Open College Network. Funding has been obtained to train a further 500 farmers over the next three years. Work is now in progress by Access To Farms to pilot the accreditation framework for farm premises.

13. Fundamental to the progress made by the agricultural sector is the willingness of farmers and organisations to work together towards common aims. This could not have taken place without encouragement and support from the DfES and Countryside Agency. Credibility has come from responding to the needs of schools.

FUTURE RECOMMENDATIONS

14. FACE recognises the importance of research to gain better understanding of education outside the classroom. There is still much to be done and support for this work is required.

15. There is inconsistency in terms of the advice provided to schools by LEAs eg level of liability a site must have can vary between £5,000,000 and £10,000,000. A single consistent set of LEA guidelines would assist.

16. Many farmers and growers are taking positive steps to minimise risk through good health and safety procedures. The insurance industry should be encouraged to acknowledge those who can demonstrate best practice.

17. Much has been done within the agricultural sector to improve the quality of educational visits as part of the accreditation training and inspection framework. Such initiatives as this can only become sustainable with continued support from government.

18. FACE acknowledges the co-ordinating role played by the Growing Schools initiative and its efforts to promote education outside the classroom. The focus should now be in the form of a proposed outdoor education manifesto to unite all stakeholders.

October 2004

Memorandum submitted by Dr Peter Higgins, Outdoor and Environmental Education Section, School of Education, University of Edinburgh

EXECUTIVE SUMMARY

1. "Learning outdoors" is an educationally significant field of study and practice which warrants support in order to maximise its potential benefits for schools and their students.

2. Evidence from the limited studies which exist indicate modest positive outcomes related to personal development and environmental education as a result of structured outdoor learning experiences. There is considerable scope and need for further research, particularly related to teaching, learning and evaluation processes.

3. There are long-term health benefits of participation in outdoor activities but the role of outdoor educational experiences at school in encouraging such activities is an area which warrants further research.

4. The history of out-of-classroom learning in the UK has been one of fragmented, intermittent provision and lack of appropriate teacher training.

5. Primarily due to the broad range of providers and interests that come under the "umbrella" of the outdoor learning sector in the UK, there is no single representative organisation (a multiplicity exist) and no commonly agreed view of its purpose.

6. The UK scenario outlined has led to outdoor education practice that is focused on provision of safe, outdoor adventure activities that have tenuous links to school curriculum and minimal means of evaluating learning processes and outcomes.

7. Whilst excellent examples of coherent programmes linked to curriculum do exist, such practice is not universal primarily because Local Authority provision and financial support for outdoor learning experiences has declined in the last 20 years.

8. Where residential "outdoor education" programmes are offered by schools these are often short-term experiences, primarily paid for by the student or their family, that are out-sourced to external providers, many of whom have limited or no formal educational training or experience.

9. Other barriers to the provision of an integrated, coherent out-of-classroom curriculum in schools relate to teacher perceptions and workloads, safety and litigation fears and the costs of providing appropriate staffing.

10. Learning outdoors lends itself to an interdisciplinary approach and could be effectively incorporated into a range of traditional discipline areas in the school curriculum. However, teachers need the knowledge and skills to be able to use the outdoor learning environment effectively and safely.

11. Teacher training in subjects which have a fieldwork dimension and outdoor education is essential to provide a coherent curriculum, high quality outdoor education teaching and to ensure that more pupils are able to access outdoor learning experiences (as recommended in the Ofsted report).

12. Suitable and successful curriculum frameworks and teacher training programmes already exist in some countries overseas as demonstrated by the Australian and Norwegian examples provided. This shows that despite some practical issues, outdoor education can be offered in schools within a coherent framework offering students rigorous, stimulating and accessible learning opportunities.

SECTION PROFILE

The Outdoor and Environmental Education Section of the University of Edinburgh has the longest tradition of such provision in Higher Education in the UK. For over 30 years this section has provided courses which balance theory and practice and has an international reputation as one of the leading providers of outdoor and environmental education in the world. The University offers a range of courses for undergraduate and postgraduate students as well as extensive opportunities for doctoral research and beyond. The central focus of our work is to encourage positive relationships between individuals and the environment through learning outdoors. However, this must be balanced with the critical thinking skills fundamental to both academic study and professional practice.

We are committed to a broad vision of *learning outdoors* as the corollary to learning indoors. In this context the outdoors offers a multitude of sensory, aesthetic, intellectual, physical, intellectual, personal, social and spiritual opportunities which can be approached in an interdisciplinary way which is very difficult to achieve in the classroom. Direct experiences of the outdoors bring us into contact with our culture and heritage, have implications for health and well-being through physical activity and personal and social development, and often take place in settings where environmental and sustainability education can be offered in a way which would be impossible in a classroom. To this end we have developed the three circles model shown in the figure below. In this context the role of the outdoor educator is seen as someone who facilitates learning in each, or all three, of the circles according to the needs of the individuals they teach and the requirements of the curriculum. A fully competent outdoor educator will feel confident to work in all three circles whilst always adhering to safe and professional practice.

Figure 1—The Range and Scope of Outdoor Education

Although section staff currently work in a Scottish University all have teaching and/or research experience in other countries, for example other parts of the United Kingdom, Australia, New Zealand and North America. In addition all have involvement in collaborative projects in these and other countries, whilst some have particular experience of outdoor education programme development through European Union funded projects. All staff are members of national or international advisory committees associated with outdoor, experiential and environmental education. These include European and Scandinavian advisory boards and a UNESCO advisory committee. The international dimension of our work is enhanced by the number of taught postgraduate and research students we attract from countries all over the world and similarly the visitors who come to work with us on short term and longer term sabbatical leave. Perhaps as a consequence of this the three circles diagram (Figure 1) has become widely accepted as the standard model for outdoor education in a number of countries around the world informing philosophy and practice.

In the following submission no academic references are provided in the text. The intention of this is to ensure that the document is as brief as possible and easily readable, however, every effort has been made to ensure that all the evidence presented can be supported by published documents or internal unpublished research. Reference sources will be provided in a separate document. There are aspects of our account for which research simply does not exist. In such cases we have based our views on consultations with colleagues in the sector who have specialist personal knowledge and have drawn on our own experience. We have little experience of outdoor play and have therefore not commented on this. Our responses primarily relate to the situation in England and Wales although reference is made to Scotland and indeed a number of other countries throughout the world.

1. HISTORY AND CONTEXT

1.1 Whilst a number of factors may have influenced current partial, patchy and inconsistent provision of learning experiences outside the classroom in the UK a central feature must be the lack of a statutory requirement for this form of education to take place. Whilst the 1944 Education Act did note the educational value of the outdoors and indeed had some influence in the post-war years leading to the 1970s, its provisions can best be described as encouragement rather than obligation on local education authorities. Furthermore an Act of Parliament of 60 years ago which provided encouragement for particular actions cannot be expected to have significant contemporary influence without supporting subsequent legislation, and in the face of curricular and budgetary constraints stemming from the 1980s.

1.2 Similar constraints existed for the Higher Education establishments which provided degree courses (in relevant specialist subject areas such as geography, science and in teacher education) in which both classroom and outdoor centre staff were trained. Furthermore the growing funding council emphasis on research output from universities has led to a reduction in contact time between academic staff and students, with teaching mainly having a lower priority than in the past. Consequently, from the 1980s to the present day there have been reduced opportunities for trainee teacher and other university students to engage with the natural heritage through fieldwork and outdoor activities. This in turn means that many of those who administer and organise educational opportunities for school pupils are neither familiar with the learning potential of such experiences, nor are they required to do so undertake the training to develop this aspect of provision.

1.3 Throughout the period since the 1944 Education Act the "outdoor learning sector" has remained internally disorganised and unable to present a consistent and coherent view of their subject area. Whilst this remains the situation today it is certainly easily understandable when one considers the breadth of provision which would come under the umbrella of "outdoor learning" (for example subject teachers in schools, outdoor education teachers in schools, local authority outdoor centres, commercial centres and those with charitable trust status, environmental educators, charitable bodies with environmental education remits etc). The two main consequences of this have been that it has been very difficult for policy makers to ascertain who to speak to in pursuit of an insight into the subject area, and a sector lacking of an effective approach to putting its case forward. Add to this the concerns, both public and political, surrounding the safety of young people on outdoor education courses and the increase in prosecutions where accidents have taken place in the outdoors, and it is little wonder then that many policy makers, local authorities and schools are not wholeheartedly supportive of outdoor educational experiences. The response of the outdoor education sector on issues of safety has been, certainly since the Lyme Bay incident in 1993, to focus almost exclusively on safety-related issues in their professional practice. Whilst such a response is entirely understandable, it has meant that curricular change has gone largely unnoticed and the resulting opportunities unexploited. This has led to a situation where although many experiences outside the classroom can be deemed to be "safe" they have little or no locus in a curriculum.

1.4 The outdoor sector has been very poorly informed by research findings. In the 30 to 40 years of higher education involvement there have been less than a dozen PhD theses written on the subject area and no major grants awarded. Substantial research has been commissioned by the Government to evaluate major schemes such as the "Summer Activities for 16 year-olds" scheme and its successors which ran from the late 1990s onwards. Furthermore, research findings on the benefits or otherwise of outdoor experiences from overseas have also been of limited value. This is perhaps because in some countries the value of outdoor learning experiences is taken for granted whilst in others countries there is limited interest in providing such experiences.

1.5 The research situation in the UK has been changing over the past five to 10 years, and paradoxically at the same time as formal out-of-classroom experiences opportunities have been in decline academic interest has been increasing. It is clearly impossible to summarise the results from this research in a few lines, however, the weight of evidence from MSc and PhD theses, projects supported by small research grants and Government commissioned studies do generally show benefits in out-of-classroom experiences. Perhaps more importantly this evidence points to a latent and undeveloped potential in relation to both curricular studies and lifelong learning. A range of qualitative and quantitative methodologies have been used to evaluate these experiences and but only a few of the more progressive studies have attempted to address the issue of the longer term benefits of educational outdoor experiences.

1.6 This interest has led to increasing publications of books and journal articles. In 1997 the peer reviewed international *Journal of Adventure Education and Outdoor Learning* was launched and currently publishes two issues per year. There are now regular meetings of a national research forum and as this group has developed there has been a significant shift to embrace research focused on "improving practice" rather than on "proving" the value of various experiences. Research from sociological, psychological, gender and philosophical perspectives is increasingly common.

1.7 Whilst a number of providers of outdoor education experiences attempt to evaluate the influence of their programmes, the majority simply conduct one-off end-of-course evaluations. The results of our own and a few other independent studies have considered whether changes in personal qualities have been sustained and these generally support the view that modest but positive changes are indeed retained at periods up to a year after the end of the outdoor experience. It should be noted however, that these studies have primarily dealt with personal and social attitudes of young people and their dispositions (respect and care for self and others, sense of social responsibility, sense of belonging). One of our studies does provide evidence that the orientation of students to academic work may be improved as a result of outdoor experiences. However, study on the influence on academic success has not yet been conducted

1.8 It should be emphasised that the poor provision of outdoor learning experiences in schools means that most young people are restricted to at best, a one week course at an outdoor centre or field-studies centre. In light of this the research evidence of generally positive but modest improvements in personal and social qualities, academic orientation and interest in physical activities seem to be an excellent return on scant educational investment. It remains to be seen what the impact might be of longer-term, more sustained programmes.

2. Cost and Funding of Outdoor Activities

2.1 For some of the reasons noted above (lack of a statutory requirement, funding issues, curricular issues etc) Local Authority provision and financial support for outdoor learning experiences has declined in the last 20 years or so. The model of teachers in schools providing out-of-classroom experiences as part of their teaching of subjects has also declined. Most schools have no member of staff who can be considered as knowledgeable about outdoor educational experiences, leave alone an outdoor education specialist. Where it still exists school-based provision is deemed to be part of the educational endeavours of the school or Local Education Authority and is essentially free at point of delivery. Residential outdoor centres have been, and continue to be used to provide such experiences and the traditional model was one of Local Authority financial subsidy for such excursions. In most cases such centres were established by the Local Authority and staffed primarily by qualified teachers together with some specialists in outdoor activities. Their salaries and the provision and maintenance of the centre would have been funded by the Education Department of the Local Authority. Whilst this was not the universal model it was the common and preferred approach.

2.2 In the past 20 years or so there has been a major change with the number of local authorities initially seeking to defray residential outdoor education costs to young people (ie their parents or guardians) for travel and food, then making more substantial charges for accommodation and finally and crucially for staffing the courses. The final stage in this process has been the closure or sale of many centres and the retreat to charitable status for a number of others. Whilst some close links remain this policy has in some cases led to a disassociation between centres and their Local Authorities and in others a completely separate status and funding arrangements. A high proportion of these have sought and successfully gained charitable trust status, placing them in a position not dissimilar to fee-paying schools (ie those attending paying fees to a charitable educational business). These changes have in essence deregulated an aspect of educational provision in the UK and the centres themselves have been susceptible to associated financial and other exigencies.

2.3 The upshot of this mixed model is that the relationship between the activities provided by the centre and the curricula is essentially one for the school to negotiate. This in turn becomes a matter of interest in and commitment to the provision of curricular opportunities on the part of the school, the teachers and the outdoor provider. As the sector does not regulate itself and it is not regulated externally (other than through the Adventure Activity Licensing Authority (AALA)—which deals exclusively with safety issues) there is no form of consistent reassurance as to the educational quality of such provision. Indeed the distinction between an outdoor educational experience which is properly and fully located in a curriculum (both academic and personal and social) and what might best be described as an "activity holiday", may not be apparent to the parent/guardian of young people attending such courses, or indeed the school or even the outdoor centre staff.

2.4 The lack of consistent local authority support and funding for such experiences, not to mention the "market place" within which outdoor educational providers now operate leads to some variation in costs. However, the standard cost for a one week residential (Monday to Friday) is likely to be in the range £200 to £280 and clearly not all can afford to pay for such experiences. The lack of direct local authority control over provision means that many disadvantaged pupils will lack the financial support to attend, and many of those from modest family backgrounds will also struggle to find the fee. This is somewhat ironic as a number of studies indicate that such young people are unlikely to meet their academic potential and may well benefit from personal and social education experiences.

2.5 Local authority funding of residential outdoor education took on a new dimension with the introduction in 1991 and 1992 of Devolved Management of Resources (DMR) also known as Devolved School Management (DSM). This system devolved responsibility for the management of budgets and spending from education departments to the heads of residential outdoor centres and heads of schools though some issues such as building capital, maintenance and employee costs remain at departmental level. This allowed centres greater autonomy in the spending of individual budgets; and allowed schools, on an individual basis, to decide whether or not they wanted to use the centre and then, whether or not they wanted to subsidise residential visits for their own pupils. Whereas previously, education departments would allocate school provision centrally, schools were now free to decide for themselves. Following the introduction of DMR, evidence of the distribution of devolved responsibility versus central control from one authority to another does not exist. This leaves an uncertain picture in which to develop an integrated approach to outdoor education provision.

3. The Place of Outdoor Learning within the Curriculum

3.1 There are, broadly speaking three obvious ways in which outdoor learning relates to the national curriculum and these match the three circles of Figure 1. Outdoor adventurous activities (OAA) can be included in the physical education (PE) curriculum (from Key Stage 3 through to A-level); in subjects such as art, geography, science and history fieldwork can provide practical experiences and a context for school-based theoretical study. Appropriately structured and reviewed outdoor educational experiences can contribute to personal and social education and citizenship. Whilst the Programmes of Study and Attainment Targets offer interesting out-of-classroom opportunities at primary and secondary levels, the National Curriculum does not prescribe nor require any such particular learning experiences, other than OAA being listed a an option. As would be expected in a non-statutory context the availability and quality of provision of such experiences through the school or centre is nationally inconsistent and there is no guarantee that even the majority of students will be offered such experiences: a finding reiterated in the recent Ofsted report.

3.2 In light of the fact that outdoor activities can be viewed as sporting activities in their own right, and indeed ones at which the UK has traditionally excelled (mountaineering, sailing, canoeing etc) the lack of emphasis in the curriculum seems puzzling. All the more so considering the well recognised long-term health benefits of such activities which are often pursued well after individuals have forsaken the team-sports which characterise school-based physical education. Perhaps this is the nub of the issue, it is much easier to organise a class into two teams to play a ball-game than to provide outdoor activities which often require specialist equipment, transport and particular teaching skills.

3.3 The health benefits of physical activity outdoors (especially walking) are now widely accepted and promoted alongside the social and psychological benefits of being in the countryside. Whilst it is widely accepted that PE in schools should encourage physical activity it should be borne in mind that long-term health is promoted by life-long commitment to activity and this is often has a social dimension. Little wonder then that walking in the countryside with friends or family is often cited as the most popular adult form of physical activity rather than the team-sports which are the basis of much PE provision in schools.

3.4 That out-of-classroom experiences should be included in subjects which have an environmental dimension seems obvious. However, perhaps for the variety of reasons noted elsewhere in this paper (a lack of "first" degree and/or teacher training, school organisational factors, insecurity about accidents etc) such provision is not widespread. To counteract this trend action is required on each of the influential factors. However, a policy expectation that schools should provide structured programmes of out-of-classroom environmental education and that this would be linked to assessments would have a dramatic impact.

3.5 Personal and social educational experiences are now often associated with citizenship and both are frequently linked to outdoor education. The argument is that encounters with challenging situations on the outdoors, which are then properly reviewed to help students make meaning from them, provide realistic metaphors for personal issues and relationships with others in society. Perhaps because this has been a common rationale particularly for outdoor centres, this issue has received some research attention and support. In light of this a more widespread use of out-of-classroom experiences would be expected. The factors mitigating against may well be similar to those noted above for environmental field-work.

3.6 As noted earlier the common model for many schools is to arrange short-term primarily residential experiences. However, whilst these are to be welcomed they are in a very real sense self-defeating. Whilst evidence points to the valuable experiences that people have during these programmes there is rarely a consistent approach to link these experiences with curricular work and/or wider issues of citizenship. Although curricular opportunities exist, there is no requirement to follow them and so provision is often as the result of enthusiastic teachers rather than consistent approaches. If these experiences are to be useful to pupils in their everyday life settings then they need to make sense of the experiences they have at outdoor centres. For this to happen it may be necessary to rethink the model of delivery in favour of an integrated approach to outdoor education provision. One way to achieve this would be to make better links between schools and outdoor centres. For example, the class teacher or school outdoor education specialist could work on a programme of lessons which use the visit to an outdoor centre as a culminating endeavour. If this were a curricular requirement then integration would depend more on programmed activity than the goodwill of teachers.

3.7 Whilst not seeking to propose outdoor educational experiences as a panacea, the argument that this approach might do all of the above would make such experiences uniquely valuable to schools. Whilst evidence exists for the value of each component there has been virtually no investment in research to assess the value of integrated learning experiences in the outdoors. What published work exists has mainly been theoretical argument.

3.8 Although the above has focused on the existing curriculum in schools it is worth noting that out-of-classroom education may provide significant opportunities for proposed developments in vocational learning. In particular the outdoor activities holidays sector has experienced rapid growth in recent years and offers increased employment opportunities.

4. EXTERNAL ASSESSMENT OF PROVISION

4.1 Before dealing with the issue of external assessment it is first important to point out that, as noted earlier, *internal* assessments are infrequently conducted and often limited to a brief conversation or questionnaire at the end of a short course. In order to conduct meaningful internal assessment the relationship between the needs of the pupil (in the context of the school and their overall academic and personal and social development) must be considered in relation to the range of activities provided in school-based or residential-based outdoor experiences. The obvious place to do this is in the school itself to which the young people will return after their outdoor experience. This requires that teachers understand the purpose, content, methods and approach which characterise the outdoor learning experience. These teachers must then relate this to curricular and other aims. The success or otherwise of these out-of-classroom experiences should then inform both school practice and that of any teachers or specialists providing outdoor experiences for the young people. In our view the generally positive nature of anecdotal comment on outdoor experiences combined with a lack of specialist teachers in the school has led to a generally uncritical approach to provision. Our studies suggest that the observation that "the kids really enjoyed themselves" can easily lead to the impression that "the outdoor course was educationally worthwhile". Whilst enjoyment and learning may well be related the one does not necessarily lead to the other. In fairness it might be pointed out that a rigorous framework for this form of internal or indeed external assessment is not required for most other aspects of the curriculum, however, few of these are in the perilous position of outdoor learning which seems to continually be required to justify itself.

4.2 As noted earlier external assessment of provision has primarily been with regard to Health and Safety inspections by AALA. Under the provisions of the Act which established AALA most outdoor providers in the UK (except schools and some others) are required to be inspected and to meet certain safety standards. In contrast there is no form of consistent or regular inspection of the quality of teaching and learning relating to outdoor educational provision. Although the recently published Ofsted report presents their findings on only 15 such centres, this constitutes the broadest external inspection in the UK. (The most "in-depth" is probably a three-year study of five centres conducted by the University of Edinburgh). Whilst a number of outdoor education centres have been inspected by Her Majesty's Inspectors (HMI) over the years the focus has been primarily on Local Authority centres and does not to any great extent cover the full range of provision in the UK. That such inspections tend to be sporadic and one-off should come as little surprise considering both the diversity and scale of such provision and that the primary responsibility of HMI is in-school provision.

4.3 In schools which do have programmes offering outdoor educational experiences whether these be provided by school teachers or by an external provider it is customary for HMIs to comment on this in their reports. However, as far as we know there are no HMIs with a background specialism in outdoor education and whilst they clearly have the analytical skills required to inspect, there would be value in some form of professional development to appraise them of the breadth and scope of out-of-classroom education. With regard to assessment of the effectiveness, the Ofsted report comments that the work of the programme in a residential centre is rarely developed further when students return to school, and therefore the long-term benefits are lost. Whilst this is in our view fair comment it should be pointed out that their own report is, presumably for valid reasons, based primarily on on-site observations.

4.4 To assess whether there are longer-term benefits or otherwise it is essential that such evaluations take place. Our own research on outdoor education centres in the UK found a lack of connection between the claims made for such experiences and the collection of data to support it. In response to this we have advocated a framework designed to encourage those involved in delivery to implement a holistic empirically-based approach to their work. This relies on considering for example the intent to develop "self-awareness" through reviewing programme *aims, assumptions, content, method, evaluation and claims.* It is intended to show that evaluation should not only be outcome based but process based as well including the planning, teaching and evaluation of outdoor education programmes. It is intended to provide a basis for developing clear educational objectives in advance of programmes taking place and to lead to successful and effective programme development rather than *post hoc* rationalism. Only through such an approach can providers have confidence in the claims made for their programme.

4.5 In light of the above it seems inescapable that in order for curricular aims to be satisfied and the effectiveness of programmes to be assessed there must be some mechanism in place to do so. However, if young people are to be taken out of school on an educational pretext it is vital that the quality of that educational experience is assured. In our view there is little or no justification for an "activity holiday" in school time, and providers of out-of-school experiences should explicate the link between practice and the academic or broader school curriculum for any parent, teacher or inspector who asks.

4.6 At the same time it is clearly inappropriate to assess providers without giving them the opportunity to be trained in quality assurance. This in turn means that the training of those who might teach outdoors, for example those on relevant single discipline (eg science, geography, history) courses, outdoor education courses and even hopefully those training in primary teaching should emphasise an understanding of the theory, practice and evaluation of education out-of-doors.

4.7 Although the sector relies on the national governing body (NGB) awards in each of the outdoor activities (for example canoeing, climbing, sailing etc) as measures of coaching competence, such courses do not, nor are they intended to, provide a training for outdoor educators in linking outdoor experiences with the educational requirements of the curriculum. The NGBs are essentially clubs for people interested in pursuing the various outdoor activities for recreation or competition and in order to do so they have developed their own coaching structures. Consequently they cannot be expected to consider the link between coaching these activities and the curriculum, nor indeed the assessment of the effectiveness in doing so.

4.8 There are very few courses in the UK which are designed to train those who teach outdoors and of these, few focus on teaching as a discipline or provide teaching or comparable qualifications as an outcome for successful graduates. The reasons for this are quite straightforward. Despite the popularity of such courses they are expensive for colleges to run and therefore few exist. There is also no national teaching structure (General Teaching Council or equivalent) requiring or even advocating such specific professional training. It is rather like having chemistry teachers selected on the basis of an interest in, but not necessarily a qualification in or teacher training in the discipline. In order to provide consistent high quality outdoor learning experiences this issue needs urgent attention.

5. ORGANISATION AND INTEGRATION WITHIN EXISTING SCHOOL STRUCTURES

5.1 As with other aspects of provision there is no consistent model for the organisation and integration of out-of-classroom experiences. This may well be for the reasons noted earlier, namely the absence of staff designated to take this responsibility, classroom teachers who may have no particular interest in taking children outdoors or others who have anxieties about the consequences of accidents. Perhaps above all though, the lack of specific curricular locations for out-of-classroom experiences provides no encouragement or requirement to do so. Where outdoor adventurous activities are noted within the curriculum (as part of the PE curriculum) they are listed as an option. As very few PE teachers will have had any training in outdoor adventurous activities this necessarily becomes an issue of individual interest on the part of the teacher. Where the out-of-classroom experiences are environmental or personal and social these too are not required as part of the curriculum.

5.2 Where a teacher does have an interest and wishes to take children out of the classroom on fieldwork there is associated an increased organisational and administrative load. It is perhaps unsurprising then that schools which do offer out-of-classroom experiences often find that organising a residential excursion to a field studies or outdoor education centre provides a convenient alternative. In doing so the responsibility for provision is devolved to the contracted provider and the task of the school is primarily to ensure that the young people arrive safely at the centre and return home at the end of the residential. This often means that the school loses one or more teachers for the duration of the residential, and that before leaving with the group teachers have to prepare lessons to allow a colleague or supply teacher to cover their classes. Upon return the classroom teacher is then usually faced with a catching up period. This can therefore be costly for the school and demanding of the teachers involved. The other major consequence of such a form of delivery is as noted earlier that the content and conduct of the programme is essentially devolved to the staff of the centre. The best arrangements are clearly where school staff make a concerted effort to ensure the delivery is of valuable educational experiences which are then followed up upon return to the school. This point is noted in the recent Ofsted Report on outdoor education centres.

5.3 Where schools do employ a specialist outdoor education teacher their role is often demanding, requiring them to find primarily local venues to deliver integrated educational experiences. However, depending on the location of the school such an arrangement can be limiting and fairly frequent access to a minibus to take groups out is usually necessary. There are other structural problems too. The ratio at which both outdoor activities and field studies are conducted (for obvious health and safety reasons) is often one teacher working with eight to 12 students and this may present difficulties for schools. Consequently the only realistic model for schools to adopt is one of extraction of groups of this size from a year group.

5.4 It should also be borne in mind that the provision of out-of-classroom experiences is not universally popular amongst school-teachers, and it is not uncommon for an extraction model or a residential week model to be resisted by teaching staff who are not convinced of the benefits and are equally unenthusiastic about any resulting increase in their own workload. Overcoming this requires transparent and demonstrably fair structures within the school, clear leadership from school managers and clarity in explaining the purpose of such out-of-classroom experiences. All the more reason then why such experiences should be properly evaluated to discern any educational benefits. In discussing the issue of getting children out of the classroom with teachers, one other organisational factor is often mentioned. This is the requirement to gain consent from the parent or guardian of each of the young people involved in the activity and also clearance from within the local authority structure. The latter usually requires details of the excursion or residential to be seen and signed by an adviser with appropriate authority to do so. This is often an extra test of the motivation of teachers to organise out-of-classroom experiences. However, with support from school management this task could be undertaken by the school's administrative team.

6. QUALIFICATION AND MOTIVATION OF TEACHERS AND THE EFFECT ON TEACHER WORKLOAD

6.1 As noted earlier there is no clear or agreed structure for the training of teachers. For those teachers whose interest is primarily in academic fieldwork the issue is somewhat more straightforward than for those interested in providing outdoor activities. In the case of the former, the academic discipline and their teacher training provide a basis for their work. Although much depends on whether they themselves have had experiences of fieldwork within their own training, it is essentially a matter of getting the young people out of school and into the environments they wish to study. Beyond this the main requirement is an understanding of health and safety related issues associated with the main fieldwork locations in the countryside and associated water bodies, seashore etc. For those who take groups into mountainous country the normal expectation is that they would hold an appropriate NGB qualification such as the Mountain Leadership Award. Whilst this is not in any sense a "legal" requirement, it would be the expected standard of training and qualification for someone conducting fieldwork in mountainous terrain.

6.2 For those who teach outdoor activities the situation is altogether more complex. First there are very few academic courses at universities in the UK which offer a teaching qualification in outdoor education. Second very few schools can afford the perceived luxury of a specialist outdoor education teacher who does not teach other subjects within the school. Consequently where outdoor educators are employed in schools they are frequently specialists in another discipline who have an interest in and some additional qualifications in a range of outdoor activities. Hence an outdoor education teacher in a school may hold a teaching qualification in outdoor education and another discipline, or may be a specialist in another discipline with no academic training in outdoor education at all. In both cases the outdoor education teacher would normally be trained and qualified to teach several outdoor activities to an introductory or higher standard. Gaining such qualifications requires first and foremost a personal commitment to the activity (ie hillwalking, canoeing, sailing etc) then attendance at training courses and then finally with appropriate experience, assessment of the ability both to perform at the necessary skill-level and teach in the environment for which the qualification is specified. This process requires commitment, is costly and takes considerable time. Some schools are very supportive of teachers who wish to gain these NGB awards whilst others are less so. Many outdoor education teachers pay for the training and qualification process themselves and often can only attend courses during holiday periods. However, in many schools such teachers provide an important focus and motivation for other staff to develop their own skills in outdoor activities, and encourage their colleagues to train and qualify and indeed accompany groups. Examples of best practice exist where this process extends beyond the school to a Local Authority outdoor education centre which will offer training and assessment courses in a range of outdoor activities for staff from their schools. This generates more fulsome understanding of the activities themselves, their educational purposes, the opportunities available in the outdoor centre and the requirements of the school curriculum.

6.3 In terms of workload it is, in our experience, uncommon to hear teachers who take young people on out-of-classroom educational excursions and residentials complaining about the increase in their teaching load. Where they exist such complaints often relate to administrative issues. Whilst some school staff who do not teach outdoors may perceive an increase in their workload they may well still be supportive. For example a major study conducted of schools and centre provision within the Lothian Region of Scotland around 20 years ago found that in schools where outdoor education was seen as an important focus of the school's efforts, staff were generally highly motivated to support such provision. Anecdotal evidence suggests that this remains the case and indeed where such provision has recently decreased staff feel something important has been lost from the school.

6.4 In one study of provision of out-of classroom education in Oxfordshire Primary schools teachers and policy makers cited lack of staff expertise, the demands of the literacy and numeracy strategies, and the need for staff who initiate such programmes to be supported as factors mitigating against further development. An unpublished Ofsted survey of "outdoor and adventurous activities" (as an option in the PE National Curriculum at Key Stages 3 and 4) in 33 schools and centres in 1999 supported the view that leadership and vision on the part of senior school staff were crucial in fostering such experiences, and that appropriate in-service training often provided the means of giving responsible staff both the skills and reassurance to do so.

6.5 If out-of-classroom learning experiences are to become more widespread and more meaningful a short to medium term approach becomes necessary and this must involve in-service training. This should provide teaching staff and school managers with the necessary knowledge of Local Authority procedures and relevant legal issues, appropriate teaching strategies for teaching outdoors and the skills (and indeed qualifications) necessary to teach various activities. Whilst this may seem unattainable this has been a very successful approach for at least one Local Authority. In the 1980s and 1990s the Lothian area of Scotland had a vibrant outdoor education programme in schools and centres which was adopted as a model by many countries. Most secondary schools (45) had specialist outdoor education teachers and a comprehensive in-service scheme operated primarily through the Local Authority centres led to over 500 teachers being qualified to assist in outdoor education provision in these schools. In the longer term, including fieldwork and outdoor education in the requirements of relevant teaching qualifications would enable staff with specialist knowledge to be recruited to schools and may also have a spin-off benefit in teacher recruitment.

7. THE FEAR OF ACCIDENTS AND THE POSSIBILITY OF LITIGATION

7.1 It is notable that this "question" does not refer to the causes of accidents nor does it include an implication that out-of-school activities should be "safer". On the assumption then that this is intentional and that the remarkable safety record of such activities is understood we will focus on the stated question.[1]

7.2 It is clear that there is a genuine fear of outdoor accidents amongst many school staff. This is perfectly understandable in light of the media interest in each high-profile case. What is also clear is that such coverage is often misleading in that it gives an impression of unsafe practice not substantiated by the accident figures. At least one teaching union has also advised members not to take groups on outdoor excursions and it takes considerable self-confidence and not a little specialist knowledge (of exposure adjusted comparative accident rates) to ignore such pressures.

7.3 When accidents are due to negligence it seems perfectly appropriate that the law is pursued and prosecutions follow. This has been the case in several recent cases. Where we believe teachers and others face additional pressures is the fear that litigation will follow an out-of-classroom excursion. It does not seem clear why there are particular fears about such possibilities when there seems to be no comparable concern about in-school accidents. It will not be easy to allay such fears but several approaches could be considered.

7.4 The support of teachers and their unions is essential, and in order to persuade them to do so a number of measures may be required. First, the educational case for going outdoors must be put forward, and this would be strengthened significantly if such activities were embedded in the curriculum requirements. Second, appointment of teachers with specialist knowledge of outdoor learning and who are able to train school staff in the background and procedures would prove a valuable resource. Third, a national insurance scheme might be considered for all those teaching out-of-doors who are working under the aegis of a school or associated outdoor education centre. Fourth, a national accident compensation scheme might be considered. It may be a long way outside the remit of this enquiry but it is worth note that in, for example, New Zealand a national accident compensation scheme sets standard fees for various injuries and this has prevented wholesale litigative action. Beyond this, and in some situations personal accident cover could be suggested for students.

7.5 One additional point needs to be emphasised and this is the cost of not going out of the classroom. The recent Ofsted report highlights the fact that young people, not to mention their teachers are often not skilled in assessing risks. One obvious way to do this is to train them to do so, and this means at least some experience of situations where risks are apparent. Furthermore, the failure of schools to encourage outdoor physical activities may have long-term health costs and the lack of direct environmental learning implications for our appreciation of our cultural and natural the natural heritage and understanding of the crucial issue of sustainability. These points have been noted elsewhere in this document, but it should be noted that little empirical evidence has yet been gathered on these issues.

8. HOW PROVISION IN THE UK COMPARES WITH THAT OF OTHER COUNTRIES

8.1 Whilst we have experience and some knowledge of provision in a number of countries we have sought below to focus on examples of what we consider to be *good practice*. Individual examples are discussed and common or thematic issues highlighted at the end of the section.

8.2 *Outdoor education in the school curriculum in Australia*

8.2.1 Outdoor education has existed in schools in Australia since the 1960s and is particularly well established in the state of Victoria where it has been taught as a discrete subject in the P-10 and senior secondary curriculum since 1989. In Victoria over 100 secondary schools offer outdoor education as a subject at senior school level and most secondary schools (approximately 460), offer some form of outdoor education. Five schools build outdoor education into the daily programme of a long-term (usually 6–12 months) rural, residential experience for students at year 9 (form 3). Outdoor education is offered in six Universities in Victoria either as a stand alone degree or as part of a teacher training or physical education degree, Postgraduate teacher training in outdoor education is offered at three Universities in Victoria and approximately one quarter of teachers who teach outdoor education in schools have specific training in this discipline. While the situation is improving this is an ongoing issue since the majority of outdoor education teachers are trained in physical education and therefore often lack the specific knowledge required to teach the senior secondary curriculum which has a strong environmental emphasis.

[1] If the issue of out-of-school accidents, safety issues and comparative accident statistics is one that the inquiry would seek evidence on, please specify the issues and we will offer comment.

8.2.2 Outdoor education is also offered in schools and is supported by curriculum frameworks in South Australia, Western Australia, Northern Territory, New South Wales, Tasmania and Queensland. The purposes and practices are varied with different emphases in each state and a range of support structures. Victoria and Queensland in particular are relatively well supported with specific education centres staffed and resourced to provide outdoor education experiences for students from government schools. This form of outdoor education is however, usually extra-curricular and therefore short term and fragmented. The inclusion of outdoor education in the school curriculum allows for a more coherent educational programme.

8.3 *Friluftsliv: The Norwegian approach to out-of-classroom learning*

8.3.1 The Norwegian term *"friluftsliv"* can be roughly translated as "outdoor nature life" and embraces a range of physical activities in the countryside, most of which have cultural and environmental dimensions. It is a widespread social phenomenon and in a sense *friluftsliv* is a defining aspect of national identity. Almost all Norwegians would have experienced it at school and many continue to do so with family and friends. In these terms it would be well understood by most Norwegians and in terms of educational policy its provision is uncontested.

8.3.2 The role *friluftsliv* plays in the Norwegian school-system is defined through the national curriculum for secondary schools. *Friluftsliv* is mentioned as a supplementary subject for a variety of school-subjects, although it is especially connected to physical education. However, this should not be taken to mean that it is considered a primarily physical pursuit, rather that the role of PE teachers is somewhat broader than in the UK.

8.3.3 In **school years 6 to 16 (Primary and Secondary Modern schools)** pupils are entitled to experience nature and learn about the interaction of man and nature in former and contemporary times. The pupils are expected to develop their outdoor skills and gain an understanding of the fragility of nature.[2] Students are requested to develop an understanding of *friluftsliv's* role in cultural identity, the joy of movement and the joy of "life". The main activities taught to do so, primarily to allow journeys in the Norwegian landscape and include introduction to canoe-paddling, winter-*friluftsliv*, camp-craft skills and orienteering. This is reflected in the training of "Secondary Modern" school teachers.

8.3.4 Many of Norwegian schools have a **one-day module out-of-doors course** (*Uteskole/Læring i friluft*) with a systematic pedagogical content. *Uteskole* is a working method where parts of daily school-life are moved outside to nearby local areas. They are supported in doing so by the national education plan which encourages schools to take students outside one day a week.

8.3.5 Norway also has a system of "local authority **outdoor education centres**" (**Leirskole**) and over 62,000 pupils visited one in the school year 2003–04. This amounts to 10% of all pupils in the secondary age-range. The aim of this provision is to achieve a deeper understanding of nature and holistic ecological understanding. The intention is that in the 10 years of secondary education every school pupil in Norway will follow a 7–10 day course at a Leirskole.[3]

8.3.6 *Friluftsliv* can be followed in-depth within the **Norwegian *"Folkhighschool"* movement**. In English, the name "folk high school" often gives a misleading impression. "Residential adult college", "residential enrichment academy", "experiential academy" or even "folk school" would be more apt modern descriptions. The typical range of age of students is between 18 and 25 years and the courses normally last for nine months. Each school has its own profile, but in general, the Norwegian folk high schools teach classes covering a variety of interest areas, including arts, crafts, music, sports, philosophy, theatre, media, photography, outdoor activities etc. With about 90 of these schools in Norway of which more than 40 offer or specialise in *"Friluftslivlinjer"*, the Folkhighschool is perhaps the deepest educational manifestation of Norwegian friluftsliv.

8.4 The cases of Sweden, Denmark and Finland are similar to that of Norway but there are specific cultural differences in approach and provision. The above examples are characterised by a depth of provision through which many aspects of curriculum are taught to as high a proportion of the school population as possible. It should be noted that whilst in many countries there is little attempt to embed out-of-school experiences in the formal curriculum there is often a stated linkage with personal and social education. In most of our studies of international approaches to outdoor learning, where a real effort is made to approach broader environmental and other curricular issues these countries develop and implement detailed curricular guidelines.

8.5 One point of interest is that in many cases the countries we are familiar with developed their national approach to outdoor learning after detailed consideration of the approach taken in the UK in the 1960s and 1970s. In particular the carefully constructed and wide-scale provision in the Lothian Region of Scotland was widely regarded as the ideal model. Several decades of erosion have left such provision in a poor state, not dissimilar to the rest of the UK, whilst several of those countries which adapted the model to suit their own situation now have extensive curricular provision.

---

[2] National Curriculum (4th and 5th form) (1997) *kroppsøving og l97: mål for mellomtrinnet (8.-10. Klasse)*.
[3] www.leirskole.no.

8.6 Further details of provision in Australia, Norway and New Zealand are provided as separate attachments and guidance on sources for a number of other countries (eg Canadian Provinces, Czech Republic, Germany, Poland, Singapore, Switzerland and a number of other countries) can be provided on request.

NEW ZEALAND: OUTDOOR EDUCATION IN THE HEALTH AND PHYSICAL EDUCATION CURRICULUM

Outdoor education makes a unique and significant contribution to the development of the essential skills described in The New Zealand Curriculum Framework. In this document the case for inclusion for outdoor education is stated as providing students with "opportunities to develop personal and social skills, to become active, safe, and skilled in the outdoors, and to protect and care for the environment".

The following extracts from the document provide both the rationale and location of outdoor education in the curriculum.

Outdoor education includes adventure activities and outdoor pursuits. Adventure activities foster students' personal and social development through experiences involving co-operation, trust, problem solving, decision-making, goal setting, communication, leadership, responsibility, and reflection. Through outdoor pursuits, students develop particular skills and attitudes in a range of outdoor settings. Outdoor pursuits include biking, orienteering, bush walking, tramping, camping, kayaking, sailing, following rope trails, and rock climbing.

In outdoor education programmes, the four dimensions of hauora are enhanced through safe, challenging, and enjoyable learning experiences in the outdoor environment.

Through the socio-ecological perspective, students will investigate the importance of the outdoor environment and outdoor activities to the well-being of all New Zealanders. They will critically examine social, cultural, scientific, technological, and economic influences on outdoor activities, on the environment, and on how the environment is used.

The enhancement of hauora through outdoor education requires school-wide policies and procedures to ensure that appropriate activities, safe practices, and the most suitable community resources are selected, used, and evaluated.

In developing outdoor education programmes, schools should:

1.   make use of the school grounds and the immediate local environment;

2.   make the most of opportunities for direct experiences that can be completed in a school day;

3.   provide relevant, challenging learning programmes that offer opportunities for reflective thinking skills (including critical reflection skills, where appropriate) and that can be provided within a realistic budget;

4.   ensure that appropriate resources and skilled personnel are available; and

5.   follow safe practices and comply with legislative requirements.

Students require a range of structured, sequenced, and developmentally appropriate learning opportunities in outdoor education. These include:

1.   adventure activities and outdoor pursuits that focus on physical skill development, fun, and enjoyment;

2.   adventure activities and outdoor pursuits that focus on the development of personal and interpersonal skills;

3.   learning about the traditions, values, and heritages of their own and other cultural groups, including those of the tangata whenua;

4.   opportunities to learn about the environmental impact of outdoor recreation activities and to plan strategies for caring for the environment;

5.   planning strategies to evaluate and manage personal and group safety, challenge, and risk;

6.   finding out how to access outdoor recreation opportunities within the community.

7.   develop and apply, in context, a wide range of movement skills and facilitate the development of physical competence;

8.   develop a positive attitude towards physical activity by accepting challenges and extending their personal capabilities and experiences;

9.   develop and apply a knowledge and understanding of the scientific, technological, and environmental factors that influence movement; and

10. develop and apply knowledge and understanding of the social and cultural factors that influence people's involvement in physical activity.

In terms of relationships with other people, students will:

1. come to understand the nature of relationships;

2. increase their understanding of personal identity and develop sensitivity to, and respect for, other people; and

3. use interpersonal skills effectively to enhance relationships.

In terms of healthy communities and environments students will:

1. find out how societal attitudes, values, beliefs, and practices affect well-being;

2. identify the functions of resources and services that support well-being, find out about their availability, and identify the roles of individuals and groups that contribute to them;

3. understand the rights and responsibilities, laws, policies, and practices that relate to people's well-being; and

4. understand the interdependence between people and their surroundings and use this understanding to help create healthy environments.

The above information was extracted from the New Zealand Curriculum Framework. For further information see:

New Zealand Ministry of Education (1995) Education Outside the Classroom. Guidelines for Good Practice.

New Zealand Ministry of Education (1992) Anywhere, Everywhere. EOTC Curriculum Guidelines for Primary Schools, Secondary Schools, and Early Childhood Centres.

OUTDOOR EDUCATION IN THE SCHOOL CURRICULUM IN AUSTRALIA

Outdoor education has existed in schools in Australia since the 1960s and is particularly well established in the state of Victoria where it has been taught as a discrete subject in the P-10 and senior secondary curriculum since 1989. For information on this curriculum framework and assessment procedures please refer to www.vcaa.vic.edu.au/vce/studies/outdoor/outdoorindex.html

In Victoria over 100 secondary schools offer outdoor education as a subject at senior school level and most secondary schools (approximately 460), offer some form of outdoor education (*see* Lugg and Martin, 2001). Five schools build outdoor education into the daily programme of a long term (usually 6–12 months) rural, residential experience for students at year 9 (form 3). Outdoor education is offered in six Universities in Victoria either as a stand alone degree or as part of a teacher training or physical education degree, Post graduate teacher training in outdoor education is offered at three Universities in Victoria and approximately one third of teachers teaching outdoor education in schools have specific training in this discipline. While the situation is improving this is an ongoing issue since the majority of outdoor education teachers are trained in physical education and therefore often lack the specific knowledge required to teach the senior secondary curriculum which has a strong environmental emphasis (see Lugg, 1999; Lugg and Martin, 2001).

Outdoor education is also offered in schools and is supported by curriculum frameworks in South Australia (see Picket and Polley, 2003), Western Australia, Northern Territory, New South Wales, Tasmania and Queensland (www.education.qld.gov.au/schools/environment/outdoor/). The purposes and practices are varied with different emphases in each state and a range of support structures. Victoria and Queensland in particular are relatively well supported with specific education centres staffed and resourced to provide outdoor education experiences for students from government schools. This form of outdoor education is however, usually extra-curricular and therefore short term and fragmented. The inclusion of outdoor education in the school curriculum allows for a more coherent educational programme.

A copy of a Benchmark study of senior secondary outdoor education curriculum has been included with this report as has a copy of the study design for Outdoor and Environmental Studies in the Victorian Certificate of Education).

FRILUFTSLIV: THE NORWEGIAN APPROACH TO OUT-OF-CLASSROOM LEARNING

The Norwegian term "friluftsliv" can be roughly translated as "outdoor nature life" and embraces a range of physical activities in the countryside, most of which have cultural and environmental dimensions. It is a widespread social phenomenon and in a sense friluftsliv is a defining aspect of national identity. Almost all Norwegians would have experienced it at school and many continue to do so with family and friends. In these terms it would be well understood by most Norwegians and in terms of educational policy its provision is uncontested.

The role friluftsliv plays in the Norwegian school-system is defined through the national curriculum for secondary schools (Laereplanverket for den 10 aarige grunnskolen). Friluftsliv is mentioned as a supplementary subject to a variety of school-subjects, although it is especially connected to physical education. However, this should not be taken to mean that it is considered a primarily physical pursuit, rather that the role of PE teachers is somewhat broader than in the UK.

In school years six to 16 (Primary and Secondary Modern schools) pupils are entitled to experience nature and learn about the interaction of man and nature in former and contemporary times. The pupils are expected to develop their outdoor skills and gain an understanding of the fragility of nature.[4]

The curriculum for "Secondary Modern" school teachers (*allmenlaererutdanning*). PE (*Kroppsoeving*) comprises four areas:

— Development of motor senses.
— Games.
— Sports, dance, *Friluftsliv* (outdoor education).
— Didactics of physical education.

Students are requested to develop an understanding for *friluftsliv's* role in cultural identity, the joy of movement and the joy of "life". The main activities taught to do so, primarily to allow journeys in the Norwegian landscape and include introduction to canoe-paddling, winter-*friluftsliv*, camp-craft skills and orienteering.

Many of Norwegian schools have a one-day module out-of-doors course (*Uteskole/Laering i friluft*) with a systematic pedagogical content, such as:

— teaching through outdoor-games;
— cooking outdoors;
— creative forming out of doors;
— mathematics out of doors;
— a stream as a biotype; and
— the forest as a biotype.

Uteskole is a working method where parts of daily school-life are moved outside to nearby local areas. They are supported in doing so by the national education plan which encourages schools to take students outside one day a week.

Norway also has a system of "local authority outdoor education centres" (*Leirskole*) and over 62,000 pupils visited one in the school year 2003–04. This amounts to 10% of all pupils in the secondary age-range. The aim of this provision is to achieve a deeper understanding of nature and holistic ecological understanding. The intention is that in the 10 years of secondary education every school pupil in Norway will follow a 7–10 day course at a Leirskole.[5]

Friluftsliv can be followed in-depth within the Norwegian "Folkhighschool" movement. In English, the name "folk high school" often gives a misleading impression. "Residential adult college", "residential enrichment academy", "experiential academy" or even "folk school" would be more apt modern descriptions. The typical range of age of students is between 18 and 25 years and the courses normally last for nine months. Each school has its own profile, but in general, the Norwegian folk high schools teach classes covering a variety of interest areas, including arts, crafts, music, sports, philosophy, theatre, media, photography, outdoor activities etc. With about 90 of these schools in Norway of which more than 40 offer or specialise in "Friluftslivlinjer", the Folkhighschool is perhaps the deepest educational manifestation of Norwegian friluftsliv.

These schools which originate from the Danish boarding-school movement of the 1860s, are using teaching principles such as Learning-by-doing, dialogue-based and experiential learning.

> "The folk high schools build on a holistic view of the students and challenge them to grow individually, socially and academically. Learning-by-doing is the basic educational philosophy of the schools. Their core methods are dialogue-based and experiential. The schools strive for challenging classes and courses, but the educational challenges are embedded in the personal and

---

[4] National Curriculum (4th and 5th form) (1997) kroppsøving og 197: mål for mellomtrinnet (8.-10. Klasse).
[5] www.leirskole.no.

social growth, too. This focus on the whole person is the strength and unique character of the folk high schools, where the point is to motivate, teach, inspire and foster commitment in you, the student. The schools give you the freedom to learn in your own way."[6]

RECENT POLITICAL MEASURES TO FOSTER FRILUFTSLIV

In 2004 the Minister for Education (kultur-og kirkeminister Valgerd Svarstad Haugland) allocated six million NOK to further the support of DNT-cabins throughout Norway (30.04.2004). These cabins are located primarily in "wild country" and are used extensively both for recreational and educational experiences (often journeys) through the landscape of Norway.

The minister acknowledged that Friluftsliv played a major role in cultural identity, physical activity and relaxation. The DNT-cabins are important Friluftsliv facilities with considerable potential to foster physical and mental health.

An amount of 33.5 million NOK is expected for the support of "leirskoler" within the new Norwegian state budget for the year 2005.

October 2004

Memorandum submitted by the British Ecological Society

INTRODUCTION

1. The British Ecological Society (BES) is pleased to provide written evidence to the Education and Skills Committee's inquiry into Education Outside the Classroom. The British Ecological Society, founded in 1913, is an independent learned society with an international membership of over 4,000. Its primary objectives are to advance and support research in ecology, promote ecological education and provide science policy advice. Our primary involvement in terms of education outside the classroom is linked to academic fieldwork.

2. The Society supports work in this area by offering a number of funding opportunities to further the education of young ecologists. The BES is helping biology teachers to develop their expertise in fieldwork through sponsoring training courses specially designed for trainee and newly qualified teachers in collaboration with the Field Studies Council. The courses include support on management of groups during fieldwork, risk assessments and practical subject-based activities and ideas. Our Education Officer provides advice to teachers about ecological fieldwork on a one-to-one basis and is involved in delivering in-service training (INSET) to teachers focusing on the effective use of school grounds to enhance science teaching. We have also developed a website: www.britishecologicalsociety.org/education to provide information and resources for teachers.

SUMMARY

3. The BES welcomes the Committee's initiative to examine students' access to experiences outside of the classroom and exploration of the barriers that prevent this from occurring. There is strong evidence that despite the clear educational and personal development strengths that it offers, fieldwork and other provision for outdoor learning is declining. This is happening at a time when there is not less but indeed more demand for people with the skills and confidence to practise ecology. There are many reasons for the decline in education outside the classroom, but the main issues that need to be addressed are:

(i) Biological fieldwork needs to be a requirement rather than an option in the Biology curriculum at all key stages whether this is in the school grounds or elsewhere.

(ii) Specific outdoor teaching experience should be within the national curriculum for science teacher training and should feature in continuing professional development opportunities for teachers to rectify the shortage of experienced biology teachers who possess the skills to promote fieldwork outside the classroom.

(iii) The fear that teachers have of losing their job as a result of the occurrence of a genuine accident remains an important barrier to the provision of outdoor experiences for young people and we are pleased that the Secretary of State for Education recognises that staff involved with school trips deserve more protection from the "blame culture".

---

[6] Cited from fælleskatalog Norges Folkehøgskole, www.folkehogskole.no/hvorfor_fhs.asp.

The Value of Education Outside the Classroom

4. The BES strongly supports outdoor classroom education as an essential part of the curriculum, because it allows students to connect abstract scientific ideas with "hands on" experiences. Biological fieldwork may provide the only opportunity for students to observe living animals and plants in their natural habitat and promote a deeper understanding of the investigatory approaches that underpin the whole of science. It places students in situations which are more unpredictable and less compartmentalised than the conditions encountered in classrooms and laboratories. Biological fieldwork is important for the future of academic disciplines like ecology, for the science skills base and for the public understanding of science and environmental change. There is currently a shortfall in practical skills, such as field surveying and identification that are required to address pressing environmental and conservation issues.

Costs and Funding of Outdoor Activities

5. Costs are known to be a major influence on fieldwork provision. Fieldwork in schools is often heavily subsidised by parents/guardians. If field studies organised by state schools cannot rely on a parental/guardian financial contribution, subsidy has to come from the school budget and compete with many other demands. This situation is not helped as the role of the Local Education Authority adviser diminishes and some Local Education Authorities reduce funding arrangements, thus inhibiting the role of centres in curriculum-related provision. Only some degree of unequivocal statutory requirement will overcome this inequality and eliminate the potential for financial discrimination. The BES recommends that Government funding needs to be ring-fenced to support this minimum entitlement.

6. Besides the cost of outdoor education activities, there is the cost of supply cover for the members of staff involved in the outdoor activity. This needs factoring into funding and money should be specifically set aside for it in addition to the direct costs involved.

7. Teachers are finding it increasingly difficult to take young people away from school outside of the regular school day. Difficulties in trying to position residential fieldwork within the curriculum often result in such activities running at weekends or during holidays. This has implications for staff time and student motivation. Students in A-level or University are often in part-time employment and are therefore less willing to attend such courses.

8. The cost of Government not funding outdoor education is significant. The ability to address important environmental issues, such as the impact of climate change, will be undermined in the future if there is not a strong skills base in certain areas such as ecology and taxonomy. This will in turn have a significant impact on our ability to understand and manage changes to biodiversity and other natural resources in the future.

The Place of Outdoor Learning within the Curriculum

9. The BES believes outdoor education is so important that Government needs to make sure that it is a part of every child's education by making it a minimum statutory entitlement. Statutory guidance should include the amount of time each child is entitled to. Part of this minimum entitlement should be earmarked for science and include first hand environmental/ecological experience.

10. Biological fieldwork should be a requirement rather than an option in the Biology curriculum at all key stages whether this is in the school grounds or elsewhere. Practical experience and observations outside of the classroom are essential for biological education. Even urban schools may be able to offer students valuable field-based educational experiences within their grounds or immediate environs.

External Assessment of Provision

11. The Office for Standards in Education (Ofsted) inspections should include observations on fieldwork activities and judgements made about schools' provision for outside learning opportunities. A guidance booklet for schools including exemplar material to provide clear advice to Head teachers on what constitutes best practise in provision of field based learning would be helpful.

Organisation and Integration within Existing School Structures

12. Good fieldwork is essential for young people's learning in biology and should be integrated into the curriculum, not viewed as an additional exercise. Opportunities for providing students with educationally valuable experiences outside the classroom already exist within present school structures but they need to be highlighted, prioritised and made more accessible to teachers and their students.

QUALIFICATION AND MOTIVATION OF TEACHERS AND THE EFFECT ON TEACHER WORKLOAD

13. There is now a critical shortage of biology teachers with the academic and professional skills to support planning and organising fieldwork in both schools and universities. Teachers, including trainees, need much more support in developing the skills, confidence and commitment to deliver out-of-classroom activities. There are presently no clear recommendations for outdoor teaching experience of biology fieldwork within the national curriculum for teacher training in science. Therefore, a minimum entitlement for every trainee teacher specialising in science to have experience in leading a fieldwork activity is needed to rectify this deficiency.

14. The opportunities for continuing professional development in outdoor education are minimal. There needs to be a programme of low cost professional development courses for teachers to address their needs. These should include workshops and manuals covering different fieldwork methodologies and project ideas as well as help with assessing and managing risk. External funding should be made available for teachers to attend these courses.

THE FEAR OF ACCIDENTS AND THE POSSIBILITY OF LITIGATION

15. Too many young people are being deprived of outdoor activities because their teachers fear being sued. Teachers have a very real fear of losing their job as a result of making an alleged misjudgement and although the perceived fear may far outweigh the reality, it remains an important barrier to the provision of outdoor experiences for young people. Schools are no longer running as many trips, especially overseas.

16. In a move to protect its members' interests, one teaching union has been advising against taking school trips since February 2004. This only serves to heighten the fear that exists among teaching staff. We embrace the statement from the Secretary of State for Education in support of being able to offer children some form of residential experience. The move expressed by the Secretary of State to protect teachers from the "compensation culture" is also most welcome.

17. The paper work required for risk assessment and planning of school trips is important but at times excessive. The extra time and burden that the preparation of these documents places on teachers' means that they are discouraged from running fieldwork. There is a need to rationalise the amount of bureaucracy involved by streamlining existing structures and providing a single, common pro-forma for risk assessment of outdoor learning activities. An established protocol should be put in place and supported by all stakeholders including teaching unions and government departments.

HOW PROVISION IN THE UK COMPARES WITH THAT OF OTHER COUNTRIES

No comment.

October 2004

Memorandum submitted by the Museums Association

OVERVIEW

Museums offer some of the most significant opportunities available to schools to extend students' learning outside the classroom. They can bring the curriculum to life. Roman history suddenly seems much more real when you can handle the pots and coins a citizen of the Roman Empire might have used. Every child learning about dinosaurs should have the opportunity to come face to face with the fossilised remains of one. A student may think that they are no good at art until they have the chance to work with a practising artist in a museum. As well as their obvious contributions to art, history and science, museums make contributions across the whole range of the curriculum.[7]

Like other out-of-classroom learning opportunities museums can engage students who are turned off by formal learning, with the chance to learn by imagining or doing. They give students the opportunity to experience a completely different environment, swapping a classroom for the kitchens of a Tudor house or a coalmine, 300 feet underground.

Recent investment has strengthened the quality and range of educational provision in museums. However, there are still barriers which prevent many schools making as much use of museums as they might. The cost of transport means that many schools in more remote or rural areas miss out on the full richness of the experience that museums have to offer. And additional resources have largely been concentrated in

---

[7] Research into the projects funded by the Department for Education and Skills, Museums and Galleries Education Programme 2, found that 45% of sessions addressed literacy, 41% citizenship, 32% ICT and 20% numeracy, as well as the more expected history, art, geography and science. (DfES, 2004)

a small number of museums, meaning that the education potential of others is seriously under-developed. This response contains some proposals for targeted investment, which would greatly increase the opportunities available in museums for education outside the classroom.

1. *Background*

1.1 The Museums Association (MA) is an independent membership organisation representing museums and galleries in the UK and people who work for them. The Association has over 5,000 individual members and 600 institutional members. These institutional members encompass around 1,500 museums in the UK ranging from the largest government-funded national museums to small volunteer-run charitable trust museums. The MA is a charity, receiving no government funding, which seeks to inform, represent and develop museums and people who work for them in order that they may provide a better service to society and the public.

1.2 This inquiry is concerned both with out-of-classroom learning in general, and with outdoor education in particular. Many museums offer opportunities for outdoor learning. Some farming museums, historic house museums, industrial museums and social history museums preserve whole landscapes and townscapes, and give children the opportunity to enjoy the particular challenges of learning in the open air. However, in this response, the MA has looked at out of classroom learning in a broader sense, in order to encompass the whole range of experiences, which museums have to offer.

1.3 Museums increasingly offer a range of outreach activities to schools and do not only interact with schools on the museum site. They support a range of out of classroom learning activities. Natural history specialists might organise fieldwork, which drew on the museum's collections. Museum archaeologists can assist with the interpretation of archaeological sites, and social historians can help children to see their own environment in a new light.

2. *Introduction*

2.1 In 2003, the MA launched a proposal that the Government should fund a free museum visit for every school child every year. We can supply the Committee with copies of the leaflet which outlines the proposal. In brief, the scheme looks at ways in which the most significant barriers to greater use of museums by schools can be overcome.

2.2 Estimates suggest that around 50% of school children already visit a museum on a school visit every year. This is encouraging, but there are clearly missed opportunities. Participation is much higher among primary schools than secondary schools, suggesting that museums' potential to provide more sophisticated and challenging learning experiences for older students is under-exploited. Transport costs are a significant barrier, meaning that children's experience of museum visiting is often circumscribed by their immediate geographical area. Many schools find it difficult to cover teachers' absences so that they can prepare for, as well as lead, school visits. And while teachers and students value sessions which are led by specialist museum educators, many museums are unable to provide such direct teaching for school groups.

2.3 The MA proposes a scheme whereby the Government would provide funding to schools to use for visits to museums. Such a scheme could of course be extended to include other out-of-school learning opportunities, such as the historic environment and the countryside. Our research suggests that an average of £10 per child each year would enable every child to enjoy a high quality taught session at a museum, or other site. The largest element of this would cover the school's costs, paying for the cost of transport and supply cover for teachers preparing and leading the visit; the remainder would pay for the delivery of a high-quality session taught by a specialist educator at the museum. A comprehensive web-based directory (which could build on existing online resources) would make it easy for teachers to find out what sessions were available at museums.

2.4 This is an average cost. Some urban schools, which could take advantage of free local transport would require much less funding, while rural schools and those in remote areas might require more. While a universal roll out of the scheme would be expensive (estimated at £64 million per annum for England, based on 6.4 million 4–16 year-olds in schools), it could feasibly be targeted in the first instance at those areas where take-up of out of school learning is poor, either because of a lack of regional facilities, or because of poverty and social exclusion.

2.5 It is important to acknowledge that improving museums' service to schools has been a major focus of the Government's investment in regional museums through the Renaissance in the Regions programme. Since this funding is still at an early stage, it is too soon to assess its impact. However, although welcome, the funding is limited to a relatively small number of regional museums. There are many more museums with the potential to provide an excellent service to schools, but which do not meet the other criteria for funding through Renaissance in the Regions.

2.6 Since 1999, the Department for Education and Stills has provided funding for education work in museums and galleries, through the Museums and Galleries Education Programme, phases 1 and 2. This investment has funded innovative projects, with a high rate of satisfaction from both teachers and students. However, a limitation of this funding was that it was project-based. Museums were only able to employ additional staff on a temporary or casual basis, which meant that skills and expertise were lost when the projects ended. They were not able to develop such strong relationships with schools as a longer-term programme of investment would offer.

2.7 One compelling argument for increasing schools' use of museums and other out of class room learning venues is that people who visit regularly as children are much more likely to return as adults. Broader school use helps to ensure that as many people as possible benefit from national cultural and natural resources throughout their lives. Museums are also increasingly developing after-school activities; school visits can help to encourage children to take up these after-school opportunities.

3. *Barriers to the development of out of classroom learning*

3.1 The inquiry's terms of reference specify a number of possible barriers to the expansion and development of out of classroom learning. This section of our response reflects on some of these in the context of museums.

3.2 *Costs and funding.* Cost is often perceived to be a non-issue as far as museum visits are concerned: since 2001, additional government funding has enabled all national museums to offer free entry; most local authority museums are also free. However, independent museums, which rely mainly on self-generated income, still have to charge for admission. Independent museums make up over a third of all Registered museums, and often offer the only museum provision in more remote or rural areas.

3.4 Furthermore, many museums make a special charge for a taught session for school groups; those that do not have to subsidise the service out of other income, and are always oversubscribed. A funding stream which allowed schools to pay for high-quality taught sessions at museums would enable museums to expand their capacity as well as ensuring that schools continued to visit independent museums: many independent museums report that their school visits are falling as schools chose instead to visit free museums in their area. If this trend were to continue it would mean that students missed out on the chance to visit some of the important surviving examples of our industrial and cultural heritage.

3.5 As with other forms of out of classroom learning, the cost of transport to museums can be prohibitive, especially for schools not able to make use of public transport. Funding which covered transport costs would allow greater equality of access, so that children growing up in rural areas can have the same opportunities to enjoy their heritage as those in urban centres.

3.6 *External assessment of provision.* The current Registration scheme for museums is run by the Museums, Libraries and Archives Council (MLA). It is about to be relaunched as Accreditation; and it provides quality control over museums and the services they offer. MLA has also developed a highly regarded framework, Inspiring Learning for All, which helps museums to improve their approach to learning provision. Nevertheless, museums remain outside a mainstream educational assessment programme. We believe that museums would welcome tougher assessment of their educational provision, if such a scheme was backed up with additional support and helped to bring them closer to the educational mainstream.

3.7 *Integration with existing school structures and the motivation of teachers.* We believe that there is great potential for museums to work more closely with schools and in particular to explore ways of providing training and development opportunities both for schools and museum educators. One possible model might be a programme of secondments whereby teachers could spend some time working in a museum, and museum educators (who are mostly qualified teachers) could spend some time working in schools. The Museums Association has experience of running a successful secondment scheme, the Sharing Museum Skills Millennium Awards and we believe that a relatively small amount of funding could unlock substantial benefits through such a secondment scheme.

3.8 We believe that there is scope for increasing the emphasis on out of classroom learning in initial teaching training. This would help to build teachers' confidence in leading visits to museums and other venues, and increase their understanding of the potential of out of classroom learning opportunities.

3.9 Museums could also help with mid-career training for teachers, including helping them revitalise their approach to their subject specialisms. The chance to work alongside experts in their specialist fields, and to work with internationally significant collections could be very motivating for teachers.

3.10 *How provision in the UK compares with other countries.* We understand that the Ministry of Culture in the Netherlands has operated a culture voucher scheme for school children to enable them to access cultural opportunities such as theatre and museum visits. The scheme provided a voucher, which could be redeemed at a range of venues, either by groups or individual children.

October 2004

Memorandum submitted by the Association of Heads of Outdoor Education Centres

SUMMARY

This submission by the Association of Heads of Outdoor Education Centres offers written evidence to the Education Select Committee Inquiry into Education Outside the Classroom. It supplies an introduction to the very long-standing tradition of high quality outdoor education within United Kingdom. It examines the costs and cost implications; the place of outdoor education within the curriculum; assessment of provision; reaction to fear of accidents litigation. It offers **five recommendations** which would both address any barriers to the safeguarding of existing and future provision of quality outdoor education as well as any expansion and development of out of classroom learning.

Contents

1. INTRODUCTION AND BACKGROUND

1.1 The Association of Heads of Outdoor Education Centres represents Heads of Centres and Deputy Heads of Centres of a wide range of outdoor education centres in the UK. The majority of which are owned and maintained by Local Authorities and charitable trusts. They provide a very varied range of both residential and day visit courses for young people and adults covering a variety of habitats, environments, field courses and adventure activities. They also provide training and assessment opportunities for National Governing Body Awards.

1.2 Outdoor Education is a general term used to embrace many and varied types of activity undertaken by primary, secondary and special school students in a wide range of contexts—outdoor and residential visits; field work; outdoor adventurous activities.

1.3 Britain has a long tradition of quality outdoor education.

These centres provide a variety of out of classroom education opportunities which include day visit opportunities and short stay residential outdoor education courses. Courses and programmes are negotiated with each participating group and can include adventure activities, personal, social, health and citizenship education, leadership and team building, examination based field work, environmental education and courses in art, music history, Physical Education etc which support curricular work in schools and enrich the educational experience.

1.4 Outdoor education and out of school visits give depth and breadth to the curriculum and make important contributions to a students physical, personal and social education.

1.5 Schools from primary, special and secondary sectors undertake a wide range and variety of out of classroom activities and outdoor education experiences for their students. This includes a wide range of day visits; participation within the Duke of Edinburgh Scheme as well as a range of commercially provided overseas expeditions. Organisations frequently require support and advice from the AHOEC

1.6 The AHOEC has an agreed and established Mission Statement which states that it will promote excellence in the management of centres providing personal development through high quality outdoor education.

2. COSTING

2.1 Outdoor education and education outside the classroom has a precarious existence due to the absence of dedicated funding. The funding circumstances of outdoor education were examined and supported by the Government during the work undertaken with reference to Modernising Local Government Finance and Fair Funding in 2000–01. Progress was made but further work is now required which would safeguard existing provision, assure sustainability and enable.

2.2 Fee levels inhibit participation by children within certain deprived socio-economic groupings. Present and short term future budget pressures will result in an increase of fee level and will exacerbate the extent of inhibition of attendance by those whose level of deprivation would benefit most from the experiences provided.

Recommendation 1

The Select Committee is recommended to look at ways of ensuring the continuing finance of out of classroom education and in particular existing outdoor education provision. Funding mechanisms need to be identified which would safeguard and maintain the financing of existing provision as well as expanding the opportunities to meet the needs of pupils who suffer social and economic deprivation.

3. Outdoor Learning Within the Curriculum

3.1 Outdoor education and outdoor and adventurous activities fail to realise the maximum positive potential in the personal development of young people within education due to the fact that there is no statutory requirement for their inclusion within the curriculum.

3.2 The curriculum is overcrowded thus limiting opportunity and making progress dependant upon the commitment and dedication of particular Local Authorities and other committed organisations and the committed work of a minority but effective core of head-teachers and teachers. There is an opportunity to address the issue through the implementation of the vision stated in the five year plan for education and through the implementation of the Tomlinson Report as announced on 18 October.

3.3 Formative out of classroom education experiences have been impaired by the gradual loss and decline in appropriate and safe outdoor spaces surrounding school locations. The sell off of land for development and income generation has had a negative impact.

3.4 However the benefits of high quality outdoor education experiences were highlighted in the recently published Ofsted Survey on Aspects of Good practice in Outdoor Education. This report focussed on a sample group of 15 outdoor centres across England and Wales.

3.5 A large number of schools have developed their own out of school education and outdoor education policies which support a rich, well designed and broad curriculum. This additional breadth of experience provides essential opportunities for learning, discovery, problem solving, risk recognition and management, creative writing, art music. In addition to opportunities to develop self confidence, social and emotional skills and maturity.

3.6 Many have a longstanding commitment to residential centres and many are dependent upon their visit to fulfil their examination syllabus field work, especially in geography and biology. However, there is concern that there has been a significant reduction in geographical fieldwork and to a lesser extent a reduction in biological fieldwork participation over the past two to three years. This is largely attributable to the curricular pressure of AS level examinations, and to the escalating cost of courses.

Recommendation 2

The Select Committee is recommended to:

 (i) examine ways of encouraging wider participation in outdoor education and education outside the classroom by enabling opportunities to support and develop use of the wider environment within the core curriculum.

 (ii) investigate further the decline in participation of examination syllabus fieldwork and look at ways of encouraging and supporting participation.

4. Assessment of Provision

4.1 Outdoor education centres provide a wide range of activities which are subject to Licensing under the young Persons Safety Act and are regularly inspected by the Adventure Activities Licensing Authority (AALA). In addition they are often subject to an LA internal Monitoring and Evaluation system, as well as external assessment by National Governing Bodies.

4.2 Both external and internal assessment do not create barriers to provision, on the contrary they both support and enable quality and safe provision. However, Ofsted inspections of schools do have a negative impact on the participation of children in out of school activities at both Key Stages 2 and 3. This is particularly evident in the lack of take up of opportunities in the weeks immediately prior to and inspection. These inspections currently take place at prime time for optimum weather and climate conditions in May .

4.3 Outdoor education centres provide courses, which have a very direct curricular relevance and contribution, however, they are often placed at a disadvantage in the fact that they do not receive directly any information and circulars from the DfES.

Recommendation 3

The Select Committee is recommended to consider:

 (i) the impact that Standard Assessment Tests and their calendar timing may have on out of classroom education opportunities.

> (ii)   the allocation of a full DfES identity number to each centre to enable them to receive routine and relevant information in the same way as it is supplied to schools.

5. QUALIFICATION AND MOTIVATION OF TEACHERS AND THE EFFECT ON TEACHER WORKLOAD

5.1 Classroom and is exacerbated by the "workforce remodelling" programme, which could limit the number of hours available for school visits.

6. FEAR OF ACCIDENTS AND POSSIBILITY OF LITIGATION

6.1 Over the past few years the Government has placed significant emphasis on the benefits and values of outdoor education and adventurous activities. This was supported in the three guidance documents Standards for Adventure, Standards for LEA's in Overseeing Educational Visits and Handbook for Group Leaders, published as supplements of the original guidance Health and Safety of Pupils in Educational Visits.

6.2 These supplementary guidances were aided by the provision of significant funding, on a time framed basis, to provide training courses in support of Educational Visits Co-ordinators which were to be in place at every school by August 2003.

6.3 The Guidance Documents and the supporting training opportunities have been positive in supporting teachers to undertake out of school visits and activities. This will be further supported through the development of a group-leader training scheme. These initiatives will assist in ensuring sound planning and risk assessment and reduce the fear of litigation.

6.4 There is however, a need to ensure that there is both opportunity and funding for Continuing Professional Development of teachers and other adults within Local Authorities to support the progress of safe and effective out of classroom and outdoor education. In addition there is a need to include out of classroom learning and outdoor education within Initial Teacher Training programmes.

6.5 There is particular concern at present with the restriction of participation by younger teachers due to the impact of Department of Transport changes to the Driving Licence categories, notably the issues surrounding a D1 Category Driving Licence. There is a need to look at effective ways of supporting young teachers to be able to drive minibuses and addressing the current financial barriers to training in order to overcome the D1 category restriction.

Recommendation 4

The Select Committee is recommended to investigate:

> **(i)   the growing problem of limitation of opportunity for out of classroom education due to the impact of changes in driving licence categories by the Department of Transport.**

> **(ii)   the support of Continuing Professional Development and removal of financial barriers to training.**

7. UK PROVISION COMPARED WITH OTHER COUNTRIES

The United Kingdom has a long tradition of sound outdoor education. It pioneered a National Governing Body training and qualification opportunity across a wide range of outdoor adventurous activities which supports safe leadership and participation in a range of potentially hazardous pursuits. This qualification and safety infrastructure is the best within Europe and the World and has been copied by many other countries that have seen the benefit of the educational enrichment and personal development opportunities provided within the UK. Many of these such as New Zealand and Scandinavia have ensured that outdoor education and out of classroom experiences are part of their curriculum entitlement.

Recommendation 5

The Select Committee is recommended to celebrate the variety and quality of outdoor education and out of classroom education opportunities in the United Kingdom and look at ways of ensuring its sustainability and future.

October 2004

Memorandum submitted by Learning Through Landscapes, the National School Grounds Charity

1. INTRODUCTION

Learning through Landscapes

Learning though Landscapes (LTL) is the national school grounds charity. Formed in 1990 following a four-year research project backed by the Department for Education and 14 Local Authorities, the organisation works to promote the importance of good school grounds for children's learning, development health and welfare and for the benefit of the wider community.

— Why?

Learning through Landscapes campaigns for children's right to decent school grounds and helps make school grounds better places. This is because children and young people who do not have access to good school grounds are not getting the best start in life.

Many people do not understand the importance of school grounds to children's learning and development. However, they are essential, providing unique opportunities for the meaningful participation of children in school life; for healthy exercise, creative play and making friends; for learning through doing; for putting children in touch with the natural world and for enhancing the delivery of subjects across the curriculum at all Key Stages from Foundation to Secondary.

— What?

LTL is the leader in the field of school grounds and provides a "one stop shop" for any issue relating to school grounds. LTL gives children and young people a say in the way their school grounds are used and improved. As a result, they learn to create and look after something valuable; their self-esteem grows and their behaviour improves, along with their potential to learn and achieve.

— Without?

Many children have few, if any, opportunities to learn and play outdoors. Without the work of LTL, we believe they could easily miss out on a vital opportunity to learn and be healthy and happy in their formative years, and to gather the experiences they need to be healthy and happy adults.

Learning though Landscapes works in partnership with government, local authorities, the private sector and the school communities themselves to improve the use design and management of school grounds.

Since 1990, LTL has worked directly with over 10,000 schools, raised over £20 million for grounds improvement and contributed substantially to school grounds research and to new legislation and good practice.

LTL developed and manages the DfES funded programme, "School Grounds of The Future", has contributed to the recent Exemplar Schools programme and worked with the Department to produce a number of Building Bulletins, including: No. 71, "The Outdoor Classroom", and No. 85, "School Grounds, a guide to good practice" *(Ref 1)*.

LTL is a founder member of the School Playing Fields Advisory Panel, which advises the Secretary of State on applications to dispose of school playing fields.

Ken Davies

— Chief Executive Learning through Landscapes since 1998.
— Member of the School Playing Fields Advisory Panel.
— Member of the former Sustainable Development Education Panel.
— Trustee Council for Environmental Education.
— Associate of The Landscape Institute.

Opening Statement

This evidence from Learning through Landscapes is put forward to support the case for improved investment in the nation's school grounds for learning outside the classroom, to identify current barriers to progress and to make recommendations to the Government as to how these might be overcome.

2. EXECUTIVE SUMMARY AND CONCLUSIONS

School grounds offer a unique and accessible resource for teaching and learning beyond the classroom which is available to all 7.8 million school children on a daily basis at reasonable cost. They also provide an excellent opportunity for engaging children and young people in the use, development and management of their own environment and for giving them a voice in the life and running of their school.

What is more, the Government has gone a long way towards protecting school grounds against unnecessary disposal and demonstrated a commitment to the outdoors as an essential component of the school community.

While this has set an excellent context within which school grounds could take their rightful place within outdoor education, there has yet to be a sufficient follow through of planning and action to make this a widespread reality. In truth, school grounds still remain vulnerable to financial pressures within the education system, particularly in respect of new capital development. They remain an area of relatively low quality associated with low investment and low academic achievement. This represents a significant waste of resources within the system and a wasted opportunity for children's all round education development and participation.

The principal blocks to progress are:

— Outdoor learning in the school grounds is not seen as sufficiently mainstream within education.

— This is an area which is significantly undervalued and of low funding priority in schools.

— Teachers are not adequately trained and experienced.

— Management and development are not sufficiently co-ordinated.

— Education outputs and outcomes are inadequately researched and measured.

— The fear of accidents and litigation can be a deterrent.

To address these issues and blockages, Learning through Landscapes would like to suggest a more effective and dynamic partnership be developed between the Government, its schools, and the many organisations and agencies that could positively contribute and influence development and good management and teaching practice.

A recommended 10 point Action Plan is set out in section 5 of the Evidence.

3. THE SCHOOL GROUNDS CASE

For learning outside of the classroom.

School grounds account for some 63% of the total education estate of 54,000 hectares in England.

Of this area, around 67% is for team games and the remainder is made up of children's playspace, informal and habitat areas and social spaces (Ref 2). These areas together support the outdoor learning, development and social needs of some 7.8 million children and young people on a daily basis.

Given that pupils can spend up to 25% of their time at school actually outside of the classroom, school grounds represent a collective site visit of around 1.4 billion child visitor days per annum in England.

School grounds are an environment designed and managed primarily for children and young people. They can be readily accessed by all pupils on a daily basis without significant additional travel and supervision costs and there is ample research and practical evidence to show that they are of great value for teaching and learning from Foundation Stage through all Key Stages (Ref 3, 4).

With the increase in traffic and fears for children's safety within local communities, school grounds also provide opportunities for vital healthy play and recreation of many kinds, as demonstrated in the recent DfES and DCMS joint study on children's play.

There are, however, significant issues of quality and suitability, teacher confidence and school management which need to be addressed (see Section 4/5).

Learning through Landscapes, own estimates are that, compared with the very best practice achieveable in schools today, the majority school grounds are used at only 30% of their true educational and social potential.

However, where improvements are made, the results are impressive.

The 2003 LTL National School Grounds Survey (Ref 5) looked at 700 schools that had improved their grounds in the past four years. It found that:

— 65% of schools reported an improved attitude to learning;

— 52% reported improved academic achievement;

— 73% said behaviour had improved;

— 64% reported reduced bullying;

— 84% reported improved social interaction; and

— 85% said that healthy active play had increased.

The recent published review of research on outdoor learning by the National Foundation for Education Research and King's College London *(Ref 4)* was also very positive in this respect. This showed ample evidence to support the role and value of school grounds in the cognitive, affective physical/behavioural and social impacts and learning associated with the use of the outdoor environment.

School grounds can also support the development of "off site" outdoor learning through linked curriculum work and by encouraging an effective outdoor learning culture in schools.

4. BARRIERS TO PROGRESS

LTL research shows that school grounds in England are being substantially undervalued and underdeveloped with the subsequent loss of opportunity, waste of precious resources and detrimental impacts on children's learning, welfare and development *(Ref 3)*.

There are a number of issues and barriers to be overcome:

1. *Finance*

Lack of capital and revenue finance for maintenance is the reason most often quoted by schools for not improving their grounds. Since the introduction of LMS, school grounds finance appears to have been pushed progressively lower in the list of the schools' spending priorities.

The significant growth in schools capital funding since 1997 would appear to offer great potential to address this problem. However, early indications are that this may not be the case owing to a backlog of other spending priorities leading to an "affordability gap".

The new capital spend under Building Schools for The Future and the Academies programme does not guarantee that LEA's and their schools can or will address this chronic school grounds problem.

LTL's observation is that some of the new schools, and particularly some of the new Academies, are coming on stream with school grounds that are still substantially below the standard that would be expected of a modern educational establishment. We suggest that the reasons for this are:

— External works budgets on capital projects (particularly the soft landscape elements) are well known to be vulnerable to cost cutting when building costs overrun because they are "last in line".

— Educational investment in the outdoors often comes within the definition of "exceptional costs".

— There appears to be a significant presumption in favour of high tech indoor learning provision which leaves little scope for investment in the outdoors.

— Architects and private education contractors seem unaware of the need to provide a balanced whole site development which includes quality outdoor learning provision, despite the encouragement to do this which is promoted by the DfES own Exemplar Schools project. (The recent CABE/RIBA report, "21st Century Schools, Learning Environments for The Future", makes virtually no reference to the value of the school grounds despite its claim to be a project stimulating debate about the design of learning environments. *(Ref 6)*

— PPP consortia often appear to have a poor understanding of the teaching and learning potential of school grounds and there is a tendency for them to design expensive aesthetic landscapes of little educational value.

In addition:

— Fundraising by Parent Teacher Associations lists school grounds as the third most popular target for fundraising, indicating the extent to which this is still dependent upon voluntary effort in the community.

2. *The Disposal of School Grounds*

The introduction of new legislation to prevent the unnecessary disposal of school playing fields *(Ref 7)* has had a positive impact and the case for any disposal now has to be well made. The Government is to be congratulated on this initiative.

However, Academies are to be largely exempt and this is worrying in view of the points made in 1. above.

Also, there is potential for the loss of the children's outdoor environment under general consents proposed for the use and disposal of land under the Extended Schools programme.

LTL would advise that both proposals should be properly evaluated in the context of possible negative impacts on children's access to school grounds.

3. *Teacher Qualification and Motivation*

Apart from specialist Physical Education, Initial Teacher Training has little or no scope to equip new teachers with the skills and experience to teach out of the classroom. There is subsequently, a considerable lack of confidence in doing this, particularly with older pupils *(Ref 8)*.

There are also cultural barriers to be overcome.

LTL research in secondary schools *(Ref 9)* indicates that teachers who take their pupils out of the classroom are perceived by colleagues to be "not working", and there is a considerable peer group pressure to comply with the norm of indoor teaching and learning.

4. *The Curriculum and Education Development Strategies*

Research shows a strong link between curriculum and education development and schools ability and willingness to use the outdoors, particularly at Key Stages 3 and 4.

Positive curriculum and other education developments that have raised the status of outdoor teaching and learning include:

— The Foundation Stage Early Learning Goals—which require that practitioners plan a learning environment indoors and outdoors that encourages a positive attitude to learning through rich and stimulating experiences *(Ref 10)*.

— "Excellence and Enjoyment, A Strategy for Primary Schools"—which encourages schools to enrich children's learning out of doors through play *(Ref 11)*.

— The introduction of Citizenship and Education for Sustainable Development and the increased emphasis on Personal, Social and Health Education.

— Specific requirements to provide children with adequate Physical Education opportunities.

— The proposed new 14–19 Curriculum which would raise the status and value of vocational education; including opportunities for teaching, learning and training outdoors.

— Specialist Schools with the opportunity to focus on areas of the curriculum where the outdoors is essential or can be used to enhance learning; such as Sport, Technology, Science, Art and Business and Enterprise.

— The introduction of the Healthy Schools Standard.

— Initiatives such as the DfES Growing Schools programme.

However, even though LTL programmes and practice over the past 15 years have shown how teaching and learning outdoors can enrich most parts of the curriculum, including Geography, Science, Design Technology and Art, this is not yet embedded in teaching practice across all relevant subjects.

Anecdotal evidence would suggest that "outdoor learning" is still too often equated with "vocational learning" ie less academic/less desireable.

This will take time and effort to turn around but the new curriculum and other developments listed above certainly hold out the hope that we at least now have the opportunity to succeed. There is now formal "permission" within the education system to teach and learn outdoors, if we choose to take it.

There are some detailed blocks to progress which need to be addressed in relation to current vocational education outdoors. For example, NVQ's do not count in league tables and this is a disincentive to investing time and effort in this area. Also, NVQ standards assume delivery to be work-place based and many schools find difficulty in getting their schools classified as such .

We have also been informed by schools that 14–16 courses do not currently qualify for vocational funding by the Learning and Skills Council.

5. *Measuring Success*

For too long, advocates of outdoor learning have not been able to provide sufficient hard facts on the benefits of this activity, particularly in relation to school grounds.

This is recognised as a difficult area of research which is also substantially underfunded. LTL believes that such an investment would lead to significant improvements in investment and training strategies.

The 2003 Ofsted study and report on Good Practice in Sustainable Development Education *(Ref 12)* made several positive comments on the role and value of outdoor teaching and learning but this has yet to be incorporated in any formal changes to the inspection framework.

6. *School Structure and Management*

Outdoor teaching and learning in the school grounds is much stronger and better represented in the primary sector where it is much easier to develop the necessary whole site and whole school approach to its development and management.

In primaries, however, this is an area which must have the specific ascent and backing of the Head Teacher and where, too often, success or failure depends on the dedication and effort of one committed and enthusiastic teacher.

It is not surprising therefore, that this is an area of school management which tends to ebb and flow with changes in staff and that it often becomes unsustainable.

Few schools have dedicated and suitably qualified grounds development managers within their staff and fewer still will have anyone with specific skills or knowledge, even though the school is largely responsible for the physical management and development of its own site.

LTL discussions with School Governor Associations has indicated a great willingness on their part to become more aware and more involved in this area of school management but, when pressed, they find it difficult to find the time or resources to respond, given the huge workload and pressing issues that fill their current agenda.

7. *Health, Safety and Litigation*

The fears of teachers and their unions are well documented in this area. In this respect, LTL has had the positive involvement of the Association of Teachers and Lecturers, but no other union to date.

The LTL 2003 School Grounds Survey indicated that accident levels were likely to fall significantly where a school improved its grounds and had positive management strategies *(Ref 5)*.

Our wide involvement in school grounds programmes over 15 years would indicate that it is perfectly possible to achieve acceptable levels of managed risk in relation to school ground activities, indeed, thousands of schools have done so.

This would appear therefore, to be an issue which can be quite adequately addressed by good planning, sound management and sensible investment strategies, including the involvement and support of parents and parent groups.

Given that exposure to low levels of risk and challenge is well known to be an essential component of children's play, learning and development, this would indicate that such procedures should be an essential component of good school management.

8. *Comparisons With Other Countries*

Given the comments above and the list of issues to be addressed, it is remarkable that the UK is highly regarded internationally for its work in developing the case for good school grounds and for some outstanding individual successes in its schools.

This is evidenced by:

— Learning through Landscapes managed and hosted the first International Conference on School Grounds in 1997, supported by the OECD.

— Work in the UK stimulated the development of the international "Learnscapes" network involving schools and their education authorities from 19 countries.

   This comes under the umbrella of ENSI, the Environment and Schools Initiative which is in turn part of an international government based network co-ordinated by the OECD's Centre for Educational Research and Innovation.

The official contact in England for Learnscapes is Ofsted, and the inspectorate has actively participated in conferences and discussions. Despite many examples of individual school success, all the partners in the Learnscapes network have identified similar barriers to the development of outdoor learning in the school grounds:

— Outdoor learning is not sufficiently mainstream within education.

— It is significantly undervalued and underfunded.

— Teachers are not adequately trained and experienced.

— Management and development are not co-ordinated.

— Education outputs and outcomes are inadequately researched and measured.

5. Recommendations to Government

Government has made a major advance in protecting school grounds from unnecessary disposal. Our recommendation is that this should now be backed by a positive strategy and programme for the effective improvement and ongoing management of this valuable public asset so that its full educational, child development and community value is realised.

We suggest that there are now sufficient resources within the education system to allow this to happen but the Government will need to show further leadership in this area if there is to be progress.

Learning through Landscapes suggests a 10 point Action Plan:

— Provide clear guidelines to Local Education Partnerships about the importance of achieving whole site design solutions, including maximising outdoor education potential in school grounds.

— Incorporate this as a key part of the financial/education assessment and decision making process in respect of capital investment in schools.

— Ask Ofsted to examine how the inspection framework might be developed to encourage greater and more effective educational use of the whole school site and ask the DfES to develop and publish a standard of excellence to which schools could aspire.

— Examining the potential for providing schools and teachers with "on site" support and guidance in outdoor learning and grounds development through an effective national/regional/local partnership with Voluntary Organisations and the wider community.

— Ask this partnership to put forward feasible and practical management options for addressing the climate of fear and litigation surrounding outdoor education in schools and facilitate a productive discussion between this partnership, the unions and the insurance industry.

— Initiate a dialogue with governor organisations to determine what role governors could and should play in maximising the educational value of all their school's assets, to include the school grounds.

— Discuss with appropriate research institutions how more effective research can be brought to bear to clarify the benefits of outdoor learning in the school grounds and what approaches are most effective.

— Discuss with business leaders how to provide greater incentives and encouragement for the private sector to support and invest in school grounds and the wider outdoor learning environment.

— Discuss with the teaching profession how to raise the status and value of outdoor learning and how this might be linked to professional development and incentives.

— Commission a base line national survey of the state and current use of school grounds and use this as the basis for a five year forward plan of action and improvement, similar to the recent research in Scotland.

6. References

1. DfES Building Bulletin 71, The Outdoor Classroom 1990, Building Bulletin 85, School Grounds, A Guide to Good Practice 1997.

2. DfES publication 0273, March 2003, Asset Management plans—Data Analysis.

3. Learning through Landscapes, a report on the use, design, management and development of school grounds, Eileen Adams 1990 and, Special people Special Places—the hidden curriculum of the school grounds, Wendy Titman 1994.

4. A review of research on Outdoor Learning, Mark Rickinson et al. National Foundation for Education Research/King's College London 2004.

5. The LTL 2003 National School Grounds Survey.

6. 21st Century Schools, Learning Environments for The Future, CABE/RIBA August 2004.

7. Section 77 of The School Standards and Framework Act 1998.

8. Grounds for Concern, Learning through Landscapes, Wendy Titman 1999.

9. Grounds for Concern.

10. DfEE/QCA Curriculum Guidance for The Foundation stage 2000.

11. DfES Excellence and Enjoyment, A Strategy for Primary Schools 2003.

12. Ofsted, Taking the first step forward, towards an education for sustainable development, HMI 1658, 2003.

October 2004

Memorandum submitted by the Adventure Activities Licensing Authority

1. About the Licensing Authority

1.1 The Adventure Activities Licensing Authority (the Authority) is a cross-departmental and cross-border public authority. It is sponsored by the Department of Education and Skills (DfES) and operates under the written guidance of the Health and Safety Commission (HSC). Its primary function is to inspect the safety management of certain adventure activity providers, with particular attention to young people, and if satisfied with the standard of safety, to issue them with a licence.

1.2 The Authority's inspectors across England, Scotland and Wales have been scrutinising the operations of adventure activity providers since 1996 and have generally been more than satisfied with the standards of safety. On the few occasions when they have not been, the Authority has withheld the licence either until satisfactory improvements have been made, or indefinitely.

1.3 "The aim of the adventure activities licensing scheme is to give assurance that good safety management practice is being followed *so that young people can continue to have opportunities to experience exciting and stimulating activities outdoors* while not being exposed to avoidable risks of death and disabling injury." (Guidance to the Licensing Authority from the Health and Safety Commission on the Adventure Activities Licensing Regulations 1996, revised 2004.) The italics are added.

2. About this Submission

Having liaised with at least some other contributors to this inquiry the Authority is satisfied that you will receive authoritative, evidence based opinion on the overwhelming benefits of Education outside the Classroom. It will not reiterate their arguments but is happy to endorse them. Nor will the submission address most of your specific topics; others are better placed to do that. Mostly it will address the issue "The fear of accidents and the possibility of litigation". On this the Authority is satisfied that it can offer an informed opinion supported by evidence.

3. Lives Lost and Lives Saved

There is a danger that society and the instruments of government, in trying to ensure greater safety in one area will inadvertently create much greater danger in other areas. For example, trying to reduce accidents outside the classroom will make it more difficult for young people to develop a fit and healthy life-style, with a corresponding dramatic increase in the risk to their future physical as well as emotional well-being. Moreover, the increased risk will overwhelm any reduction.

No attempt is made to suggest that any one death is more tragic or more important than any other. The only morally robust argument is to attempt to reduce all sudden and premature deaths.

4. Accidents on School Visits

Appendix 1 shows figures for fatal accidents on school visits since 1985. There have been a total of 57. From the figures we can see that:

  51 were pupils and 6 adults.

  20 were abroad and 37 in the UK.

  23 were drownings.

  17 were road traffic accidents.

  19 involved adventure activities (approximately 1 a year).

The Authority has summary details on file for most of these.

Whilst these figures may at first appear alarmingly high they need to be set in the context of other causes of death amongst young people and the population in general.

5. Causes of Death in the UK with Particular Attention to Young People

5.1 To our knowledge no single government body collects figures on all causes of sudden, premature or accidental death. As a result, there appears to be no clear overview of the Health and Safety of the Nation, let alone the Health and Safety of Young People.

5.2 By necessity the figures have also been extrapolated or adjusted to take account of differing recording categories etc so as to present the best overall picture. Sources for the data are shown and more information on the sources is available to you if you wish.

5.3 Appendix 2 sets out the main findings for causes of death in all age groups (adults, children and young people). It includes fatalities in all adventure activities, under all circumstances (ie led groups, peer groups, and individuals) and compares this figure with fatalities in other areas.

Significant findings include, per annum:

   130,000 deaths for cancers.

   120,000 deaths from heart attacks.

   110,000 deaths from smoking related illnesses and conditions.

   30,000 deaths from obesity related condition. (This figure is rising rapidly and the age group considered most at risk is our current school leaving generation.)

   25,000 deaths from alcohol related illnesses and conditions.

These are the "Big 5" causes of death, and they are all, one way or another, life-style causes. In other words we could choose to reduce or eliminate our exposure and that of our children. The most effective way of reducing the risk from each of the "Big 5" would be to encourage young people to develop a fit and healthy life-style.

By comparison there are, per annum:

   10,000 deaths from accidents;

   4,000 deaths from accidents at home;

   350 deaths from accidents at work;

   150 deaths from adventure activities (under all circumstances); and

   1 death on school visits as a result of adventure activities.

Appendices 2 and 3 give further statistics which help to provide the missing over-view.

5.4 *Obesity*

Ian Campbell, Chair of the National Obesity Forum is reported (in Children Now magazine—6 October 2004 issue) as saying that while healthy eating campaigns in schools and on television had achieved "an awful lot of impact", the Government had been slower to wake up to the fact that physical activity was equally important.

5.5 Clearly there is a recognition that the Government's focus on fitness and health will have to increase dramatically. There is no simple solution to the obesity problem, and equally no risk-free solutions. However the benefits, in terms of lives saved and money saved by the Department of Health etc, are self-evident.

5.6 *Suicide*

Appendix 3 shows the annual causes of death for our young people. Significant amongst the data are the facts that:

Twice as many young people commit suicide than are murdered. Moreover, the great majority (five out of six, some commentators say) of the murders are committed by someone within, or close to, the victim's family. The occurrence of "stranger danger" is therefore very low but society's reaction to it is overwhelming to the point that we will not allow our children the opportunity to develop a fit and healthy life-style. Ironically, the reasons given are purported to be in the child's greater interest. The statistics do not support this.

There are approximately 1,000 suicides annually in the age range 15–24 years. (Many coroners will agree that the figure is almost certainly much higher. For one thing, it is very difficult to prove "beyond all reasonable doubt" that someone found dead actually committed suicide.) The Samaritans report that the greatest single cause, particularly among young men, is leaving school with low self-esteem and no sense of self-value.

5.7 Adventure activities (and indeed many activities outside the classroom) are well known for improving self-esteem and a sense of self-worth. Many lives can clearly be saved by not only allowing, but actively encouraging young people to become involved in these activities.

5.8 At any given time there are 10,000 pupils permanently excluded from school. Again, adventure activities and similar, have a proven record for helping young people to re-engage. The cost in terms of human lives of this disengagement, as manifested in street crime, car crime, drug crime etc is assumed to be high, although difficult to quantify.

5.9 *Conclusions*

   (i)   Government needs to encourage, to a much greater extent than at present, all young people to develop a fit and healthy life-style both physically and emotionally in order to combat the enormous threat they face tp their future health and well-being.

   (ii) Government need to recognise that there are no risk-free solutions to these problems.

6. LITIGATION

6.1 There is disagreement over whether the occurrence of litigation is increasing. The 'official' view seems to be that it is not. (There is however, evidence that court-assigned damages are increasing towards more realistic levels, for example, for the cost of life long disability.)

6.2 There is little or no evidence that a typical individual teacher is at specific risk. A recent insurance survey (*see* appendix 4) concluded that teachers were more likely to take an action against their employer than the reverse. Moreover, criminal charges against individual teachers are extremely rare. Even when they have occurred, once the circumstances are understood, the charges seem to have been totally justified. Much more often Local Authority are prosecuted for management failures, not individual employees for implementation failures.

6.3 Confusion has been generated, at least in part by the media, about the difference between a momentary oversight and gross negligence.

6.4 While occurrences of litigation may not be increasing, the fear of litigation certainly is. Teachers and others report this as a significant reason for them not doing more to encourage adventure activities and other education outside the classroom. Thus while the cause may be debatable the outcome is observable.

6.5 Local Authorities could do much to alleviate the problem by shouldering this largely non-existent risk rather than passing it on to sub-contractors such as adventure activity centres. This can add £10,000 to an activity centre's insurance premium.

6.6 *Conclusions*

(i) While an increase in the occurrence of litigation may be debatable the fear of it is very real, and damaging.

(ii) Local and central government could do more to alleviate this damage by assuming more of the largely non-existent risk.

7. INSURANCE

7.1 A number of reports (see appendix 4) support the view that it is becoming increasingly difficult to get (and pay for) liability insurance in certain sectors including adventure activities. There are a number of well-recognised causes for this other than an increase in litigation rates.

7.2 Again this real and costly outcome seems to be driven by the fear of litigation rather than an increase in occurrence.

7.2 *Conclusions*

(i) There is little or no evidence to support the widespread fear of civil or criminal charges against typical individual teachers.

(ii) There will be no cheap solution to the problems facing our young people. Accidents will, on occasions, continue to happen and on the rare occasions where a public authority or similar is found culpable there may be a financial cost. However, the cost to the public purse of not engaging with, and seeking solutions to, the problems facing our young people will be enormous.

8. FINAL CONCLUSIONS

(i) The Government should continue to provide assurances (and guidance) that good safety management practice is being followed.

(ii) Employers, particularly in the public sector, are under a clear obligation to help to improve the future fitness and health of our young people in terms of their physical, mental and social well-being.

(iii) When we compare like with like, either lives lost and saved, or money lost and saved, the arguments in favour of adventure activities and other education outside the classroom are overwhelming. In other words, in terms of lives and money lost and saved we cannot afford not to increase provision.

(iv) Evidence suggests that the typical individual leader has little or nothing to fear either in terms of criminal prosecution or civil litigation.

(v) The cost/benefit approach to justifying adventure activities and other education outside the classroom should not be seen as overriding compared to the educative benefits, but merely complimentary to them.

APPENDIX 1

FATAL ACCIDENTS ON SCHOOL VISITS

Incident	Date	Venue or description	Our reference	Number of casualties	UK	Abroad	Adults	Pupils	Road Traffic Accidents	Winter Sports	Drowning	Murder	Natural causes	Fall from Height	Adventure Activity
1	May-85	Land's End		4	4			4			4				4
2	Apr-88	Austria sledging		4		4		4		4					
3	Mar-93	Lyme Bay		4	4			4			4				4
4	Nov-93	M40 Minibus crash		13	13		1	12	13						
5	May-95	Grand Union Canal		1	1			1			1				
6	Jun-96	Buckden		1	1			1			1				
7	Jul-96	Brittany Youth Hostel		1		1		1				1			
8	Jul-97	Buckinghamshire		1	1			1	1						
9	Jul-97	Shell Island		3	3			3			3				3
10	Jul-97	Albertville, France		1		1	1			1					
11	Jun-98	Dinas Rock		1	1			1			1				1
12	Jun-99	Le Touquet, France		1		1		1						1	
13	Sep-99	Portsmouth Harbour		1	1			1			1				
14	Jan-00	Nevada, USA		1		1		1						1	1
15	Oct-00	Stainforth Beck		2	2		1	1			2				2
16	Feb-01	Austria, toboggan ride		1		1		1						1	1
17	Apr-01	Valloire		1		1	1			1				1	
18	Jul-01	Vietnam		1		1		1			1				
19	Jul-01	Dieppe		1		1		1	1						
20	Jul-01	Malvern Hills		1	1			1						1	1
21	Aug-01	Vale of Neath, S Wales		1	1			1			1				1
22	Aug-01	South Africa		1		1		1					1		
23	Nov-01	Blackpool		1	1			1			1				
24	May-02	Glenridding		1	1			1			1				1
25	Jun-02	Dijon, France		1		1	1		1						
26	Jun-02	Surrey		1	1			1					1		
27	Jul-02	Northumberland		1	1			1					1		
28	Jul-02	Glynneath		1	1			1			1				
29	Jul-03	Caen, France		1		1	1		1						
30	Jul-03	Val d'Aosta, Italy		1		1		1		1				1	
31	Jun-03	Aberdeenshire		1	1			1						1	
32	Apr-04	Hamburg		1		1		1					1		
33	Jun-04	The Lizard, Cornwall	INF133	1	1			1			1				
		Total		57	37	20	6	51	17	7	23	1	4	7	19

APPENDIX 2

CAUSES OF DEATH (ALL AGES)

The average number of fatalities in the UK (all ages) include:

Heart attacks 130,000 (the UK's number one killer)	(Dept of Health)
All cancers: more than 120,000	(Dept of Health)
Smoking related illnesses 110,000	(Home Office)
Obesity and unfitness 30,000. Obesity in under 15's has tripled in the last 10 years. One in two obese children will become obese adults and so this is set to become the biggest single cause of premature death for our current school-leaving generation.	(National Audit Office)
Alcohol related deaths 25,000	(Home Office)
Breast cancer 15,000	(Dept of Health)
Total accidental deaths 10,000	(HSE)
Suicides 6,000, spread fairly evenly across the age groups from 15 years upwards. Thus there are approximately 1,000 in the age range 15–25.	(Samaritans)
Class A drugs 1,200 (mostly heroine)	(Home Office: Reducing Drug Deaths)
Road Traffic Accidents (RTAs) 3,500	(The total is down but deaths of young people are up.) (Dept of Transport)
Train crashes or derailments 8	(HSE Railways Inspectorate)
Trespassing on railway lines. About 120.	(HSE Railways Inspectorate)
Asbestosis (the result of asbestos stripping) 3,000. (We know the cause, we're just working through the consequences.)	(HSE)
Sun-bathing 1,400 (ie skin cancer caused by over-exposure to sun)	
Asthma 4,000	(Dept of Health)
Allergic reaction to aspirin 200	(Rescue Emergency Care)
Accidents at work 350	(HSE)
Accidents in the home 4,000. (Of these approximately 200 are under 18 years of age.)	(DTi HASS/LASS)
Do-it-Yourself 70	
Epilepsy 1,000. (500 of these were previously undiagnosed, and of these the vast majority are children. Ie 1 child death from epilepsy every day!)	
Drowning 450, but steadily falling.	(RoSPA)
Under 5 year olds drowning in a domestic bath 5	(Dti HASS/LASS)
Canoeing 5 (all ages, all situations)	

Adventure activities (all activities, all situations) approximately 150

APPENDIX 3

AND FOR OUR 13 MILLION YOUNG PEOPLE

THE LEADING CAUSES AMONGST CHILDREN FROM 28 DAYS TO 15 YEARS

Total	3,200
Injury and Poisoning	590
Congenital anomalies	468
Cancers at least	430*
Cot death and similar ill-defined conditions	375
Disease of the nervous system	315
Infections and parasitic diseases	264
(all other conditions)	up to 750*

ACCIDENTAL OR SUDDEN DEATH AMONGST YOUNG PEOPLE (UP TO THE AGE OF 19)

1,420 *All accidents*

700	Road Traffic Accidents (Massively the biggest single cause)
470	Congenital anomalies
430	Cancers
375	Cot deaths and similar ill-defined conditions
315	Diseases of the nervous system
264	Infectious and parasitic diseases
215	Under 14s from accidents in the home.
200	Skin cancer caused by Sunbathing
140	Suffocation
125	Poisoning (a quarter of which are from taking Class A drugs)
110	Suicide (Not part of the 1,400 total, but twice as common as child murders)
90	Drowning
80	Fire (When did you last change the batteries in your fire detectors?)
70	Falls (Kids fall a lot, but it is not often fatal)
50	Homicide (Not part of the 1,400 total. The vast majority by someone from within the direct or extended family.)
3	On school trips (The average since 1,985—Mostly Road Traffic Accidents)
750	All other medical conditions

AND BY COMPARISON . . . . .

School visits 3 (A third of which are road traffic accidents)

Adventure Activities on school visits 1

SET AGAINST THESE FIGURES

There are probably 3 million school children who are involved in adventure activities each year, and 7–10 million days of school visits.

The Duke of Edinburgh Award schemes have an accident rate of 1 serious accident (eg broken leg) per 1½ million overnights.

The Scouts have ½ million members involved in adventure activities.

The biggest cause of death in boys aged 5–15 is accidents.

The biggest cause of death in girls aged 5–15 is cancer.
(Office of National Statistics)

In 1921 child mortality (death under 1 year) was 84 per 1,000 live births

In 2000 child mortality (death under 1 year) was 6 per 1,000 live births

October 2004

Memorandum submitted by the English Outdoor Council

Thank you for the opportunity to express our views on learning outside the classroom. First, to explain where we fit in to the complicated world of the outdoors, the Council is an umbrella body of English representative bodies across the whole range of outdoor education. Our members are listed on the letterhead.

We have seen the evidence of a number of our member organisations and we support their views. In order not to burden you unnecessarily, I have tried not to repeat points that have already been well made. Our points may therefore seem somewhat idiosyncratically diverse—I hope you will understand why!

We assume you do not need convincing of the value of outdoor education. If you do, we now have the evidence, which is available on request. A consortium including the Council commissioned the National Foundation for Educational Research to carry out a study which was completed in March 2004. One reported finding is that "adventure programs have a major impact on the lives of participants and that this impact is lasting".

In its very positive account of the impact of outdoor education, the Ofsted report published in September 2004 states "Outdoor education gives depth to the curriculum and makes an important contribution to students' physical, personal and social education. However, not all students in schools benefit from such experiences."

This is unacceptable. Ofsted agrees—one of its six points for action is "Ensure the benefits of outdoor education can be experienced by all students". To be fair, there have been great strides forward in provision over the last five years, primarily funded through the National Lottery. Summer Activities for 16 Year-Olds (later the Uproject), Positive Activities for Young People and Get REAL have all made a very positive contribution.

The London Student Pledge is another excellent example of an innovative step which broadens students' experience in a way which was surely intended in the definition of the purpose of the national curriculum. While it does not specifically mention outdoor education, it does give an entitlement to an educational visit or overnight stay, one of the most powerful ways of delivering outdoor education. This too is being funded at least in part through the Lottery.

However, Lottery funding is inherently time limited and cannot form a permanent solution unless the rules are changed. We appreciate that you are looking for potential solutions—this is one. Change the Lottery rules so that, in certain exceptional circumstances, valuable provision that has never been supported by Exchequer funding can be supported on a long-term basis.

We appreciate that schools have many demands on their funds. For outdoor education, this has been particularly difficult as LEAs have been required to delegate more and more of their funds to schools. Central LEA provision, through which much outdoor education used to be provided, is clearly able to deliver less and less.

Delegating the budget to schools in theory gives them a choice but, in practice, the difficulty of setting up out of classroom opportunities and the competing demands on funds make it more likely that this valuable opportunity will be squeezed out. We need to challenge schools to state that out of classroom activity should be an entitlement for all their pupils and to plan the extent and depth of such activity in a progressive way over the years that a pupil progresses through the school.

We also appreciate that schools have many demands on their time and recognise the difficulty of adding to an already crowded curriculum. We are therefore not proposing this—we recognise we need to persuade, not impose.

The effect of the numerous demands on schools is to put outdoor education almost in a market situation where it must compete with many other priorities. Happily, many teachers know from their own direct experience how powerful an experience outdoor education is and what an impact it can have on classroom performance. Despite the pressures, there is no lack of enthusiasm—a straw poll taken at a recent conference of advisers representing most of the country's LEAs showed that educational visits were increasing in just under half of the authorities and stable in a similar proportion. There were only a tiny number of authorities in which they are declining.

Educational Visit Co-ordinator training has helped in this and proposed Visit Leader training will help further. However, while in-service training has been very effective in recent years, we are not convinced that initial teacher training does a good enough job in terms of giving trainee teachers the confidence they need to take their pupils out of the classroom. Standards for Qualified Teacher Status require trainees to be able to plan out-of-school experiences but, in the context that so much needs to crammed into so little time, we are not convinced that this is in practice being delivered consistently and effectively.

This is something that Ofsted could be asked to report on. Indeed, they could be asked to place more weight on reporting on the extent and value of out of classroom activity in all school inspections.

If we acknowledge that persuasion rather than imposition is the answer, the more encouragement schools get to deliver out-of-school activity, the better. At the invitation of DfES and DCMS, the English Outdoor Council is currently in the process of producing a document entitled "High Quality Outdoor Adventure", which will help in this process. Other practical help is needed.

For example, society must find a way to reassure teachers that they will not be held personally liable for accidents unless they are criminally negligent and make that reassurance strong enough that NASUWT will change its advice to its members. It must also find a way to support teachers as they voluntarily commit time over and above the classroom day. Recommendations that 14-19 Reform should provide an entitlement to "Wider Activities" need fleshing out into a way of ensuring that a theoretical entitlement is backed up by practical ways of making sure it is available to all.

To help in the process of reassuring teachers, much more could be done to publicise the findings of the Better Regulation Task Force report "Better Routes to Redress". This clearly finds that a compensation culture is not taking root but that the problem is one of perception. Fear of litigation is undoubtedly a problem but the solution is to remove that fear by loud, clear and repeated presentation of the facts. If the message were clearly communicated that judges are throwing out "silly" cases and not allowing a compensation culture to develop, that might help significantly. It would also be very helpful if the undisputed fact that school trips are significantly safer than everyday life were better communicated.

Returning to the question of making Lottery funded provision sustainable, we suspect that a change to Lottery rules will not happen and that, inevitably, there will be a need for more Exchequer funding if these really valuable educational experiences are to continue in the long term. This need not be an impossibility—it can be argued for on the basis of value for money in terms of the change it achieves. Pupil behaviour is a huge problem and problems exacerbated by low self-esteem include drug abuse and violence. Never before has whole person development, growth in self-confidence and responsibility been more important.

Outdoor education excels in its ability to deliver these qualities. Ministers have shown by their actions that they clearly value the learning that derives from outdoor education, particularly in a residential context. We regret however, that insufficient steps have been taken to evaluate the long-term impact of steps that have been taken over the last five years. We argued that the evaluation of Uproject should include an assessment of the value for money of that intervention in comparison with the value for money of other ways of tackling the problem of uncommitted 16 year-olds. We also argued that the proactive cost of prevention should be compared with the costs of remedial action if the young person concerned slips into a life of crime and unemployment. It is not too late to carry out such a study—we are told that the data exists.

We anticipate that the findings of such a study would form a good case for investment of Exchequer funding. We have been campaigning for five years for a residential experience to be an entitlement for all young people. Lottery funding has provided this in the short term. We must now make the opportunity available to all on a sustainable basis.

October 2004

Memorandum submitted by the Health and Safety Executive

SUMMARY

This memorandum sets out HSE's approach to the risks that could arise during school trips and seeks to address the question raised by the inquiry on "the fear of accidents and the possibility of litigation".

Fatalities on school trips are very rare. In England last year, there were around 7–10 million pupil visits/year involving educational/recreational activity but only one fatality.

HSE encourages a sensible approach to health and safety—managing risk not trying to eliminate it altogether.
The way ahead is managing the risks through proper planning, not prohibiting school trips.

HSE works with others, especially DfES which leads on pupil health and safety, to ensure schools and education authorities learn the lessons and are well supported to manage risks effectively.

INTRODUCTION

1. HSE's policy on school trips is to encourage them as a valuable component of children's overall development, not least as a means of teaching the principles of risk awareness, an essential life skill. We do not demand completely risk-free school trips but ones where risks are properly understood and managed. We promote a sensible and proportionate approach.

2. We firmly concur with the conclusion of the recent Ofsted report, 'Outdoor education: aspects of good practice', that outdoor education makes an important contribution to students' physical, personal and social development. We welcomed the statement of the Chief Inspector at the report's launch that 'the benefits of outdoor education are far too important to forfeit and by far outweigh the risks of an accident occurring. If teachers follow recognised safety procedures and guidance they have nothing to fear from the law'.

3. Several recent prosecutions and the perceived increase in personal injury claims have led to concerns among teachers. Some are being advised not to lead school trips for fear of the legal consequences if anything goes wrong. HSE believes this is an unhelpful development. A certain amount of planning and management is necessary for any successful and safe school trip. HSE's risk-based approach can be shown to aid good planning without being onerous and at the same time satisfy health and safety requirements.

4. Responsibility for education in England falls to the DfES but is devolved to the Scottish Executive and the National Assembly for Wales in those territories. DfES has, therefore, published comprehensive guidance on planning and managing school trips in England. The National Assembly for Wales has published its own virtually identical, dual-language version and the Scottish Executive is also preparing its own version. HSE has collaborated with DfES on the guidance so schools can meet their health and safety duties by following it.

ABOUT HSE

5. The Health and Safety Executive was established by the Health and Safety at Work etc Act 1974. It reports directly to the Health and Safety Commission which has overall responsibility for policy on occupational health and safety. The Commission is sponsored by the Department for Work and Pensions.

6. Working under the direction of the Health and Safety Commission, HSE's role extends well beyond just inspection and enforcement activity. We also work closely with representatives of employers, employees and other stakeholders to carry out research and provide information and advice.

HSE's ROLE IN SCHOOL TRIP SAFETY

7. A fundamental principle of the legal framework is that responsibility for health and safety lies with those who own and manage workplaces, normally employers. In general, the Local Authority is the employer in state-controlled schools and the Governing Body in independent schools. Employers must assess the risks attached to their activity and take appropriate action. This "goal-setting" rather than "prescriptive" approach takes account of what is reasonably practicable and encourages innovation.

8. While the focus of the Act is upon ensuring the health and safety of employees, there is also a general duty for employers to manage their work in such a way as to not harm members of the public (including pupils at school) affected by it. This is reinforced by the duty in the Management of Health and Safety at Work Regulations 1999 to make a suitable and sufficient assessment of risks. The DfES guidance ("Health and Safety on Educational Visits" 1998 and its supplementary guidance "Standards for Local Education Authorities in Overseeing Educational Visits", "Standards for Adventure" and "A Handbook for Group Leaders" published in 2002 (available at www.teachernet.gov.uk/wholeschool/healthand safety/visits/)) offers advice on the practical fulfilment of those duties.

9. This framework of health and safety legislation is limited to Great Britain (GB) but there is a virtually identical framework in Northern Ireland overseen by the Health and Safety Executive Northern Ireland (HSENI). HSE cannot investigate accidents occurring overseas but may investigate any activities carried out in GB to support a particular visit, eg how the trip was planned.

THE RISK OF SCHOOL TRIPS

10. It has been estimated that across England there are 710 million pupil trips per year involving educational/recreational activity. The majority of trips are carried out safely and responsibly, and fatalities are very rare.

Table of fatal accidents to schoolchildren while on school trips reported to HSE—1999 to date

Year	Total number of fatalities on school trips	Number occurring in Great Britain	Number occurring overseas
1999–2000	4	1	3
2000–01	4	2	2
2001–02	6	4	2
2002–03	2	2	0
2003–04	0	0	0
2004 (p)	1	1	0
Total	17	10	7

(data include off-site swimming activities)

11. Not all risks can be eliminated from school trips. HSE does not expect this but does expect a proper risk assessment to be undertaken and the consequent control measures to be followed.
Advice to schools

12. The DfES guidance on school trips was recently supplemented with new material, which introduced a new role, the Educational Visits Co-ordinator (EVC), within a school to oversee the planning of all trips. There is also comprehensive advice on how to put the risk assessment into practice during the trip so that it does not remain a paper exercise. It explains how to set up systems and procedures that better support teachers and others leading visits. It sets out good practice on:

— the role of the local authority outdoor education adviser;

— the role of educational visits co-ordinator in a school;

— roles of governors and head teachers;

— risk assessment; and

— competence, delegation and monitoring.

13. The guidance incorporates the lessons learnt from the double fatality at Stainforth Beck in 2001. HSE has worked with DfES to bring this to the attention of schools and we are continuing to work with the department in promulgating the lessons learnt from the more recent fatality at Glenridding in 2002.

14. There are many people working in education who have built up a good deal of expertise in running visits safely. HSE encourages them to share their expertise with those who still have some way to go and is pleased to report increasing evidence of this happening.

— The Outdoor Education Advisers Panel (England and Wales) pioneered and piloted a training course for Educational Visits Co-ordinators (EVCs) in schools. The Panel is providing training to LEA staff across England and Wales to enable them to train EVCs in their schools. DfES has provided pump-priming funds in 2002–03 to encourage LEAs to take this up.

— LEAs are drawing up generic risk assessments for common types of visit to reduce the workload on schools. Many LEAs are sharing these assessments with each other.

— Some LEAs are looking at setting up electronic web-based monitoring systems to replace the current paper-driven systems. There is much willingness to share these systems with others to save costs and to have common systems.

HSE's Approach to Investigation of Incidents

15. If a fatality occurs on a school trip, HSE carries out an exhaustive investigation to find out what preventative action could have been taken.

16. Our approach to inspection and enforcement is informed by the principles of better regulation: transparency, accountability, targeting, consistency and proportionality. This approach is set out in the Commission's Enforcement Policy Statement (www.hse.gov.uk/pubns/hsc15.pdf). HSE takes enforcement action that is proportionate to the risk, and accords priority to the most serious hazards that are poorly controlled. In order to enforce, there must be clear evidence of a breach of health and safety law and a demonstrable, foreseeable risk to the health and safety of those at work or members of the public. Schools may be inspected as part of an overall audit of a Local Authority. Inspection of the systems in place for managing school trips may be a part of this.

17. Where appropriate, HSE will prosecute and works closely with the Police under the work-related deaths protocol. Under HSE's overall enforcement policy, prosecutions are taken against employers who do not manage health and safety effectively. Under certain circumstances individual employees may also be subject to prosecution. Within the last five years, HSE has prosecuted only one teacher. The Crown Prosecution Service (CPS), however, did prosecute a teacher last year on grounds of negligence, and he was subsequently convicted of manslaughter.

18. HSE has established memoranda of understanding with other regulators to ensure that potential boundary issues, overlaps and omissions are properly addressed. One of the bodies we work with is the Adventure Activities Licensing Authority. This is an independent, public authority funded by the DfES, and operating under the written guidance of the Health and Safety Commission, which oversees the delivery in GB of certain outdoor adventure activities for young people. Commercial (as distinct from wholly voluntary) providers of such activities must be licensed and satisfy the Licensing Authority that they comply with nationally accepted standards of good practice. The Licensing Authority inspects providers, on behalf of the DfES, and has powers to withdraw or alter the conditions of a licence.

Conclusion

19. School trips remain an effective way of developing children's' physical and personal skills. HSE believes that we must learn the lessons arising from the tragic accidents that have occurred, but not deny future opportunities to children because teachers have withdrawn for fear of making a mistake. Organisers and leaders who act professionally and conscientiously have no need to fear the law.

October 2004

Memorandum submitted by the Association of British Insurers

Executive Summary

This paper discusses the ways in which insurance, and the risk assessment and management techniques which underpin insurance, can enable schools to undertake a varied programme of activities outside the classroom, enhancing our children's education. It covers insurance practice in dealing with both the maintained and independent sectors.

Insurance provides both the means to fund legitimate claims for compensation following accidents or injury in schools or during educational activities and advice and expertise in minimising the likelihood and impact of such events. For example, the leading insurer to the maintained sector assisted the Department for Education and Skills (DfES) in developing the guidance "Health and Safety of Pupils on Educational Visits" and supplementary publications.

In pricing the cover offered to Local Authorities and schools, insurers do not differentiate between in-school activities and those outside the classroom. Similarly employers are able to include students on work placements within their Employers' Liability covers. Insurance therefore enables the full range of educational opportunities.

In the maintained sector, Local Education Authority's insurance is provided as part of the wider Local Authority's cover. Only around 3% of Local Authority bodily injury claims arise from educational activities (inside and outside the classroom). The cost of this insurance to a Local Authority is therefore almost entirely driven by non-educational services.

Recent legal and market developments have led to increases in the cost of liability insurance generally. Claims inflation currently stands at 10–15% per annum. The Association of British Insurers is working with the Government, voluntary sector and others to ensure that good risk management minimises the impact of those engaging in or providing educational activities outside the classroom.

Insurers also provide direct support to schemes offering young people educational, development and sporting opportunities.

INTRODUCTION

This Memorandum is the Association of British Insurers' (ABI) contribution to the Education and Skills Select Committee inquiry into education outside the classroom. ABI has 400 members which together account for about 97% of the business of insurance companies in the UK. (Lloyd's syndicates which are not ABI members also write significant volumes of liability insurance).

In the event of an accident or other incident causing injury or death, school staff, pupils and visitors to the school site can be compensated either directly by the Local Education Authority or school, or via insurance cover. The same is true when staff and pupils are engaged on an activity which takes them away from the school site.

Inevitably activities outside the classroom take place in a less controlled environment where the possibility of accidental injury is greater. Some activities, such as Outward Bound trips, are considered beneficial precisely because they expose pupils to, and teach pupils to manage, risk.

BACKGROUND

Every year, millions of pupils are involved in school sports, school field trips and outward bound activities and 95% of students now go on some form of work placement with an employer. This activity is vital in extending pupils' experience and in undertaking practical tasks that build knowledge, test skills and add an element of fun. It can develop young personalities and prepare young people for the world of work.

Any activity in life involves risks and some educational activities deliberately expose pupils to risk as part of the learning process. But risk can be assessed and managed to acceptable levels and the consequences or impact of accidents reduced by taking sensible precautions. On occasion something will happen that results in the injury or, exceptionally, the death of a pupil or staff member. In these situations the legitimate claims for compensation by the injured party can be met from insurance, thus protecting the school or Education Authority's budget from unexpected liabilities.

INSURANCE COVER

Insurance provides financial protection to staff and pupils whether in the UK or travelling abroad. Three main types of insurance are relevant:

> *Employers' Liability*—meets the costs of claims resulting from an accident at work (or an occupational disease). Normally this provides cover for paid employees only, but can be extended to include volunteers. In addition, employers offering work placements can extend cover to students on their premises.

This insurance is compulsory, although Local Authorities are exempted and may choose to self-insure.

Public Liability—meets the cost of claims for injury or illness, or damage to property, for those not employed by the insured. It is not a compulsory insurance except in a few very particular cases, such as riding schools.

Personal Accident—provides specified cover for a defined list of injuries. It can be bought by individuals or as a group cover. For example, many Local Authorities and independent schools purchase this cover for their pupils whilst they are engaged in school activities, including sports, outdoor pursuits and field trips.

In addition Local Authorities and schools may choose to take out travel insurance (including medical cover, lost baggage, accommodation and return travel costs) particularly for foreign trips.

Risk Assessment and Management

Risk assessments have been widely adopted as good practice by Local Education Authorities and schools. Insurers can give advice on the factors that should be considered and the way to approach risk assessment in conjunction with members of the Association of Local Authority Risk Managers (ALARM).

Normal insurance practice in the maintained sector relies on schools adhering to good practice guidelines, for example the Department for Education Skills publication "Health and Safety of Pupils on Educational Visits" and supplementary guides. These were developed with the assistance of underwriters from Zurich Municipal Insurance. By requiring the use of these guidelines insurers promote Government's own defined good practice, but do not impose further restrictions.

Some Local Authorities may adopt health and safety policies that go beyond DfES guidance, but this is not at the behest of insurers.

In the independent sector insurers similarly expect schools to follow recognised standards of care and risk management. Typically these would include using facilities licensed by the Adventure Activities Licensing Authority where appropriate, or activities such as climbing or abseiling to be supervised and instructed by a suitably qualified person using practices in line with British Mountaineering Council guidelines or a suitable equivalent.

Underwriting Practice

In the maintained sector insurance is usually provided through a comprehensive contract covering the whole of the Local Authority's activities. Rating is determined by the mix of services the Local Authority provides and the particular claims experience of that authority. No specific information on the number or nature of educational activities is requested and education outside the classroom is not considered a material fact in assessing the risk profile of the authority or in pricing.

Zurich Municipal, the market leader in this sector, reports that just 3% of Local Authority bodily injury claims relate to educational activities. They do not record the division between on-site and external activities and therefore are not able to separately assess this.

Claims Handling

Where an accident or injury occurs and relevant insurance is in place the insurer will undertake the administration of the claim, including handling legal action should the claimant decide to pursue this route. Many insurers offer rehabilitation services to help people back to work after an injury. Clearly rehabilitation benefits the employer and may reduce overall claims costs, particularly where further injury or impairment is avoided by early therapeutic intervention.

In the maintained sector, Local Authorities may choose to retain a substantial share of the risk by taking an "excess" of up to £150,000. In these cases it is common practice for the insurer to take on the claims handling even where the Local Authority is funding the compensation directly.

Recent Developments in the Liability Insurance Market

The cost of compensation for liability claims in the wider economy is increasing substantially. For example, the cost of the average Employers' Liability claim increased almost threefold between 1996 and 2002. Legal changes like "no-win no-fee" arrangements have added to the legal costs of pursuing a claim. At the same time, legal judgements have increased the scope of liability.

For a number of years, insurance companies absorbed a large proportion of these increased costs with the result that they incurred significant underwriting losses, a situation which could not be sustained in the long term. Premiums have consequently increased substantially, particularly from 2000 to the end of 2003. Premium increases for 2004 are likely to average 10–15%, a figure that is broadly in line with claims inflation.

Whist these factors affect the cost of all liability insurances, they will have least impact where effective health and safety practices, and hence low claims records, are in place.

INSURANCE AND WORK EXPERIENCE

Insurers play a significant role in facilitating work experience placements for school pupils and students. ABI has been party to a long-standing agreement with the DfES that, as a matter of convention, students on work placements should be treated as employees for the purposes of insurance against personal injury (that is they will be covered by the Employers' Liability policy). Employers should of course notify their insurers that they are taking on placements.

A copy of the DfES booklet "Work Experience: a guide to employers" is attached. This includes some useful checklists for employers to notify their insurers of their intention to take on work placements and for the school to confirm that the employer is properly insured.

INSURANCE INDUSTRY ACTION FOR THE VOLUNTARY SECTOR

Many off-site educational experiences are provided through the voluntary sector. ABI has been working with the Home Office Insurance Cover Working Group to examine how the Voluntary and Community Sector (VCS) can better access the insurance market, given that they do not normally employ specialist insurance and risk management services, in contrast to Local Authorities and large companies. ABI arranged two seminars in 2003 to bring insurers, brokers and the VCS together. These identified that the VCS and other sectors need more information on what insurers are looking for in terms of risk management and ABI is working with the Home Office to this end.

INSURER ACTION AIMED AT PROMOTING EDUCATIONAL AND OUTDOOR ACTIVITIES

Many insurance companies contribute to initiatives, which facilitate learning outside the classroom. In addition to offering work placement opportunities, examples include:

— In 2001 the RBS group, which includes Direct Line and Churchill, established a three year £10.7 million partnership with the Prince's Trust. Some of these funds go to Route 14/25 which helps thousands of young people learn new skills, develop confidence and get into work.

— Norwich Union have entered a five year partnership with NCH, the children's charity, to help educate and build confidence in the UK's most vulnerable young people.

— Norwich Union also sponsor UK Athletics which is devoted to the development of the sport at grassroots level and the "do the right thing" campaign is aimed at creating more opportunities for children to do sport.

— Zurich sponsor Weston Spirit's Cyberspace a high technology centre for children in Leeds aimed at improving access to information technology.

— Co-operative Insurance Society sponsor the Young Driver of the Year Award and have made and distributed a video promoting safe driving aimed at the 15–24 age group.

In addition insurers supported initiatives enhancing or extending education by bringing the outside world into the classroom. For example, Axa, Swiss Re and CIS all support one to one reading schemes and mentoring. Zurich Municipal, in conjunction with ABI's Arson Prevention Bureau, sponsors the "Arson Combated Together" drama programme which teaches Key Stage 3 pupils the dangers of arson whether at school or in the community.

The Arson Prevention Bureau has also launched "kids zone" an on line educational tool which currently provides activities and lesson plans for Key Stage 1 and 2 pupils on fire safety and arson. This will be extended to Key Stage 3 in 2005.

October 2004

Memorandum submitted by the National Association of Head Teachers

INTRODUCTION

The National Association of Head Teachers welcomes the opportunity to present evidence to the Committee on this important matter. Staff, pupils, parents—indeed the whole school community can benefit from increased opportunity for learning that such activities can supply. However, there needs to be an awareness of the implications for the school that the organising and running of out-of-school activities can have.

COSTS AND FUNDING OF OUTDOOR ACTIVITIES

The increased demands on school budgets means that priorities for allocation are contentious and budget allocation hard-won. Any activity organised by the school must be able to demonstrate a favourable cost-benefit analysis. This applies to any out-of-school activity as much as in-school curriculum enrichment opportunities. There is no doubt that out-of-school activities can incur substantial costs in time, financial and human resources. Schools need to budget carefully for these and consider the "value for money" aspect.

Just to arrange a one-off, offsite visit for a day has implications for transport costs, staff cover costs, preparation time and debrief time. A residential visit has the potential to increase these costs exponentially and also residential costs must be incorporated. There is no opportunity for schools to recoup these costs other than through voluntary contributions from parents. Needless to say, these may or may not be forthcoming! Where they are not forthcoming, the school can only resort to placing the whole trip in jeopardy.

Staffing costs for out-of-school visits can vary hugely, but it is fair to say that there is always an expense over and above that normally incurred if the pupils were to remain in the classroom. In ensuring that the degree of extra risk inevitably associated with off-site visits is kept within acceptable limits, the adult : pupil ratio is generally higher. Where pupils with special needs are involved, this can also lead to additional costs to cater for the pupils' needs. All of these costs have to be met from the school budget and/or voluntary contributions. This can produce an unacceptable drain on already stretched budgets.

THE PLACE OF OUTDOOR LEARNING WITHIN THE CURRICULUM

There is an expectation that learning objectives will be specified for any educational provision: for education outside the classroom the imperative is to specify clearly what is to be learnt, and how, and to indicate why such learning needs to happen outside of the classroom environment. The value of such activities in terms of character-forming exercises, team-building, development of leadership qualities cannot be overestimated. However, consideration of such benefits must also be weighed against the costs and the fact that, in general, they not central to the school's curriculum and learning objectives.
Examples of activities that have historically formed part of the off-site provision are:

— science and geography field trips;

— PE/games activities off-site, like orienteering, horse-riding etc;

— historical activities, such as museum visits;

— visits to places of worship as part of religious education;

— Theatre trips;

— Visits abroad, to support modern foreign languages; and

— exhibitions, art and music events.

In general, many of these experiences could not be replicated adequately in classrooms. They should be considered as essential off-site activities and should be funded as such.

EXTERNAL ASSESSMENT OF PROVISION

The adequacy and quality of specialist outdoor provision is the responsibility of the employer—the LEA for community and voluntary schools, the governing body for foundation and voluntary aided schools. Obtaining information about providers is not always straightforward but is necessary. Some routes are reasonably easy, such as those providers that are covered by the Adventure Activities Licensing Scheme. Others are less so, though equally important.

External accreditation of providers should be more widespread. Staff involved in organising off-site activities should be expected to undertake appropriate training.

ORGANISATION AND INTEGRATION WITHIN EXISTING SCHOOL STRUCTURES

Planning for even the most straightforward of off-site visits can be extensive. If the off-site visit starts and/or finishes outside the normal times of the school day, for example, this may mean arrangements for delivery and collection of pupils, checking on availability of parents/carers to meet the timings, additional opening hours of the school grounds. Work experience placements can provide their own challenges.

Where not all children from a particular class participates in an activity, this can add pressure to the resources of the school. Any children left on the premises must be catered for. This can happen on a regular basis for sporting activities off-site, for example, but is not confined to such activities.

Though the setting may be different, the management, control and authority issues with regard to the pupils still remain the same as on site. In some cases, they become more acute. Sufficient staff must be present, emergency procedures should be in place and well communicated to all participants, medical needs must be catered for, playtime must be arranged etc. Managing these out of the pupils' usual environment can present additional challenges.

QUALIFICATION AND MOTIVATION OF TEACHERS AND THE EFFECT ON TEACHER WORKLOAD

Training is available for leaders of off-site activities, for example, OCR's training course, "Off-site Safety Management Scheme" is aimed at those who organise off-site visits of any nature and covers all aspects of planning, including risk assessments, pre-planning etc. Any staff members organising and planning off-site visits should be expected to undertake such training, as this will better prepare them for the task they are undertaking.

Although staff are generally motivated to plan and undertake off-site visits, it is true to say that this is not as wide spread as it was. Teachers undoubtedly have concerns about the possibility of litigation. These may be unfounded but they are very real. The idea that, if an accident occurs, then someone must be to blame and that person, in the eyes of the parents, must be the teacher, does nothing to assist with willingness to organise off-site visits. Lack of clarity with regard to what can be expected in terms of right to participate for children with special educational needs can also cloud the issue.

Workload issues must be taken into consideration when looking at the additional burden put on all staff. Planning and organisation is in addition to the normal work undertaken by staff. Where an educational visit is arranged over an extended period, for example, staff may be considered to be "on duty" for the whole period, day and night, as they continue to be responsible for the pupils in their care. Organising off-site visits is potentially a great drain on the staff concerned.

In the context of workload issues, it is not unreasonable to mention work experience. The organisation, monitoring, assessment, on-site visits to pupils, can reach nightmare proportions, and not always to great effect. The value of such placements should be balanced against the huge effort required to set these up.

THE FEAR OF ACCIDENTS AND THE POSSIBILITY OF LITIGATION

There is no doubt that there is ever-present concern with regard to both accidents and the possible litigation that may arise. It is also true that the compensation culture mentality does nothing to encourage schools to undertake the additional workload that off-site visits require. Although the vast majority of activities take place successfully and without incident, the tiny minority where problems occur are reported so widely that the effect is greatly skewed.

Training of staff will help to minimise the likelihood of things going wrong. Some form of protective insurance would assist in reassuring understandably nervous staff that they will not be made the scapegoat for any potential untoward incident. It might also be helpful if a positive publicity campaign were to be mounted to demonstrate the value of education outside the classroom and also how successful and safe almost all activities can be. The current advice document, Health and Safety of Pupils on Educational Visits, is seen as very helpful and should be commended to all those involved with the planning and running of school visits.

HOW PROVISION IN THE UK COMPARES WITH THAT OF OTHER COUNTRIES

We have no comment to make in this area.

CONCLUSION

We would not wish to see education outside the classroom diminish. Its value both in supporting the curriculum and in character development is immense. However, unless adequate training, sufficient funding and explicit protection/insurance can be identified, it seems unlikely that schools will be able to maintain the current provision, let alone increase it. An accreditation scheme for specialist providers should be more widespread.

October 2004

Memorandum submitted by the National Foundation for Educational Research

INTRODUCTION

1. The National Foundation for Educational Research (NFER) is the country's largest independent body specialising in educational research. The Foundation has a considerable portfolio of research on education outside the classroom, including work on outdoor learning, environmental education and education for sustainable development (http://www.nfer.ac.uk/research/env.asp).

2. This submission draws particularly on a recent review of outdoor learning research undertaken by NFER and King's College London (Rickinson *et al*, 2004). This synthesised the findings of 150 pieces of research on fieldwork/visits, outdoor adventure, and school grounds/community projects, published internationally in English between 1993 and 2003. It was funded by the Field Studies Council, DfES, English Outdoor Council, Groundwork, RSPB, and Wildfowl and Wetlands Trust.

3. The submission is also informed by two other research projects undertaken by NFER in collaboration with King's College London and the University of Bath. These include a review of research on "*Improving the Understanding of Food, Farming and Land Management Amongst School-age Children*" (Dillon *et al*, 2003), and an empirical study of "*The Outdoor Classroom in a Rural Context*" (currently underway).

4. Given the terms of reference of the enquiry, this submission focuses on the question "*what barriers exist to the expansion and development of out-of-classroom learning*".

BARRIERS TO OUTDOOR LEARNING PROVISION

Summary

5. It is clear that the provision of outdoor learning in schools and universities is affected by a wide range of barriers and opportunities. Notable barriers include:

(i) fear and concern about health and safety;

(ii) teachers' lack of confidence in teaching outdoors;

(iii) curriculum requirements in schools and universities limiting opportunities for outdoor learning;

(iv) shortages of time, resources and support; and

(v) wider changes within and beyond the education sector.

6. A frequently-cited challenge for outdoor learning provision is *fear and concern about young people's health and safety*. One source of such fear has been "*a number of well-publicised accidents involving school children*", which have served to overshadow "*the educational benefits of the off-site and outdoor classroom*" (Thomas, 1999, p 131). In her discussion of the impact of the Lyme Bay tragedy in which four teenagers died on a sea kayaking trip in 1993, for example, Jacobs (1996) reports that:

> some headteachers stopped sending their pupils on activity holidays because their confidence in activity centres had been undermined. Many centres reported that there had been a fall in business by up to one-third in the 15 months following the incident. (p 296)

7. Concern has also arisen in relation to farm visits, following a civil court case concerning a child contracting an *E. coli* infection during an organised school visit to an "Open" farm in 1997 (Richardson, 2000). This is reported to have led to heightened anxiety amongst "*parents, teachers, educational employers [as well as] many farmers and organisations involved in farm visit schemes*" (*ibid*, p 62). This point is well illustrated by one of the largest teaching unions (NASUWT) advising "*members against taking school trips because society no longer appears to accept the concept of a genuine accident*" (Clare, 2004).

8. Studies that have investigated school teachers' thinking about teaching beyond the classroom suggest that health and safety issues represent one of a number of difficulties facing school staff. This was the case, for example, for 65 physical/outdoor education teachers in southern England (Harris, 1999), 59 elementary school teachers in and around Chicago (Simmons, 1998), and 28 secondary school science teachers in Darwin, northern Australia (Michie, 1998). It also featured as one of several barriers reported by teachers and outdoor educators involved in the current Growing Schools Initiative in England (Scott *et al*, 2003).

9. It is important to recognise that concerns about children's well-being and safety are part of what Thomas (1999) calls "*a prevailing social trend, not only towards making things safer, but also towards seeking compensation for acts or omissions that result in personal injury*" (p 131). In other words, the growth of a litigation culture is a further dimension that has added to educators' and schools'/centres' concerns about outdoor learning.

10. A major challenge is the level of *teachers' confidence and expertise in the use of teaching and learning strategies outdoors*. An Ofsted survey of Outdoor and Adventurous Activities (OAA) in 33 English schools noted "teachers' experience" as a key factor affecting the quality of OAA in different schools (Clay, 1999). This was particularly evident in the differences between primary school and secondary school provision:

> *The teachers with more experience of working in the outdoors made greater demands on pupils . . . Enthusiastic but less experienced teachers—usually in primary schools—tended to opt for lower levels of challenge well within the capacity of the pupils.* (p 84)

11. This is echoed by Beedie (1998) who argues that the delivery of OAA by schools is constrained by "*limited perspectives from PE staff*", possibly as a result of "*lack of training*" (p 19). In a UK project called Farmlink, which aimed to facilitate long-term relationships between schools and local farms through educational visits, one of the problems encountered was teachers' lack of knowledge about farming (Groundwork, 2002b). The recent evaluation of the Growing Schools Initiative made a similar point (Scott *et al*, 2003). The same seems to be true for teaching and learning in school grounds. A qualitative study of 32 secondary schools in England found that one of the barriers to working in the grounds cited by teachers was "*personal and professional limitations [such as] lack of training [and] fear of lack of control*" (Titman, 1999, p 10). This is echoed by more recent school grounds research in England and Australia (Skamp and Bergman, 2001; Malone and Tranter, 2003a and b; Rickinson *et al*, 2003a and b), as well as studies into teachers' ability to provide opportunities for active citizenship within and beyond the school (Kerr and Cleaver, 2004, forthcoming).

12. The prospects for addressing the needs of teachers in this area, however, are not encouraging. In the UK, Barker et al. (2002) point out that:

> *The decline in fieldwork is also evident in initial teacher training [. . . and . . .] in-service experience is becoming less likely.* (p 7)

These challenges have not been helped by the increasing number of non-specialists teaching secondary school subjects especially at key stage 3 and the decline in advisory support for outdoor learning within many LEAs.

13. Similar issues are raised by Simmons (1998) in her research on Chicago teachers' willingness to use outdoor natural settings (rivers, ponds and marshes, deep woods, country parks and urban nature) for environmental education. Based on interviews with 59 elementary school teachers "*with widely differing experiences in providing EE in natural settings*", the study found that:

> *the teachers did not believe that they were particularly well trained to teach in natural areas . . . they seemed to believe that their classes were too large to manage and that they lacked the necessary background to teach in [such places].* (p 31)

14. The requirements of school and university curricula and timetables are a further reported constraint on outdoor learning. Researchers identified various manifestations of these constraints:

— Secondary school teachers in England in 1999 indicated that "*the main reason for not using the [school] grounds was the belief that the National Curriculum neither prescribes nor provides sufficient flexibility to permit the use of school grounds for teaching*" (Titman, 1999, p 10).

— The constraints of secondary school timetables in various countries meant that teachers had insufficient time to undertake work in the school grounds during a single lesson period (Titman, 1999), or were said to be unwilling to extend field trips beyond a double lesson period for fear of "*incurring the wrath of their peers for taking students out of their classes and/or generating relief lessons*" (Michie, 1998, p 47).

— According to many researchers and commentators, the English National Curriculum's focus on "Outdoor and Adventurous Activities" as primarily within the remit of Physical Education appears to have resulted in an overemphasis on the physical (as opposed to the personal/social, and environmental) aspects of outdoor education (Humberstone, 1993; Beedie, 1998; Clay, 1999).

— Changes in secondary school science syllabus requirements have meant that "*coursework and individual investigations now take precedence [over] developing a sense of place*" (Barker *et al*, 2002, p 7).

15. Alongside curriculum constraints are difficulties due to *shortages of time, resources and support* for outdoor learning. Harris' survey (1999) of 65 secondary school/teachers in the south of England noted "*a lack of time and a lack of money*" as the top two obstacles to outdoor education (p 8). In Australia, Michie (1998, p 48) reports that "*time and effort on the part of the teacher were often seen as negative factors*" associated with organising and undertaking fieldwork. Tasks such as visiting venues, contacting resource people, preparing resource materials, organising relief lessons, collecting students' money and using one's out-of-school time were all noted as difficulties. Another issue raised by the secondary school science teachers in Michie's (1998) study was transportation.

> *Class sizes in junior secondary science were generally greater than the size of the group that could be transported with a small bus . . . Bigger buses are not only more expensive to buy and maintain, but also they require different licensing arrangements.* (p 47)

16. The same issue is reported as a difficulty for undertaking farm visits (Groundwork, 2002b). The recent Growing Schools evaluation, for example, highlighted a number of barriers relating to fund-raising, transportation, and costs to parents (Scott *et al*, 2003). Likewise, Fisher (2001), writing about research into fieldwork in science based on interviews with teachers and administrators in 30 secondary schools in south-west England, noted that:

> *For students aged 11–16 years, structured scientific fieldwork away from the school grounds may now be rare. For students aged 16–18 years . . . fieldwork has become regarded as a luxury and is usually limited to the minimum required by the examination scheme and to the extent students can fund these activities themselves. (p 76)*

17. Even with outdoor learning on the school site, the question of resources in terms of the availability of well-designed facilities and curriculum-resource materials remains a challenge for many secondary schools. As noted by Titman (1999), "other than provision for sports, there was little evidence of school grounds having been designed initially to support the formal, informal and hidden curriculum" (p 8). A key issue in this study, though, was the support or otherwise of the school senior management team.

> *Schools which had made most use of sites correlated in the main with those where the head was actively involved in and committed to the concept. In these schools the grounds had status and profile. On a practical level interested headteachers are also more likely to facilitate use through management structures, for example by creating a special responsibility post/allowance. (p 10)*

18. Related to this are schools' and teachers' philosophies of learning and the extent to which these incorporate a conception of learning as an indoor and outdoor activity. As Malone and Tranter (2003b) found in their study of Australian primary schools:

> *The school ground design, although instrumental in the potential for extending curricula, is not as vital as having a view of learning that does not distinguish between the indoor-outdoor environments. (p 299)*

19. Finally, outdoor education is subject to wider changes within the education sector and beyond, and this can be another area of challenge. This is well illustrated by the fate of fieldwork within UK university degree courses over the last decade. Clark (1997) highlights a number of ways in which the purpose and role of geography fieldwork have been affected by "the emergence of a new higher education system". He draws attention to the impact of changing:

— student/staff numbers—*"rising student numbers and student/staff ratios mean that staffing levels on fieldwork have fallen [and] staff-led small-group teaching is often no longer practicable"*;

— course structures—*"it is difficult to specify learning objectives, and to devise realistic and fair methods of assessing fieldwork, when students are drawn from a wide range of backgrounds and may be studying varying amounts of geography within loosely-knit modular degree schemes"*;

— timetabling—"institution-wide timetables, in which the working day is divided into a series of two- or three-hour blocks, commonly limit the opportunities for field excursions in the local area"; and

— resource levels—*"reductions in resources and increasing student indebtedness threaten residential fieldwork, especially in overseas locations"*. (Clark, 1997, p 390; *see* also McEwan, 1996)

20. Another example is outdoor adventure education in the secondary school sector. In an article exploring "school-based" and "residential" delivery of Outdoor and Adventurous Activities (OAA), Beedie (2000) makes clear that the debate has been shaped by "a climate of change in secondary education".

> *School managed budgets, legislation following high profile tragedies such as Lyme Bay, undermining of LEA power, changing perceptions of risk and financial pressure on outdoor centres have all contributed to our present educational circumstances in ways which have a direct bearing on potential OAA programmes. (p 18)*

A similar point is made by Barker *et al* (2002) about the negative effects that "changes in school management" have had on field studies.

IMPLICATIONS FOR POLICY

21. *Summary*

Those with a statutory and non-statutory responsibility for policy relating to outdoor education should be in no doubt that there is a considerable body of empirical research evidence to support and inform their work.

— Policy makers at all levels need to be aware of the benefits that are associated with different types of outdoor learning. The findings of this review make clear that learners of all ages can benefit from effective outdoor education. However, despite such positive research evidence and the long tradition of outdoor learning in this country, there is growing evidence that opportunities for outdoor learning are in decline and under threat.

— There is an urgent need for policy makers at all levels and in many sectors to consider their role in:

— tackling barriers that stand in the way of the provision of effective outdoor education for all students;

— encouraging good programmes and practices and capitalising on policy developments, for example, by linking initiatives in different sectors; and

— supporting research, development and training so that good practice can be understood, disseminated and fostered.

— This has implications for action across a range of policy sectors nationally, regionally and locally, including education, health, environment and science.

22. Those with a statutory and non-statutory responsibility for policy relating to outdoor learning should be in no doubt that there is a considerable body of empirical research evidence to support and inform their work. This speaks to a wide range of individuals and institutions including teachers, school governors, non-governmental organisations, local authorities, LEAs, teacher unions, subject associations and politicians at all levels, all of whom may be involved directly or indirectly in developing and evaluating policy relating to outdoor learning.

23. We believe that policy makers at all levels need to be aware of the benefits that are associated with different types of outdoor learning. In particular, they need to appreciate that:

— fieldwork and field studies, properly planned, delivered and followed up, provide powerful opportunities for cognitive and affective learning;

— outdoor adventure education can provide unique opportunities for personal and social development with long-lasting impacts; and

— school grounds/community projects can enrich curricular and cross-curricular learning, and build stronger links between schools and communities.

In short, learners of all ages can benefit from effective outdoor learning.

24. However, policy makers need to recognise that despite positive research evidence and the long tradition of outdoor learning in this country, there is growing evidence that opportunities for outdoor learning are in decline and under threat. There is therefore a need for policy makers at all levels and in many sectors to consider their role in increasing access to outdoor education that is challenging, effective and that meets the needs of society while being sensitive to the needs, feelings and culture of the individual. It is crucial that policy makers consider ways to:

— tackle barriers that stand in the way of the provision of effective outdoor education for all students;

— encourage good programmes and practices and capitalise on policy developments, for example, by linking initiatives in different sectors; and

— support research, development and training so that good practice can be understood, disseminated and supported.

25. This raises a number of questions for several different policy areas, including education, health, environment, and science.

26. In the education sector, policy makers need to address these questions:

— To what extent are there policies in place that promote high quality outdoor education as an entitlement for all students at both primary and secondary schools?

— To what extent do policies ensure that fieldwork at undergraduate level is actively encouraged and supported?

— To what extent do institutional policies support outdoor education through training?

— To what extent do such policies in schools, universities and LEAs result in adequate funding for safe and effective residential in a range of relevant subjects?

— To what extent do curriculum and assessment policies fully support outdoor education?

— To what extent are there policies in place to ensure that the networks of new subject learning centres organise outdoor learning training courses for teachers?

— In what ways can the expertise and confidence of new and experienced teachers be improved through pre-service, in-service and leadership training?

27. For policy makers in the health sector, the following questions warrant consideration:

— To what extent do existing policies ensure that outdoor education is designed to enhance personal health while reducing any concomitant risk?

— In what ways can activities in school grounds promote healthy lifestyles?

— To what extent do existing institutional health and safety policies promote and enhance outdoor education for all students wherever relevant?

— To what extent are policies in place that result in adequate training in safety and teaching methods for all appropriate staff?

28. In the environment sector, policy makers need to address the following questions:

— To what extent do existing policies ensure that outdoor education results in positive experiences of the countryside and develops an understanding of rural/urban livelihoods?

— What policy changes might result in greater connections being made between schools and communities in urban and rural areas through outdoor education?

29. Science policy makers need to address the following kinds of questions:

— What policy initiatives might result in all students appreciating the role that fieldwork plays in the physical and the life sciences?

— To what extent is there a need for fieldwork to be a mandatory part of physical and life science courses wherever appropriate?

— To what extent is there a need for the Council for Science and Technology to consider the place of fieldwork in science education up to and including postgraduate level?

30. Underpinning all of these questions is a need for the benefits of outdoor learning to feature more prominently in debates about schools of the future (Bentley, 1998), social inclusion and "personalised learning" (Miliband, 2004), healthy schools and communities, and education for sustainable development (DfES, 2002a).

REFERENCES

Dillon, J, Rickinson, M, Sanders, D, Teamey, K and Benefield, P (2003). *Improving the Understanding of Food, Farming and Land Management Amongst School-age Children: a Literature Review* (DfES Research Report 422). London: DfES.

Rickinson, M, Dillon, J, Teamey, K, Morris, M, Choi, M, Sanders, D and Benefield, P (2004). A Review of Research on Outdoor Learning. Shrewsbury: Field Studies Council.

October 2004

Memorandum submitted by William Scott and Alan Reid, University of Bath, and Nick Jones, Council for Environmental Education

Attached you will find a submission to the Education and Skills Committee enquiry into Education outside the Classroom. This submission comprises the report which we wrote for the DfES into aspects of its Growing Schools Initiative (GSI)—a programme extensively concerned with work that children do "outside the classroom". Although of restricted focus—on food, farming and growing, the countryside, and the environment, the initiative, and the evaluation, do highlight issues that we think are germane to your enquiry. We hope you find the report useful.[8] A word version of the report is also attached. This is available at: http://www.teachernet.gov.uk/docbank/index.cfm?id = 5655.

SUMMARY

The attached document reports on the evaluation of the Growing Schools Initiative's Innovation Fund Projects (2002–03). Six flagship Projects were supported through the Innovation Fund as part of the Department for Education and Skills' (DfES) larger (and continuing) Growing Schools Initiative. The report is based on an external evaluation commissioned by the Department as an integral aspect of the Innovation Fund's programme of activities (2002–03), and carried out by the Council for Environmental Education and the Centre for Research in Education and the Environment at the University of Bath with the co-operation of the organisations that managed the Projects.

The evaluation team, in welcoming the achievements of the Projects in what is emerging once again as a significant area of the curriculum, noted that it was clear that food, farming and growing, the countryside, and the environment are important issues for schools to include in their work with young people. However, we also noted that when the Government's commitment to sustainable development, and schools' roles in setting out to address this, are taken into account, these issues take on a far greater significance.

In this report, Section A.2 outlines the genesis of the Growing Schools Initiative, presenting a summary chronology of the actions of government, NGOs and other interested parties.

Section A.3 details the emergence of the Innovation Fund, describing its relationship to the wider Growing Schools Initiative.

Section A.4 sets out the Aims and Objectives of the Innovation Fund projects, exploring the choices available to the co-ordinating organisations for the six flagship Projects in deciding which foci to adopt.

---

[8] Not printed.

Section B1.1 describes the evolution of the role of the external evaluation, detailing the options that emerged and the choices that were made.

Section B1.2 sets out how evaluative data were gathered, detailing how this related to Projects' own evaluative work.

Section B2 provides details of the five organisations which managed the Innovation Fund Projects.

Section B3 summarises what Projects regard as their major outputs and outcomes, grouping these according to the aims and objectives of the Innovation Fund, and identifying a number of general points about how Projects reported their work.

Section B4 examines a number of critical issues arising from the Innovation Fund projects, setting out recommendations about the conduct of future work in this field.

Section C draws together recommendations for the Department for Education and Skills, NGOs, external Agencies and others, presenting these under a number of themes which relate to the Innovation Fund project's aims and objectives.

In conclusion, we recommended that any future work within the Growing Schools Initiative needed to place a greater emphasis on the following:

1. Learning and the Nature of Evidence of achievements, participation and barriers in Growing Schools-related Initiatives (Recommendations 1 and 2).

2. Concepts and Curriculum Mapping in the Growing Schools "field", eg how ideas relating to food, farming, growing, countryside, environment, development, and the like relate to each other, and to other ideas (Recommendations 3 and 4).

3. Conceptualising the Outdoor Classroom, in terms of how pedagogical and learning theory inform its use (Recommendation 5).

4. The nature, differentation and contextualisation of barriers, and how they are overcome (Recommendation 6).

5. What Research tells us in designing learning and professional development initiatives in relation to the field of Growing Schools (Recommendations 7 and 8).

6. Working with Teachers, in terms of their funding, involvement and professional development in Growing Schools Initiatives (Recommendations 9–11).

7. Working with Students, to identify, develop and extend learning gains from Projects (Recommendation 12).

8. Working with Partners, to maximise the contribution that each can make to the work of the other (Recommendation 13).

9. Working with Farmers, through existing, quality-assured routes (eg Stewardship schemes) (Recommendation 14).

10. Communicating Achievements effectively and efficiently to diverse audiences, through training, support, funding and evaluation mechanisms (Recommendations 15 and 16).

11. Constructing Case Studies that enable readers to think critically and reflexively about their own work, refine their practice in ways appropriate to need and context, and make effective use of internal evaluations (Recommendations 17 and 18).

12. Due consideration of the Timing and Growing of projects and opportunities for student learning and teacher professional development (Recommendation 19).

13. Reconsidering and ensuring Value for Money (Recommendation 20).

October 2004

Memorandum submitted by the Commission for Architecture and the Built Environment (CABE)

1. INTRODUCTION

1.1 The Commission for Architecture and the Built Environment (CABE) is a Non-Departmental Public Body, established by the Government in 1999. Its role is to promote the creation of high quality buildings and spaces that transform people's quality of life. The Department of Culture Media and Sport and the Office of the Deputy Prime Minister co-sponsor CABE. CABE engages with a range of stakeholders throughout the public, private and voluntary sectors (see www.cabe.org.uk).

1.2 CABE Education was established by CABE as a separate charitable foundation in 2002 (see www.cabe-education.org.uk). The Foundation aims to inspire young people to get more from the buildings and spaces around them. Our ultimate ambition is to nurture a generation of confident and demanding citizens to play an active role in improving the villages, towns and cities that we live in. CABE Education is presenting its evidence to the Select Committee as it believes that buildings and spaces provide a rich, (potentially) easily accessible and stimulating educational resource. Through learning how places come to be built and how they change over time, young people can better understand how they can be improved.

1.3 CABE Space is a key CABE programme relating to the experience of young people outside the classroom. It is the national champion for parks and public spaces (see www.cabespace.org.uk). CABE Space sees creative play as crucial for children's development and is concerned that increasing urbanisation has left our children with far fewer opportunities than previous generations to play freely outdoors. Good-quality parks and green spaces can help to address this concern, providing children with opportunities for fun, exercise, learning and social development.

2. Access to Experiences Outside the Classroom

2.1 We recognise that the main thrust of this enquiry is to look at the issues and barriers that currently prevent children and young people from engagement in outdoor activities in less-familiar surroundings. However, we would suggest that getting young people out of the classroom to actively experience their immediate built environment is equally crucial. The issues and barriers which prevent greater access from schools—even to places that are more local and more familiar—are very often similar to those which prevent children from participating in more physically adventurous outdoor activities. We urge the Committee to take a broad view because whether children are engaged in adventurous outdoor activities or using the outdoors for more academically focused educational work, the experience of school visits is very valuable. Interests and enthusiasm nurtured on school visits can form the basis of interests and enthusiasms that can last a lifetime. Children tend to remember school outings because they can be stimulating and fun at the same time as being educational. Every effort therefore needs to be made to make it easier for schools to get children out and about.

2.2 "The built environment is a resource that is perennially available to all, and one with which everyone has a relationship. It has an immense physical and intellectual range that can provide rich, shared learning experiences. Since the built environment is outside of the windows of classrooms and surrounding streets its learning applications are simple to access and need to be promoted more widely." (Letter to Ministers from JACBEE, 20 September 2004.)

2.3 The Joint Advisory Committee on Built Environment Education (JACBEE) was set up by DCMS and DfES in 2003. The Committee included representatives from CABE Education, English Heritage, Heritage Link and the Citizenship Foundation and made its recommendations to Ministers this autumn. In their joint response this October, Charles Clarke and Andrew McIntosh agreed that a "compelling argument for the educational value of the built environment" had been made. We therefore think it appropriate to bring this to your committee's attention.

2.4 As well as producing teaching materials and supporting a network of educators (see our postcard, 360° magazine and publications attached as Appendices I–IV), CABE Education undertakes research into teachers' use of the built environment and the views of young people, in order to better understand how to achieve our aims. We have carried out some research which we consider of considerable relevance to the subject of the current enquiry.

2.5 In September 2004 CABE Education received the results of a research study gauging reactions from teachers and key organisations to its planned programme to encourage more out-of-classroom visits to buildings and public spaces (*Research Study for the Get out there campaign*, Williamson, Chittendon and Catchpole, September 2004). A representative sample of 25 teachers and Head teachers across England were targeted within Geography, Citizenship, Art and Design, Design and Technology and History at secondary level. Representatives from 26 central and local government, union, subject and teacher training organisations were also interviewed. The key findings relevant to the Committee's enquiry are outlined below:

(a) All teachers and organisations recognised that off-site trips "make an essential and irreplaceable contribution to the teaching and learning of their subject area as well as pupil's development". Particular benefits identified by teachers included: contextualised learning; development of students' and teachers' knowledge and understanding; increased student motivation; improved relationships and behaviour; new opportunities and broader horizons; a wider range of learning experiences; development of social skills; resonant experiences; interaction with other professionals; professional development; and increased confidence for teachers.

(b) Almost all of the schools surveyed took students out on visits, in each of the subject areas, at least once during the school year. Visits were primarily organised to enhance a subject area's programme of study. However, the majority of trips tended to be to galleries, museums or other more distant locations. Few schools from the sample took trips within walking distance. Teachers also reported that there has been a tendency to reduce the number of visits over recent years.

(c) The majority of teachers appreciated the relevance of the built environment although some did not feel they had the necessary resources or subject knowledge to make full use of it.

(d) Organisations in the survey all referred to the vital and positive aspects of out-of-classroom learning including enriching the curriculum, inspiration, promoting confidence, providing new perspectives and points of view and providing lifelong learning skills.

(e) However, concerns were expressed by both teachers and organisations about the many factors which make organising visits complicated and time consuming.

2.6 CABE Education believes there is a real need for user-friendly guidance for teachers on how to plan and prepare for school trips using the built environment. CABE Education intends to produce such guidance in the near future. We recognize that such a guide would need regular updating. We also believe that through our 360° magazine we can feature a regular slot promoting best value or good places to visit, that are perhaps not the most obvious destinations, as a way of encouraging more schools to undertake visits. We do believe that if teachers feel confident about arranging visits effectively, problems can be minimized. It has to be acknowledged, however, that so far as the built environment is concerned, there is a shortage of educationalists able to interpret the built environment to children. CABE Education has an important role to play here in developing, nurturing and encouraging those who can communicate ideas about the development of our towns and cities in an engaging, creative and yet realistic way to young people. We recognize this challenge and are seeking to address it.

2.7 In an earlier piece of research for CABE Education (*Using the Built Environment as a Teaching Resource*, MORI, March 2004) it emerged that teachers saw that "the built environment has the potential to engage students [. . .] because students do enjoy learning about their surroundings. Trips to look at local buildings are seen by teachers as a way of enabling students to better understand topics that are covered in the classroom [. . .] and are constantly looking for more innovative ways to engage their students".

2.8 Further research for CABE Education by MORI (A Research study among 11–16 Year Olds MORI, March 2004) showed that 58% of pupils wanted to go on visits to interesting buildings. As a demonstration that children were interested in becoming more involved in their own neighbourhoods it emerged that 43% of those polled were already, or wanted to be, involved in changes to the area where they lived. CABE Education views this latent interest by children in their surroundings as extremely positive and believes that there is much more that can be done to stimulate this interest and encourage interest to translate into positive engagement, thus aiding a growing interest in and awareness of what it means to be a responsible citizen.

2.9 A summary of research on urban spaces for CABE Space (*The value of Public Space*, CABE Space, March 2004, attached as Appendix V) showed the importance of play opportunities for the acquisition of social skills, from experimentation and the confrontation and resolution of emotional crises, to moral understanding, cognitive skills, and, of course, physical skills.

2.10 In the introduction to *What would you do with this space?* (CABE Space/CABE Education, May 2004, attached as Appendix VI), Yvette Cooper, Parliamentary Under Secretary of State, Office of the Deputy Prime Minister, states that "the interactions that take place in public space provide children with a rich education about the world around them". The 16 case studies of good practice in the guide showed the many benefits young people can get from being involved in changes to their local environment including judging risks, decision making, understanding needs of others and increased confidence. These are very much the same kinds of benefits that children can obtain through more adventurous outdoor activities but it needs to be remembered that there is considerable scope for benefits to be derived from visits near to schools as well as to places further away.

2.11 A further key finding outlined in this publication was that there was often a change in the perception of young people by the wider community who saw them as a positive force for change rather than a menace. However, territory in the urban environment that young people felt ownership of and responsibility for was needed to produce the benefits outlined above. Often this is not the case.

3. Barriers

3.1 The Committee's terms of reference are to consider what barriers exist to making the most of the potential for education outside the classroom. Our comments, picking up on your areas of interest, are as follows:

Costs and funding

3.2 Studies of local buildings and public spaces are relatively low cost as transport costs are very much less than they would be to destinations further away. In many instances there are opportunities for schools within walking distance so transport costs can be avoided. More should be made of such opportunities. However, transport costs can be a real issue for schools and a real deterrent to the running of school trips. More funding should be made available to make it easier for schools to arrange visits. The pioneering work in Wales in recent years of the Gateway Project is a model that could be emulated elsewhere. The Gateway Project is a registered charity which, with the support of the HLF and other donors, is able to pay for the transport costs to enable groups of disadvantaged people, both adults and children, to visit the gardens of Wales. It keeps overheads to a minimum but has none the less reached a wide audience and had a remarkable impact. There is great scope for the Gateway model, already being extended into the West Midlands, to be rolled out elsewhere. Whilst Gateway's focus is essentially based around the concept of the benefits to be derived from visiting significant gardens (eg historic gardens or the Welsh Botanic Garden), the model could readily be adapted to encompass visits to buildings or other places of interest, most particularly to buildings, streets or neighbourhoods.

3.3 Our *Get out there* research (referred to in 2.5 above) showed that, transport costs apart, there are still associated costs of teacher cover, teacher training and research and suitable fieldwork equipment, which apply to any visit. When funding school visits, Gateway provides help to teachers and to schools with this aspect which is enormously valued. This means that children can make the most of any visit.

The place of outdoor learning within the curriculum

3.4 Moving on from the issue of the transport costs of visits, an analysis of the National Curriculum 2000 undertaken by CABE Education with support from subject associations (*The Place of the Built Environment in supporting the National Curriculum*, Cabe Education, November 2003) showed that there were strong links between the built environment and almost all subject areas and all key stages. However, these are often not made explicit in QCA Programmes of Study and so teachers are not always aware of the potential of their local area. This is something CABE Education intends to address through the production of resources.

3.5 This view was endorsed by JACBEE's findings and its recommendations that "DfES and DCMS work with QCA to promote and endorse the potential of the built environment" and that "CABE, English Heritage and interested parties work together to produce a proposal for the creation of a one-stop-shop for built environment education information". Further to this, the Attingham Trust report *Opening Doors: Learning in the Historic Environment* (Giles Waterfield, June 2004) called on DfES and DCMS to extend their work on realising the educational potential of the historic environment and also for the establishment of a "one-stop-shop" for information on built environment education encompassing both the historic and contemporary. CABE Education is now embarked upon a programme of work to test the feasibility of this. Whilst CABE Education's magazine, 360°, which comes out three times a year and which is widely distributed, contains a great deal of information about what is going on in the sector, there is a clear need for greater investment and for a more comprehensive approach to encouraging teachers and schools to make the best use of the built environment.

External assessment of provision

3.6 From our *Get out there* research, it is clear that the educational value of the local built environment was often not recognised and secondary school teachers were not always confident in how to use it. This was a major factor in reducing the number of local visits. QCA promotion of the built environment as a resource and the one-stop-shop mentioned above would most certainly improve this somewhat depressing situation.

3.7 The Real World Learning Alliance have identified the lack of consideration of out of classroom learning in school inspections. If there were such external evaluation of the whole school approach to visits this would undoubtedly encourage schools to make more of the opportunities available. We would suggest that your committee consider the desirability of including an assessment of out of school activities as part of regular school inspections.

Organisation and integration within existing school structures

3.8 For any off-site excursion, schools are required to meet health and safety guidelines issued by the LEA, the trip venue/site and the school. Our *Get out there* study showed that some schools feel well supported while others are less confident of procedures. Tasks include: making a risk assessment; arranging transportation; providing medical certification; establishing parental/carer consent; obtaining insurance; providing emergency telephone number lists; negotiating time off-timetable with other subject areas; setting cover work where absent from lessons; arranging cover teachers; conducting a pre-visit recce; planning and preparing teaching resources. Teachers in Schools that had strong, clear policies and established practices and procedures for out-of-classroom learning felt more confident and were therefore able to carry out more visits and gain more from them. This approach should be encouraged through training and models of good practice. CABE Education is actively working in this area with a view to providing guidance for schools on how to organise a school visit to a local built environment destination. This will be of enormous use to teachers, classroom assistants and other administrative staff.

3.9 Similar organisational tasks apply to a trip whether it is a walk across town or to a destination much further afield. Our research showed that this was another factor in teachers deciding that if they were going to go to the effort of arranging a visit it might as well be to a well-known "destination". Such destinations (eg a major museum, art gallery etc) have the advantage, in teachers' perceptions, of having ready made educational facilities (education staff, education room, and ready prepared educational materials for example) which facilitated organisation. Whilst visits to major destinations are a vital part of any child's education, there is a real role for other types of visit. Suitable guidance and resources need to be made available through a one-stop-shop (as outlined in para 3.5 above) providing inspiring and practical models for the type of short local safaris recommended in *A child's place: why environment matters to children* (Green Alliance/Demos, May 2004). Some support of this nature is becoming available through the growing number of members of the Architecture Centre Network which CABE actively supports through its regional grants programme (see www.architecturecentre.net).

Qualification and motivation of teachers and the effect on teacher workload

3.10 Planning opportunities for pupils to learn in out-of-school contexts, such as school visits, are a requirement of Qualified Teacher Status (Standards for the Award of Qualified Teacher Status 3.15). Provision of support is from the training college and on teaching practice. In order to promote educational experiences outside the classroom a positive and practical approach is essential for trainee teachers. Materials and support are needed for teacher trainers. In our *Get out there* research concern was expressed that there is a wave of Newly Qualified Teachers coming into teaching with the view that trips are just too risky. This is a matter of very serious concern to us.

3.11 Supporting this view a further JACBEE recommendation is that "DfES and DCMS work with the TTA to produce built environment education training packages". CABE Education believes these should include, or relate to, training and support on making visits which instills a "can do" approach.

3.12 Once teachers are practicing in schools our *Get out there* research found that there are a number of factors that help to encourage the organisation of trips. A school ethos that encourages trips backed up by workable policies are vitally important: easy to use proformas, practical advice, mentoring by experienced teachers, support of head and of governors, senior management attending trips and being supportive, cooperation of parents and administrative support. All these contribute to the likelihood of trips taking place and of their being a success.

Fear of accidents and possibility of litigation

3.13 These fears were very prominent in our *Get out there* research. Teachers were concerned about risking their careers due to litigation, whether such legal challenges were well-founded or not. Union recommendations against organising trips were ignored by some and heeded by others.

3.14 CABE Education believes that a systematic framework that ensures legal accountability at the LEA level is needed. This would improve confidence and competence and could assist in reducing teachers' workload and do much to reduce the climate of nervousness and fear about the possibility of teachers being blamed if something goes wrong.

4. SUMMARY

4.1 In summary, CABE Education would like to suggest the following as recommendations:

4.2 Teachers should be encouraged and enabled to make more of the educational value of the buildings and spaces in their local environment through:

(a) Provision of a framework for legal accountability at the LEA level that raises confidence and competence and reduces teachers' workload. LEAs/DfES should provide teachers with personal liability insurance.

(b) Linking the above to clear, practical and reliable support and guidance for conducting risk assessments.

(c) Establishing school trip coordinators in every school and LEA with expertise in organising short local visits as well as longer day trips and residential trips. This role could be combined with that of the suggested DCMS Cultural Entitlement coordinator.

(d) Provide further support to teachers through the training of classroom assistants or administrative staff to take on a greater role in organising visits.

(e) Provision of curriculum support materials such as case studies for subjects making links to curriculum and exam criteria and exploring a range of models for trips, eg one hour, two hour, half and full day.

(f) The TTA should work with key agencies in the sector such as CABE Education and English Heritage to produce built environment education training packages which inspire Newly Qualified Teachers to increase the amount and quality of classroom learning in this area.

(g) Identification and dissemination of best practice models in school policy, practice and procedures.

(h) Local venues/sites including buildings and parks should be helped and encouraged to work with teachers to provide support in the form of advice on preparation, resources, InSET, clarification of roles, clear curriculum links and links with students' previous knowledge and experience and evaluation methodologies. The Gateway Project provides a cost effective model for achieving this.

(i) Establishment of a one-stop-shop for information on exploring the built environment which incorporates (e), (f), (g) and (h) above.

(j) QCA should be engaged in further promoting and endorsing the potential of local out-of-classroom experiences of the built environment.

4.3 A greater number of diverse and stimulating environments for play should be created in each neighbourhood that are accessible to children and young people both within and outside school grounds. These should be developed with the involvement of children and young people.

4.4 Inspection of schools should include greater consideration of the quality and quantity of out-of-classroom learning and how it is integrated into the curriculum.

October 2004

Memorandum submitted by Play Wales/Chwarae Cymru

1. Play Wales/Chwarae Cymru is the national organisation for children's play in Wales; an independent charity funded by the Welsh Assembly Government. Our aim is to act as a champion for children's play, to increase awareness and understanding of the critical importance of play to children's development. It is our belief, that play which is freely chosen, personally directed and intrinsically motivated is vital in a child's development.

2. Our role is that of a critical friend, to influence the policy, strategic planning and practice of national and local government. We work with all agencies and organisations that have an interest in, and a responsibility for children's play, as well as those whose decisions have an impact on children's play.

3. We promote high quality play provision for all children, and provide support for all aspects of staffed playwork, playground development and maintenance, and the development of playwork education and training.

4. Our services include advice and consultancy on training, playground design and playground management; seminars and conferences; support for the continued development of staffed adventure play provision; playground inspections and risk assessment; an expert witness service for playground-related issues; a newsletter for all involved in play in Wales; a website (www.playwales.org.uk); a play reference library and information service; practical support for organisations wishing to provide for children's play needs; and developing pioneering materials to improve the quality and understanding of playwork theory and practice.

One day Wales will be a country where every child's right to play is recognised and fully provided for.

5. Our response is prefaced with a statement with respect to children's play and the barriers that our society has created to militate against that need for play being met.

CHILDREN'S BASIC PLAY NEEDS

6. All children are developing and growing human beings. Their needs are special and from a very early age there is a need—an instinctive need and urge—not only to play games and develop physical skills, but also to:

— crawl, jump, swing, slide, run, roll around, and play rough and tumble, hang from items and move from item to item, to hide, to seek, to prod and probe;

— take risks, seek excitement and challenge—discover their potential capacity for doing things, and understand their limitations through testing their abilities in a variety of ways, and making mistakes;

— create and construct: deconstruct and reconstruct, change and move the content of the environment around them;

— engage in fantasy and make believe, role-play and imitative play;

— experiment with the elements, such as earth, water, air and fire; experience for example; different textures, forms, colour, smells, taste and sounds, warmth and cold;

— experiment with different perspectives, heights and levels—hollows and mounds, climbing, balancing, and going through, up, over and onto things;

— develop social relationships with one and other; by being able to create opportunities for co-operation and interaction, exploring and dealing with conflict and realising the benefits of collaboration;

— individualise and personalise their play in which they can express themselves and be themselves;

— experience adventure, challenge, encounter, confront and manage risk, by exploring and experimenting to find out about things for themselves in their own time and at their own pace and within any parameters they determine; and

— establish a sense of physical and social independence whilst also establishing a social identity.

7. Play encompasses children's behaviour which is freely chosen, personally directed and intrinsically motivated. It is performed for no external goal or reward, and is a fundamental and integral part of healthy development.

BARRIERS TO CHILDREN'S PLAY

8. In Wales there is an acceptance by the Welsh Assembly Government that children need to play. However, where, how and when children play is determined by a range of circumstances, the physical environment and attitudinal perspectives of the society in which children live.

9. It is an often-expressed view that children will play anywhere and everywhere, whenever an opportunity presents itself. To a large extent this is true because of the innate and irrepressible urge that children have to play. However, over recent years, a number of external restraints, intentional and un-intentional, have been increasingly applied which have directly and detrimentally affected the level and quality of play opportunities now available to children.

10. The main causes of the erosion of children's access to quality play experiences include:

— parents attitudes to safety in the outdoor environment and the comparatively limited understanding of the value of play generally;

— the pressures of an increasingly litigious culture emerging throughout the UK which "discourages" local authorities and communities to provide play areas.;

— the poor quality and limited number of dedicated play spaces in residential areas and the inexorable colonisation of all open space for adult use, including that of leisure, recreational, sport, and vehicle and travel convenience;

— adults reactions to play provision in local communities is often hostile, children at play being perceived as noisy, messy, boisterous, aggressive and a general nuisance;

— an absence of consideration of children and young people's outdoor spatial requirements in the modern environment, for example; the lack of priority given to play space in new housing developments;

— attitudes to social status, cultural background, race, disability and economic circumstances that have an impact on access to and perspectives of play; and

— children's play has no readily or easily definable and measurable outcomes, often regarded as a trivial diversionary activity against a backdrop of formal education.

WELSH ASSEMBLY GOVERNMENT PLAY POLICY

11. The Welsh Assembly Government adopted a Play Policy in 2002, (Appendix 1) and it will shortly be launching a national consultation on the recommendations of the Play Policy Implementation Group, to translate the Policy into a reality for children in Wales.

12. These Recommendations identify a range of issues, of which some touch on the work of the Education and Skills Committee Inquiry.

13. For example with respect to the fear of accidents and the possibility of litigation, possibly the greatest challenge the Government faces in providing for children's play needs in the 21st century is the perception that risk is regarded as something to be avoided, and an emerging expectation that there should be the facility for litigation to provide compensation in the event of an accident.

14. *A major difficulty for play is that its universally-recognised as having positive attributes, they are hardly measurable scientifically. It is hard to quantify scientifically the fulfilment of "a child's right to play," though few would dispute its legitimacy. It is also hard to measure the psycho-social and developmental benefits of play, whether or not it enhances creativeness or a healthier life style in later years, or even its potential for enabling children and young people to learn about how to handle risk. It is difficult to prove that the provision of playgrounds lowers total risk to children and young people by moving them away from more dangerous places and activities. Thus, whereas the benefits of play are mainly assessed qualitatively at best, the disbenefits are measured in terms of cost of provision, injuries, law suits and the like, and are far more tangible. Achieving a balance between tangibles and intangibles is difficult and, particularly in a science dominated culture, is in singular need of human intervention and judgement. Furthermore if play is accepted as being as important as is commonly said, then more research would appear warranted on the different kinds of play opportunities which can be provided and the benefits for different age groups. At present the danger is that safety concerns, real or perceived, and litigation, have a bigger hand in determining the types of play facilities made available than does any consideration of play benefits. (Playgrounds—risks, benefits and choices Professor David J Ball, 2002)*

15. "Managing Risk in Play Provision" developed by the UK Play Safety Forum, outlines the low level of play injury and stranger danger and asserts that a certain amount of risk is necessary for the healthy development of children and young people. However, the document is aimed at planners, managers and workers and does not speak to parents directly. Ultimately parents and carers have the power to let their children play freely.

16. It is useful to consider that there are numerous sport and leisure activities where the risk of injury is automatically accepted. In relative terms, the number of injuries in such activities far outweighs those experienced in play provision. Participation in football, rugby, hockey, netball and basketball for instance, results in a high number and wide variety of injuries. Such high records of accidents however, have not discouraged continued participation, on the contrary, it is encouraged on the premise that it is seen to be of benefit to the health, social and psychological well-being of those involved.

17. This has become an issue of critical importance, as play providers are finding that they must pay increasingly exorbitant insurance premiums to obtain public liability insurance. There is evidence that the decision of play providers to increasingly limit the play opportunities they provide for children is based upon the insurers reluctance to provide cover, rather than upon the play needs of the children with whom the play providers work.

18. Clearly there is an urgent need for the Government to create a climate in which play providers can responsibly offer opportunities for children to experience risk taking without the fear of subsequent litigation. This might be achieved by the introduction of legislation that enables play providers to state that the activity in which the child participates has an inherent risk, that is a necessary aspect of the activity, and that such a statement with militate against claims that might arise from what one might call a "natural accident".

19. Such are the benefits that accrue from play and the opportunity for children and young people when playing, to experience risk taking, that those benefits outweigh the concomitant possibility that a child might hurt themselves.

20. As a consequence of this development, the future possibility of litigation in the event of accident will not detrimentally affect the quality of children's play experience, thus reflecting a more appropriate balance between opportunity and consequence.

21. We would assume that the Committee will be familiar with the current work of the Home Office Active Communities Unit on INSURANCE and SPORTING, RECREATIONAL and ADVENTUROUS ACTIVITIES.

22. With respect to playing out in schools; schools, as places of learning, are well placed within the community to provide a range of opportunities for children's play. School playgrounds and playing fields can often represent the only open space in urban areas.

23. If well designed, landscaped, and managed, they can offer children and young people a rich environment and a constant stream of stimuli, ideas and resources through their contact with the natural landscape and environment. However, the present reality is generally one in which the school site is a barren wilderness when compared with for example a natural woodland setting, devoid of all bar the most rudimentary play value.

24. Historically playgrounds were developed as "training yards", flat in order to facilitate the formation of lines when children were engaged in group exercises.

25. Over the past 15 years, the UK charity "Learning through Landscapes" has worked with schools undertaking considered landscaping of their grounds (except those specific areas designed for sporting activities) to create play environments that compensate for the loss of natural space. Such landscaping can provide changes in level, opportunities to learn through the elements, and plantings that offer progressive play opportunities to meet the needs of all children and young people.

26. Significantly, "Learning through Landscapes" work with children and young people within the community to encourage ownership of the environment created, in order to ensure its sustainability. Furthermore, once hard landscaping and planting has been completed there can be significant reductions in maintenance costs as a result of the reduced area of flat grass requiring fortnightly gang mowing.

27. *Creating a sense of "ownership" of public and community spaces is a precondition of successful use, care and maintenance. The key stake-holders in a secure public realm are the public themselves, including children and young people, and their involvement at all levels is essential. ("No particular place to Go")* (Groundwork Trust 2003).

28. Play Wales would ask that the Government commit itself to supporting the transformation of those areas of school grounds not dedicated to sports activities, by landscaping and planting, to create compensatory natural spaces that provide children with a rich play environment. These environments will be designed to provide a broad range of play opportunities.

29. This development will not be limited solely to supporting the delivery of the Foundation Stage and Foundation Phase in England and Wales respectively. It will provide spaces which serve to enable children to interact with the environment and each other. The spaces will include loose parts to provide for the experience of a range of play types, both for use by the children attending during the school day and for children and wider community use out of school hours.

30. This development will complement and contribute initiatives, to open up schools as community resources, to meet the needs of children, their families and the wider community, outside the school day.

31. With respect to school staff; Play Wales recognises that as a result of changing social trends many children lack the opportunity to play freely outside of school time, therefore, school playtime can contribute to compensating for this loss, offering children the opportunity to experience a range of play types appropriate to their developmental needs.

32. It is an irony that in many schools "wet play" in schools is neither wet nor play. Children tend to be kept inside and occupied with videos or adult led activities at break time during bad weather. It is recognised that the Play Policy in Wales would be better served if children and young people were encouraged to experience all types of weather, and that schools can contribute to this experience.

33. . . . *overall children felt that other school activities were prioritised at the expense of play . . . (Listen Up, Save the Children 2003).*

34. Furthermore all people who work with children and young people should be encouraged to develop a deep understanding of the philosophy and practice of play. This will include knowledge of play types, play behaviour, play needs, and appropriate intervention styles.

35. Play Wales would recommend that Government ensures that all teacher training courses for new teachers and nursery staff, include content that addresses the most recent developments in the understanding of children's play as children's self-directed learning and how playwork facilitates that process.

36. Comparison might be drawn between the perception of play in schools (whereby the child's drive to play is harnessed by the teacher to be used in activities with an expressed outcome identified in the National Curriculum) and the concept of play as embodied by the Welsh Assembly Government Play Policy. That is to say, play as children's behaviour which is freely chosen, personally directed and intrinsically motivated and performed for no external goal or reward. Neither is wrong. However, they are different, and they serve two distinct yet complementary purposes.

October 2004

Memorandum submitted by the Children's Play Council

"I Have a Dream"

"I have a dream that one day children will be able to roam freely without fear of cars. A day when children will not be told "that's too dangerous!" or "stop that racket!" as soon as they walk out the door. A day when they are not treated sub-humanly. A day when they are not penned up in houses or tiny "playgrounds". . .

Laurie Hedge, 12 years, October 2004. School project.

2. Laurie lives in south London. The park where he lives is designed primarily for adults and children are banned from cycling and skating. Most of grassy areas have "no ball games" signs and the low branches are cut off trees to stop children climbing them. For Laurie and many other children in his area break-time at school is one of the main times to run around freely and play with friends.

3. Laurie is typical of many children whose experience of outdoor play is severely limited by the circumstances in which they live. A recent survey from Learning Through Landscapes and the Royal Bank of Scotland found that 35% parents said their 7–12 year old children never played out with their friends when not at school.[9]

4. This submission from the Children's Play Council to the select committee argues that national and local government and schools must do more to:

— recognise the importance of children's free-play opportunities during school play/break-times, valuing free-play as an important part of a child's school day,

— accept that free-play during play-time should not be expected to have measurable outcomes for children's learning,

— design and develop outdoor playgrounds which offer children choice and a range of environments and experiences,

— acknowledge and accept that children playing need to be able to stretch themselves and take risks, possibly resulting in minor accidents,

— ensure playground staff are valued and trained in playwork principles and skills.

---

[9] *Supergrounds for schools,* press release, Royal Bank of Scotland, October 2004.

...en's Play Council (CPC) is a leading voluntary organisation promoting better play ...d services for school-aged children and young people in England. CPC is a membership ...r members include national and regional voluntary organisations, play associations and ...authorities and EYDCPs. CPC is concerned about all areas of children's lives where play is important including the school day.

6. CPC currently has a policy development and research contract with the Department of Culture Media and Sport, is supported by the Department for Transport for work on Home zones, co-manages a Big Lottery Fund programme with Barnardos (Better Play) and receives project funding from charitable trusts and the Housing Corporation for other work. We are also part of a coalition of organisations, led by the Association of Teachers and Lecturers, developing work on children's play at school.

CPC works under the aegis of the National Children's Bureau.

THE IMPORTANCE OF PLAY-TIME FOR SCHOOL CHILDREN

7. Playing freely, making their own choices and having fun must be the primary aim of play/break-times for school children. All children need time and space to play during the school day. Playing allows children a break in the rigid structure of the school day, gives them a chance to enjoy themselves, run around, talk with their friends, try new ideas, develop relationships and expend pent up energy.

Physical exercise

8. In addition, evidence shows that play-time is a crucial time for children to get physical exercise. Research from University College London with children of nine to 12 years old shows that, during the school break, children used 1.9 activity calories per minute compared with 0.6 during lesson times. Whilst this was less than PE and games lessons (3.1ac/m) it was more than many sports clubs and out-of-school activities.[10] The children also spent significantly more time getting exercise during play-time at school than playing out after school or at the weekend This research confirmed other findings that amongst children of five to 11 years old their highest energy expenditure occurred during school break-times.[11] Research from overseas shows similar patterns.[12, 13]

Testing boundaries and taking risks

9. Children learn through experience, testing themselves and others and taking risks. School play-time is one important time when children can do this in a relatively "safe" environment. Good school playground provision and management offers children a stimulating, challenging environment for exploring and developing their abilities whilst managing the level of risk so that children are not exposed to unacceptable risk of serious injury.[14]

Developing social skills

10. Research drawing on experience from the UK shows how important break time at school is for children's developing social skills and relationships. It is a time when children form and maintain friendships and social networks, develop strategies for conflict and "find freedom and a social life independent of the classroom, where the rules of conduct are their own, and where activities stem from their own initiative".[15] The significance of playground play and games in developing friendships has been widely reported.[16]

Encouraging creativity

11. Allowing children the opportunity to develop and adapt their own games and play provides crucial opportunities for creative development and expression. Playground games are often rooted in culture and tradition but change over time to fit children's needs and interests. Time, space and suitable resources, including skilled adult facilitation can ensure better creative opportunities.

---

[10] *Making children's lives more active,* R Mackett *et al,* Centre for Transport Studies, University College London, 2004.

[11] Physical activity levels of 5–11-year-old children in England: cumulative evidence from three direct observation studies, M Sleap and P Warburton, *International Journal of Sports Medicine,* 17(4), 1996, pp 248–253.

[12] "Active school playgrounds—myth or reality? Results of the 'make it groove' project", A Zasks *et al* (Australia), *Preventive Medicine,* 33 (5), 2001 pp 402–408.

[13] "Physical activity during free play and physical education", J Sutterby, University of Texas, conference presentation, 2003.

[14] *Managing risk in play provision:* a position statement, Play Safety Forum, Children's Play Council, 2002.

[15] "Friendships at school, the role of break times", P Blatchford, Education, 3 (13), 1999, pp 6–65 (cited in *School Grounds Literature Review: phase one of the Scottish School Grounds Research Project,* T Casey, Play Scotland, 2003.

[16] *School Grounds Literature Review: phase one of the Scottish School Grounds Research Project,* T Casey, Play Scotland, 2003.

FACILITATING FREE-PLAY

12. To get the maximum benefit from their play-time children need enough space, a suitable environment, sufficient time, a choice of activities and oversight by skilled staff who understand playwork values and skills.

13. If not managed properly play-time can be a time of increased bullying and difficult behaviour for some children. However, schools which have acknowledged the importance and benefits of free play have also been able to provide an environment which reduces difficult behaviour whilst still allowing choice and control to children. Working with children to re-design play spaces, "zoning" playgrounds, developing a more "natural" environment, training staff and raising the status of playground staff have all enhanced the experience of children and the school population.[17]

ISSUES OF CONCERN

14. Despite a general understanding of the importance of free-play for school children Children's Play Council is aware that, in some schools,

— play-times have been reduced over time;[18]

— structured activity is preferred over free play;

— the benefits of play-time are measured in learning outcomes and;

— normal vigorous play is restricted because schools fear repercussions if children have minor accidents.[19]

15. We were also extremely concerned that the Government has not understood the value of play-time and school ground to children. One example of this occurred when the DfES was commissioning Exemplar Designs for the new school building programme. In the design brief to architects there was no mention of playgrounds and school play-time.[20]

16. We are concerned that, with these restrictions and lack of understanding, children's opportunities for free-play and all the attendant benefits they get are under threat.

CONCLUSIONS

17. The evidence cited in this memorandum draws us to the following conclusions which we hope will be supported and championed by the Education and Skills Committee:

— Time for free-play during the school day is vital for children and should be preserved or re-instated where it has previously been reduced;

— Children should not be expected to achieve learning goals set by adults during their play-time;

— School children should be encouraged to play outside during play-time as much as possible and given the chance to be physically active;

— Children's playground activity should not be unnecessarily restricted by the school's fears of threats litigation from parents. Where this is a potential problem parents, children, school staff and governors should work together to agree "acceptable levels of risk" for children's playground activities;

— Playground environments should include some natural elements and offer the choice of a range of active and quiet play opportunities which suit the needs and interests of children of different ages, abilities and cultural backgrounds;

— Playground staff should be trained in playwork values and skills and recognised as skilled and valued members of the school staff team.

18. Finally, perhaps members of the Select Committee would like to cast their minds back to their own childhood experiences and fond memories they may have of playing with friends. Children today need the same or better opportunities for play at school as, for many, their out of school play activities are severely restricted compared with those of previous generations.

October 2004

---

[17] See note 16.

[18] "Time for a break", A Pellegrini & P Blatchford, *The Psychologist,* 15 (2) 2002, pp 60–61.

[19] Reports and anecdotes collected from playworkers and the media.

[20] *Schools for the future: Exemplar Designs concepts and ideas,* Department for Education and Skills, 2004.

Memorandum submitted by the National Trust

INTRODUCTION

1. The National Trust welcomes the Committee's inquiry into education outside the classroom and the opportunity to contribute to the debate in this area. The National Trust is Europe's largest conservation charity and a major provider of out-of-classroom learning—indoors and outdoors. We currently welcome 540,000 formal learning visits by school students and a further 450 working holidays to our built and natural properties in England, Wales and Northern Ireland. Our practical experience in welcoming 50 million people to our countryside properties every year and a further 13 million to our houses, museums, gardens and pay for entry properties, means that we have the infrastructure and experience to facilitate safe but not "sanitised" experiences across the curriculum. Many of these visits are by families with school age children. Although the motivation for informal visits is not often for learning, research in 2003 suggests the vast majority (as many as 93%) deliver informal learning outcomes. Likewise out of hours activities for school age children—for example through summer clubs supporting transition between the different key stages for those at risk of disaffection, or youth club projects—are an important tool in supporting formal learning. A number of National Trust case studies are included with our submission.

2. The Trust believes that there is no substitute for learning outside the classroom with real people, whether that is in the great outdoors, a museum or a historic building. Our practical experience, evaluation and research suggests that young people of all ages derive enormous benefits from such experiences and that when these experiences are structured and sustained they can have lasting impact on the individuals and support teaching.[21] We are partners in the Real World Learning Campaign which believes that out-of-classroom learning should be an integral part of every child's education. The campaign seeks to raise awareness of the benefits of out-of-classroom learning and to address the barriers which prevent us from growing our potential to reach more young people.

3. School hours account for a tiny fraction of our lives. Learning is a lifelong process and a source of fun, inspiration and physical and mental well-being. We believe education outside the classroom is a powerful catalyst for creating a lifelong thirst for learning and for building a knowledge economy grounded in creativity and an understanding of the world around us. Whilst there is increased awareness and support for out-of-classroom learning, not least due to the Real World Learning Campaign, much more could be done to make the most of the opportunities out there. We believe this inquiry provides a welcome vehicle to encourage this to happen—both through challenging current misconceptions (eg risk) and by finding solutions to barriers to growth. In particular we recommend the Committee calls for:

— A statutory entitlement in schools for every child to have regular, structured out of classroom experiences to support curriculum work.

— A clear and unambiguous statement from the Government that out-of-classroom experiences are an important and integral part of every child's education and should be integrated across the curriculum. This could take the form of a Manifesto for Education Outside the Classroom developed in partnership with the relevant sectors.

— DCMS and DfES should work in partnership with the historic environment sector to develop a specific heritage and learning proposal.

— A similar approach to the natural environment to be explored in greater detail by the *Growing Schools* initiative.

— A scheme to address transport costs in schools where parents are unable to contribute—schools should be able to bid into a fund supplemented by private sponsorship.

— The development of an information gateway for subjects across the curriculum, drawing on the *Growing Schools* model, which would promote better sharing of information on the opportunities available, and the cost-effectiveness and benefits of visits.

— Cross-curricular entitlement to these experiences embedded in guidance to schools and Local Education Authorities.

— The introduction of out-of-classroom learning across the curriculum as a key part of every Ofsted school inspection.

— Development of universal guidance to schools encouraging them to develop a whole school policy on out-of-classroom learning which recognises its multiple benefits across the curriculum.

— Support for resources such as education visits co-ordinators, to be made available where possible, perhaps for a cluster of schools.

— Sufficient opportunities being made available during initial teacher training and through continuous professional development to build confidence, competence and experience amongst teachers in planning and undertaking out-of-classroom learning.

---

[21] FDS International (2003), *Teachers Needs and Wants: research for the National Trust.*

— Providers to work in partnership to raise public awareness of the benefits of education outside the classroom to challenge misconceptions.

— The Government, teacher trade unions and providers to work together to address issues of concern over taking children out of the classroom. This should involve the development of a common template for risk assessment as proposed by the Real World Learning Campaign and a recognisable standard such as the farm education standards being piloted by the Access to Farms Partnership.

THE NATIONAL TRUST: LEARNING AND DISCOVERY

4. The National Trust's strategic plan puts lifelong learning and education at the heart of everything we do. Our approach is to foster learning through self-discovery. We enable pupils to enjoy practical activities, encouraging them to experience the "real thing" and to care for the built and natural environment around them. The Trust has 300 experienced learning staff and 1,300 dedicated education volunteers whose passion and professional knowledge for their subjects is contagious. We support learning and teaching across the curriculum, with particular strength in History, Science, Arts, Geography, Citizenship and Education for Sustainable Development. This activity occurs at a huge variety of locations across the UK: local or remote, built or natural, indoor or outdoor, work-based or recreational, rural or urban. In each case real issues—past or present—are used to inform debate and discussion.

5. The Trust runs a number of significant education programmes, including:

— School Guardianships which builds long term "stewardship" relationships between schools and their local properties. Some Guardianships have been running as long as 15 years and are mentioned in schools' Ofsted reports as playing a significant part in supporting the curriculum.

— The Redrow School Partnership linking schools in rural and urban communities to explore the curriculum together.

— A highly subsidised Education Group Membership open to all schools.

— Specialised outdoor/environmental activity centres at Stackpole in Pembrokeshire and Brancaster in Norfolk.

— The National Trust Touring Theatre which has been running for 25 years and engages people in complex issues through performing arts.

— Untold Story—a three year interpretation project supported by the Heritage Lottery Fund that brings non-traditional audiences to interpret our properties.

Further details are attached.

6. Further property-based programmes include:

— *Sutton House, Hackney:* Winner of two Sandford Awards for Heritage Education, Sutton House was shortlisted for this year's Gulbenkian Prize for museum of the year. Presenting a diverse range of arts-focused learning programmes for all age groups, Sutton House is particularly strong at community outreach and has established a significant following in and around the London Borough of Hackney. Sutton House hosts more than 4,000 education visitors a year, reaching 251 local schools and enabling a broad range of experiences from life in Tudor times to personal heritage exploration and interpretation. Recent workshops with the local Caribbean community and events for Black History Month have been particularly successful, but long term funding is a perennial concern.

— *Morden Hall Park, Merton:* This property offers a very strong schools' environmental programme and last year played host to 6,483 education visitors, from 90 primary and secondary schools. Sessions are designed to compliment the National Curriculum Geography Key Stages and are strongly environmentally focused making particular use of access to the River Wandle and surrounding habitat. The property's Snuff Mill Environmental Centre has just received grant funding for refurbishment and there are plans to extend community outreach efforts to the nearby Phipp's Bridge Estate. In 2003, the property hosted visits from 82 primary schools.

— *Osterley Park, Hounslow:* Osterley Park is both a historic mansion house and vital green lung for the largely Asian population in this part of West London. The property houses an exhibition space, dedicated study base, is developing links with Hounslow Primary Care Trust and has an over-subscribed community youth drama group. The property fields around 1,500 education visitors a year and presents an unusually strong offer in terms of both cultural and natural learning opportunities.

— *Hughenden Manor, High Wycombe:* Possessed of a sizeable and excellent study base, Hughenden Manor has developed a strong schools' programme offering both cultural and natural heritage learning opportunities. Benjamin Disraeli's country home now frequently plays host to costumed school children enjoying immersion in Victorian life that enables them to experience the work that would have taken place to prepare the estate for the visit of Queen Victoria. The ability to handle Victorian artefacts is a strong point of this property's educational offer and one that is a particular thrill for all those that have had the opportunity of experiencing it.

7. It is our experience that participants in these programmes make return visits and tend to bring their family and friends with them, spreading the benefits to those who might not have had such experiences previously. In addition those pupils visiting regularly as children are more likely to return as adults and play an active role in caring for their historic and natural environment.

GROWING THE POTENTIAL; MEETING THE DEMAND

8. In a recent survey of schools, nine out of 10 teachers said they do not take as many school trips as they need to.[22] They would like to take their pupils out more but budgets and curriculum timetabling get in the way, even though 80% of the same sample cited the curriculum as the primary reason for going on trips. This is reflected by our own experience, with some programmes oversubscribed or even influencing parents' choice of schools. A mapping exercise of National Trust learning provision in 2003 suggests that there is significant potential to increase opportunities for school-children to visit our properties if these, and other barriers, are overcome. Typically, these barriers include: the limited ability of voluntary sector bodies to subsidise learning programmes; an increasingly crowded and prescriptive curriculum leading to fewer opportunities; fear of accidents and subsequent litigation; low status of out-of-classroom teaching; defensive attitudes of some teaching unions; and cost (including transport) to poorer schools.

9. The need to make the most of the educational potential of our rich cultural heritage through structured visits for young people is a clear Government message.[23] This includes access to both our built and cultural heritage as well as the natural environment. In 2002, in response to Government recommendations in its vision for the historic environment, *A Force for our Future*, the National Trust published proposals for providing free access for all children to heritage sites (see *Making History Matter*, copy enclosed). This sets out initial thoughts on how such a scheme might be funded and administered. Our preferred option is to develop a dedicated programme of activity which supports schools in undertaking structured school visits, rather than a voucher scheme.

10. Despite this potential, and the clear objectives of *A Force for our Future*, we still have a long way to go. Whilst free access for children to national museums and English Heritage sites (about which we have some concerns), has made some progress, little has been achieved for the wider historic environment sector. In addition to addressing the specific barriers to growth explored below, we believe a clear and unambiguous statement is needed. This could take the form of a Manifesto for Education Outside the Classroom developed in partnership with the relevant sectors.

11. We also believe DCMS and DfES should work in partnership with the historic environment sector to develop a specific heritage and learning proposal. Similar scope exists in relation to the natural environment and we would like to see the potential to do this explored in greater detail by the Growing Schools initiative.

COSTS AND FUNDING

12. The Trust currently subsidises formal learning outside the classroom to the tune of £2 million per year and levers in a further £3 million in external funds and generous sponsorship. We make a nominal charge to schools under our Education Group Membership scheme which does not reflect the true cost of the experiences. This pattern is repeated elsewhere in the voluntary sector. The costs borne by the National Trust are very high and mean that we are unable to offer more opportunities despite having the infrastructure to do so—which is what makes it cheaper for others to use our resources in the first place.

13. In addition schools in disadvantaged rural and urban areas struggle to pay for transport costs. The Trust has a number of pilot bursary schemes for transport costs, such as the North West Minibus Scheme where funds are raised by local members groups and private sector sponsors. The scheme has so far benefited 8,000 students, but despite an alliance with a commercial operator continues to run at a loss. We would like to see better provision made nationally to address this inequality and propose that where parents are unable to contribute, schools should be able to bid into a fund supplemented by private sponsorship. Our research suggests that, based on five visits to a property, transport costs are estimated at £25 per child over three years, although this could be significantly reduced if more capacity for outreach was developed and pilot phases adopted in key areas.[24]

14. Though cost is a barrier, it is not prohibitive for many schools and our survey suggests it is not the deciding factor in taking a school trip. This is particularly the case for secondary schools where timetable considerations were the deciding factor for 50% of the sample schools.[25] Those teachers who have developed long-term relationships with our properties are overwhelmingly supportive of the wide benefits and cost effectiveness of such experiences, in both curriculum and pastoral terms, for their schools. Where teachers

[22] FDS International (2003), *Teachers Needs and Wants: research for the National Trust.*

[23] "*England's historic environment is one of our greatest national resources . . . The historic environment is something from which we can learn, something from which our economy benefits and something which can bring communities together in a shared sense of belonging.*" Tessa Jowell and Stephen Byers, Foreword, *The Historic Environment: A Force for Our Future*, DCMS/DTLR, December 2001.

[24] *Making History Matter: how children can discover heritage*, National Trust 2002.

[25] FDS International (2003), *Teachers' Needs and Wants: research for the National Trust.*

do not have the confidence or experience to plan and undertake school visits, other barriers are cited. This could be addressed through the development of an information gateway for subjects across the curriculum, drawing on the *Growing Schools* model, which would promote better sharing of information on the opportunities available, and the cost-effectiveness and benefits of visits.

THE PLACE OF OUTDOOR LEARNING WITHIN THE CURRICULUM

15. Where out-of-classroom learning is a statutory requirement, take up is strongest, for example in Geography. A strong statutory requirement is also reflected in the content of Ofsted inspections. According to Ofsted's recent report, "good and very good teaching in outdoor education shares the same general characteristics as teaching in normal classrooms but some of these are particularly important including . . . crossing subject boundaries to broaden students' understanding". Despite this there is no statutory requirement to undertake school visits in many curriculum subjects or to meet cross-curriculum objectives. The Trust's experience suggests that carefully planned trips can address more than one subject and engender much wider benefits in students' basic and key skills such as creativity, motivation and confidence:

> "Any project that sends my pupils home with that much energy and enthusiasm must be creating a real learning experience." *Teacher participating in Dance in Trust.*

> "I said to my mum that the visit to Formby was the best day of my life. I loved the sand blowing in our faces, and the woods where we could imagine going on a lion-hunt." *Child with special needs.*

16. Where teachers are inexperienced in taking classes on school trips, they may not understand the extent to which it can be a substitute for class work or meet the demands of more than one curriculum subject at any one time.

> "The biggest impact I can think of from the guardianship project, is the fact that my planning and therefore the children's learning, is now completely integrated with having the Sheffield Park Garden as an extension of the school. I/we look on it as a fantastic natural resource which enriches so many aspects of the children's work. If you think how many subject areas we have covered through the garden, science, literacy, ICT, maths, art, PHSE and geography, I now wonder how I would cover the curriculum as efficiently if we didn't have the guardianship project! I know the pupils and staff look forward to each visit, which in itself is quite amazing as the responsibility of 'off site' visits usually sends teachers into dread mode, but because the garden doesn't feel 'off site' any more, I feel really comfortable organising the trips. This is due to the friendly, helpful nature of the staff at Sheffield Park Garden and because we have been able to familiarise ourselves so much with the garden and the risks can therefore be easily catered for. I think the children appreciate the garden far more now they see 'behind the scenes' and some of them have said that it makes them notice more when they visit gardens, which they thought were boring before." *Head teacher of school visiting Sheffield Park Garden, East Sussex*

In addition to a Government statement on the value of learning outside the classroom, we would like to see cross-curricular entitlement to these experiences embedded in guidance to schools and Local Education Authorities.

EXTERNAL ASSESSMENT OF PROVISION

17. Many teachers are not aware of the positive outputs and outcomes of out-of-classroom learning. These typically include improvement in social and communications skills, increased motivation, positive changes in the relationship between pupils and accompanying teachers, and improved behaviour being transferred to the classroom.

> "Having over 25 years teaching experience, I can say without hesitation that this project is by far the best thing I've ever been involved with since I began teaching. It was tremendous." *Head of art department, Derby*

Being inspected for these benefits would raise awareness and promote best practice, while taking the pressure off other curriculum burdens. We believe that out-of-classroom learning should be introduced as a key part of every Ofsted school inspection and integrated across the curriculum and that the broad benefits this would bring would offset the cost of implementation.

ORGANISATION AND INTEGRATION WITHIN EXISTING SCHOOL STRUCTURES

18. Learning outside the classroom is not only a powerful and creative antidote to the target driven and academic focus of school work, if done well, it can have a lasting impact. Research by the NfER suggests that this impact increases with time and in particular if there is a choice of activities and regular follow up work.[26]

---

[26] Rickinson, M. *et al* (2004), *A review of research on outdoor learning*, National Foundation for Educational Research.

19. Putting enjoyment back into learning is a stated aim of the current Government, yet our experience suggests that schools and teachers need more incentives to undertake successful trips, especially where they have little experience or there is no requirement to do so. As Ofsted state, "Outdoor education continues to thrive where head teachers and individual enthusiasts provide leadership ...They recognise the importance of outdoor education experiences in giving depth to the curriculum and to the development of students' personal and social development". If such experiences are poorly integrated into the whole school curriculum or as an *"end of year activity"* many children lose precious opportunities to develop and prosper during their school years and teachers forgo opportunities to build strong relationships with their class. We would like to see universal guidance to schools encouraging them to develop a whole school policy on out-of-classroom learning which recognises its multiple benefits. Support for resources such as education visits co-ordinators, should be made available where possible, perhaps for a cluster of schools.

QUALIFICATION AND MOTIVATION OF TEACHERS AND THE EFFECT ON TEACHER WORKLOAD

20. Negotiating timetable cover and paying for supply cover, are a major barrier cited by teachers who are trying to organise trips. This appears to have become more of a problem as courses have become increasingly modularised, reducing flexibility. The Trust has run a successful *Guardianship* programme for over 10 years which develops long-term relationships with local schools, taking much of the burden off teachers whilst building their confidence to take part. We are currently undertaking research to explore the long-term impacts of these relationships[27] but believe them to be very profound. At Errdig near Wrexham, our estate maintenance costs which were high because of vandalism, have reduced as a direct result of involving young people in working alongside our estate staff. We would like to see these lessons picked up in any dedicated heritage or natural environment learning programme sponsored by DfES.

> "I love those light-bulb moments where just by watching the children's faces you suddenly see this click—they've got it. They realise that the tree they're standing under travelled across the ocean as a seed and has grown here for 120 years. It's like magic." *Community Education Volunteer, Windermere and Troutbeck*

21. There is added value for children and teachers in working alongside other adults of varying ages, backgrounds and professions, such as museum staff, countryside wardens or community education staff and volunteers, who can share their passion and enthusiasm for a subject. Measures should be taken to ensure that sufficient opportunities are available during initial teacher training and through continuous professional development to build confidence and experience amongst teachers in planning and undertaking out-of-classroom learning.

THE FEAR OF ACCIDENTS AND THE POSSIBILITY OF LITIGATION

22. There is a very real climate of fear surrounding school trips triggered by recent tragic accidents and stoked to some extent by media coverage. In reality, the number of incidents occurring on visits with quality providers is very small. It should be recognised that curriculum pressures or costs are more significant in deciding whether to take trips.

23. Most providers take responsibility for providing safe and secure environments for school trips very seriously. All directed activities at National Trust properties have first been checked for safety through rigorous risk assessments. We also recommend that all schools undertake their own risk assessments and provide guidance to them on the types of risk or hazard participants are likely to encounter. As far as possible, developing an understanding of risk is integrated into the learning objectives of a visit. All pre-booked educational trips to National Trust properties are also entitled to a free planning visit to support teachers in preparing for risk and build their confidence.

24. Providers should continue to work in partnership to raise public awareness of the benefits of education outside the classroom and to challenge current misconceptions. However, they should also seek to work closely with the Government, and teacher trade unions to address issues of concern over taking children out of the classroom. As the Real World Learning Campaign suggests, this could involve the development of a common template for risk assessment that is recognised by unions and schools alike.

25. At National Trust countryside properties we are developing largely science based field work programmes such as our Plot to Plate initiative (see attached case studies). We are a member of the Access to Farms Partnership which is piloting new farm standards for schools so that schools can be reassured that the farm they choose to visit has passed certain Health and Safety standards and where the farmer has the necessary training and accreditation.

October 2004

---

[27] A recent survey of schools working in partnership with the Trust revealed that over 90% recorded satisfaction rates with our programmes as "good" or "excellent".

Memorandum submitted by The Duke of Edinburgh's Award

1. The Duke of Edinburgh's Award welcomes the opportunity to submit evidence to the Committee and will be pleased to follow up this written submission orally, if invited to do so.

2. The Duke of Edinburgh's Award was founded in 1956. Since then, over three million young people have taken part in it.

3. The Award is a programme of activities for young people aged 14–25. It is available at three levels— Bronze, Silver and Gold—and has four sections— Expeditions, Skill, Physical Recreation and Service. At Gold level there is also a Residential Section. The programme is delivered by schools, youth services, voluntary organisations, colleges' E2E providers, universities, young offender institutions and businesses operating under licence from the Award. In 2003–04 almost 138,000 young people joined the Award programme in the UK. Through the International Award Association, the programme is available in over 100 other countries.

4. The aim of the Award is to provide an enjoyable, challenging and rewarding programme of personal development for young people. Its guiding principles are that the Award is:

— Non-competitive

— Available to all

— Voluntary

— Flexible

— Balanced

— Progressive

— Achievement-focused

— A marathon not a sprint

— Enjoyable

5. Young people undertake education outside the classroom in all sections of the Award programme, not just the expeditions and residential sections. We therefore have enormous experience on which to draw in making this submission to the Committee. We work in partnership with all the major voluntary organisations (eg Scouts, Girlguiding UK, cadet forces); are represented on national bodies to do with outdoor education, such as the Outdoor Education Advisers Panel, and our advice on safety and child protection is sought by bodies such as CCPR. We are represented on the Wales Youth Agency and Youthlink in Scotland and in England are in membership of the National Council of Voluntary Youth Services (NCVYS).

6. The Award has recently been commissioned (jointly with the Scouts) by the Department for Education and Skills to map existing provision for residential education and advise on expanding capacity to enable all young people in Key Stages 2–4 to have access to residential experience. (This exercise will be submitted to DfES in December 2004). The present Secretary of State for Education and Skills is a Gold Award holder.

THE PLACE OF OUTDOOR LEARNING WITHIN THE CURRICULUM

7. In this context, the curriculum should be seen as the full range of formal and non-formal learning environments, not just of school and college students but all young people, many of whom—particularly the disengaged and vulnerable—learn most effectively through youth services and voluntary organisations. This has been recognised most recently by the Tomlinson Working Group Report on 14–19 reform which places "wider activities" within the core of the proposed diploma system as an entitlement for all. Wider Activities are defined in the report as "activities which take place outside the formal classroom or other learning environment, including community work, sports and arts, part-time work or work experience, and personal awards such as Duke of Edinburgh". The value of outdoor education was also confirmed in the recent Ofsted report "Outdoor education; aspects of good practice" (September 2004). Outdoor education supports the principles of Every Child Matters and the Children Bill and should feature prominently in the forthcoming Youth Green Paper. It is a vital part of the Government agendas on sport, the arts and health. Specialist schools, for example through their community development plans, and Extended Schools are placing increasing emphasis on a range of non-formal learning activities. In our experience sport and the arts are particularly effective media for engaging young people in inner-city areas. We have just launched, through an event at the Barbican, a major arts project in London, supported by the DfES, Connexions and the London Challenge, in which specialist arts colleges play a prominent part.

8. It is the Award's experience that parents, employers and higher education value the contribution of wider activities to the "development of wider key skills such as working with others". Some universities use them as a supplementary admissions criterion.

COSTS AND FUNDING OF OUTDOOR ACTIVITIES

9. Sport is comparatively well-funded, but there is no mechanism in central or local government for a strategic approach to funding outdoor education in the round. Moreover, there remains a need for extra funding, particularly in the voluntary and community sectors, which would make the notion of entitlement a reality and open the full range of activities to a wider spectrum of the community.

10. Costs of outdoor education are higher with commercial providers than with leaders who are teachers, youth workers or from the voluntary sector. They are also higher when based at staffed residential centres than when using self-catering accommodation (including camping) or non-residential activities. This situation needs addressing.

11. See below for comments on the funding of training for leaders of outdoor education.

ORGANISATION AND INTEGRATION WITHIN EXISTING SCHOOL STRUCTURES

12. There is a pressing need, acknowledged by Tomlinson, to create more space in school and college life for wider activities. This can be done by reducing the burden of assessment on teachers and by encouraging attestation, of learning by adults other than teachers. There is a shining example of appropriate infrastructure in the way the Youth Sport Trust supports specialist sports colleges and their partnerships. A parallel infrastructure should be developed for all schools, with a broad approach to wider activities, not just sport.

13. A minority of schools and local authorities encourage the provision of programmes such as the Award by rewarding teachers with a management point, sessional payment or reduced teaching load, but in too many cases delivery is dependent entirely on the goodwill of teachers and others volunteering beyond the call of duty.

QUALIFICATION AND MOTIVATION OF TEACHERS AND THE EFFECT ON TEACHER WORKLOAD

14. There are schools and youth projects without any member of staff qualified to lead any outdoor activities. If all young people are to have a chance of an outdoor experience, there must be at least one qualified person in every organisation that works with young people. This might require the employment of enrichment activity specialists. An added barrier in urban areas is the high turnover of teaching staff and persistent shortage of youth workers. This factor creates added disadvantage for young people from the most deprived backgrounds.

15. In theory, the Learning and Skills Council has generous funding for outdoor leader training courses. In practice this funding only reaches colleges, and then only if they choose to run the courses. Small specialist providers, such as the Outdoor Education Centres, can only get a share of this funding by franchise agreements, and they depend on the willingness of a college.

16. The DfES offered a Standards Fund 317 in January 2003. This was intended to support training for The Duke of Edinburgh's Award leaders as well as for those dealing with challenging behaviour and those organising educational visits. Regrettably there was no guidance on how SF317 should be allocated, so that in some areas it was not divided among the three purposes outlined.

17. There is an urgent need for funding to support outdoor leader training. It would make sense to establish an Outdoor Leader Funding Agency to take over responsibility for this work and discharge it with minimal bureaucracy.

18. The Award has pioneered, with Cambridge University, the University of East Anglia, Oxford Brookes University and Trinity College Carmarthen, modules on under graduate and postgraduate education to give future teachers and youth workers knowledge and skills for outdoor education. We would like to expand these courses and would welcome government support.

19. The Award is currently bidding to DfES, under the NVYO grant scheme, to strengthen its provision of training, with particular reference to the training of outdoor education leaders.

THE FEAR OF ACCIDENTS AND THE POSSIBILITY OF LITIGATION

20. The key to reducing the fear of accidents is the provision of effective training for both young people and adults. The Award has an enviable record in this area, achieved by insisting that young people undertaking expeditions are thoroughly prepared and equipped. The Award also promotes a training framework for group leaders, supervisors and assessors.

21. The possibility of litigation is responsible for many teachers, youth workers and volunteers ceasing or not even starting to lead outdoor activities. Fortunately, however, many thousands are committed to the development of young people through outdoor activities, especially if they are supported by advice and training. It has been encouraging recently to see that a judge in Newcastle County Court threw out a case by a young woman who got sore feet on a $0 mile Gold Award expedition, and that all the associated media coverage was supportive of continuing to undertake challenging activities.

CONCLUSION

22. The Committee's inquiry is timely. It provides an opportunity to comment on a number of related education and cross-departmental initiatives and make recommendations for unified action and redirected funding in the interests of young people and the well being of the United Kingdom.

October 2004

Memorandum submitted by the British Activity Holiday Association

The British Activity Holiday Association is the trade body for the leading commercial providers of outdoor education, training and recreation in the UK. The activity programmes operated at member centres contribute significantly to both formal and informal learning outside the classroom. Some members provide courses linked directly to the curriculum, whilst others act as facilitators to enable teachers to seek the educational outcomes they desire; and still more welcome children on an individual basis during school holidays, where they learn activity, social and personal skills during a recreational experience.

1. COSTS AND FUNDING OF OUTDOOR ACTIVITIES

BAHA members are not subsidised, so we seek to recoup costs from participants or their sponsors. Courses and holidays that are inclusive of board and accommodation, instruction, supervision and equipment are not cheap to provide, but we estimate that 50% of the potential market can afford the full market rates. At the other end of the spectrum, we estimate that 10% of children are from families on benefit. That leaves a further 40% that do need financial support in order to be able to benefit from the same enriching experiences. The commercial sector can help in this situation, by offering shoulder space vacancies at marginal rates. This can be a cheaper option for parents and LEAs than funding an infrastructure within the LEA.

2. THE PLACE OF OUTDOOR LEARNING WITHIN THE CURRICULUM

There are so many benefits for pupils to gain away from the classroom. In terms of citizenship, they can learn how to support, lead and follow and develop those skills back at home and school. They are faced with many new challenges, which help to develop self confidence and self esteem. They are introduced to new ideas for physical exercise, not the standard team games and ball sports normally on offer at school. What's more, some of these new activities provide the potential for a future healthy lifestyle of exercise in the outdoors. On the safety side, they can become more risk conversant and understand that risk can be identified and managed safely. And last, but not least, they can have fun and enjoyment in a stress-free environment embodying the true meaning of "re-creation".

3. EXTERNAL ASSESSMENT OF PROVISION

Where activities fall within the scope of the Adventure Activities Licensing Regulations, all BAHA members must of course apply for a licence and submit their operation to inspection. Of course, licensing is restricted in application, so BAHA also requires members to submit to additional or replacement inspection by its team of independent, external inspectors. This is in addition to submission to any voluntary inspection by such National Governing Bodies as the British Canoe Union, the Royal Yachting Association, the British Surfing Association, the British Horse Society etc. Members have not historically been inspected by Ofsted, but they are subject to personal inspection by the Outdoor Education Advisers from LEAs throughout the country. From a health and safety perspective, centres are also subject to enforcement by the local Environmental Health Office.

4. ORGANISATION AND INTEGRATION WITHIN EXISTING SCHOOL STRUCTURES

We are delighted to say that many schools have established their activity week as an integral part of the school calendar. Teachers recognise the many benefits that pupils and themselves gain from such residentials. They are therefore prepared to make sacrifices to ensure that they continue to happen, despite any barriers that LEAs and/or unions place in their path. Education is about preparation for life, not just classroom learning. In this context, we encourage the Committee to support whatever adjustments are required to allow them to fit in with school structures.

5. Qualification and Motivation of Teachers and the Effect on Teacher Workload

Taking groups of pupils on outdoor education visits is a voluntary exercise on behalf of school teachers. Those that participate are already motivated and BAHA members do all they can to assist them. We can help with the provision of risk assessments and all other forms of information. We can provide proformas for distribution to parents; payment cards; and templates for various other requirements. We can book transport from and back to school; arrange insurance cover and provide staff to help with the supervision and motivation of pupils. In short, we can divest teachers of much of the administration and routine, leaving them free to ensure that their pupils gain maximum educational benefit from the experience. Teachers need have no technical competence of their own, other than rudimentary first aid for the journeys from and back to school. We can make the whole experience pleasurable for teachers as well as pupils.

6. The Fear of Accidents and the Possibility of Litigation

The "blame culture" and over-reaction in the media have totally distorted the statistics relating to risk on outdoor activity trips. We all need to work together to keep the few accidents that do occur in perspective. Obviously the loss of a young life is extremely distressing for all concerned, but such fatalities are really extremely rare and compare very favourably with accidents at home, in the street or even in the playground. It's an interesting fact that most accidents at activity centres take place during "down-time" between activities, not on the activities themselves. If teachers follow the HASPEV guidance issued by the DfES in 2002, they really have nothing to fear, but it's very difficult to get that message through to them. There is hope, though. Even the NASUWT recognises that teachers are best advised to take pupils to AALA, BAHA or LEA centres, rather than taking them off on trips by themselves.

Conclusion

The last word should be left with Marcus Bailie, Head of Adventure Activities Licensing Authority Inspections: "Let young people get on with activities which statistically cause them very little harm, but which are likely to prolong their lives and radically enhance their expected quality of life. To deny them these things would be to deny them the inalienable big three—the right to life, liberty and the pursuit of happiness."

October 2004

Memorandum submitted by the Council for Environmental Education

About CEE

The Council for Environmental Education (CEE) is the national strategic organisation for environmental education in England. Founded in 1968, CEE's membership includes 73 national organisations and an ever-increasing, diverse network of organisations with interests in education, the environment and sustainable development. Our work seeks to add value to the sector and create a supportive policy climate. For example, CEE acted as special adviser to the Environmental Audit Committee inquiry *Learning the Sustainability Lesson*. CEE is grateful for this opportunity to contribute to the Committee's inquiry.

Out of Classroom Environmental Learning

CEE is particularly concerned with educational experience of natural and built environments, and educational experiences in education centres, visitor centres, and museums relating to the environment. This will be referred to throughout this submission as "out of classroom environmental learning", (OoCEL) reflecting elements of the useful categorisation of the range of interests in education and the environment developed by Scott and Gough (1).

An Historical Perspective

Since the expansion of mass schooling, a strand of educational thinking has stressed the importance of learning outside the classroom. Patrick Geddes' Outlook Tower in Edinburgh at the end of the 19th Century set out a model for the field and urban studies centres that developed in this country, particularly after 1945. Specialist provision for young people to study the world beyond the classroom became widespread.

The Field Studies Council (FSC) noted in 1972 that between 1941 and 1969, the number of Local Education Authority (LEA) field centres grew from about five to about 110. It identified nearly 200 centres run by schools, the Youth Hostels Association, FSC and other organisations.

However, at that time, as the authors of *Out and About* (2) observed, many schools still reflected a belief that school life and life in the "outside world" should be separate:

"Windows were high, often frosted, so that pupils should not be distracted by the outside view from concentrating on the 'essentials' taught within classrooms . . . History, geography, science, English and mathematics were subjects to be studied from printed books and blackboard summaries; they bore no relationship to the town, the countryside, and the communities of the children's outside life."

The CEE report to the *Countryside in 1970* conference referred to schools "exploding into the environment". *Streetwork, the Exploding School* (3) made a significant contribution to thinking on OoCEL. "It is a book about ideas: ideas of the environment as the educational resource, ideas of the enquiring school, the school without walls . . ."

Throughout the 1970s the diversification and development of opportunities and professional expertise continued throughout a network of residential and day centres, and public institutions supporting OoCEL. By 1980 it was common for LEAs to have at least one centre, in the case of Birmingham, a dozen. With budget restrictions, LEA provision began to wither; the introduction of Local Management of Schools (LMS) significantly reduced the number of LEA centres and advisers focusing on OoCEL. This decline is demonstrated by the reduction in membership of professional bodies, the Environmental Education Advisers Association and National Association for Environmental Education. Education policies since the start of LMS have continued to erode public provision of services supporting OoCEL and the ability of teachers to make use of them. Other local authority departments, NGOs, private centres, museums and other providers have strived to replace or supplement LEA work but coherent, professional and inclusive provision of OoCEL is now patchy. Speakers and delegates at CEE's 2001 conference, *The Power of Place,* argued persuasively for the necessity of OoCEL to contextualise the curriculum, whilst reflecting on barriers to its adoption and development: concentration on a limited core curriculum and quantitative evaluation, low status in inspection, funding changes, a decline in teachers' expertise and LEA support, safety concerns and fear of litigation.

Recent attempts to support such learning fail to address many of the barriers to more challenging, effective and inclusive OoCEL. FSC, the British Ecological Society (4) and others have raised the prospect that at least one aspect of OoCEL, biology fieldwork, "risks extinction", and evidence gathered by the Real World Learning Campaign (5) suggests a decline in takeup of OoCEL in specific subject areas, at specific phases, and amongst disadvantaged user groups.

The Value of Out of Classroom Environmental Learning

When highly valued by participants, integrated into the curriculum, well planned and professionally supported, OoCEL has great educational value. In *A Review of Research on Outdoor Learning* (6), researchers at The National Foundation for Educational Research and Kings College London conclude that there is strong evidence that OoCEL has significant cognitive and affective impact, and, critically, provides an opportunity for mutual reinforcement of knowledge, understanding and affective experience. Academic benefits include strong support of curriculum requirements in geography, science, history, citizenship and significant contribution to education for sustainable development (ESD). The Government's Sustainable Development Action Plan for Education and Skills (7), launched in 2003, has as its primary aim that "all learners will develop the skills, knowledge and value base to be active citizens in creating a more sustainable society". Existing opportunities, including those provided by CEE members, make a clear contribution towards this goal. A more supportive policy climate would allow this contribution to be strengthened.

A recent Ofsted report (8), though concentrating on adventurous outdoor education, draws attention to the role of direct experience of new environments or new experiences in familiar environments in contextualising aspects of the curriculum.

Research also points to the importance of direct experience in valuing and developing understanding of the environment. The Demos/Green Alliance report *A Child's Place* (9) concludes that:

"Many children have a surprisingly good grasp of environmental issues but gain their most powerful understanding through exploration of their own natural environment."

Such understanding is empowering, and critical to achieving sustainable development.

Policy

Department for Education and Skills (DfES), government agency, LEA and school policy needs to support OoCEL if it is to be effective. There is little evidence that current policy sufficiently supports integration of challenging, effective OoCEL into the curriculum. Within the National Curriculum Geography Programme of Study, "appropriate" fieldwork is required, but no guidance is provided on its location or duration. Geography is itself marginalised in many schools; Ofsted has identified serious weaknesses (and evidence of schools failing to meet curriculum requirements for fieldwork) in primary geography (10). There are no curriculum requirements for fieldwork or educational visits in other subjects, such as science, citizenship and history.

This low profile is also reflected in the Qualifications and Curriculum Authority (QCA) model Scheme of Work: a concern when such a high proportion of schools are using the model as the basis of their curriculum planning. OoCEL is not specifically assessed in most school inspections, and is not specified by most GCSE, A Level or vocational examination specifications.

There is limited guidance available for schools and providers on quality in OoCEL is limited. Whilst good materials are available, including those provided by some LEAs, CEE's *Measuring Effectiveness: evaluation in Education for Sustainable Development* (11), and *Quality, Safety and Sustainability* (12), published by the National Association of Field Studies Officers (NAFSO), further research is needed on the contribution of OoCEL and aspects of quality provision.

Specific recognition within the Ofsted inspection framework of the value of OoCEL and further guidance from QCA on integrating OoCEL into the curriculum would be beneficial.

DfES has provided useful guidance aimed at minimising risk to pupils' health and welfare, including *Health and Safety of Pupils on Educational Visits* (13), *Standards for LEAs in Overseeing Educational Visits* (14), *Handbook for Group Leaders* (15) and *Group Safety at Water Margins* (16).

This welcome focus on minimising risk is not, however, balanced by sufficient emphasis on the benefits of OoCEL, on supporting teachers in developing relevant expertise, and in protecting schools and teachers from financial risk when accidents, regrettably, occur. This lack of support is understandably reflected in the approach of teaching unions. NASUWT currently advises its members not to lead educational visits; in response to HMCI David Bell's statement at the launch of Ofsted's report on outdoor education that "if teachers follow the recognised safety procedures and guidance they have nothing to fear from the law", NASUWT issued the following: "As NASUWT casework has demonstrated time and time again, following the procedures and guidance is no protection against litigation".

A more robust legal and practical framework is required, within which teachers can feel confident to operate and support OoCEL. The framework should allow for action commensurate with risk, and reflect a consensus between government, providers and the profession (including the teaching unions). Furthermore, more research is needed on the efficacy of LEA and school policies designed to support learning outside the classroom.

Teacher education has a vital role in developing teachers' expertise and confidence in accessing, integrating, and leading OoCEL. Anecdotal evidence suggests a decline in the status of fieldwork and other OoCEL in BEd and PGCE courses, and a decline in relevant experience expertise amongst teacher trainers. More research is required to identify good practice and the extent of relevant learning in initial teacher training and continuing professional development activities. A commitment from DfES and the Teacher Training Agency to ensure suitable support within teacher education would be of great benefit.

FUNDING

Before LMS, subsidised LEA provision enabled many pupils from low income areas to benefit from OoCEL experiences. Currently some groups are excluded from such opportunities. Research is needed to assess this trend and to explore models of inclusive national and local support. Specific funding may be required to allow inclusive access to opportunities, and Government needs to research the possibility of introducing an entitlement to OoCEL.

Providers of OoCEL opportunities also require support. Funding for so many activities is not currently available directly from DfES or DCMS, and funding changes including the end of education project funding from the Landfill Tax Credit Scheme, changes to National Lottery funding programmes, and a shift away from education in the latest round of Defra's Environmental Action Fund, have left many providers facing great uncertainty.

DfES has funded some providers through the Growing Schools scheme. The initiative, which "aims to use the 'outdoor classroom' as a context for learning, both within and beyond the school grounds" has been cited by ministers (17) (18) (19) in responses to Parliamentary questions on fieldwork and out of classroom learning. CEE welcomes the initiative. However, an independent evaluation of pilot projects carried out by CEE and Bath University's Centre for Research in Education and the Environment (20), raised generic issues on OoCEL, and questioned whether the scheme recognises, or significantly addresses, barriers to challenging, effective learning outside the classroom.

SUMMARY OF RECOMMENDATIONS

— DfES and agencies need to identify and address barriers to OoCEL.

— Government, LEA and schools policy needs to support OoCEL.

— A robust, fair, legal framework for OoCEL is required.

— Research and action is required on ITT and CPD for teachers.

— Central and local government needs to adequately fund inclusive provision.

REFERENCES

1. *Sustainable Development and Learning: Framing the Issues;* Scott W and Gough S, RoutledgeFalmer, 2003.

2. *Out and About: A Teachers' Guide to Safety on Educational Visits;* Schools Council, Evans/Methuen, 1972.

3. *Streetwork, the Exploding School;* Ward C and Fyson A, TCPA, Routledge and Keegan Paul,1973.

4. *Teaching Biology Outside the Classroom: Is it Heading for Extinction?;* Field Studies Council/British Ecological Society, 2003.

5. Personal communication, 2004.

6. *A Review of Research on Outdoor Learning;* Rickinson M, Dillon J, Temey K, Morris M, Mee Young Choi, Sanders D, Benefield P, Field Studies Council.

7. *Sustainable Development Action Plan for Education and Skills;* DfES, 2003.

8. *Outdoor Education: Aspects of Good Practice;* Ofsted, 2004.

9. *A Child's Place;* Demos and Green Alliance, 2004.

10. *Ofsted Subject Reports 2002–03 Geography in Primary Schools;* Ofsted, 2004.

11. *Measuring Effectiveness: Evaluation in Education for Sustainable Development;* CEE, 2004.

12. *Quality, Safety and Sustainability;* NAFSO, 2004.

13. *Health and Safety of Pupils on Educational Visits;* DfES, 1998

14. *Standards for LEAs in Overseeing Educational Visits;* DfES, 2002.

15. *Handbook for Group Leaders;* DfES, 2002.

16. *Group Safety at Water Margins;* DfES, 2003.

17. Science Teaching: Response by Baroness Ashton; 10 Sept 2003: Column WA130.

18. Natural Environment: Response by Mr Stephen Twigg; *Hansard* 16 Jul 2004: Column 1372W.

19. Non-Classroom Learning: Response by Mr Stephen Twigg; *Hansard* 14 Sept 2004: Column 1566W.

20. *Growing Schools—The Innovation Fund Projects (2002–03): an External Evaluation;* Council for Environmental Education, University of Bath Centre for Research in Education and the Environment, 2003.

October 2004

Memorandum submitted by SkillsActive

BACKGROUND INFORMATION ABOUT SKILLSACTIVE

1. SkillsActive is an employer led organisation recognised and licensed by Government as the Sector Skills Council for Active Leisure and Learning. We have been charged with leading the skills and productivity drive within the Sport and Recreation, Health and Fitness, Playwork, The Outdoors and the Caravan Industries.

2. We are working with and for the Sector to:

— Advise Government and influence decision makers.

— Promote the image of the Sector to the public.

— Ensure the quality of training and qualifications.

— Help people find the jobs and training they need.

— Help the industry attract and retain the right staff.

— Attract funding to meet employers training needs.

3. SkillsActive is a registered charity and a membership organisation for employers and voluntary organisations in our Sector. We receive funding for our core functions from the Sector Skills Development Agency, as a result of being licensed by Government.

4. We work in close partnership with the Department for Education and Skills, the Department for Culture, Media and Sport, the Devolved Administrations and the Home Country Sport Councils to deliver our programme of activities. SkillsActive's work is directed by the Board of Trustees, which meets every two months.

5. SkillsActive works with employers to set National Standards for training and qualifications in the Sport and Recreation, Health and Fitness, Playwork, The Outdoors and the Caravan Industries.

6. SkillsActive also provides a secretariat, jointly with the CCPR, to the Adventure Activities Industry Advisory Committee (AAIAC), which is an industry reference committee on safety issues and provides an advisory role to the Adventure Activities Licensing Authority (AALA).

The Value of Out Of Classroom Learning

7. As the Sector Skills Council for the Active Leisure and Learning Sector, SkillsActive develops the training and offers the expertise to make out of classroom learning programmes work. It is our role to ensure enough skilled professionals exist in the public, private and voluntary workforce by ensuring that the supply of funding provision for training and qualifications reflects the demands made by business.

8. Play, Sport and Outdoor Activity are key components to the balanced development of young people. SkillsActive fully support the recent Ofsted report on Outdoor Education and believes there is real educational value in out of classroom learning which cannot be replicated or achieved in the classroom. Informal, kinaesthetic and experiential learning develop essential skills for life, making an important contribution to physical, personal and social development.

9. Similarly, such out of classroom learning can be a tool for engaging children and young people who for whatever reason do not respond to education in a classroom setting. The Department for Education and Skills initiative "Playing for Success" is one such scheme which demonstrates the value of the out of class room experience. Playing for Success has established out of school hours study support centres at football clubs and other sports grounds. The environment and medium of football, rugby and other sports is used as a motivational tool to help raise literacy, numeracy and ICT standards amongst Key Stage 2 and 3 pupils who are de-motivated and struggling with study.

10. Such initiatives work, but they should not only be employed in a remedial capacity. Out of classroom learning should be used as a motivational tool throughout the curriculum to encourage greater engagement from all pupils.

11. It must also be realised that, contingent on geographical and socio-economic factors, not all children have equal access or opportunity to partake in outdoor learning in their lives. It is therefore essential that the opportunity to participate in out of classroom learning is delivered through the school system, so that all children, regardless of their background, can access the valuable learning experiences out of classroom education can offer.

12. SkillsActive believe that out of classroom education should be an integral part of the extended schools concept but not just confined to extra curricula activities. It should include curriculum time allocation for residential experiences, and day and part day trips. Schemes such as the Duke of Edinburgh's Award Scheme, and the activities of the Scouts and Guides should be included within the concept of the extended school.

Costs and Funding of Outdoor Activities

13. Cost is a major barrier to young people's access to outdoor education. According to SkillsActive members in the Outdoor Sector, the message from schools and colleges is that the outdoor residential courses they offer are ideal, but not easily afforded. If all young people are to have equal access to participation in outdoor learning measures must be taken by Government to ensure that all schools and all pupils can afford the valuable experience they can offer.

14. SkillsActive therefore calls for funding provision to be given to enable all young people to have access to an outdoor residential experience, in addition to other out of classroom learning experiences.

15. It should be noted that the Ofsted report only looked at LEA run outdoor centres. These centres are in the minority in terms of numbers of participants, in addition they usually operate in a privileged financial environment with at least support for capital resources and often have heavily subsidised direct costs.

16. Other out of school activities such as sports clubs and after school clubs rely heavily on volunteers and teachers working after hours to run them. It is important that enough subsidised or free courses for volunteers exist so that there are enough properly trained volunteers available and willing to supervise such out of school learning.

The Place of Outdoor Learning Within the Curriculum

17. SkillsActive believes there is real educational value in out of classroom learning which cannot be replicated or achieved in the classroom. Informal, kinaesthetic and experiential learning develop essential skills for life, making an important contribution to physical, personal and social development.

18. One of our members, the British Canoe Union (BCU), reports that children are frequently unable to judge distance such as the width of a river, or assess the speed of a moving object. Whilst these issues are swiftly addressed by instructors it emphasises the importance of education outside the classroom.

19. Similarly, such out of classroom learning can be a tool for engaging children and young people who for whatever reason do not respond to education in a classroom setting. The Department for Education and Skills initiative "Playing for Success", in partnership with professional sport, is one such scheme which demonstrates the value of different learning formats and the value of linking with sport. The scheme has established out of school hours study support centres at football clubs and other sports' grounds which use the environment and medium of football, rugby and other sports as motivational tools, and focus on raising literacy, numeracy and ICT standards amongst Key Stage 2 and 3 pupils who are struggling a little and often demotivated. Such initiatives work, but they should not only be employed in a remedial capacity. Out of classroom learning should be used as a motivational tool throughout the curriculum to encourage greater engagement from all pupils.

20. It must also be realised that, contingent on geographical and socio-economic factors, not all children have equal access or opportunity to partake in outdoor learning in their lives. That is why it is essential that the opportunity to participate in out of classroom learning is delivered through the school system, to ensure that all children, regardless of their background, can access the valuable learning experiences out of class room education can offer.

21. SkillsActive believe that out of classroom education should be an integral part of the extended schools concept but not just confined to extra curricula activities. It should include curriculum time allocation for residential experiences, and day and part day trips. Schemes such as the Duke of Edinburgh, and the activities of the Scouts and Guides should be included within the concept of the extended school.

22. Currently better performing schools are integrating outdoor personal development into the curriculum, whilst lower performing schools are not. It is unfair that some pupils should have access to the valuable experiences outdoor learning can offer and SkillsActive recommend that best practice should be replicated across all schools.

EXTERNAL ASSESSMENT OF PROVISION

23. It is essential that any external assessment is sensitive to the particular field of out of classroom learning. SkillsActive have been working with Ofsted inspectors to develop a specialised training programme for Play to help them understand the nature of Playwork so they are better able to carry out fair assessments in this equally specialised field.

24. The Adventure Activities Licensing Authority (AALA) already licences adventure activities in a number of outdoor education establishments.

25. SkillsActive should be authorised to establish a training programme for Ofsted Inspectors to ensure that the concept of specialist training which has so benefited the Play sector is replicated within the Outdoor Learning Sector provided by LEAs.

ORGANISATION AND INTEGRATION WITHIN EXISTING SCHOOL STRUCTURES

26. SkillsActive acknowledges the importance of the role of School Sport Co-ordinators and Educational Visits Co-ordinators. Both have a role to play in extending the opportunity for out of classroom learning. These Co-ordinators should also be responsible for ensuring access to specialised training and qualifications for teaching staff so that each school has the capacity to offer a full range of out door learning opportunities. They could also play a role in motivating staff in schools and ensuring they have the right support in the form of insurance and additional training to assist with school trips.

QUALIFICATION AND MOTIVATION OF TEACHERS AND THE EFFECT ON TEACHER WORKLOAD

27. SkillsActive do not perceive a lack of motivation as a major deterrent to teachers participating in out of school learning, although teacher workload may have an effect. The main barrier to teachers participating in outdoor learning is a genuine fear of litigation. This fear is one which, as mentioned in the recent Ofsted report, is largely unfounded, and yet it is one which is exacerbated by the messages given out in the media and by certain teaching unions. Many of the concerns teachers hold about litigation can be overcome with proper support and training.

28. Teachers should have access to whatever training they feel necessary to enable them to participate in or oversee out of classroom learning. This could be anything from a teacher volunteering to help coach the school rugby team having access to a refereeing course, to a geography teacher completing a mountain leadership course so they feel confident in supervising physical geography field trips. SkillsActive also supports the CCPR's call for a minimum of 30 hours dedicated to physical education within initial teacher training for primary teachers.

29. The National Governing Bodies (NGBs) of sport should be encouraged to provide courses specially aimed at teachers assisting skilled professionals in the outdoor learning sector on school trips. A good example of where this is happening is with the British Canoe Union (BCU). The BCU has developed tailored courses in "Bell Boats" for teachers helping on school trips. A PE teacher does not need to be a level four canoe coach to assist with an outdoor learning week at a residential activity centre—skilled professionals

will be on hand at the centre to provide this support. A confident and informed teacher is well placed to imbue a healthy perspective towards risk in their class. Greater availability of such courses would enable and motivate teachers to become involved in such activities. The added advantage is that teachers who are able to participate in this way then have the insight to follow up the learning experience with the pupils in the classroom.

30. The SkillsActive role is to work with the industry outside of school to ensure that enough skilled professionals exist with appropriate qualifications in Playwork, Outdoor Activity and Coaching to facilitate this. However, we would be happy to extend this role to work with the Sector to develop training specifically for teachers to work alongside specialists.

THE FEAR OF ACCIDENTS AND THE POSSIBILITY OF LITIGATION

31. Risk is an essential element of many outdoor education experiences. Indeed, managing risk and learning about how to behave outside of the school environment are essential life skills which young people must be given the opportunity to learn for themselves. Although to completely eliminate risk would be to dilute the experience of out of classroom learning, risk can be calculated and managed with the right training. A confident and competent teacher with the proper training and qualifications should have no reason to fear participating in out of school learning.

32. The level of anxiety associated with out of classroom education is not proportional to the risk. Teachers need to be reassured that if they have been trained and have attained the necessary qualifications the likelihood of an accident occurring is greatly reduced. The message needs to be given that the benefits of learning opportunities out of school far outweigh the possibility of an accident occurring. This message will be much more palatable for teachers if they have the support of the school in obtaining the necessary qualifications.

33. SkillsActive would offer to work closely with Unions and NGBs to ensure the insurance cover offered by teaching unions and NGBs can include and cover teachers volunteering in out of class room learning. Affordable and appropriate insurance must be linked to and reflect training and qualifications.

CONCLUSIONS AND RECOMMENDATIONS

34. SkillsActive calls for ring fenced funding provision to be given to enable all young people to have access to an out of classroom residential experience, in addition to other out of school learning experiences.

35. It is important that enough subsidised or free courses for teachers and volunteers exist so that there are enough properly trained teachers and volunteers available and willing to supervise in out of classroom learning activities.

36. SkillsActive supports the CCPR's call for a minimum of 30 hours dedicated to physical education within initial teacher training for primary teachers.

37. SkillsActive should be authorised to establish a training programme for Ofsted Inspectors to ensure that the concept of specialist training which has so benefited the Play sector is replicated within the Outdoor Learning Sector provided by LEAs.

38. SkillsActive would be happy to extend its role to work with the Sector to develop training specifically for teachers to work alongside specialists in out of classroom learning and encourages National Governing Bodies to follow the example set by the British Canoe Union in this respect.

October 2004

Memorandum submitted by the Heritage Lottery Fund

1. BACKGROUND TO THE HERITAGE LOTTERY FUND

1.1 The Heritage Lottery Fund (HLF) distributes money from the National Lottery to heritage projects across the United Kingdom. It is administered by the Trustees of the National Heritage Memorial Fund, a Non-Departmental Public Body sponsored by the Department for Culture, Media and Sport.

1.2 Our Strategic Plan 2002–07, *Broadening the Horizons of Heritage,* identifies three broad aims:

— to conserve and enhance the UK's diverse heritage;

— to encourage more people to be involved in and make decisions about their heritage; and

— to ensure that everyone can learn about, have access to, and enjoy their heritage.

We also aim to bring about a more equitable spread of our grants across the UK.

1.3 Our funding supports all aspects of heritage from museums and archives to nature conservation to oral history and traditions; from local community activities to multi-million pound capital projects (see Appendix A for details for our grant programmes).

2. HLF's Funding for Education

2.1 HLF welcomes the Education and Skills Committee's inquiry into Education Outside the Classroom. HLF provides a significant amount of funding to support education projects across all heritage sectors in the UK. Our submission to the select committee is thus from the perspective of a funder of a wide range of projects run by heritage sector organisations, and others, which deliver education outside the classroom.

2.2 HLF defines education in broad terms to include formal and informal learning across the lifespan. Our funding helps individuals develop their understanding of heritage in an active way appropriate to their needs, interests and background.

2.3 In formal learning, HLF-funded projects usually link their work to a taught curriculum in schools, colleges or universities and include activities such as:

— a school visit programme organised by a heritage site;

— support and development for teachers to work at a heritage site or with a heritage collection; and

— creating learning resources and activity programmes.

2.4 In informal learning, HLF-funded projects include organised activities and resources which help people understand heritage sites or collections such as:

— open days;

— family activities;

— heritage skills workshops;

— interpretation panels and leaflets; and

— heritage trails.

2.5 Recent research into HLF funding for education has shown that between 1994 and 2003:

— over £400 million of HLF funding has been awarded to 1,166 education projects;

— we have funded over 220 education spaces; and

— over 530 education posts.

Within this overall picture, a huge range of educational activity and outreach programmes have been funded which involve children and young people in schools and colleges learning outside the classroom, for example, at museums, galleries, wildlife sites and parks.

3. HLF's Research into Heritage Education Projects

3.1 In spring 2004, HLF commissioned the Scottish Centre for Research in Education to undertake evaluation of the impact of our funding for curriculum linked learning for 5–19 year olds. A sample of 50 projects, taking place across the UK and involving all heritage sectors, is under evaluation. They range from "Hands-On Heritage", a Groundwork project involving young people in Cumbria, to a multi-cultural education project at the Abbeydale Industrial Hamlet in Sheffield. This research is still underway and a final report is due in summer 2005. However, interim findings from the first stages of the research have been used to inform this submission.

4. Defining Education Outside the Classroom

4.1 From an HLF perspective, it is clear that education outside the classroom is not necessarily outdoor learning. Learning which takes place in museums, archives, galleries, libraries, discovery centres and at industrial heritage sites can be termed "education outside the classroom" but does not necessarily have an outdoor element. To avoid confusion we suggest that the Committee carefully defines what it means by Education Outside the Classroom. To truly represent the range of activity that happens outside of school, HLF would like to see the widest definition adopted.

5. Costs and Funding of Outdoor Activities

5.1 HLF does not fund schools directly to carry out heritage learning activities. Nevertheless, the scale of our funding to heritage sector organisations and others for work with the formal education sector is an indication of the level of need which is not being met from elsewhere.

5.2 Education outside the classroom is often run by charitable or voluntary organisations that do not have access to core funding for their educational work. Set up and delivery costs of education outside the classroom often have to be found from short term project funding such as that provided by the HLF. Absence of secure funding makes these educational services vulnerable.

5.3 With HLF funding, sometimes heritage organisations are able to offer educational services free of charge (43% of the projects in our research sample made no charge). Where a charge is made this is usually at a subsidised rate and does not reflect the true cost of provision. Charges vary considerably and appear to range from £1 to £5 per pupil for a half day session. Yet such charges can be a barrier to participation for some schools.

5.4 Heritage organisations and teachers report transport to sites as another key barrier to participation. Of the projects consulted in our research, 68% reported that coaches and minibuses were the main form of transport used by their participants to reach their sites. Where an HLF project has planned a programme designed to widen access by reaching out to deprived or excluded communities, HLF will support transport subsidies for schools and youth groups.

5.5 Working outside the classroom generates additional costs for providers beyond the obvious ones of transport and service charges. On-site access to good quality learning spaces with adequate toilets and covered spaces for lunch is essential. There is a need for high quality, relevant and up-to-date learning materials and lesson plans to ensure that site based learning can be embedded into the curriculum. HLF has funded a range of learning spaces from pond dipping platforms to flexible indoor classrooms. Learning projects funded by HLF tend to be activity based but often result in the production of additional learning resources.

5.6 Anecdotal evidence from heritage education officers suggests that many teachers lack the skills, equipment and confidence to deliver high quality learning in the field and appreciate the added value offered by a professional heritage service. We suggest that it is unrealistic to expect classroom teachers at primary level to have the necessary degree of expertise in the full range of curriculum subjects which might be covered in learning outside the classroom. Subject teachers at secondary level may not have the particular expertise related to a specific site or collection to extract the maximum benefit. There is a need, therefore, for co-professionals who are experts in using sites and collections for educational purpose to work alongside classroom teachers to deliver high quality learning sessions. Our research, and that of others (see, for example, Museums, Libraries and Archives Council, *What did you learn at the museum today?*, 2004), suggests that children place particular value on having access to such "experts" who share their specialist knowledge and open their eyes to new ways of learning and, indeed, new recreation and career opportunities.

6. THE PLACE OF OUTDOOR LEARNING WITHIN THE CURRICULUM

6.1 Our research has found that HLF funded projects that provide learning outside the classroom are helping to deliver most curriculum areas, with the exception of Modern Foreign Languages. The most commonly cited subjects were Local History, History, Art and Design, Science, Geography and Environmental Studies. Literacy, numeracy, PSHE and citizenship are also delivered at heritage sites.

6.2 Heritage projects provide rich resources for interdisciplinary and innovative learning experiences, stimulating and exciting both teachers and students into new ways of thinking. Heritage sites and collections provide a special experience which cannot be duplicated in the classroom. Children and young people are inspired simply by being in a place and seeing things that are outside their day-to-day experience. Taking just a few examples from the portfolio of recent HLF projects, such experiences include:

— the amazing scale, and hidden mathematics, of Norwich Cathedral;

— the fragility and beauty of the dingy skipper butterfly and its place in the ecosystem;

— the earth shuddering power of a beam engine in full swing and the story this has to tell about the early Industrial Revolution; and

— the horror of a slave chain.

6.3 As our research has shown, work outside the classroom is inspiring oral and written language development, understanding of mathematics and interest in science. It is also supporting citizenship education. In participating in HLF funded projects, children and young people are being offered the opportunity to greater appreciate the value and importance of heritage to our future well-being and sense of identity and understand our individual and collective responsibility to define, value and look after our shared environmental, cultural and social heritage.

6.4 Teachers report the difference such visits can make in engaging those students who are less keen to learn in classroom settings or who are studying alternative curricula. Attitudinal and behavioural improvements in students can result from learning in new and exciting settings. Heritage contexts provide students with practical opportunities for group work which have tangible outcomes, for example researching and designing an exhibition at a museum or building and installing bat boxes at a nature reserve. Such experiences can provide useful support for young people in the transition to work.

6.5 Some other examples of HLF-funded projects supporting education outside the classroom include:

— The Countryside is our Classroom project (HLF award: £44,000) funded an officer to work with the Bedfordshire Community Council to link farms and schools to help children learn about healthy living, country life and how food is produced.

— The Education and Community Action project run by Lincolnshire Wildlife Trust (HLF award: £365,000) has funded three education officer posts. They are providing a wide range of learning opportunities for all Key Stages at wildlife sites across Lincolnshire including pond dipping, species identification and food webs for younger students and residential weeks supporting biology field work at Gibraltar Point for older students.

— At Cressing Temple Barns in Essex, primary school children working on the shelters unit of the geography curriculum explore how the barns were constructed and then make their own model timber framed building from real materials, and learn some practical wattle and daubing techniques (HLF award: £70,000) .

— The Cultural Co-operation Year Round Education Project (HLF award: £409,000) delivers artistic residencies to schoolchildren in London to explore cultural traditions. The project includes provision for subsidised transport to take children with special needs to museums.

6.6 Some projects have benefited from the support of their Local Education Authority, for example in facilitating teacher secondments to heritage organisations to develop curriculum materials, providing a classroom space for an education officer from a wildlife charity to carry out her teaching, or providing access to INSET programmes. Other projects have found LEAs to be uninterested and unresponsive.

6.7 HLF can fund projects that promote vocational education. There is some indication that heritage sector organisations are becoming more proactive in offering work experience placements for young people at school and in college. Where this happens it is usually linked to the business or leisure studies curriculum. However, there is scope to extend this type of provision to other curriculum areas linked to vocational GCSEs and A Levels, even more so if the Tomlinson recommendations are agreed by the Government. We would like to see more awareness within Education Business Partnerships of the heritage sector as a venue for work experience and hence, an increase in the number of opportunities available to young people.

6.8 Heritage organisations often build on contacts with young people in formal educational settings by offering "progression" activities such as volunteering, participating in youth forums and young people's clubs. We believe that enabling young people to build a longer term relationship with heritage organisations can have a profoundly beneficial effect on personal development and raise aspirations. This has been demonstrated by a separate strand of research at HLF which is evaluating our Young Roots grants programme. Young Roots aims to promote the involvement of young people (aged 13–25 years) with the heritage of the UK. The scheme is subject to a four year longitudinal evaluation which will consider the success of the scheme in meeting its aims and explore the impact of the scheme on participants, on communities and on partner delivery organisations.

7. QUALIFICATION AND MOTIVATION OF TEACHERS

7.1 Continuing Professional Development (CPD) for teachers to help them make effective use of heritage sites and resources to deliver out of class activities is provided by many of our grantees. CPD activities take the form of INSET days, open evenings, advisory groups brought together to design curriculum materials, secondments, formal training and student teacher placements. Grantees report that teachers often lack confidence and experience in working out of class and rely heavily on the expertise of heritage education staff. Team delivery by teachers and these co-professionals helps to build confidence and share good practice.

7.2 Projects in our research have reported that they would like more input to CPD programmes to explain what is on offer and to develop innovative ways of working together. With CPD becoming the responsibility of the Teacher Training Agency there is an opportunity to open up development opportunities to all providers of curriculum-linked learning whether they are school based or based in heritage or other organisations.

7.3 In the Mermaid's Purse project (HLF award: £88,200), the HLF-funded education officer worked with teachers and their pupils from a range of schools and with staff at St Martin's College. The project developed and piloted learning activities linked to environmental issues at Morecambe Bay, using an innovative teaching approach based on principles of philosophical enquiry. The young people learned about the complexity of the ecosystems within the Bay area and also extended their critical thinking skills. As part of the project a learning pack was made available to teachers across the counties involved and to new teacher trainees. Innovative, risky activities such as these build capacity within the teaching community and promote a willingness to explore new methods of curriculum delivery, increasing motivation of teachers and students.

7.4 Teachers need good support from school managers and earmarked budgets to encourage them to undertake education outside the classroom and get the most out of these experiences. We suggest that more could be done to encourage all schools to participate in these valuable enrichment activities.

8. FEAR OF ACCIDENTS AND THE POSSIBILITY OF LITIGATION

8.1 Our grantees report concerns that health and safety guidelines constrain visits to heritage sites. Whilst children, their parents and teachers have the right to expect safe practices to be in place, there appears to be a tendency to assume that all out of classroom learning carries the same degree of risk. In extreme cases this has led to schools adopting a "no visits" policy. Many of our heritage sector grantees are supporting their teacher colleagues by carrying out their own risk assessments and making these available for schools to use, thus alleviating some of the work involved in meeting health and safety standards.

Dr Sharon Goddard
Education Advisor, Policy and Research Department

APPENDIX A:

THE HERITAGE LOTTERY FUND'S GRANT PROGRAMMES

Repair Grants for Places of Worship

This is a replacement for the Joint Places of Worship Scheme (which only applied in England) and aims to manage the enormous demand for our funds in this area of heritage. The new scheme will focus on urgent repairs and bring about a better balance between funding and conservation priorities across the UK.

Heritage Grants

This programme offers grants of £50,000 or more to organisations which aim to look after and enhance the UK's heritage; to increase involvement in heritage activities; and to improve access to and enjoyment of heritage. It caters for a wide range of projects, including the very largest and most complicated.

Project Planning Grants

These grants of between £5,000 and £50,000 are available to help in the early planning of projects which are expected to lead to an application for a Heritage Grant.

Your Heritage

This programme offers grants of between £5,000 and £50,000 for projects which either care for heritage or increase people's understanding and enjoyment of it. Projects should also make it easier for people to gain access to heritage and benefit the community and the wider public. The application form is much simpler than that for Heritage Grants.

Young Roots

Young Roots promotes the involvement of young people, 13 to 25 years old, in their heritage. The programme offers grants of between £5,000 and £25,000. To be eligible for a grant, a project must increase opportunities for young people to learn about and get involved in their heritage, and be delivered through partnerships.

Awards for All

We run Awards for All along with other Lottery distributors at a local level. Through this scheme, we give grants of between £500 and £5,000 to small community groups, including new groups. We can fund up to 100% of the project costs.

Local Heritage Initiative

This initiative helps local groups to investigate, explain and care for their local landmarks, landscape, traditions and culture. Through grants of between £3,000 and £25,000, the scheme helps local groups with a range of small-scale projects.

The scheme is run on our behalf by the Countryside Agency in England and is being piloted in Scotland by partnerships led by Scottish Natural Heritage, and in Wales by the Countryside Council for Wales.

October 2004

Memorandum submitted by the Museums, Libraries and Archives Council

1. INTRODUCTION

1.1 The Museums, Libraries and Archives Council (MLA) is the national development agency working for, and on behalf, of museums, libraries and archives and advising government on policy and priorities for the sector. MLA's roles are to provide strategic leadership, to act as a powerful advocate, to develop capacity and to promote innovation and change. Museums, libraries and archives connect people to knowledge and information, creativity and inspiration. MLA is leading the drive to unlock the wealth, for everyone. MLA is a Non-Departmental Public Body sponsored by the Department for Culture, Media and Sport.

1.2 Museums, libraries and archives have an important role to play in enhancing learning opportunities for school age children. Not only can they provide innovative and imaginative ways of delivering the curriculum, but they can provide unique spaces for learning away from the classroom with input from experienced and professional staff focused on delivering inspirational and creative learning opportunities, working alongside teachers and classroom assistants. In addition to this, early years activity has been demonstrated to have a positive impact on child development and learning once children reach school age.

1.3 The museums, libraries and archives sector is significantly engaged in supporting the delivery of the curriculum and providing inspirational learning opportunities to school students of all ages. Some examples may include:

— Visiting an exhibition, or taking part in a specific activity at a museum, gallery or archive as part of the school day.

— Using school and public libraries to help with homework, or as part of the school day.

— Participating in summer reading schemes in public libraries during the summer holidays.

"The positive change in attitude to learning, level of involvement and quality of work seen during this cross-curricula project has been amazing. It is clear to us that creativity in the curriculum is the key to learning"[28]—Mandy Staines, Teacher, Bessemer Grange Primary School. Participant in a project working with Dulwich Picture Gallery as part of phase 2 of the Museums and Galleries Education Programme.

2. BACKGROUND

2.1 Providing education outside of the classroom is a key activity for museums, archives and libraries. This not only means providing learning opportunities both inside and outside the school day for students, but it also means providing training and learning opportunities to teachers to enable them to make maximum use of museums, archives and libraries as part of their teaching practice.

2.2 Recent government investment, particularly via Creative Partnerships, where partnerships have been encouraged between schools and cultural and creative institutions and organisations to enhance the life of the whole school, and via programmes such as Renaissance in the Regions and the DfES funded Museums and Galleries Education Programme, has enhanced the capacity of our sector to deliver inspirational learning opportunities outside the classroom. However, many barriers still exist which prevent schools from engaging with museums, archives and libraries providing learning opportunities outside of the classroom.

2.3 As part of the Renaissance in the Regions vision for England's regional museums, each regional Museum Hub has developed an Education Programme Delivery Plan (EPDP) which establishes how it proposes to deliver a Comprehensive Service to Schools. This forms the basis of a national offer; providing every school with an entitlement to museum learning, enriching learning for every school age child through museum and gallery activity.

2.4 The EPDPs were developed after significant consultation with teachers, pupils, LEAs and other stakeholders to determine what schools want from museum and gallery education to enhance the curriculum.

2.5 The EPDP research positions museum education within the context of key national policies which are driving the development of the wider education sector. The DfES' priorities focus on:

— Providing high-quality early education and childcare for more children.

— Continuing the progress already made in primary education.

— Transforming secondary education.

— Developing a flexible and challenging 14–19 phase of education.

— Increasing and broadening participation in higher education.

— Developing the skills of the workforce—particularly the basic skills of some adults.[29]

---

[28] Wonderful Things, ALM London 2004.
[29] Future Learning, MLA 2004.

2.6 Although the main focus for the EPDPs was school age learning between five and 16, the EPDP analysed the contribution museum education makes to these wider agendas, identifying strengths, weaknesses and priorities for development.

2.7 In particular the EPDP research demonstrated the potential of museum education in addressing themes, which the unique character of museum education can make a particularly strong impact on:

— Maximising the impact of strong links with the primary sector . . . demonstrating the depth and strength of established services at Key Stage 2.

— Realising the potential of working with early years and Key Stage 2.

— Using resources and skills to develop cross curriculum learning.

— Exploring identity and citizenship.

— Inspiring creativity.

— Developing new programmes to support out of school hours learning.

— Celebrating diversity and tackling exclusion.[30]

3. BARRIERS

3.1 Several issues and inhibiting factors have been identified by museums and libraries relating to the development and take up of learning opportunities outside the classroom.

3.2 While the barriers outlined below were identified as part of the Future Learning[31] report, synthesising the issues identified in the Hub museums EPDPs, they have relevance across the museums, libraries and archives sector as a whole. For example, there is a clear parallel between the need for school libraries to raise their profile within the wider school community to enable them to achieve their potential in enhancing learning opportunities outside the classroom, and the need identified in the table below to develop greater awareness of what museums offer.

3.3 In order to raise the profile of school libraries and school library services, MLA, in partnership with the Arts Council of England, the Teacher Training Agency, the regional museum, library and archive agencies and the Association of Senior Children's and Education Librarians (ASCEL) is developing a programme involving Initial Teacher Training providers and School Library Services in delivering training to trainee teachers aimed at raising awareness of the role of school libraries and children's literature in promoting learning opportunities with school age pupils. This can be seen in the same context as developing continuous professional development (CPD) opportunities as outlined in the table. Summarised, the barriers identified are:

Barrier	Strategic Development Theme
Relevance	Develop services relevant to schools and young people that are central to museums' development.
Logistical	Simplifying procedures and information provision, service provision in various and virtual spaces.
Skills in schools and museums	Develop skills through CPD and engagement with ITT for museum and school staff.
Awareness of what museums offer	Positioning of museum education as a mainstreaming education activity through new partnerships and advocacy.
Environment and facilities	Redesign museum facilities and invest in new facilities.
Capacity	Invest in creation of additional museum education capacity.

4. CURRENT PRACTICE

4.1 MLA have developed a national framework entitled Inspiring Learning for All[32] aimed at helping museums, libraries and archives provide the best possible learning experiences for everyone.

4.2 The framework identifies best practice in museums, libraries and archives. Focusing on the learner, it:

— Ensures effective learning opportunities are provided.

— Describes the processes and approaches that support learning.

— Explains how organisations can demonstrate their impact on learning.

---

[30] Future Learning, MLA 2004.
[31] Future Learning, MLA 2004.
[32] www.inspiringlearningforall.gov.uk, MLA 2004.

4.3 Inspiring Learning for All will provide organisations with the tools to enable them to become effective learning organisations, with learning at their heart. It will also enable them to quantify the learning outcomes on their users. An innovative method has been developed quantifying learning outcomes into five key generic areas:

— Knowledge and understanding.

— Skills.

— Attitudes and values.

— Enjoyment, inspiration and creativity.

— Activity, behaviour and progression.

4.4 These generic learning outcomes have been used to evaluate and measure the impact learning activity within museums, libraries and archives has upon the learner, and allow the sector and the wider learning community to develop an understanding of the unique role of museums, libraries and archives in delivering inspirational learning opportunities to all.

4.5 As part of Renaissance in the Regions, the Department for Education and Skills (DfES), and the Department for Culture, Media and Sport (DCMS) have committed £12.2 million funding to Hub museums to deliver a comprehensive service to schools. Year 1 education programme activity in phase 1 Hubs (North East, South West, West Midlands) was evaluated by the Research Centre for Museums and Galleries on behalf of MLA utilising the generic learning outcomes developed as part of Inspiring Learning for All.[33] The evaluation established:

— 95% of teachers thought museums were important to their teaching.

— 89% of teachers using the museums felt that the visit had increased their confidence to use museums again.

— 94% of teachers agreed that their visits were linked to the curriculum.

Of surveyed pupils aged between 6–11:

— 90% agreed they had learnt some new things.

— 87% agreed that a visit was useful for school work.

Of surveyed pupils aged between 11–28:

— 87% agreed that they had learnt some interesting things from their visit.

— 82% agreed that museums are good places to learn in a different way to school.

— 58% agreed that a museum visit makes school-work more inspiring.

"Without the museum visit we would not be able to deliver the (History) syllabus and exam marks would fall . . . Students tend to get better marks in coursework related to the museum visit than in exams"[34]

4.6 The evaluation also discovered high levels of use of Hub museums during the summer holidays, with 31,800 children and 32,006 adults taking part in summer activities in 36 museums during the summer of 2003.

4.7 Overall, since Renaissance funding, the evaluation identified a 28% increase in schools use of museums in September and October 2003, compared with figures for usage in September and October 2002.

4.8 The evidence from the evaluation of the Phase 1 Hubs education programme was also confirmed by evidence from the evaluation of Phase 2 of the DfES funded Museums and Galleries Education Programme conducted by the Centre for Education and Industry at the University of Warwick.[35]

4.9 Phase 2 of this programme ran between 2002 and 2004 and received £1 million funding from the DfES. The aim of the programme being to develop effective partnerships between schools and museums and galleries, using the collections and spaces of museums and galleries to enhance the curriculum and provide inspirational learning opportunities for pupils. Over 130 projects and over 30,000 pupils were involved in the programme.

4.10 As part of the evaluation:

— 93% of surveyed Key Stage 2, 3 and 4 pupils stated they enjoyed or very much enjoyed their activity.

— 90% were very pleased or satisfied with their work.

— 82% learnt a lot or learnt something.

— 82% were engaged or quite engaged in the activity.

— 87% had worked very well or reasonably well.

— 58% felt more confident as a result of their project.

---

[33] What did you learn at the museum today? MLA 2003.

[34] What did you learn in the museum today? MLA 2003.

[35] MGEP Executive Summary, DfES 2004.

4.11 Libraries have a vital role to play in supporting education outside the classroom. School libraries help pupils develop much needed information literacy and selection skills to enable critical thinking. Many schools offering extended coverage via breakfast and after school clubs also provide extended access to library facilities.

4.12 Within the context of extended schools, libraries provide an important facility to enable learning to continue outside of the classroom, providing the opportunity for students to pursue their own learning interests in a self directed and personalised manner, enhancing teaching in the classroom. Less able students, and those unengaged in classroom learning can also find that school and public libraries provide opportunities to continue learning in an alternative and supportive learning environment which is different to the classroom.

4.13 69% of all public library authorities run homework clubs or activities to support continued learning outside the classroom, and 97% of public library authorities offer a regular programme where classes can visit public libraries during the school day. The purpose of these visits is not only to develop the information literacy skills of pupils, but to develop awareness of the role of books and a love of reading both to enhance school work and for pleasure. Additional activities in school holidays are also offered by 95% of library authorities, with 88% taking part in the summer reading challenge during the summer holiday period, also running additional complimentary events and activities.[36]

4.14 600,000 children between the ages of four and 11 took part in the 2003 summer reading challenge in 88% of UK library authorities. The evaluation, Inspiring Children, undertaken by the Reading Agency[37], and utilising the generic learning outcomes developed as part of Inspiring Learning for All, discovered:

— 78% of surveyed children felt they were "better readers" after the challenge. Four in 10 felt they were "a lot better".

— 59% of surveyed children said they found out something new from a book they didn't know before.

— 96% of surveyed children enjoyed reading the books and 98% liked choosing the books for themselves.

4.15 The intervention made by public libraries via programmes such as the summer reading challenge highlights the significant role they can play in providing learning opportunities outside of the classroom which have a positive impact on learning within the classroom.

4.16 Public libraries are also engaged in early years work. With a focus around Bookstart, and many library authorities delivery popular early years activities such as storytelling and rhymetime. A significant proportion of library authorities have dedicated early years staff working with children and their parents.

4.17 Eppe research[38] has found that "Parents reading to children was associated with high scores in all outcomes, and teaching songs/nursery rhymes to their children showed a significant impact on language at school entry. The biggest predictor at age three of reading ability at age 10 is vocabulary—especially knowledge of rarer incidence words".

4.18 As part of Framework for the Future, the DCMS 10 year vision for public libraries an "early years offer" is being developed for families across the country. The basis of the "offer" being that libraries become more family friendly and welcoming to enable the potential of an early intervention to be realised throughout their school life.

5. Conclusion

It is essential that a cultural entitlement embodies activities out of the classroom both within and outside school hours. MLA and its sectors are working together to extend this entitlement to all children and learners.

October 2004

Memorandum submitted by Zurich Financial Services

Zurich Financial Services is an insurance-based financial services provider with an international network that focuses its activities on its key markets of North America, the United Kingdom and Continental Europe. Founded in 1872, Zurich is headquartered in Zurich, Switzerland. It has offices in more than 50 countries and employs approximately 64,000 people (of which around 16,000 are based in the UK).

---

[36] Library Services to Schools and Children in the UK 2002–03, Creaser and Maynard, LISU, Loughborough University.

[37] Inspiring Children, the Impact of the Summer Reading Challenge: Key Findings, The Reading Agency 2004.

[38] The Effective Provision of Pre-School Education (Eppe) Project: findings from the pre-school period 1997–2000, Institute of Education.

The Inquiry is wide-ranging and touches on a number of areas upon which it would neither be relevant or appropriate for us to comment. However, we will attempt to give some clarification as to the role of insurance in education outside the classroom, particularly in relation to the possibility of accidents and the fear of litigation.

In the UK, Zurich Municipal is the leading provider of risk and insurance solutions to Britain's public services, including Local Authorities, Local Education Authorities and schools. Local authorities, LEAs and schools protect themselves from the risk of litigation following accidents through Public Liability (PL) policies. The services provided by local authorities are many and varied. PL claims emanating from educational activities form only a very small part of the claims initiated against local authorities (around 3%). The largest proportion by far are those from "slips and trips" on public highways (around 43%). This is illustrated by the two charts below.

2000-2003 Claim numbers (aggregate)

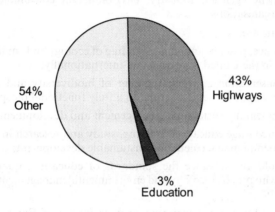

2000-2003 Claims costs

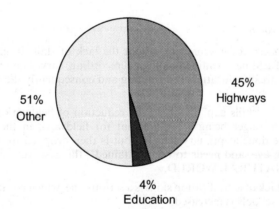

Furthermore, the majority of this 3% of "education" claims relate to those accidents by pupils and visitors which take place on the school premises, rather than claims for activities outside school activities. As the proportion of education claims is small there is not a necessity to individually price for "education outside the classroom". Furthermore we would not require details of out-of-school education as we appreciate such activities are an essential part of education.

In providing risk solutions and advice to our customers, we encourage schools and LEAs to adhere to Department for Education and Skills guidance on out-of-school activities, outlined in the "Health and Safety of Pupils on Educational Visits" publication. For areas outside the Local Authority's direct control, such as work placements, we would expect the host organisation to take responsibility. However, the authority must be mindful of placing a pupil in an environment where that pupil would potentially be at risk. If the local authority had failed to undertake a proper risk assessment in advance, they could be liable but, again, as we consider this to be an integral part of normal activities and therefore we do not consider it necessary to seek details of such arrangements nor individually price.

For Zurich Municipal, then, we consider that fear over a lack of available insurance cover or a perceived rise in premiums is unfounded. We reiterate our belief that "education outside the classroom" is an essential part of education that, while it should be safe and mindful of potential risks, should be encouraged.

October 2004

Memorandum submitted by the Institute of Ecology and Environmental Management

INTRODUCTION

The Institute of Ecology and Environmental Management (IEEM) welcomes the opportunity to comment on the Education Outside the Classroom inquiry.

IEEM is the professional Institute supporting professionals in the fields of ecology and environmental management. The Institute was established in 1991 and currently has around 1,600 members drawn from local authorities, government agencies, industry, environmental consultancy, teaching/research, and voluntary environmental organisations.

The objects of the Institute are:

— to advance the science, practice and understanding of ecology and environmental management for the public benefit in the United Kingdom and internationally;

— to further the conservation and enhancement of biodiversity and maintenance of ecological processes and life support systems essential to a fully functional biosphere;

— to further environmentally sustainable management and development;

— to promote and encourage education, training, study and research in the science and practice of ecology, environmental management and sustainable development;

— to establish, uphold and advance the standards of education, qualification, competence and conduct of those who practise ecology and environmental management as a profession and for the benefit of the public.

IEEM is a member of the European Federation of Associations of Environmental Professionals, the Society for the Environment and the IUCN.

IEEM INQUIRY RESPONSE

Education Outside the Classroom

The IEEM has been concerned for some time about the lack of skills in graduates coming onto the employment market. The IEEM has identified biological recording, survey and monitoring as an area that has been neglected in mainstream education and training and consequently the growing demand for these skills is not being met.

Part of the reason for this "skills gap" has been the reduction of fieldwork undertaken at schools, in particular, due to there no longer being a requirement for fieldwork in the National Curriculum at A Level. Fieldwork may be done at primary schools, but is then dropped for other subjects. Children's interest is kindled at young age, and needs to be maintained—the best way to do this is with DIRECT CONTACT WITH THE NATURAL WORLD.

The IEEM feels that this lack of identification skills is a serious one, which is only likely to get worse unless the amount of fieldwork in schools is increased.

The IEEM apologises for the very short written response to the inquiry but we were only informed about it a very short time ago. The IEEM's Training, Education and Career Development committee (TECDC) would be very happy to discuss this matter further.

October 2004

Memorandum submitted by the Countryside Stewardship Scheme: Educational Access

Defra's Countryside Stewardship Scheme (CSS) makes grants to farmers and other land managers for using environmentally friendly farming methods to enhance and conserve English landscapes, their wildlife and history. There is also a scheme option to improve opportunities for countryside enjoyment, including educational access visits. Under this option land managers allow use of their land for learning purposes, and visits to farms can be linked to National Curriculum subjects, such as:

— using the landscape to stimulate creative writing and artistic expression;

— mapping, land use and conservation studies;

— close contact with the farming industry and the chance to learn about activities such as lambing, harvesting, and livestock management and how the food we eat comes from the crops grown or animals reared;

— the relationship between the farming industry and the countryside, and how Countryside Stewardship aids conservation, the landscape and the protection of historical features.

Each educational access site has a Teacher's Information Pack, which shows how a visit can be used to help studies in various subjects and where it would fit within the school curriculum. The pack has been devised in association with Farming and Countryside Education (FACE). A Farm Facts Leaflet, with more general details about what the site has to offer, is provided for other visitor groups. Defra works closely with DfES, through membership of the Access to Farms partnership (ATF), which is an umbrella organisation for providers of farm educational visits.

There are currently around 1,000 CSS educational access sites in England and payments to agreement holders are expected to reach £1 million this financial year. Payment arrangements were reviewed recently and are now based on each farm visit, up to a maximum of 25 per year. This should encourage more visits than the previous system, which paid a flat rate per annum, irrespective of numbers of visits. The total paid in 2003–04 was £800,000. In addition, details of over 450 CSS educational access sites will shortly be displayed on the DfES "Growing Schools" website widely used by teachers organising visits.

Agreement holders are being encouraged to participate in a new accreditation scheme, the Countryside Educational Visits Accreditation Scheme (CEVAS), provided by ATF. Accreditation is designed to encourage better uptake of visits by schools and colleges. CEVAS provides training and accreditation package for individuals dealing with school farm visits, and includes a health and safety inspection. Following a successful pilot, the scheme has secured funding from Defra's Vocational Training Scheme (VTS) until 2006.

Agreement holders are provided with HSE guidance on farm visits by the public and are required to have appropriate public liability insurance. They are also encouraged to carry out appropriate risk assessments, depending on visitor groups. And agreement holders are encouraged to arrange security vetting by the Criminal Records Bureau, where this might be appropriate, for instance to meet the needs of local schools.

CSS educational access details can be found on the Defra country walks website at http://countrywalks.defra.gov.uk

Although the Countryside Stewardship Scheme closed to new applicants in 2004, Educational Access will continue in the new Environmental Stewardship (Higher Level) Scheme, which is due to replace Countryside Stewardship in 2005.

November 2004

Memorandum submitted by The Royal Society

1. INTRODUCTION

1.1 The Royal Society is an independent academy promoting the natural and applied sciences. Founded in 1660, the Society has three roles; as the UK academy of science, as a learned society and as a funding agency. Working across the whole range of science, technology and engineering, one of the Society's main aims is to support science communication and education. Its education programme considers formal education in science and mathematics from primary level through to higher education. As with all Royal Society programmes, the education programme upholds the values of excellence in science, leadership, independence, equality of opportunity, inclusiveness, and scrupulous attention to evidence.

1.2 In December 2003, a Royal Society working group[1] was established under the chairmanship of Sir Patrick Bateson FRS to examine the broader place of fieldwork in science education and concerns that it was being diminished. Following the first meeting of this group in January 2004 the statement (see section 2) was prepared. The comments and conclusions that follow are based on discussions emerging from this meeting and are focused specifically on issues relating to science fieldwork. The Society continues to engage with organisations and individuals taking these issues forward, and awaits the Committee's report with interest.

2. ROYAL SOCIETY STATEMENT ON THE PLACE OF FIELDWORK IN SCIENCE EDUCATION

2.1 The Royal Society considers that the skills and knowledge developed through fieldwork can be integral to the purposes of science education: to train experts able to serve science and society through research; to educate all young people in the fundamental processes of scientific investigation; and to prepare citizens of the future for responsible management of their environment. The Society is therefore concerned that the available research data (from small scale studies[2, 3]) suggest that fieldwork is being diminished throughout the education system by a number of pressures on schools, colleges and universities. To assess accurately the decline, it is crucial that large-scale data relating to the extent and type of fieldwork provision on offer is obtained. To take appropriate action, it is important that the benefits of fieldwork are thoroughly researched, reliably documented and widely communicated.

2.2 The Society recognises that out-of-classroom activities place demands on teachers, students and institutions but thinks that, with proper support and management, such demands can be accommodated within the existing education system. The Society also considers that, whilst health and safety risks are involved in fieldwork, such risks vary greatly between activities and can be managed by professional teaching staff given appropriate training and support in risk assessment and fieldwork provision. In Higher Education, the Society is concerned that as undergraduates are increasingly expected to pay for their degree education, the cost of fieldwork, for the individual and the institution, may increasingly impact on the availability and uptake of such opportunities.

2.3 The Royal Society welcomes work done by organisations like the Field Studies Council and British Ecological Society in raising awareness of a decline in biology fieldwork, particularly residential experiences for post-16 students. It is interesting to note their comparisons with geography in which fieldwork appears to have been more effectively sustained in recent times. This suggests that many of the barriers related to science are not insurmountable. The Society also welcomes curriculum developments that strongly encourage fieldwork as part of science courses, particularly in the biological sciences. Its potential benefits suggest that the place of fieldwork within science education needs to be thoroughly reviewed to ensure that, where appropriate, the opportunities fieldwork offers young people become entitlements.

3. Key Issues for the Committee's Consideration

3.1 *Definition and purpose*

As the Committee notes, "Education Outside the Classroom" is a very broad term encompassing a range of activities, some of which more obviously support the objectives of formal classroom teaching and learning than others. While we restrict our comments in this submission to science fieldwork, even this narrow definition masks a diversity of possible activities, from an hour in the school grounds exploring the physics of shadows to a week's residential course surveying heathland ecology. Indeed for some schools the definition extends to trips to leisure parks to explore scientific concepts.[4] The definitions and purposes of these activities need to be made clear not only by those involved in shaping and implementing education policy, but also at the practitioner level in schools and colleges. Such clarification should give as much attention to benefits as is currently given to risks, to enable young people, their parents and their teachers to make the best possible decisions.

3.2 *Coherence and co-ordination*

The Society notes other efforts being made to raise the profile of fieldwork in science[5] and the significant, positive support given to fieldwork by some key policy-influencers[6,7,8,9] despite some unions advising their members otherwise.[10] It should therefore be both possible, and timely, to apply a greater degree of coherence and co-ordination to these efforts. This would require leadership, a statement of purpose and intention, a plan of action and success criteria. Whether this be a "manifesto" led by Government or a campaign led by NGOs may be an interesting discussion for the Committee, but without doubt any such action needs to be based on evidence and be conducted as openly and honestly as possible.

3.3 *Evidence*

In 1998, Roger Lock of the University of Birmingham concluded that despite the opportunities offered, "Evidence about the provision and success of fieldwork as a teaching and learning opportunity is scant".[11] Six years later, Steve Tilling of the Field Studies Council again noted "there is a remarkable dearth of national data which would enable effective assessment of the levels and quality of fieldwork" and states that there is "no published evidence in secondary biology to support improved academic performance or other personal development measures".[12] In 2004, a thorough "Review of Research on Outdoor Learning"[13] concluded that while substantial evidence exists as to the opportunities offered through high-quality fieldwork, "Poor fieldwork is likely to lead to poor learning" and, perhaps as a result, "there is still a need for more work on the outcomes of fieldwork in science education". The Committee would do well to establish exactly where and how these gaps in knowledge are being filled.

3.3.1 As part of the inspection and monitoring process, regulatory authorities such as the Qualifications and Curriculum Authority (QCA) and Office for Standards in Education (Ofsted) collect a large amount of information on what goes on in schools. But the continuing difficulty in identifying reliable, large-scale data on fieldwork, alongside evidence from limited studies such as those undertaken by the Field Studies Council, suggest that tracking trends in the quality and quantity of fieldwork provision should be given a higher priority by the relevant agencies. If this is thought to add a burden to schools then some other sampling method should be considered, but the Society would like to see a swift resolution to the ongoing questions regarding the validity of evidence and accurate benchmarking of fieldwork provision.

3.3.2 In addition to such information, a greater understanding of the role fieldwork plays in strengthening science learning at all stages, and any hard evidence of de-skilling or reduced supply of skilled, professional fieldworkers in scientific research and development, would enhance our ability to assess how much needs to be done. However, suggesting that more research is needed before significant changes are made to national policy should not be taken to imply that no action is needed at all. The Committee will be aware of the vicious circle in place whereby lack of fieldwork experience in school and higher education produces new teachers who themselves lack confidence and/or competence to offer the next generation these experiences. In science, some subjects such as systematics and taxonomy cannot be taught without fieldwork, and in 2002, the House of Lords Science and Technology Committee urged that "education must emphasise the importance of taxonomy".[14]

3.4 *Opportunities and threats*

3.4.1 Ideally no science teacher who feels a fieldwork experience is vital to their pupils' education should feel that barriers to achieving their aims are insurmountable. Experience with the 250 schools who have received a Royal Society Partnership Grant to work with a scientist or engineer has shown that money can overcome a significant barrier to undertaking exciting, inspiring science in the field. Indeed we are grateful to the DfES for their current funding of this scheme.

3.4.2 Undoubtedly the Committee will receive a great deal of information about the opportunities for, and threats to, education outside the classroom. The Society suggests that the most important consideration when assembling the priorities for action, and associated recommendations, will be equality of opportunity for all young people throughout the UK education system. Whilst many believe the only way of ensuring this is through affecting statutory regulation and ring-fenced funding, the Society notes that such reactions are not favoured by the current Government. If the only way forward is through the identification and promotion of "best practice", then the Government must show that all teachers have equal opportunity and adequate support to profit from that best practice.

4. CONCLUSIONS

It is hoped that the outcome of this inquiry will help to:

4.1 establish the extent to which Government and its agencies give priority to fieldwork, and where and how this priority is communicated to teachers and the wider education community;

4.2 ensure messages regarding Health and Safety risks, and procedures for assessing and managing them, are clear and consistent across Local Education Authorities and Learning and Skills Councils;

4.3 understand and develop the role of teaching unions in being both responsible to, and responsible for, the actions of their members with regard to fieldwork;

4.4 encourage multi-agency partnerships in:

    4.4.1 agreeing appropriate entitlements for all young people to high-quality fieldwork as part of their statutory science education;

    4.4.2 improving monitoring of fieldwork provision and brokering an agreed set of definitions and criteria to establish good baseline data;

    4.4.3 research into the effects of fieldwork on science learning;

    4.4.4 investment in the sustained development and delivery of resources and training to support Primary and Secondary teachers, as well as FE lecturers (particularly involving Science Learning Centres and other CPD providers, subject associations and professional bodies);

    4.4.5 obtaining more reliable knowledge regarding the effects of changes to university science courses on secondary science teachers' ability to undertake fieldwork, particularly the implications that changes to funding and fees may have on availability of fieldwork in undergraduate courses;

    4.4.6 development work regarding changes to GCSE and A level specifications offered by awarding bodies to ensure the place of fieldwork in science qualifications is unambiguous;

    4.4.7 delivery of the DfES' Growing Schools and London Challenge initiatives;

    4.4.8 exploring the opportunities inherent in proposals for 14–19 reform.

It is vital to raise the profile of fieldwork throughout the education community and tackle the need for an evidence-based approach to its implementation. We look forward to taking an appropriate role in any outcomes from this inquiry and assist progress on securing the place of fieldwork in science education.

REFERENCES

[1] Full details of membership and terms of reference can be found at http://www.royalsoc.ac.uk/page.asp?tip=1&id=1991

[2] Barker, S, Slingsby, D and Tilling, S (2002) *Teaching biology outside the classroom. Is it heading for extinction?* Field Studies Council/British Ecological Society.

[3] Lock, R and Tilling, S (2002) *Ecology fieldwork in 16–19 biology*, School Science Review, **84** (307).

[4] *Science 2002–03 annual report on curriculum and assessment* (2004) Qualifications and Curriculum Authority.

[5] "Save our Biology" campaign—Field Studies Council and British Ecological Society (http://www.field-studies-council.org/campaigns/biologyfieldwork/index.aspx) and "Real World Learning" campaign—Field Studies Council, RSPB, National Trust, 3D Education and Adventure and the Wildfowl and Wetland Trust.

[6] "Teachers should not abandon school visits—safely conducted and properly supervised, they are an important part of any child's education", David Miliband MP, Schools Standards Minister, DfES Press Notice 2003/0195.

[7] The London Student Pledge, launched by Stephen Twigg MP, Schools Minister, in November 2003, aims to offer every secondary student in the capital the opportunity to "take part in a residential experience or visit that will further their education. This could include a geography fieldtrip, an overseas exchange, or a Duke of Edinburgh Awards trip", DfES Press Notice 2003/0222.

[8] "Practical work, including fieldwork, is a vital part of science education. It helps students to develop their understanding of science, appreciate that science is based on evidence, and acquire hands-on skills that are essential if students are to progress in science", *Science Education from 14 to 19, Volume 1: Report and Proceedings of the Committee* (2002) House of Commons Science & Technology Committee, p19.

[9] The Growing Schools initiative is a Government-funded programme which aims to encourage, support and inspire all schools (nursery, primary, secondary and special) to use the outdoor classroom, both with and beyond the school grounds, as a context for learning across the curriculum.

[10] "NASUWT reaffirms advice to members to avoid taking school trips", Press Release issued by the National Association of Schoolmasters Union of Women Teachers, 18 February 2004.

[11] Lock, R (1998) Fieldwork in the life sciences, *International Journal of Science Education,* **20,** 633–642.

[12] Tilling, S (2004) Fieldwork in UK secondary schools: influences and provision, *Journal of Biological Education*, **38(2),** 54–58.

[13] Rickinson, M, Dillon, J *et al* (2004) *A Review of Research on Outdoor Learning*, National Foundation for Educational Research and King's College London.

[14] *What on earth? The threat to science underpinning conservation. Third Report* (2002) House of Lords Science & Technology Committee.

November 2004

Printed in the United Kingdom by The Stationery Office Limited
2/2005   992148   19585